… THE FOURTH DIVISION

1939 TO 1945

THIS BOOK IS DEDICATED

TO ALL MEMBERS OF THE DIVISION, 1939 TO 1945

WHO TOGETHER MADE THE HISTORY

HEREIN DESCRIBED

HUGH WILLIAMSON

THE FOURTH DIVISION

1939 to 1945

The Naval & Military Press Ltd

Published by

The Naval & Military Press Ltd
Unit 5 Riverside, Brambleside
Bellbrook Industrial Estate
Uckfield, East Sussex
TN22 1QQ England

Tel: +44 (0)1825 749494

www.naval-military-press.com
www.nmarchive.com

In reprinting in facsimile from the original, any imperfections are inevitably reproduced and the quality may fall short of modern type and cartographic standards.

Contents

		Page	
	Foreword		vii
	Preface		ix
	Sketch maps		xiii
Chapter 1	The Outbreak of War		1
2	Brussels and Dunkirk		13
3	Home Forces		32
4	The Tunisian Campaign: Béjà		40
5	Operation Lilac Blossom		55
6	Peter's Corner		66
7	Dunkirk avenged		80
8	Algeria and Egypt		94
9	Italy: The Garigliano salient		99
10	Sant' Elia		108
11	Garrison in Cassino		115
12	The Gustav Line: preparations		122
13	The assault on the Gustav Line		129
14	The pursuit: Palombara		158
15	The Trasimene Line		163
16	The Arezzo Line		175
17	From Tuori to Montevarchi		183
18	From Ricasoli to Gaville		190
19	The Chianti mountains		196
20	Incontro Monastery		210
21	The Gothic Line		219
22	Cesena and the River Savio		236
23	The River Ronco and Forli		247
24	North of Forli		268
25	Between Forli and Faenza		277
26	Between campaigns: Taranto		294
27	Civil War in Athens		300
28	The rest of Greece		312
	Epilogue		322
	Appendices		324
	Glossary		327
	Index		329
	Photographs		337

Foreword

By H. E. Field-Marshal Lord Alexander of Tunis
KG GCB GCMG CSI DSO MC

This is the story of a great fighting division, and I am pleased to have the privilege of writing a foreword to it. I am glad to pay my tribute to the 4th Division because they served for a considerable period of the war under my command, and I owe them a debt of gratitude for the part they played in our victories.

The 4th Division formed part of the British Expeditionary Force which saw service in North-west Europe in 1939. Although those early days of the second World War ended in local defeat, they enabled us to gain time for the raising of the great Allied forces which were finally to gain complete and absolute victory over the enemy six years later. The evacuation from Dunkirk was an epic of heroism in which this splendid division shared. British courage and staunchness against a stronger and better equipped foe made possible the accomplishment of what appeared at the time to be an impossible task—the successful evacuation of our Regular Army. Over three hundred thousand of Britain's professional soldiers were saved, to form the great armies which, from the battle of El Alamein on, never lost a battle. This alone is a proud record, but it is only the beginning.

In March 1943, the division again came under my command in North Africa, and after many hard-fought battles against a most formidable opponent, had their reward in sharing in the fruits of the battle of Tunis. This great victory gave the Allies control over the whole of the North African shores, together with a bag of just on a quarter of a million prisoners.

The stage was now set for the assault on Europe. Although the division did not take part in the early stages of the campaign, they entered the fighting in Italy at the beginning of 1944, and from then onwards played a distinguished part in the hard fighting which followed during the advance up the Italian peninsula.

The battles they fought and won are too numerous to mention in a short foreword. These deeds of a great fighting formation are well recounted in the pages of this book. But I would draw to the reader's attention the actions of the assault on the Gustav Line and the capture of Monte Scalari, together with the capture of Incontro Monastery and that of the airfield at Forli.

In December 1944, when I was faced with a serious and fast deteriorating situation in Athens, I withdrew the 4th Division from Italy and sent them to Greece to restore the situation. Suffice it to say that they fulfilled their task, as I knew they would, in the shortest time and in the most successful manner.

Six years of war found many fresh battle honours added to those of the past, to be proudly borne by the units which composed the 4th Division. Every decoration and every battle honour has been well and truly gained. Every man who had the honour of serving with the 4th Division may well feel proud that he fought with such a fine formation.

Canada, 20th February 1951   ALEXANDER OF TUNIS, F.M.

Preface

This is the unofficial history of an infantry division during the second World War. It has been written for those who served in the division, as a record of their service and as a description of events whose course and purpose may not have been clear to all who took part in them. The book has been published in order to provide a complete and reasonably detailed account of the division's part in its four campaigns.

The accuracy and even the interest of the narrative has been limited by space and by the material available. The history of any formation ought to deal with every aspect of the formation's duties —command, administration, supply, communications, maintenance, and so on. But the tactical history must come first: and there has been room here for little more than the tactical history.

The story that follows, therefore, is one of infantry actions. The work of supporting arms and services is not generally described, but it is unlikely that any member of the division will forget the importance of that work. Wherever possible, the names of individual officers and other ranks have been brought into the history. The records, however, mention few names, and of all those thousands who served in the division with efficiency and courage, only a very few are named.

Any formation history is remarkable as much for what is left out as for what is put in. In addition to those aspects of the division's work already mentioned, much of interest has had to be passed over —the personality of individuals, the state of morale, the character of the country-side, the weather, the plans that went wrong, details of strengths and losses, and many other circumstances which, like descriptions of noise, discomfort and weariness, might make those half-forgotten days live again in the reader's mind. Few of the most interesting incidents appear in the official records from which most of this book has been compiled; and on points of fact the war diary of one unit or formation sometimes contradicts that of another.

The photographs, including that on the cover, show troops of the 4th Division only; the one exception is that of the Ark bridge at

Cesena, in which the tank-destroyers were under command. Photographs taken outside 4th Division's boundaries might have provided a more spectacular choice, but would have been less suitable for a book of this kind. The two photographs of guns of 77th Field Regiment were provided by Mr Martin Le Quesne; the rest were supplied by the Imperial War Museum, and are Crown copyright. Thanks are due for permission to reproduce these photographs.

Little mention has been made of awards for gallantry and efficiency, since such awards are to be regarded as a result of the events recorded rather than as a part of those events. Many of the incidents described, however, are taken from the citations filed at the War Office. All ranks of the division earned and won a good proportion of awards; as an example, the headquarters and infantry of 12th Brigade in Italy alone won one bar to the DSO, six DSOs, six MBES, seventeen MCS, eight DCMS, thirty-six MMS and one BEM.

Losses generally have not been stressed, though they have been mentioned where recorded. Nobody needs to be reminded of what it meant to an infantry battalion to lose a quarter of its strength in one day. It is perhaps worth recording that in Italy alone the division's infantry battalions lost in killed, wounded and missing nearly 100 per cent of their total strength.

That part of the narrative which deals with the campaigns in France, Belgium and North Africa, and with the period of training in Home Forces, is based on the war diaries of various headquarters and of infantry battalions. The training periods in Algeria and Egypt, the various sea journeys, most of the Gustav Line battle (from May the 12th onwards) and the chapter on Palombara were also written from records of this kind. In describing the campaign in France and Belgium, I was greatly helped by notes and sketch-maps lent by Major-General D. G. Johnson VC CB DSO MC, and by the personal diary of the late Colonel Basil Dening MC; I am most grateful to Mrs Dening and to Major-General Johnson for permission to use this material.

For the period from the division's arrival in Italy until the end of the first day of the Gustav Line battle, and from mid-June 1944 until the end of the war—including the campaign in Greece—I have followed and adapted the account of operations written by Captain Kenneth Biggs, who was appointed Divisional Historian in May 1944.

I have used, in addition to this material, the dispatches on *The*

Allied Armies in Italy from 3rd September 1943 to 12th December 1944 (published when this book was finished and all but ready to go to the printer) by His Excellency Field-Marshal the Viscount Alexander of Tunis KG GCB GCMG CSI DSO MC, and on *Operations in North-West Africa from 8th November 1942 to 13th May 1943* by Lieutenant-General K. A. N. Anderson CB MC; *12th British Infantry Brigade in Italy, March to November 1944* by Captain D. O. Henley; *The 2nd Royal Fusiliers, March 1943 to May 1945* by Lieutenant-Colonel C. A. L. Shipley DSO; *The 91st Light Anti-aircraft Regiment, April 1940 to December 1944* by Captain R. D. Birch; and *The War Diary of 104th Field Battery R.A.*

I owe many thanks to Major-General Johnson, Major-General A. D. Ward CB CBE DSO, Lieutenant-Colonel H. P. Braithwaite DSO, Major T. G. Harrison MBE, Major George Gneditch MBE and Captain R. D. Tyler MC for reading the typescript and the proofs, and for much help and many suggestions; to Brigadier H. B. Latham of the Cabinet Record Office for help in obtaining war diaries; to Major Lord Wynford for help with maps; to Miss Gladys Workman for the index; and to the Officers in Charge of Records at several depots for their help and patience. Particular thanks are due to Major Gneditch for the decorations he has drawn for the text.

H.W.

Sketch maps

In these maps, the approximate movements of British forces are shown for every important action in which the division took part. Except in the map of Italy on page *xx*, grid north is always straight up the page.

Two shades of grey have been used to indicate comparatively high ground and very high ground. The scale of miles, and sometimes of yards, appears in the frame round each map. The scale of reduction varies from map to map, and two maps which appear on the same page are usually on different scales. Irrelevant details have, of course, been left out.

The maps were drawn by the author.

CHAPTERS 1 AND 2

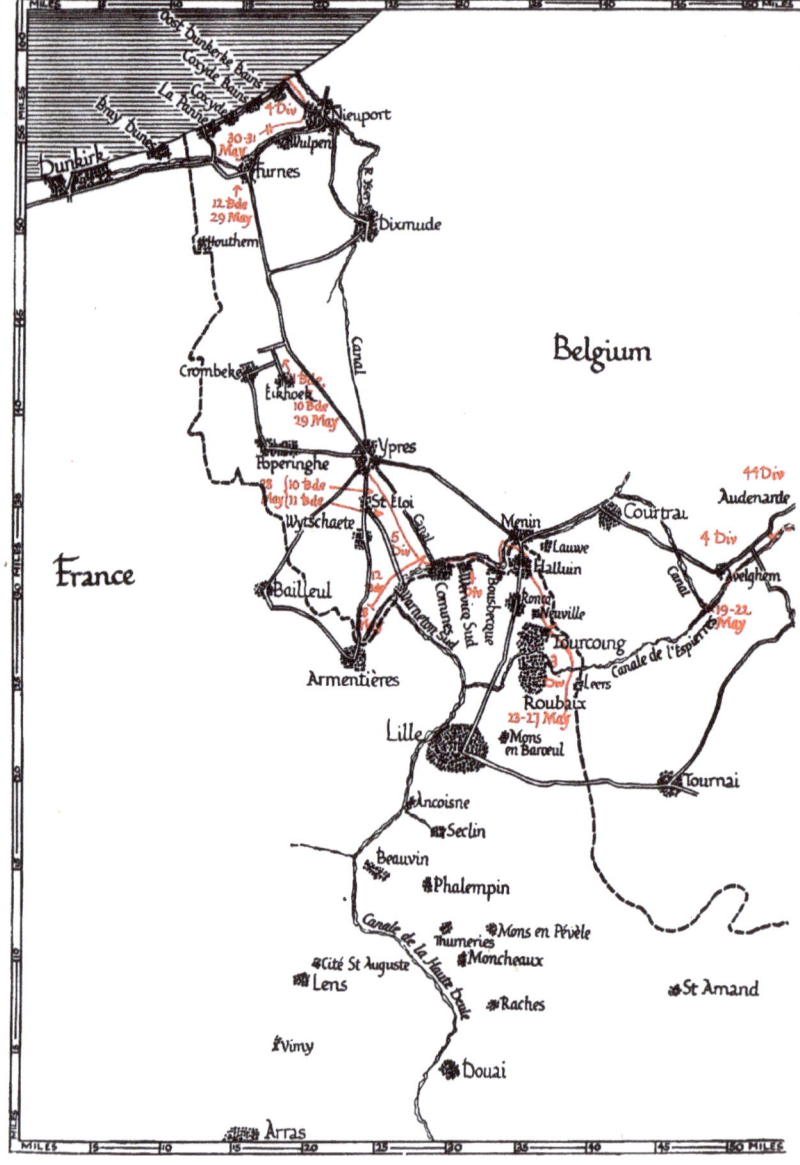

CHAPTERS 1 AND 2   xv

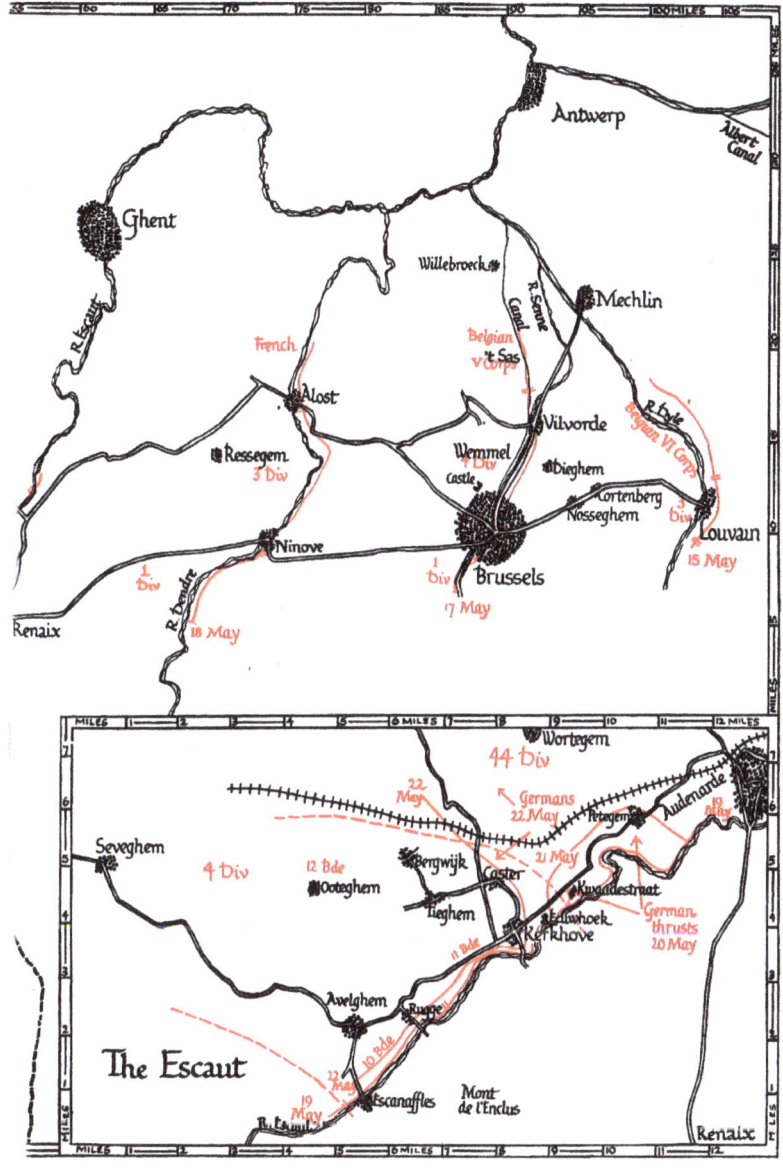

CHAPTER 4

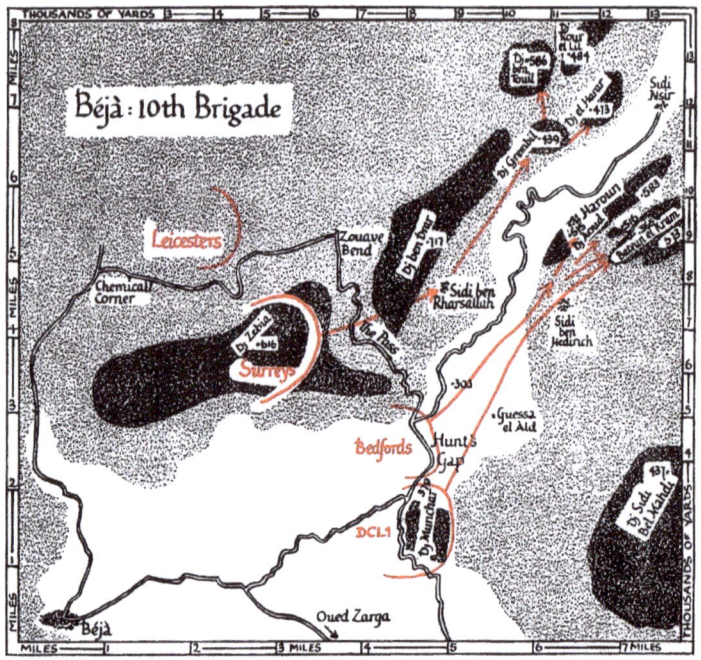

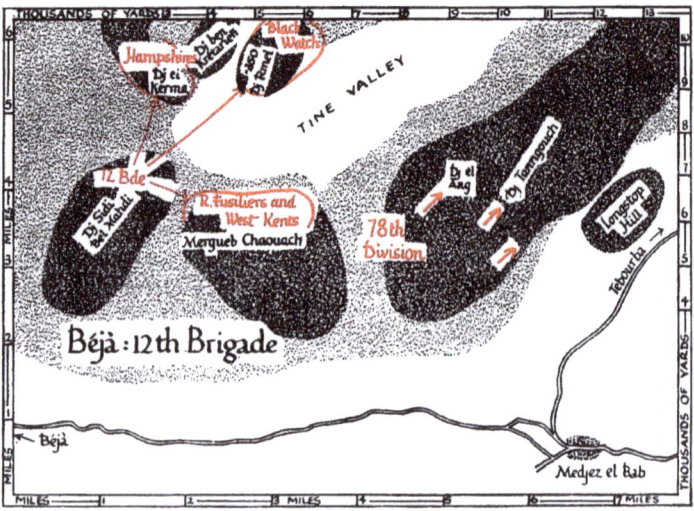

CHAPTERS 5 AND 6   xvii

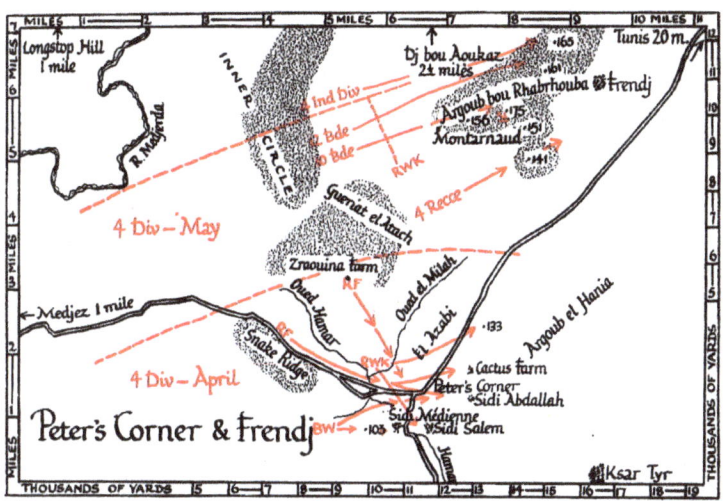

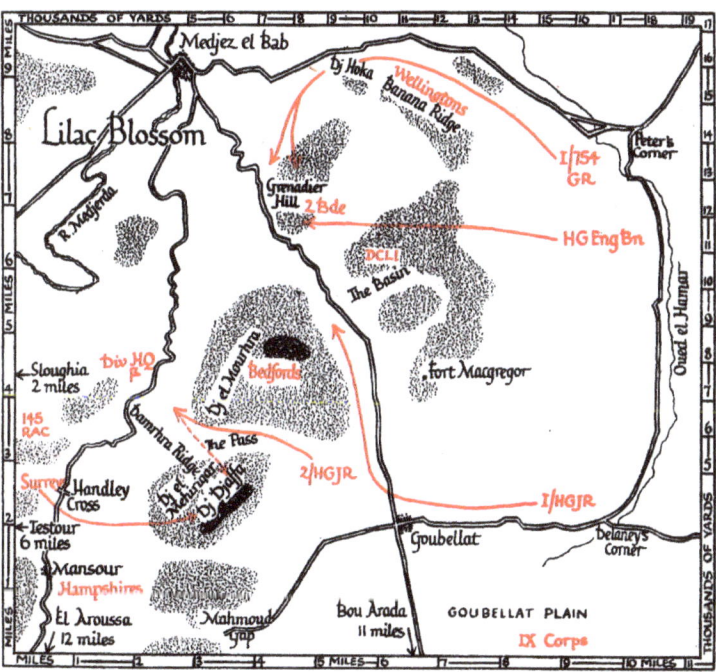

CHAPTERS 4 TO 7

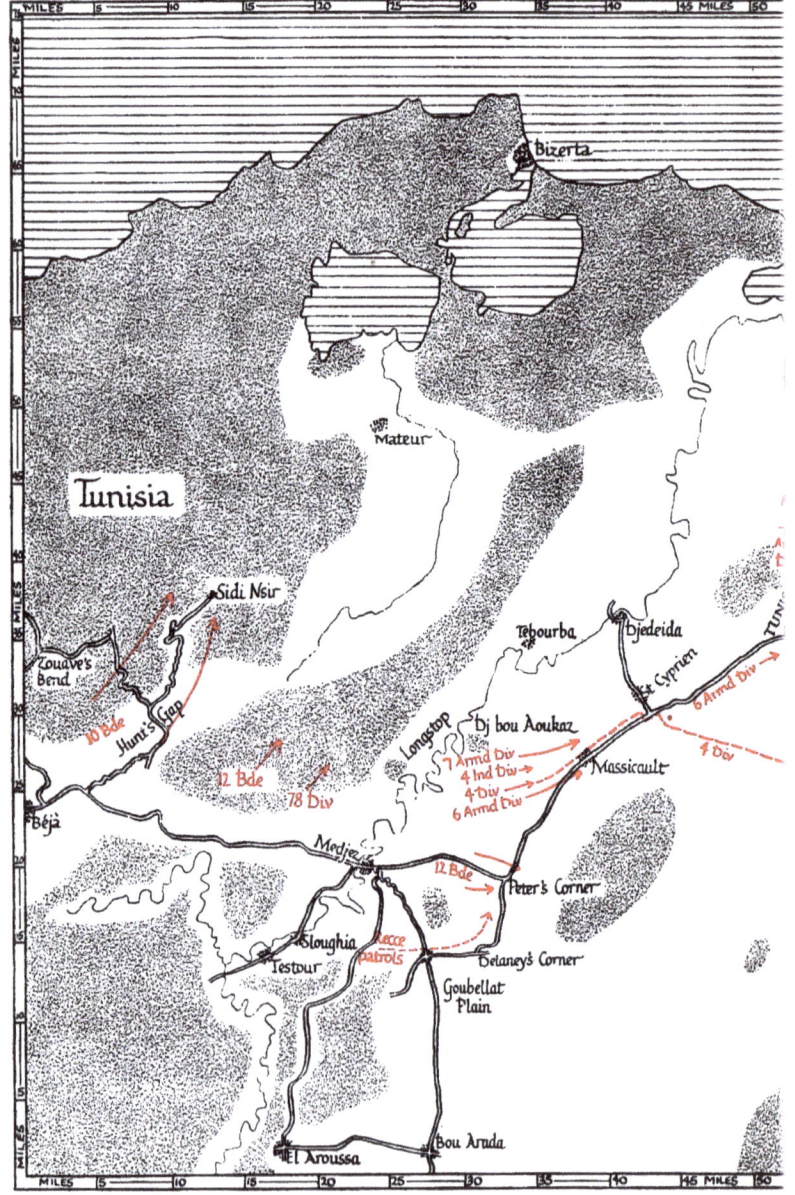

CHAPTERS 4 TO 7

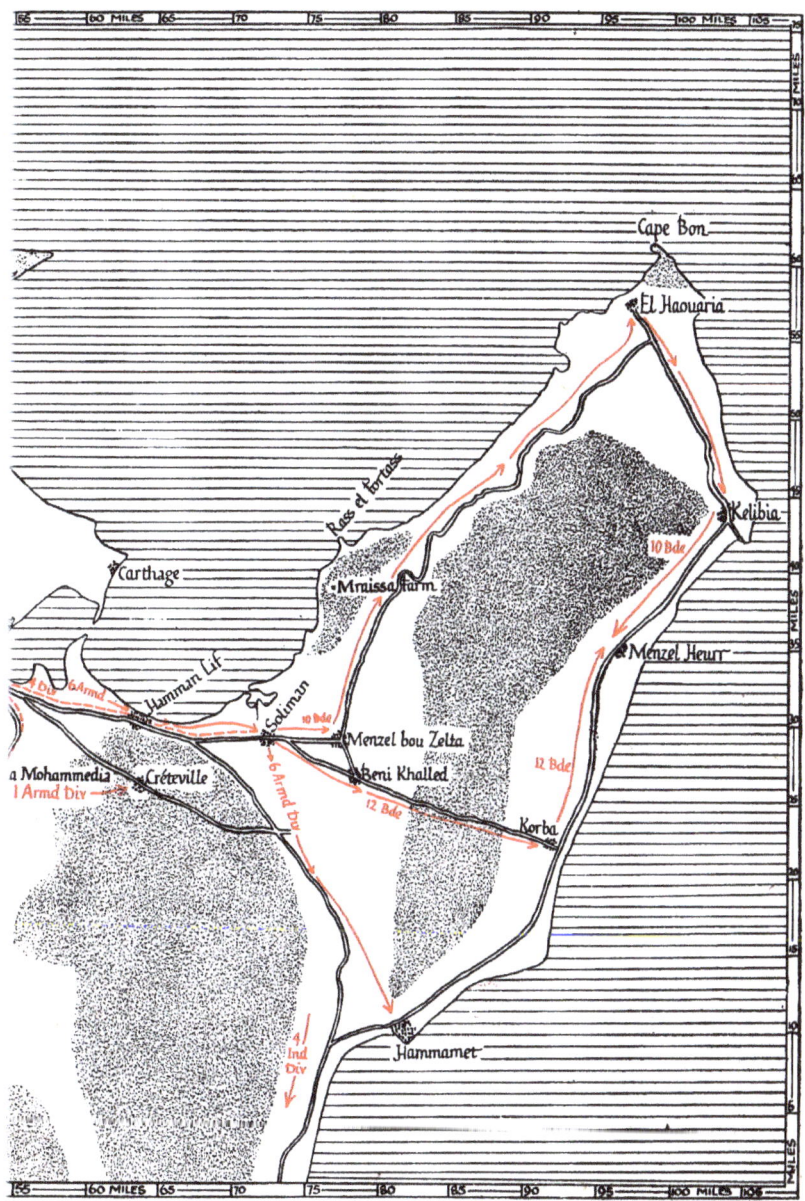

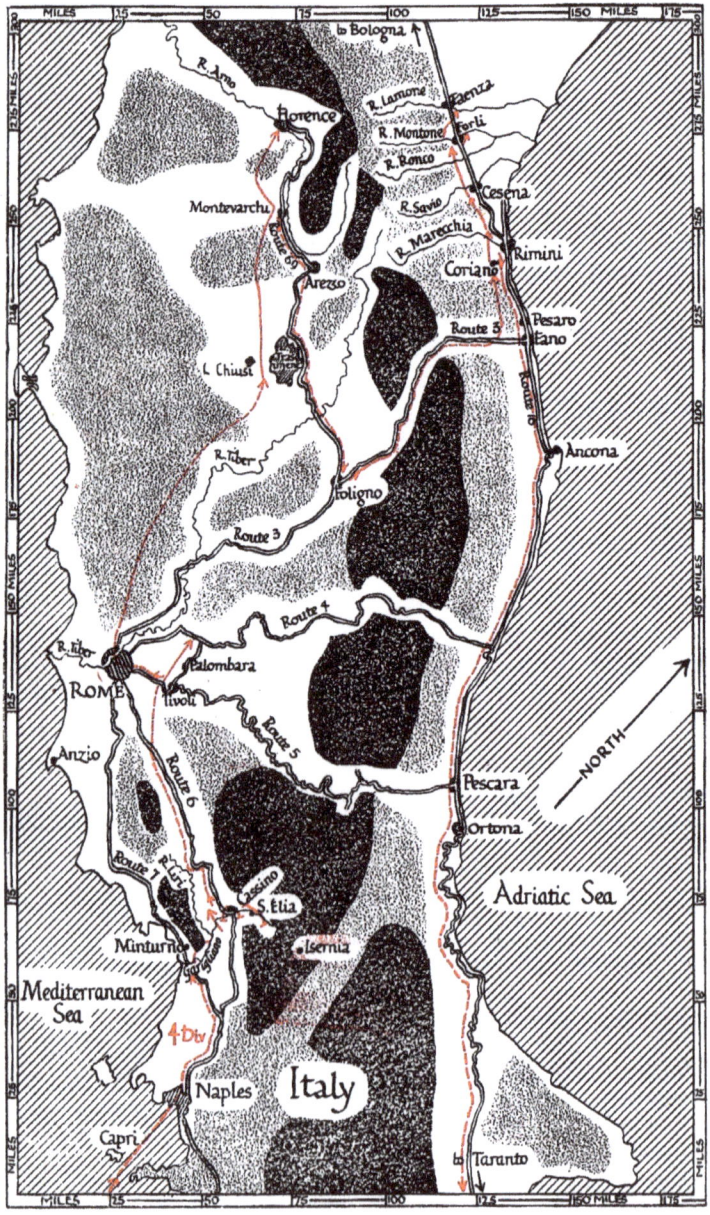

CHAPTERS 9 TO 11

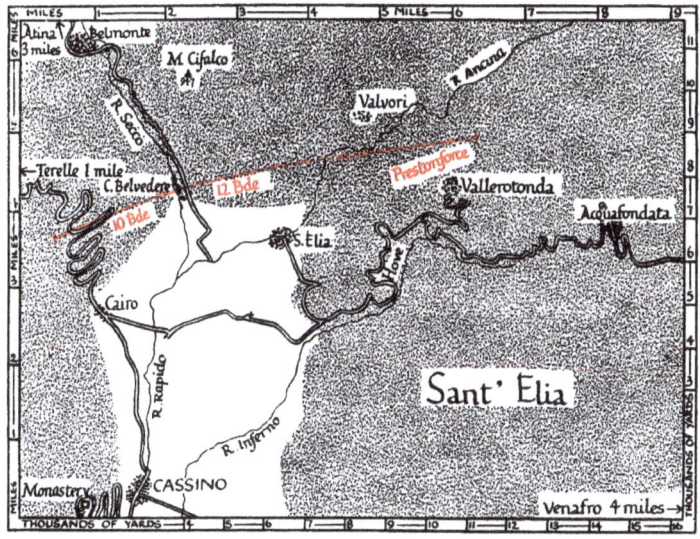

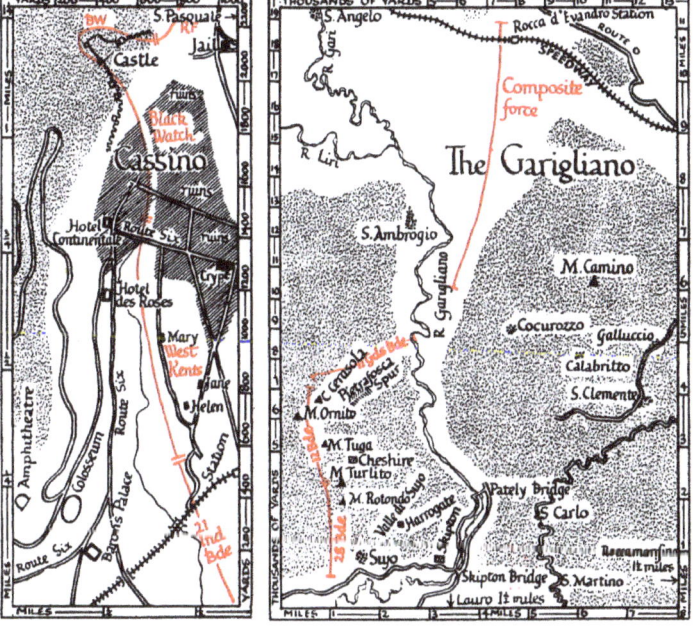

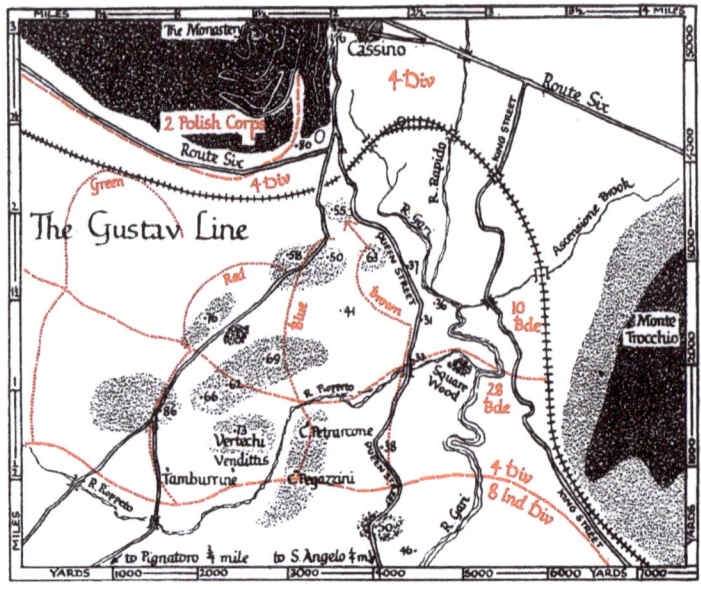

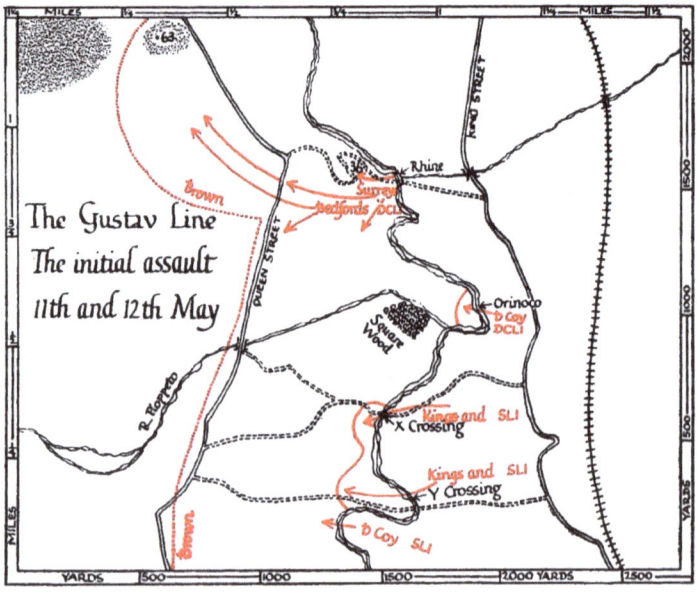

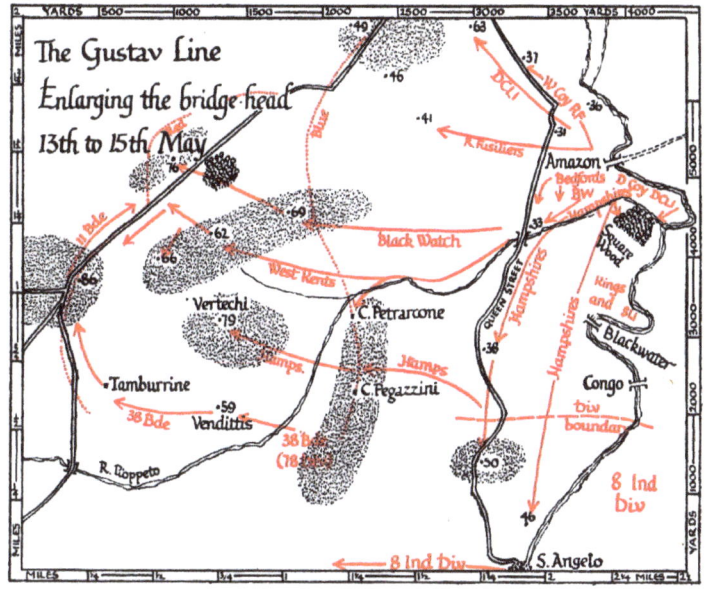

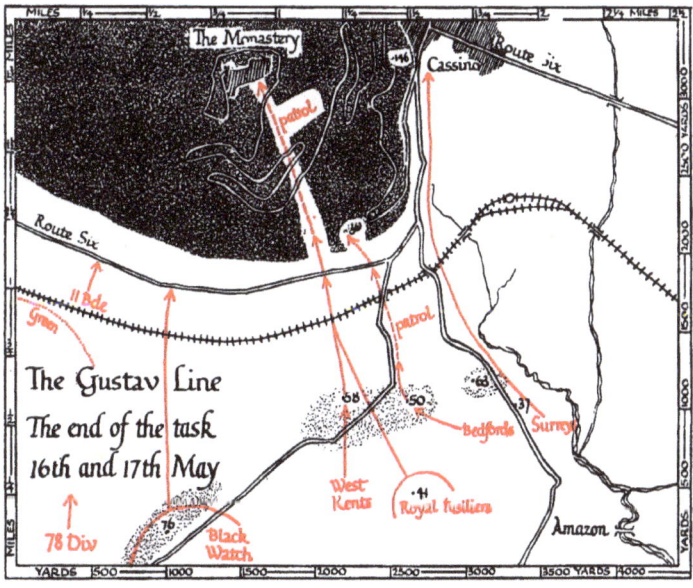

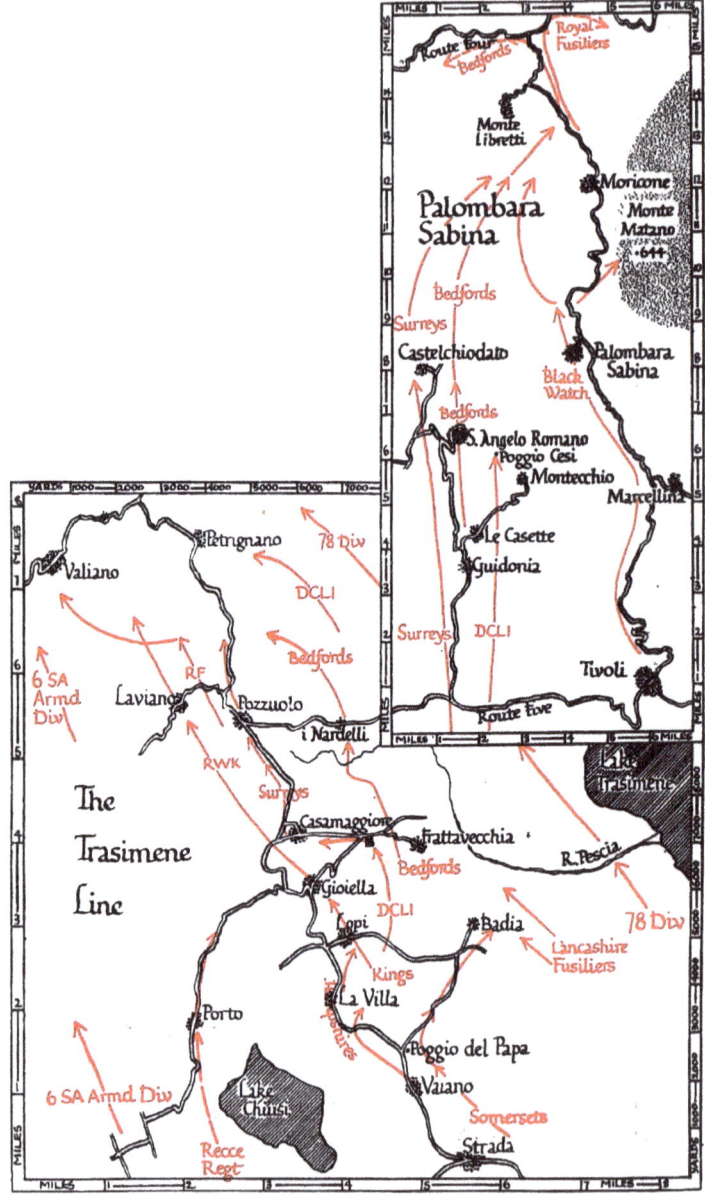

CHAPTERS 14 AND 15

CHAPTER 16

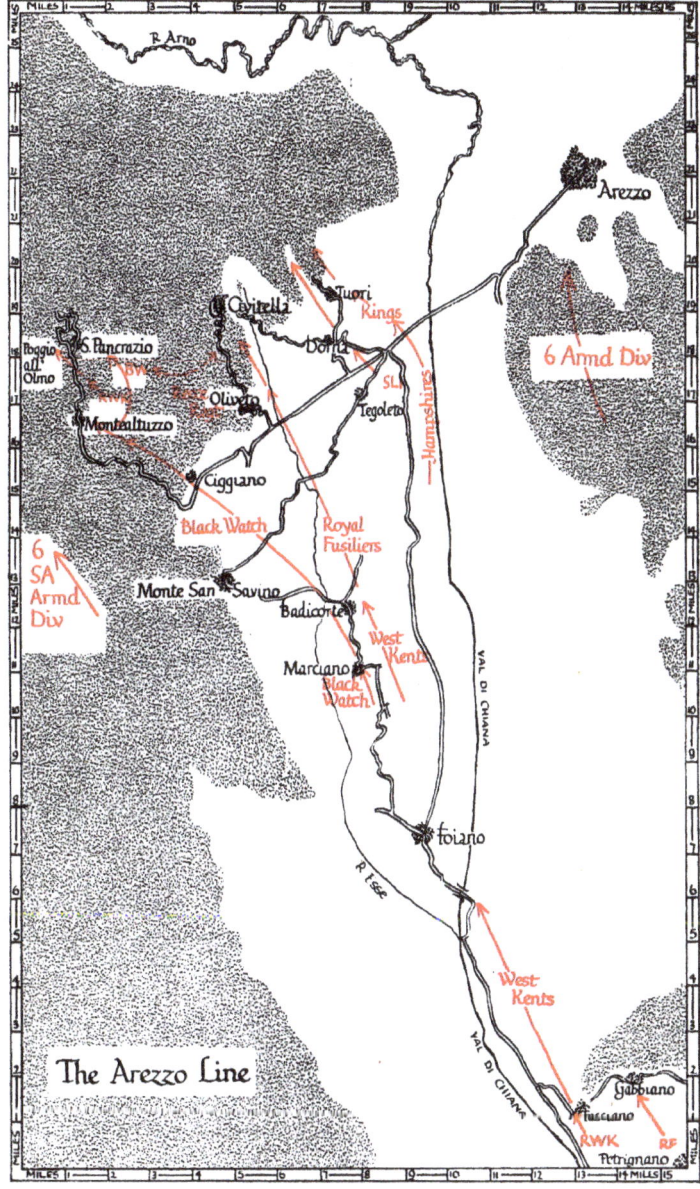

The Arezzo Line

CHAPTERS 17 AND 18

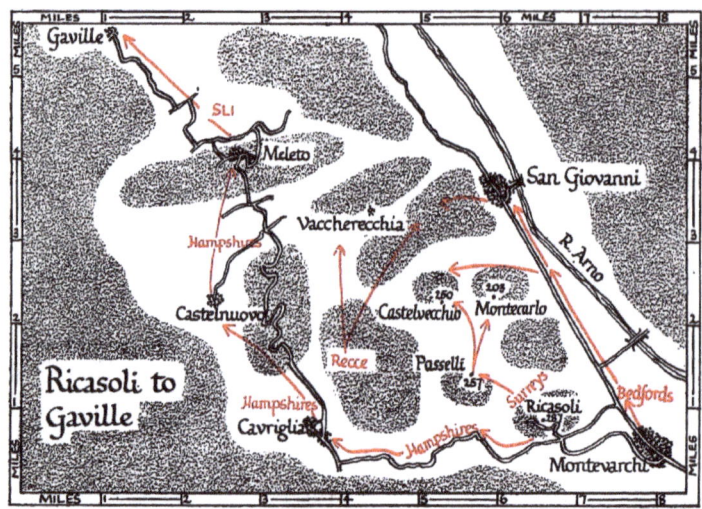

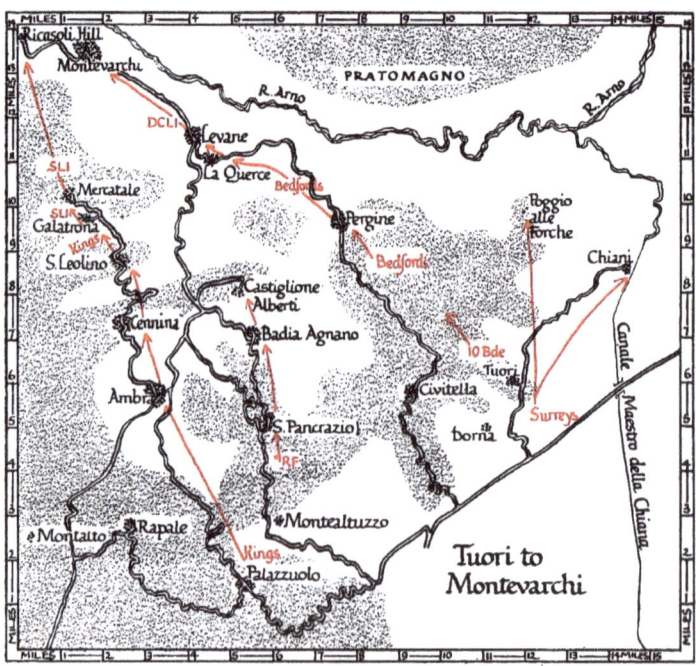

CHAPTERS 19 AND 20   xxvii

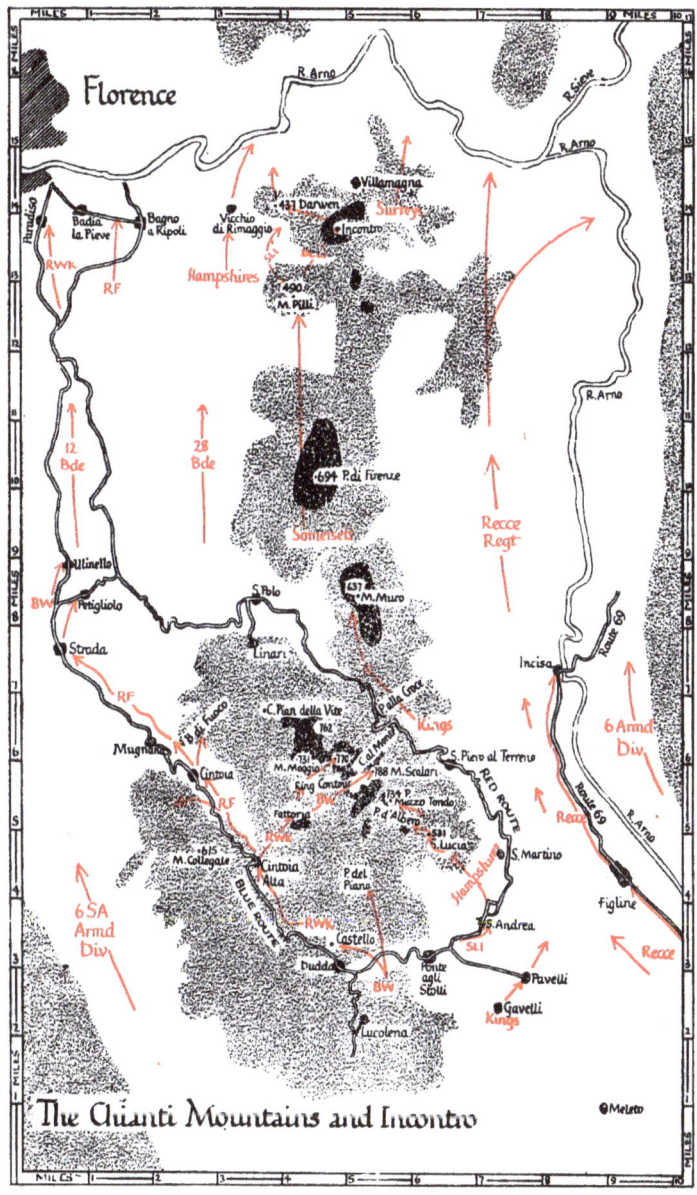

CHAPTER 21

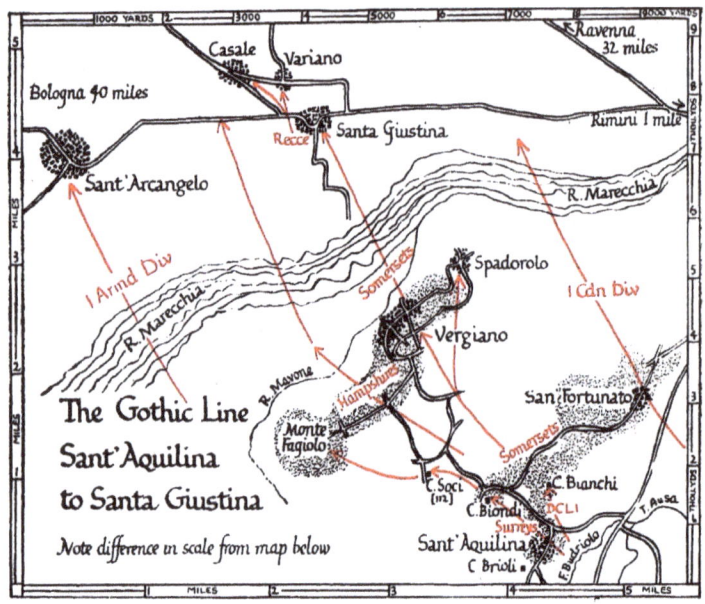

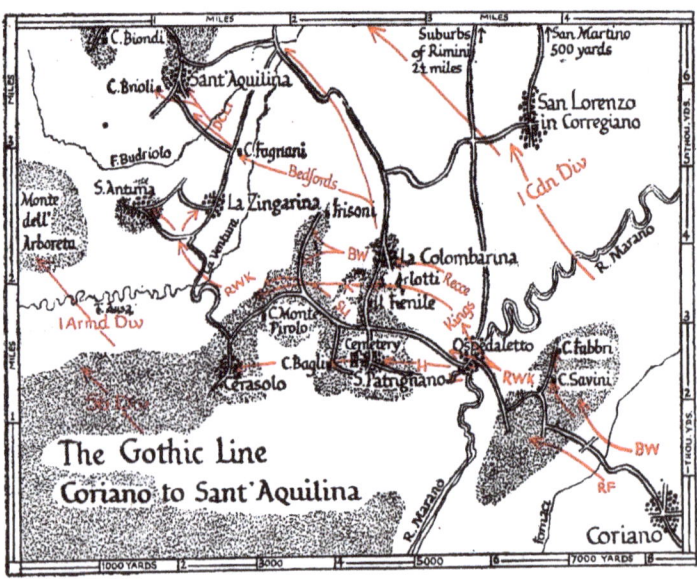

CHAPTERS 22 AND 23

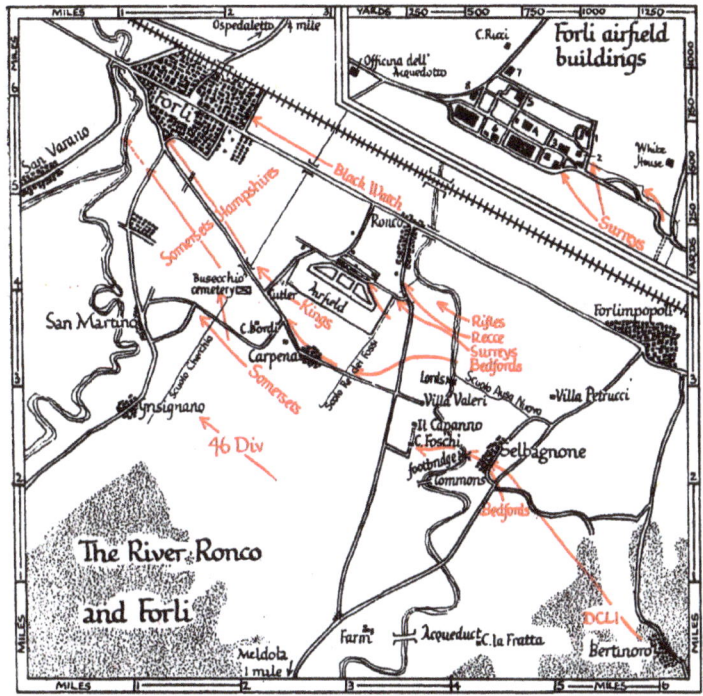

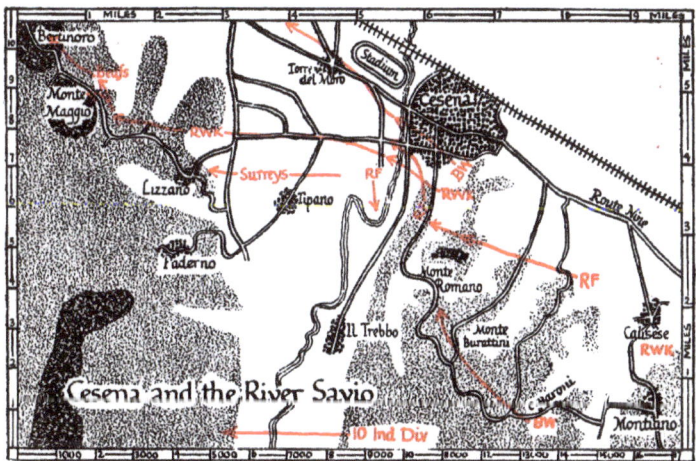

CHAPTERS 24 AND 25

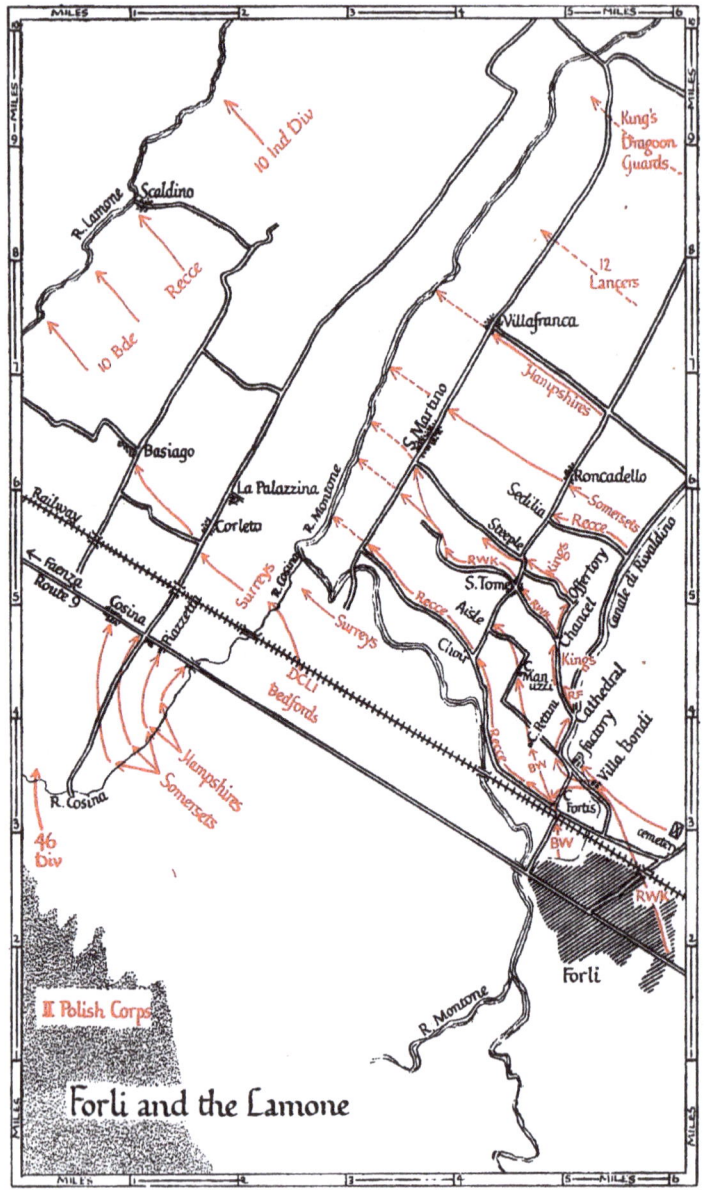

Forli and the Lamone

CHAPTERS 27 AND 28   xxxi

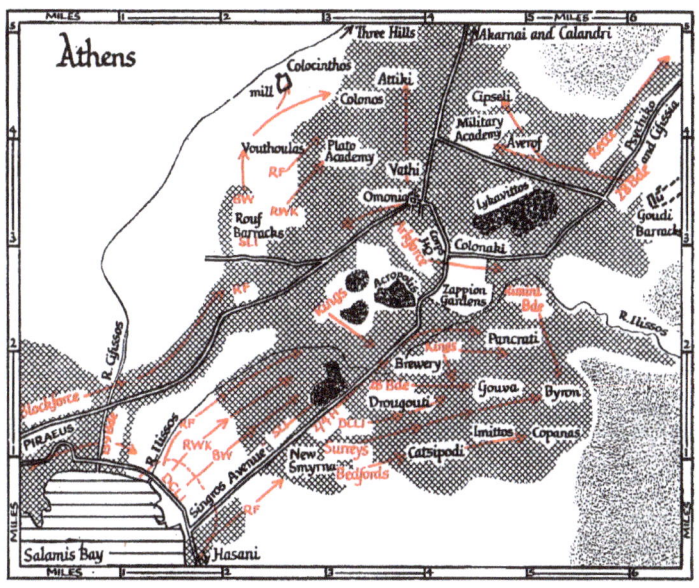

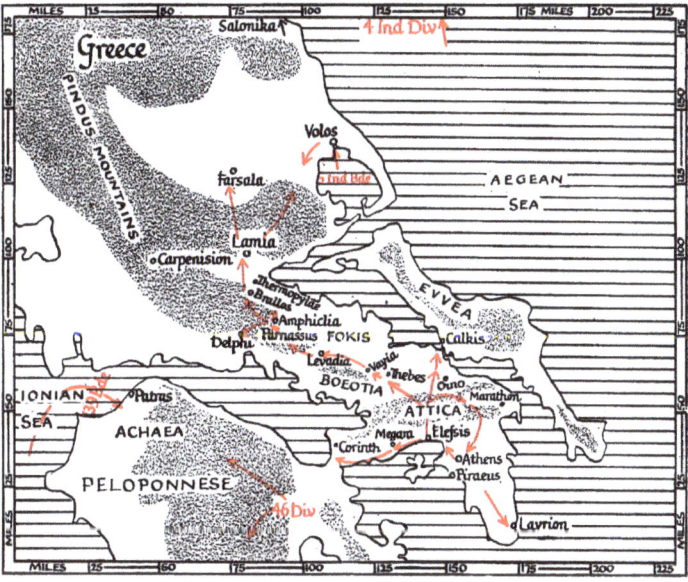

1. The Outbreak of War

In the autumn of 1939, the British Regular Army included only five divisions of infantry. The 1st and 2nd Divisions were ready for immediate mobilization, and, as the imminence of war set the planners to work, these two divisions were detailed to form the British Expeditionary Force, to fight overseas. The 3rd and 4th Divisions were only partly prepared, for they had been 'bled' of experienced officers and NCOs, posted to stiffen the Territorial Army. It was not until a few days before the outbreak of war that the 3rd and 4th Divisions were included in the Expeditionary Force.

The first days of September 1939 found the 4th Division[1] in its peace-time barracks in south-east England. Divisional Headquarters and 11th Brigade Headquarters were at Colchester; 10th Brigade Headquarters was at Shorncliffe, 12th Brigade Headquarters at Dover. The division was commanded by Major-General D. G. Johnson VC CB DSO MC, 10th Brigade by Brigadier Barker, 11th Brigade by Brigadier K. A. N. Anderson MC, and 12th Brigade by Brigadier J. G. W. Clarke MC. When war broke out, all units were on their peace-time establishment of men and equipment, and the division itself was not organized for fighting purposes, lacking for instance its Divisional Signals. 54th (East Anglian) Divisional Signals (Territorial Army) came under Major-General Johnson's command in the first week of September. The artillery regiments existed in cadre only; the services were non-existent, though the RASC and RAOC had lists of men who could drive but had no military training.

In the small hours of the morning of September the 1st, each

---

[1] The composition of the division on September the 17th is given at Appendix A.

headquarters received a telegram from Headquarters Eastern Command at Sevenoaks, ordering them to call out all troops—the Regular Army Reserve was to be called up, and men on leave were to rejoin their units.

At ten-thirty in the morning, the BBC announced the German invasion of Poland; and at eleven-fifteen on September the 3rd the Prime Minister, the Right Honourable Neville Chamberlain, told the country that Great Britain was at war with Germany. The intervening days had been a time of some disorder, for the Army had naturally had no recent practice in mobilization. Orders were no sooner given than cancelled or amended; and the announcement of the declaration of war did not filter through military channels to brigades until nearly eight hours after the Prime Minister's announcement. Area Headquarters had not yet been set up to relieve Major-General Johnson's staff of the administration of the peacetime garrison, and the same staff was required to cope with the extra housing, food, clothing and equipment needed by the Reservists who were flooding in, and with the issue of equipment of every kind to prepare the division for war.

During the five days that passed before the details were all settled and the operation order ready for issue, mobilization and re-equipment continued. Not all units could be completely mobilized during this time, since there were vehicles and stores still to come, and medical units were short of men. The G 1098—scale of personnel and equipment—for brigade anti-tank companies had not been available when mobilization began, and since vehicles could not be indented for at once they were unlikely to arrive for some time. The guns and stores of these companies would therefore have to be carried by the Divisional Ammunition Company.

On September the 17th, Major-General Johnson gave out his orders for the move. In brief, a road party consisting mainly of drivers was to take the division's vehicles to Newport, where they would be embarked. The troops of the division were to travel by train to Aldershot, and thence to the embarkation ports, of which the chief was Southampton. The move was to begin on September the 21st.

Those who were members of the division at that time will doubtless remember the feelings with which they faced the months ahead. The reputation of the German Army had been described in various ways by the daily newspapers since Hitler came to power six years before—there were the stories of cardboard tanks and wooden guns, for instance; but the British Army had heard very different reports from observers who had watched with professional eyes the growing strength of the German forces. The military talent of a warlike nation had been directed to research into new methods of warfare, and there were stories of a novel theory and of strange weapons and methods. Nobody knew exactly what they were up against. Many must have expected something like the war which had begun just over twenty-five years before—trench warfare, punctuated by murderous positional battles like those of the Somme and Passchendaele, and by doubtful victories like that of Cambrai.

In spite of this uncertainty, most of the division must have faced the future with plenty of confidence. The 4th Division had beaten the Germans before, and had remained in being through the years when no German Army of any significance existed. The solidity of the British soldier and the dash of the French seemed likely once more to be too much for German theories and German discipline.

There must also have been members of the division who looked forward to the opportunities that war would bring. Many of the older men would not be glad to leave home and family, but younger men, rising junior officers and NCOs, could hope for a chance to make use of their training, and to advance more rapidly in their profession than they would have done in peace-time. All must have been expectant—except perhaps a few of the older soldiers who remembered the Flanders campaigns of a quarter of a century before, and who had already achieved the *blasé* attitude to fighting which almost the whole division would have achieved five years later.

After a period of strenuous training—Bren classes, gas drill, map reading, first aid, gun drill, deployment, route marches and so on—the division moved to its concentration area in Aldershot Command. Officers and men resigned themselves to the difficulties and discomforts that always afflict units which have been separated from their vehicles and heavy equipment.

Embarkation and voyage went according to plan, in spite of unfamiliar problems of organization; the units of the division collected their vehicles and drove towards the BEF sector in north-eastern France. The troops were in good heart, in spite of the discomforts of the crossing; the countryside was interesting, and the French people welcoming.

France's frontier with Germany—more than two hundred miles long—was guarded by the Maginot Line, an elaborate system of fixed defences reputed to be impregnable. The right flank of the Line was protected by the Swiss mountains; the left flank, opposite the Belgian frontier, was fortified by Belgian neutrality and by little else. Along this frontier, there was a single anti-tank ditch, with concrete pill-boxes built into it at intervals. On this, and on German respect for neutrality, depended the life of France.

The Germans, too, had their fixed defences—the Siegfried Line, facing the Maginot. On the right flank of the Siegfried Line, beyond Luxembourg and Belgium, German armies waited for their moment. Belgium and Luxembourg, lying between two great armies, firmly declared themselves neutral.

A sector of some thirty miles, between Saint-Amand on the right and Armentières on the left, had been allotted to the Expeditionary Force. The sector was held, from left to right, by 1st, 2nd and 3rd British Divisions, and by 51st French Division; 4th Division at first was in reserve round Lens, behind the centre of the sector. French Armies very thinly held the line extending on the left to the sea near Dunkirk, thirty-five miles from Armentières, and on the right to the Maginot Line. Along the whole Allied front of four hundred miles, some eighty Allied divisions faced a German Army which by early 1940 would have grown to nearly double that number. French divisions, moreover, had to watch the Italian frontier between Switzerland and the Mediterranean, more than a hundred and fifty miles long.

In strength, therefore, the Germans outweighed the Allies. Other factors placed the initiative on the German side. The Allies would not enter Belgium or Luxembourg without invitation, and they would not be invited in until the Germans had violated the frequently asserted neutrality of those countries. The Germans, unfettered by respect for neutrality, could strike first into Belgium if they wished. They might on the other hand seize Holland first, or go for the Maginot Line. The Allied policy, formulated at the headquarters of General Gamelin, was to place in front of any attack a defence as strong in numbers, weapons and position as might be possible.

The political and military history of the three contending nations during the last six years had made this policy inevitable. Since Hitler's rise to power in 1933, the military strength of Germany had been developed to the full. The better part of the nation's manpower had been submitted to severe and skilful military training, while the country's economy had been adapted to the uses of war. Professional commanders, whose lives were dedicated to revenge for Versailles, had evolved new theories of warfare and tried them out in Spain. New kinds of weapon, such as the infantry gun and the dive-bomber, had been built to take their part in a new kind of attack.

Meanwhile, France had been completing the Maginot Line, designed to keep the Germans out of France, and so to save France from such ruin as that of 1914. As the defences rose, there rose among the French people the idea of a defensive war, in which France would hold the enemy at bay beyond the impregnable frontier. The effect of this, and of political instability and class distrust, blunted the striking power of the French Army and converted it into little more than garrison troops.

In Britain, the nation had long since reverted to its traditional peace-time disregard of the armed forces, aggravated by the Government's policy of the appeasement of the dictators. Parliamentary limitation of expenditure on defence had enfeebled the forces in numbers, equipment and training. The Regular Army had been inadequately equipped for proper training, and had been required to post many experienced officers and NCOs to the Territorial Army. The 'Terriers', also suffering from lack of equipment, could be trained only as a defensive force. The high level of skill essential to an effective striking force can be achieved only by long and rigorous training in battle conditions.

While the British Expeditionary Force in France was slowly being built up to a total strength of ten divisions, the people at home were lulled into a sense of security. A song-writer cashed in with a popular ditty which began 'We're going to hang out the washing on the Siegfried Line . . . if the Siegfried Line's still there!' Experts on military and political affairs, deceived by apparent inactivity of the enemy, attempted to prove that Germany would not attack westwards. For instance, Germany *must* have oil—there would be deadlock in the West, while Hitler struck south-eastwards through the Balkans towards the Middle East, or eastwards into Russia.

It was not only the British public who believed that the war could be won by starving the Germans out. From private soldier to general officer, all ranks of the Army disagreed with each other about the future. All through the bitterly cold winter, the men of the BEF discussed and wondered about what was to come.

While the Allied General Staff laid plans to meet every kind of attack that could be foreseen, the BEF settled down to its task of strengthening the frontier defences. Divisional Headquarters opened on October the 8th at Cité Saint Auguste, a suburb a mile from Lens, and received orders from II Corps that the division was in GHQ reserve. II Corps was commanded by Lieutenant-General Alan Brooke, and held the centre of the BEF sector. The right was held by I Corps. The Commander of the BEF was General Lord Gort vc kcb cbe dso mvo mc; and the BEF was itself under the French Commander-in-Chief, General Gamelin.

On the right of 4th Division, 10th Brigade, commanded first by Brigadier Barker and later by Brigadier J. L. I. Hawkesworth, and 11th Brigade, commanded by Brigadier Anderson, began to prepare defensive positions in front of, and guarding, the Canale de la Haute Deule, which runs from Douai some fourteen miles roughly north-west to Beauvin, ten miles south-west of Lille. These reserve positions were primarily for defence of canal lines against an armoured thrust through the main BEF positions, some twenty-five miles farther forward. The positions were eventually to be merged into an elaborate system of defence in depth.

The countryside was still a peaceful one, which the armed forces were not free to disorganize with road-blocks or forbidden zones. Preliminary arrangements were, however, made to blow all bridges and to block roads through such obstacles as woods and villages. Posts for anti-tank guns and rifles were built; and all road-blocks and posts were covered by section posts and belts of wire. Great care was taken, by the use of camouflage and discipline, to hide these preparations from enemy aircraft.

Digging was not a cheerful task when heavy rainstorms flooded the trenches and walls caved in for lack of revetting material. When the rain stopped, bitterly cold winds would blow from the North Sea across the exposed positions. The troops were, however, living in billets, not in the open, and suffered from the weather only while on duty. The people of the mining district—who included a high proportion of miners from countries as far away as China and Persia, as well as from Poland and elsewhere in Europe—were reasonably friendly, more so perhaps than during the 1914-18 war, and prices were favourable enough to allow the troops a pleasant evening in a café for a few shillings.

From time to time there were false alarms, varying in importance from air-raid alarms followed by no enemy aircraft to official warnings that the Germans were about to invade the Low Countries.

On October the 28th, 11th Brigade handed over the division's left front sector to 17th Brigade. Two days later, the brigade moved off—part of it travelling by train—to take over part of 51st French Division's sector. This sector, some ten miles north-east of Lille, was close against the Belgian frontier, and covered a front of four miles between Halluin and Tourcoing. The brigade came temporarily under the command of the French division.

During November, detailed orders were given out for the advance into Belgium, which would of course take place only if the Germans were to invade the country from the other side.

Towards the end of the month, further divisions from England began to arrive to reinforce the BEF. II Corps was now able to release 51st French Division, and 4th Division left Corps reserve and moved into the line north-east of Lille, where 11th Brigade was already in position.

On reconnoitring the new sector, Major-General Johnson found that the French division's plan of defence was cleverly arranged and clearly marked on the map, but simply did not exist on the ground. It was in fact what the French called *projet*. This seemed to be typical of the French Army at that time; the staff worked out the most excellent *projets*, about which little or nothing was done by the troops. The backwardness of the sector's defences, and the fact that the other divisions of the BEF had been working on theirs for two months, meant that 4th Division would have to work very hard to catch up, and so would have little time for training in mobile warfare.

In the two great industrial towns of Roubaix and Tourcoing, and in the rest of the country-side within the division's sector, life was going on as usual. Farms and factories were working full time; workers from France and Belgium crossed the frontier daily to work in factories on the far side. Troops at the frontier road posts examined everyone who came in. At night there was a certain amount of smuggling traffic which tried to dodge the patrols between the road posts. Smuggling was of course no concern of the army, but military information could also cross the frontier in the hands of smugglers. The division, therefore, had to organize a patrol system, to work with the French frontier police. This arrangement worked well, but was not entirely effective until a wire fence was erected along the whole frontier.

General Lord Gort, meanwhile, had begun to feel that war without an enemy within reach might be bad for the morale of the BEF. He therefore evolved a plan by which the infantry of one British brigade at a time was to go down to the Saar, two hundred miles south-east of Lille, to take over, under command of the French, a brigade sector in front of the Maginot Line. 12th Brigade went off first, in December, high-spirited in the hope of a fight. The new positions were in the rolling country north-east of Metz, between the Saar and the Moselle. The sector was the centre brigade sector of a French infantry division, and consisted of defences in depth between the Maginot Line and the German frontier. The most forward battalion position, known as the *Ligne de contact*, was round the village of Grindorff-Ewig, facing north-east across a stream. 12th Brigade's part of this line was two miles wide, and consisted of a chain of mutually supporting outposts and observation posts. Most of the outposts were held by a platoon, and were protected by breastworks of logs and sandbags, and sometimes by trenches; they were nearly all in the front edges of woods. The garrison lived in log huts. Between a mile and two miles to the front, the German frontier zigzagged across the fields and through the woods. Between the *Ligne de contact* and the frontier was No-man's-land, at first dominated by German patrols. The French had established an unenterprising policy of 'Live and let live', and had allowed the Germans to win a reputation for skilful and aggressive patrolling. The *Ligne de contact* was supported by three batteries of French 75-mm field guns, which had proved their value nearly a quarter of a century before, and by a battery of 155-mm medium guns. In reserve was a French battalion of infantry. The South Lancashires, commanded by Lieutenant-Colonel D. M. W. Beak VC DSO MC, were first to occupy the *Ligne de contact*, and so became the first of 4th Division's troops to see action since 1918.

Four miles behind the *Ligne de contact* was the *Ligne de recueil*. Two miles of this line, on the brow of the rising ground, were taken over by a second battalion. The third battalion held the *Ligne d'arrêt*, six miles farther back still, among the fortresses of the Maginot Line.

The Maginot Line was a chain of underground fortresses; unlike the field defences occupied by the 4th Division in front of Lille, it was a marvel of construction but not of planning. The defences were all concealed underground; weapons could be raised mechanically to fire through the smallest possible aperture, and when not in use could be lowered and covered by a cupola. Every hill was a fortress in itself, and relied for defence not only upon its own weapons but upon those of neighbouring forts—in case of dire need, a fort could batten itself down and call by telephone for fire to be directed on to its roof.

This was all very well, but these defences were neither in depth nor thick on the ground. In any case, it is doubtful whether defences of this kind are fit for any use other than as a firm base for an aggressive field force. The defences had cost about £600,000,000 to build; it is possible that the expenditure of that sum on tanks and other offensive weapons for the French Army might have had an interesting effect on the forthcoming campaign.

The many war correspondents who had been growing more and more restless during the BEF's long wait for the enemy at last had something to write home about, and routine patrols became headline news. But in the reports of the battalions in the line, day after day and night after night were reported uneventful; three Germans and a dog might have been seen crossing a distant field, or a concrete-mixer might have been heard, grinding away in a village several thousands of yards off. From time to time, small groups of British and German soldiers on patrol shot at each other, usually without result. On Christmas Eve, the Germans could be heard singing hymns and carols in a wood not far away. The weather grew colder, and before the end of the year the troops were enduring twenty-seven degrees of frost. Snow was lying on the ground when 12th Brigade handed over the sector to a brigade from another division of the BEF, and gratefully began the journey back to billets at Tourcoing.

On the main divisional front, the troops worked hard at the defences, though frost and snow interfered with concreting. Home leave began, ten days each for those who had been in France on October the 1st. Christmas was celebrated in traditional style, with officers serving their men and all ranks drinking as much as they wanted and sometimes more than they could hold.

At the end of January, the division, which until then had consisted of units of the Regular Army, began to be diluted with Territorial units. The 1st Oxfordshire and Buckinghamshire Light Infantry left 11th Brigade, and were replaced by the 5th Northamptons. During the next few weeks, 9th Field Company left the

Divisional Royal Engineers, and was replaced by 225th Field Company. The 1st Black Watch left 12th Brigade, and the 6th Black Watch came from 51st Highland Division in exchange. 17th Field Regiment, armed with the modern 25-pounder gun-howitzer, went to the 51st Highland Division, who sent back in exchange the 77th (Highland) Field Regiment. This regiment was armed with twelve 4·5-inch howitzers and twelve 18-pounder guns. These weapons, designed and built for use more than twenty years before, had to be used for the next eighteen months because of the amount of ammunition that would otherwise be wasted. The ammunition for the 18-pounders was forty per cent shrapnel, though the British Army had generally discarded the use of shrapnel, as complicated to use and comparatively ineffective. Both the howitzers and the guns were outranged by several thousand yards by the new German field artillery.

In February 1940, 10th Brigade in its turn went down to the Saar. The Bedfords, commanded by Lieutenant-Colonel J. S. Davenport MC, took over the *Ligne de contact*; the West Kents, commanded by Lieutenant-Colonel J. S. Sharpin, took over the *Ligne de recueil*; and the DCLI prepared to take over the *Ligne d'arrêt*. The thaw had set in; the air was clear and warm, and the ground sloppy with mud. After a few days the battalions changed round, and the DCLI came up to the front line.

The quiet routine of sentry-posting and patrolling was abruptly broken. Just after dawn one morning, a sudden crash of gunfire burst on and round one of the DCLI's posts in Hartbuch wood; as the unseasoned men, taken by surprise, crouched in their trenches, the Germans came storming in with grenades and automatics. Platoon Sergeant-Major Larcombe and Corporal Killick of the DCLI's 17 Platoon were killed, Private Durrant was wounded, and sixteen men were captured; a German corporal was shot dead.

There were no more attacks of this kind during 10th Brigade's tour of action. The Germans were, however, more active than they had been during the more difficult weather of 12th Brigade's time. Their working parties and observers could be seen moving about, and German patrols and artillery were increasingly active.

In the second week of March, 10th Brigade rejoined the rest of the division near Lille.

The winter weather became abominable, with bitter winds, icy rain, frost and snow succeeding each other. From time to time the weather stopped all work, and the troops joined the civil authorities in helping to clear snow from the streets. When weather permitted, work on the defences went on, and with it a certain amount of route-marches and of training with grenades and small-arms. A major 'flap' stopped everything, including leave; the Belgian frontier guards cleared away their wire obstacles and said they had orders to allow troops into Belgium. The Germans, however, put in no attack, and the frontier was closed once more.

On February the 26th, Major-General HRH the Duke of Gloucester was attached at his own request to Major-General Johnson's headquarters, for a stay of eight weeks.

The only incident of note during 11th Brigade's tour of duty in front of the Maginot Line during March was a spirited patrol action during the night of March the 19th. The battle patrol of the Lancashire Fusiliers, consisting of Captain J. H. Hudson and five Fusiliers, set out to climb the hillside in front of Grindorff-Ewig. The patrol was lying-up in a gully, waiting for the moon to go down, when nine or ten Germans appeared, making their way down the gully. After a short uproar of automatic fire and bursting grenades, the Germans began to make off, and the Fusiliers rushed their position. Three of the Germans, including a Second-Lieutenant, were dead and three were wounded. More Germans were coming up, and the patrol withdrew with a prisoner. Captain Hudson and Fusilier Worsley were afterwards awarded the Croix de Guerre by the commander of the French division, and Captain Hudson was also awarded the Military Cross. These were the first awards made to men of the 4th Division during the war.

There was still more snow to come, but the worst of the foul weather was over. Large-scale exercises began, some of them lasting four days, practising brigades and units in movement, counter-attack and tank co-operation. As these were the first exercises of their kind that the division had been able to carry out since 1935, they were of inestimable value.

The weather grew better as March gave way to April, and the ground began to harden. Colonel Dening, the GSO 1 of the division, calculated that, despite the complacency of newspaper 'experts', the Germans would attack in May or June. 11th Brigade came back from the Saar. Young officers began to reach the infantry battalions; they were civilian volunteers, who had gone through the Officer-Cadet Training Units set up very soon after the outbreak of war, and who had been granted emergency commissions.

The sea-borne attack, which the Germans had long been known to be preparing, fell on Norway, after German troops had marched into Denmark at dawn on April the 9th. This assault on neutral countries naturally led to a 'stand by' for the troops on the Belgian border, but the excitement in France soon died down, although the German press accused the Allies of planning to invade Sweden, Holland and Belgium. At the same time the Italian press began to be unpleasantly aggressive.

Colonel Dening forecast that since the weather was very hot and dry, operations in Belgium might start at any moment. At home, a foreign affairs 'expert' wrote that there would be no attack in the West because there was no new weapon powerful enough to break a strongly defended front.

On May the 4th, the last of the Territorial units arrived, when the 1st/6th East Surreys came from 44th Division at Bailleul to take the place of the 1st Royal West Kents in 10th Brigade. There was at first a certain amount of confusion between the 1st/6th East Surreys in 10th Brigade and the 1st East Surreys in 11th Brigade.

The first days of May were hot and still. Formation commanders and their staffs began to feel anxious. The voices at home which had so glibly prophesied a stale-mate on the Western Front fell silent. The division put the finishing touches to its defences, and British divisions to left and right did the same.

On May the 10th the storm burst. At half-past four in the morning the German divisions flung themselves into Holland, Belgium and Luxembourg.

2. Brussels and Dunkirk

During the twenty-one years of peace which had followed the Great War, France and Britain had gratefully relaxed after their supreme military effort. There were minor campaigns on the borders of empire, but the Armies of the two nations had been engaged in no struggle that would have exercised their full strength. Nor had the approach of another war in Europe been obvious enough to infect the people of France and Britain with a sense of urgency. Warning voices had been raised, but, in the weary aftermath of the most terrible of all wars, they had been ignored.

The Armies of these two countries, then, pursued a course normal in time of peace, preparing vaguely for another war which might never come. France spent most of her military budget on fixed defences, and trained her Army to occupy them. Britain mechanized her Army, and brought into use new types of equipment, but achieved few tactical revolutions.

But the bitter resentment that followed defeat and Versailles, and the resurgent nationalism that had raised Hitler to power, had stung the ever active military thinkers of Germany to strenuous endeavours. New theories had been developed, and new weapons manufactured to put them into effect. Both theories and weapons had been tried out in Spain, and perfected before they were turned on Poland.

The German forces were organized and equipped first to deal a shattering blow at the weakest point of the defence, then to burst through at this point, and finally to fan out to right and left behind the defenders. Since the weakest point might be no bigger than a company position, a German company commander might be able to call on tanks, self-propelled close-support artillery, assault engineers and ground-attack aircraft. Once the breach was open, tanks were ready to pass through, and mobile infantry in armoured lorries were ready to follow up. The infantry would drive up behind the tanks, dismount at the last moment to smother any resistance, and remount as soon as the tanks could go forward once more.

The Germans had furthermore worked out plans for the softening-up of the defences opposing them, in preparation for the main attack. Spies, saboteurs and rumour-mongers were planted among the civil population of the country to be attacked; traitors in high places were subsidized. By these means, the people were to be poisoned with panic and disorganization which would infect and hinder the armed forces defending them. The morale of soldiers and civilians was to be undermined by false rumours and continual propaganda. Shortly before the main attack, airborne troops—in uniform or in disguise—would be dropped to seize vulnerable points, such as bridges which were to be preserved for the advancing German tanks.

The German commanders, urged on by the Nazi Party, had trained their assault troops to disregard everything but victory. Every advantage, for instance, was to be taken of the non-combatant; helpless peasants were to be urged or driven on to the roads to hinder the Allied troops, disaffected officials of local and central government were to be bribed or intimidated into assisting the machine that would destroy their country. The invasion, within a period of a few weeks, of no less than five neutral countries was entirely consistent with this theory of Total War.

The German assault had been carefully prepared; there was to be no halt on the Marne this time. The first target was of course to be the left flank of the Maginot Line—the lightly-defended frontier of France between the Ardennes and Dunkirk. Three neutral countries were in the way. Holland could early be crippled by floods; Belgium had suffered too cruelly as the battle-field of the Great War to want to resist for long; and Luxembourg was said to be defended by one infantry battalion.

The second target would be the Channel Ports, particularly those from which the BEF might hope to escape.

Against this attack, the Allies, who now of course included the Dutch and Belgians, prepared to defend a succession of lines which followed, as far as possible, the line of natural anti-tank obstacles. The Belgian Army was to defend the Albert Canal from Antwerp to Maastricht, and the River Meuse from Maastricht to Liège. Behind this line of rivers, the French were to defend the river line from Antwerp to Mechlin; the BEF was to hold the River Dyle from Mechlin to Louvain; and the French were to come up on the right to hold the line from Louvain through Gembloux to Namur. Between Louvain and Namur there is no natural anti-tank obstacle, and this part of the line was known as the Gembloux gap. The right flank of the Belgian line south of Liège, and of the Anglo-French line at Namur, was comparatively lightly held, as the country was too difficult for a rapid thrust; and farther still to the south rise the Ardennes, said to be impassable to tanks.

The BEF began to move forward into Belgium as soon as news of the German attack was received, and 3rd Division reached the Dyle at Louvain that night. Since 4th Division was initially to be in II Corps reserve, zero hour for the division's advance was not until the night of May the 13th.

4th Division moved into Belgium along two roughly parallel roads. Route G, on the right, ran through Tournai, Renaix and Ninove to Brussels; Route H, on the left, ran through Audenarde and Alost to Vilvorde, a small town on the River Senne six miles north-east of the centre of Brussels.

The move was comparatively successful, since German aircraft made no attack on the long, carefully spaced columns of lorries and guns. Alost, however, had been heavily bombed, and Route H had to be altered to avoid the ruins. The move was far from easy, since level-crossings interrupted the columns, and growing throngs of Belgian refugees, plodding blindly towards France, began to crowd the roads. The presence on the roads of these refugees was to a large extent arranged by the German exponents of the Total War. German agents had spent months spreading rumours to the effect that the only safe thing for civilians to do was to clear off the battle-field. Townsmen and peasants passed these rumours on, and flocked on to the roads, every yard of which was needed by the armed forces.

Major-General Johnson went forward to reconnoitre the Vilvorde neighbourhood, and found it already crowded with no less than three Belgian divisions of the Belgian I Corps. These divisions had already withdrawn from the Albert Canal defences, leaving many of their weapons behind. Their commanders told Major-General Johnson that they must find somewhere to reorganize; he agreed, but pointed out that he needed Vilvorde, and advised them to reorganize elsewhere. The Belgian V Corps, which was supposed to be holding the River Senne on the left of 4th Division, appeared to be properly organized, but did not look convincingly battle-worthy.

4th Division began to arrive in Brussels and Vilvorde during the morning of May the 14th, and took up its reserve positions. 12th Brigade spread along the Willebroeck Canal on each side of Vilvorde. 11th Brigade began to reach the north-western suburbs of Brussels at four in the morning of May the 15th, took up positions along the canal on the right of 12th Brigade, and began to prepare its defence.

10th Brigade had reached Vilvorde during the evening of May the 14th, and crossed the canal to take up positions stretching from Vilvorde south-westwards to the Brussels-Louvain road. The reason for this curious diagonal position was that the battle was not going well; 3rd Division was going to withdraw from Louvain, and 10th Brigade was to guard 3rd Division's left flank during the withdrawal. The brigade was placed under the command of 3rd Division for this purpose.

One of the first and most rapid German thrusts was from Aachen in Germany to Maastricht in Holland, less than twenty miles away. At Maastricht, German parachutists and saboteurs made sure that the Dutch would fail to destroy the bridges over both the River Meuse and the Albert Canal. The German tanks raced through Maastricht into Belgium, making for the Gembloux gap and for the junction between British and French divisions; meanwhile, the Belgian troops on the Albert Canal to the north-west, ferociously attacked by dive-bombers and outflanked, fell hurriedly back on the line of the River Dyle, running through Louvain, forty miles behind Maastricht.

To the right front of the BEF, therefore, the German assault was gathering speed and force. To the left front, the Dutch were falling back in front of an equally fierce attack, while Stuka dive-bombers pounded the cities behind them. But the most dangerous thrusts of all had cut through the supposedly impassable Ardennes to cross the River Meuse, in Belgium south of Namur, and in France at Sedan.

The thrusts south of Namur and towards the Gembloux gap were threatening to outflank 3rd Division on the River Dyle at Louvain. What was more dangerous still, Major-General B. L. Montgomery, commanding 3rd Division, could not rely on the Belgian VI Corps on his left to hold fast. It was essential, therefore, that 4th Division should put out 10th Brigade like a shield, facing towards the left front where the Germans were nearest and the defence least resolute, so that 3rd Division could withdraw behind it to take up positions in Brussels. The Germans reached the River Dyle at Louvain on May the 14th, but made no co-ordinated attack; and on the following day, while 3rd Division was beating back Germans from the river, Holland surrendered.

On May the 16th, the Germans forced their way through the Gembloux gap, completely turning the right flank of the BEF. The British I Corps fell back. Lieutenant-General Brooke ordered 3rd Division to withdraw from the River Dyle at Louvain, across the River Senne at Brussels to the River Dendre between Alost and Ninove, a distance of nearly thirty miles. 4th Division was to cover the withdrawal by holding fast on the Senne at Brussels. 4th Division was to be strengthened for this role by 32nd and 60th Army Field Regiments, 4th Medium Regiment's battery of 6-inch guns, and a battery of 51st Heavy Regiment. The 2nd Armoured Reconnaissance Brigade, consisting of the 15th/19th Hussars and the 5th Inniskilling Dragoon Guards, who had been on the right of 10th Brigade, were to come under Major-General Johnson's command as soon as they crossed the canal in Brussels. 4th Division was to blow up the bridges over the canal as soon as 3rd Division was across.

That night, 3rd Division withdrew from Louvain, and, followed by a rear-guard consisting of 10th Brigade and the Armoured Reconnaissance Brigade, crossed the canal in Brussels during May the 17th. The sappers of 7th, 59th and 225th Field Companies, under the CRE, Lieutenant-Colonel Coxwell-Rogers, destroyed twenty-three bridges and one tunnel under the canal between eight in the morning and two in the afternoon, a colossal task for three companies. The great bridge in the centre of Brussels was destroyed only at the second attempt. The Germans were hard on the heels of the rear-guard, and their leading troops were already on one of the Vilvorde bridges when it exploded under them. 10th Brigade withdrew across the river and into reserve.

The first Germans appeared at half-past one in the afternoon, when motor-cyclists and armoured cars came to reconnoitre the crossings at Vilvorde. Troops of 12th Brigade opened fire, and destroyed several vehicles. The Germans gathered up an attack on Vilvorde bridge, but were held off by a company of the Royal

Fusiliers, backed up by carriers, mortars and some men from the reserve company.

Enemy reconnaissance units were filtering through Brussels at the same time, and soon there was a brisk rattle of fire across the canal from both sides. The 3-inch mortars of the Northamptons knocked out an armoured car.

During the evening, General Lord Gort gave orders that the whole BEF was to withdraw at midnight across the River Dendre. The heavy guns and 60th Army Field Regiment reverted to the command of II Corps. 3rd Division was to hold the line of the Dendre, while 4th Division passed through into reserve.

At midnight the infantry began to march out of Brussels. The withdrawal was covered by the Armoured Reconnaissance Brigade. The Hussars and the Inniskillings held Line A just behind Brussels, and two batteries of 14th Anti-tank Regiment and the machine-guns of the 4th Gordons held Line B farther back. Both Lines were supported by 32nd Field Regiment. The right flank was secured by the rear-guard of 1st Division, which was withdrawing at the same time. The left was to be guarded by the Belgians on the Willebroeck Canal.

The withdrawal had already begun, and Divisional Headquarters had closed down and was on the move, when Major-General Johnson heard that the Belgians had withdrawn from the canal. He at once sent off a message by despatch-rider to warn the rear-guard, but it never reached them. As 11th and 12th Brigades abandoned the canal and withdrew through Line A, the Germans followed up rapidly, found the northern flank open and cut in between the rear-guard and the River Dendre. The Hussars lost forty-three armoured vehicles—the whole of the unit except one squadron and two troops; a company of the Gordons and seven of the anti-tank guns were also lost.

The withdrawal of the main body went better, though the roads were already jammed with refugees and withdrawing Belgian and French troops. The division was making for the country round the village of Resseghem, which lies six miles behind Alost, between Routes G and H, along which the division had advanced four days earlier.

During the night, while the division was still withdrawing behind the River Dendre, Lieutenant-General Brooke told Major-General Johnson that he was to continue the withdrawal to positions behind the River Escaut, south-west of Audenarde. The infantry were tired out after their march of more than twenty miles from Brussels to Resseghem, but two Troop-carrying Companies were provided.

By the end of May the 18th, 10th and 11th Brigades were behind the Escaut. 12th Brigade crossed during the following day.

The division's front lay along the River Escaut from Eeuwhoek, a farm four and a half miles south-west of Audenarde, to Avelghem, a village five miles farther up the river. Avelghem is only ten miles north-east of Leers, the suburb of Roubaix which had been on the right flank of the division's prepared positions. The country-side on the north-western or BEF side of the river is flat and open; a mile beyond the river, on the enemy side, the wooded Mont de l'Enclus rises to more than three hundred feet above the rest of the country-side, looking down on the whole divisional sector. Already stretched out along its five-mile front, 4th Division could not spare the infantry brigade that would have been necessary to hold the hill.

44th British Division was already holding the river on the left as far as Audenarde. 3rd Division was withdrawn from the Dendre during May the 19th, crossed the front of 4th Division and took up positions along the Escaut on the right. The BEF had three more divisions along the river to the south, where it runs through Tournai. Another three divisions, making nine in all, were in reserve. 4th Division now came under III Corps, commanded by Lieutenant-General Sir Ronald Adam.

4th Division's front was held by 10th Brigade on the right and 11th Brigade on the left. 32nd Army Field Regiment and 4th Medium Regiment were under the command of the CRA, Brigadier Leventhorpe. 12th Brigade was in reserve round Ooteghem, three miles behind the river in the centre of the sector.

From left to right, the division's front was held by the Northamptons, the 1st East Surreys, the Lancashire Fusiliers, the DCLI and the Bedfords. The 1st/6th East Surreys were in brigade reserve, north of Avelghem.

After 3rd Division had crossed the river, the four bridges in the division's sector, which had been prepared for demolition by sappers of 44th Division, were blown up. The infantry and the gunners, and various service and headquarters units less accustomed to digging, spent the day digging in; all positions were overlooked by the Mont de l'Enclus, except for those of Divisional Headquarters and administrative units.

The night of May the 19th was quiet, but at ten in the morning of the 20th the enemy appeared, reconnoitring the river and registering roads in the divisional area with his guns. The German force on the far bank of the river began to grow in strength and aggressiveness, testing the defence for weak points. Just outside 4th Division's sector to the left, in front of 44th Division, the Germans won a foothold across the river, penetrated to a depth of nearly half a mile, seizing the farm of Kwaadestraat, and also crossed the river a mile farther to the left, near Petegem village. German attempts to cross the bridge in 4th Division's sector by the bridge at Escanaffles were unsuccessful. A German attack developed behind the bridge at Rugge, and was broken up by 4th Division's guns.

There were some curious manifestations of the Total War. A group of nuns, in black robes and yellow sashes, suddenly opened fire on one of the infantry battalions, and turned out to be Germans, subtly disguised. Captured British soldiers were stripped of their uniforms—presumably to be used by the enemy—and set free in their underclothes. Guards on blown bridges hesitated to fire on civilian cars driven by girls, until the car was near enough for the Germans in the back to be seen—or for the 'girl's' stubbly jaw to show through the powder.

The news from beyond the right flank of the BEF was growing more and more unnerving. The Germans were through the Gembloux gap, had passed Mons and entered France. Worse still, their advanced troops had reached Arras, fifteen miles behind Douai, which had been the right flank of 4th Division's first positions in France.

After a quiet night, the Germans began on May the 21st to press hard on 44th Division on the left, enlarging the bridge-heads they had already won. Before long, the bridge-head was a mile deep and nearly three miles wide. The Northamptons had to face left to meet this new threat, and the Black Watch came forward during the evening to guard the left flank from positions behind the Northamptons, on the ridge between the village of Caster and the railway line. The South Lancashires came up to Berewijk farm, on the ridge, two thousand yards farther to the west. Both battalions hurriedly dug in during the night.

The Germans also attacked 4th Division's front on the river in the early morning. An early morning attack by fifteen men across the canal by the broken bridge at Escanaffles was broken up by artillery fire and thrown back by the Bedfords. During the afternoon, another attack came across at Rugge and forced a section of the DCLI out of position. By nightfall, however, the near bank was clear, and the DCLI were relieved by the 1st/6th East Surreys under continuous shellfire, after suffering considerable losses.

The whole area was shaken all day by heavy and accurate fire from German guns and mortars. The fire seemed to be directed partly from the reconnaissance aircraft flying overhead, and partly by observers on Mont de l'Enclus, and it burst with particular force on cross-roads and possible observation-posts such as church towers. Most of the German guns concentrated on the British gun-positions and brigade headquarters. 11th Brigade Headquarters was forced to move. Telephone cables were repeatedly cut; maintenance became increasingly difficult and eventually impossible. 77th Field Regiment, which, owing to the short range of its guns, had had to be placed well forward in an exposed position, suffered particularly heavily, and lost several guns.

The enemy's attacks across the river on May the 21st were all pushed back by 10th and 11th Brigades. Enemy raids during the night were equally unsuccessful.

The morning of May the 22nd was ominously quiet. Heavy shelling began at one in the afternoon, and the battalions began to lose men. Major Lawton, the second-in-command of the 1st East Surreys, was among the killed. The Black Watch on Caster ridge tried to get in touch with 44th Division on the left and the Northamptons on the right, failed to do so and lost some men.

The change of front which had been forced on the Northamptons gave the Germans the chance they needed, and soon they were across the river in 4th Division's sector, thrusting diagonally into the Northamptons' front towards the village of Kerkhove. At the same time, an astonishing number of guns began to fire at Kerkhove, the fire being directed to some extent from an observation balloon. The East Surreys in and round Kerkhove held fast, though almost every building was hit. The Germans reached the orchards two hundred yards beyond the river, but there were pinned down by fire from both the Northamptons and the Surreys.

The main German attack began at three in the afternoon, and its weight fell on the junction between 4th and 44th Divisions. The Germans drove back the right flank of 44th Division to the village of Wortegem, three miles from the river, and pushed the Black

Watch back from the railway line on to Caster ridge. Two companies of the Black Watch were all but cut off, and had to fight their way out.

But it was useless to defend the Escaut when seventy miles to the right rear the Germans had captured Amiens and were within forty miles of the Channel Ports. The division was ordered to withdraw during the evening of May the 22nd, and to take up positions between Tourcoing and Halluin, to some extent in the positions which the division had prepared during the winter.

The retreat in face of German attacks was by no means easy. All non-essential transport, and with it a field ambulance and 77th Field Regiment, were sent back in daylight. 77th Field Regiment had to be withdrawn because it had already lost nine guns and had run out of ammunition for the 4·5-inch howitzers.

The withdrawal was carried out with a vehicle density of ten to the mile. This wide interval between vehicles was made necessary by the enemy's command of the air, and had the unfortunate result of compelling the artillery to withdraw at a time when the infantry still needed help.

The first companies had to withdraw in daylight, an extremely difficult business over open ground and under attack. Lieutenant-Colonel C. M. Rougier MC of the Lancashire Fusiliers and Lieutenant-Colonel Green, commanding the Northamptons, were among the killed. After dusk the Germans pressed the division hard, and were toughly resisted. By ten at night, all the telephone lines had been cut, and Divisional Headquarters was in touch only by wireless with 12th Brigade Headquarters.

At eleven o'clock at night, very fortunately, the German attacks slackened. The enemy settled down to a desultory shelling of roads and some air bombing, but did not follow up. At one in the morning of May the 23rd, the infantry abandoned the line of the Kerkhove-Avelghem road, each brigade covering its own withdrawal. The whole division wheeled backwards to the right rear, and was across the Courtrai Canal by half-past two in the morning. By the time the rear-guards had reached the new positions, there was no sign of the enemy. The infantry had marched twenty-three miles.

The new line extended from the north-eastern outskirts of Tourcoing to the canal a mile north-east of Halluin, a front of four miles. 3rd Division was on the right, and 3rd and 4th Divisions were now both in II Corps again. On the left was the Belgian Army, holding a line running at right-angles to the left front of 4th Division, along the canalized River Lys to Courtrai and thence north-east along the river. The German armoured divisions in the rear had not been having it all their own way, and had been thrown out of Arras and Amiens, but since there were still German tanks between the BEF and Boulogne the situation was no less grave.

The division was back where it had started from, the men were tired, and units had suffered losses both of men and of equipment. On the whole, however, the division was in good heart. The Belgian expedition had been unsuccessful, but now the party was back things would doubtless settle down. The Tourcoing-Halluin line was to be firmly held, and probably the French would know how to deal with the four German armoured divisions which had got round to the rear. When reinforcements arrived, the Allies would soon be able to fight back again. This optimism was strengthened by orders that there was to be no further withdrawal, and by a breathing space which allowed of rest, wash, food and sleep.

The situation was in fact worse than ever, for the Germans in the rear, still going strong, had reached Boulogne, and on the left the Belgians were faltering more and more. For the time being, however, 4th Division felt able to deal with events.

10th Brigade was on the right, and 12th Brigade on the left. Neither brigade was holding all its prepared positions, since the divisional front was rather farther forward than it had been a fortnight before. 11th Brigade was in reserve round Roncq.

May the 23rd was a quiet day, except that German aircraft were almost constantly overhead, on their way to support the armoured divisions behind. A few shells fired at extreme range burst in 12th Brigade's area. The digging troops sweated in the still heat of the summer day. German cyclists rode into view, were shot at and rode out of view again. The night was equally quiet. But during the day the Belgians had withdrawn from Courtrai, on the division's left front, almost as far as Halluin.

May the 24th was only slightly less quiet; the enemy advance was continuing, but seemed to be passing by the division to the left. By noon the Germans were across the River Lys between Courtrai and Menin, and the Belgians were still withdrawing. The Belgian commander assured Major-General Johnson that his troops would soon make a stand, but there was no sign of a halt. Before long, the

Belgians had been pushed off the banks of the Lys, except that at Menin they still joined up with 4th Division's left flank.

12th Brigade on the left could see long columns of German vehicles coming slowly towards Menin. RAF aircraft were diving on the columns at Wevelghem and Lauwe, on each side of the Lys only three miles away.

During the night, the division was reinforced by the 1st/7th Middlesex (machine-gunners), a battery of 20th Anti-tank Regiment and two companies of the 8th King's Own.

On May the 25th, the Belgian commander said he was being forced to withdraw to the north. Major-General Johnson sent a liaison officer out on a motor-cycle to see what was happening to the Belgians. This officer found that they had given up all thought of fighting; within two or three thousand yards of a precarious front line, Belgian troops were sitting about in cafés drinking coffee or beer.

The situation was now growing desperate. To the left rear, German tanks were advancing to join the German divisions advancing to the left front. If they were to join up, 4th Division and the rest of the BEF would be surrounded and cut off from the sea. The Belgians were still withdrawing, and soon the enemy columns could be seen moving through Menin towards Ypres. 4th Division's guns smashed up a number of German vehicles, but the advance went on. More and more German forces were moving across the division's front from right to left, and wheeling round the division's flank to the left. The left flank was completely open.

Major-General Johnson at once put the Lancashire Fusiliers into Halluin, with the 1st East Surreys on their left holding the canal almost as far as Bousbecque, two miles to the west. The Middlesex held Bousbecque itself. On the left of the Middlesex, the Black Watch came up on May the 26th to hold the canal through Comines as far as Warneton Sud. Fortunately this new front of more than eight miles, running across the division's left flank, was on the frontier and had already been thoroughly dug in.

A British brigade from II Corps reserve was put in on the left of the division, under Major-General Johnson's command, with the duty of holding the Ypres Canal between Comines and Ypres, to cover sappers preparing demolitions along the canal.

During the afternoon of May the 26th, a corporal's patrol of the Middlesex shot up a German staff car. The staff officer got away, but had to leave his dispatch-case behind. The contents of the case showed why there had been no attack on the division's front; the German plan was to encircle the prepared defences, and to get round behind Lille from right and left.

That evening Major-General Johnson learned from the corps commander that the campaign was lost; the Germans had all but encircled the whole BEF and some eight French divisions. There was no longer any hope that this Allied force could break out to the west, and take up a stand on the coast. There was nothing for it but to make northwards for the coast near the Franco-Belgian frontier, and there to embark in whatever craft could be found to carry the troops across the Channel. In case the main body was unable to get away, a few picked officers and NCOs were to go home at once; around these men, new units would be formed at home. Secret papers were to be burnt; equipment and weapons would be destroyed when no longer needed.

During the evening of May the 26th, 5th Division came up on the left to take over the line of the canal from Comines to Ypres.

Early in the morning, the Field Companies went up to the River Lys between Warneton and Comines to prepare positions facing south from which 4th Division's northwards withdrawal would be covered. Early in the afternoon, the Germans broke through 143rd Brigade in front of Comines and reached the village. The CRE, Lieutenant-Colonel Coxwell-Rogers, placed 7th and 59th Field Companies under the command of the Black Watch; the sappers took up their rifles, and with the infantry put in a spirited counter-attack. The commanders of both companies, Majors Gillespie and Macdonald, were wounded while leading their men in this gallant action. The attack was successful, and the Germans were driven away from their threatening position at the division's left rear. The Black Watch and the Middlesex were fighting hard much of the day to make the Germans stay on the right side of the canal, and so keep them away from the division's flank.

By now the Germans were across the Ypres Canal in 5th Division's sector. Major-General Johnson had hurriedly to take 10th Brigade out of the line on the right and send it across the Lys to the hamlet of Wytschaete, three and a half miles north-west of Warneton and about the same distance behind the Ypres Canal, in order to strengthen 5th Division and hold open 4th Division's line of retreat. The sector on the right of 4th Division, thus vacated, was taken over by a battalion of the Coldstream Guards. The Bedfords had to beat off a fierce German attack on the frontier positions before handing over. 10th Brigade had some sharp fighting in its new positions.

12th Brigade moved back along the Lys to take up its role of rearguard for II Corps. The brigade was to face south-east along the canal from Warneton to Armentières—a front of more than five miles—until the rest of 4th Division and the whole of 3rd Division had passed through.

11th Brigade in turn withdrew across the Lys during the night of May the 27th, and took 10th Brigade's place in the defence of Wytschaete. 10th Brigade withdrew, and was sent off towards the coast. By seven the next morning the brigade was concentrated round Eikhoek, a village eleven miles north-west of Wytschaete.

The Belgians had laid down their arms during the day. This meant that the BEF's route to the coast was undefended against any German attack which might cross the Yser at Dixmude, less than ten miles from 10th Brigade at Eikhoek.

On May the 28th, therefore, the Field Companies were sent out to blow all the Yser bridges from Dixmude to Nieuport, eight miles to the north-west and only two miles from the sea. 59th Field Company, commanded by Lieutenant Calvert, found the roads to Dixmude packed with Belgian troops carrying white flags and moving towards the enemy, but nevertheless reached the town. The Germans were already arriving, and the company lost some men. The bridges, however, had already been blown, and Lieutenant Calvert took his company on to join 12th Brigade at Coxyde, eleven miles to the north-west.

225th Field Company blew the bridges between Dixmude and Nieuport, and went off to Furnes, six miles south-west of Nieuport, to destroy all the bridges there. 7th Field Company found the Germans already in Nieuport, and in spite of making every effort could not blow the bridges. The sappers took up their rifles once more, and held the exits from the bridges until the infantry arrived on the following day.

The German threat to the BEF's withdrawal route compelled the rear-guard to withdraw more rapidly still. During the afternoon, 3rd Division completed its withdrawal across the Lys. 12th Brigade blew up the bridges and hurriedly began to withdraw through the areas of 5th and 3rd Divisions. The Black Watch, however, were facing the enemy between Warneton and Houthem; since the battalion could not safely be withdrawn, it was left behind under command of 5th Division.

The Royal Fusiliers and the South Lancashires sent a company each, with field and anti-tank guns, to help hold the Yser from Dixmude to Nieuport. The rest of the two battalions made for Poperinghe, twelve miles from Warneton, but on arrival there it was redirected to Furnes, fifteen miles to the north.

The immense mass of traffic on the roads, however, delayed the brigade column, and when day broke on May the 29th it was still near Poperinghe. The vehicles became hopelessly mixed up with those of other units and formations, but the mass of traffic kept moving slowly towards the coast. The extent of the disaster became more and more obvious as the lorries and buses passed medium guns and heavy anti-aircraft guns spiked beside the road. Food was short, and the sky was swarming with German aircraft on their way back from the beaches ahead.

By mid-morning, however, 12th Brigade had reached the perimeter of the BEF's last position. The perimeter ran from the mouth of the Yser to Nieuport, then turned south-west along the canal to Furnes, and east to Dunkirk, where it returned to the sea. The position was eighteen miles wide, and at Furnes, its deepest point, was three and a half miles deep. Into this small space were crowded all the troops who had not yet been embarked. Clouds of black smoke rolled into the sky from vehicles set on fire by their drivers or by the German bombs which burst thunderously along the beaches and roads from time to time. Outside the perimeter, the fields were littered with smashed and smoking equipment—lorries drained of oil and left with their engines screaming at full throttle, guns with barrels grotesquely splayed out at the muzzle, motor-cycles crushed by the tracks of Bren carriers. Here and there among the débris lay the dead whom nobody had had time to bury.

12th Brigade destroyed its vehicles at the perimeter, and at once took over the extreme left flank, along the Yser between Nieuport and the sea. The South Lancashires, commanded by Lieutenant-Colonel D. M. W. Beak VC DSO MC, were on the left; the Royal Fusiliers, commanded by Lieutenant-Colonel Allen, relieved the sappers of 7th Field Company at the Nieuport bridge on the right. The Black Watch had not yet rejoined the brigade. The Germans were already across the canal at Nieuport, and the Fusiliers, weary as they were, had to be vigilant and quick on the trigger.

During the evening 10th Brigade, which had been moving from Eikhoek all day, reached the perimeter, and relieved the weary troops on the right of 12th Brigade, along the canal between Nieuport and Wulpen, three miles to the south-west. German reconnaissance troops reached the canal at about the same time as 10th Brigade; it was going to be a desperately close thing. The Bedfords were on the right and the DCLI on the left; the 1st/6th Surreys were in reserve. During the night, 11th Brigade arrived, having been relieved at Wytschaete, and went into action on the right, along the two and a half miles of canal from Wulpen to Furnes. The Northamptons were on the right, the 1st Surreys in the centre and the Lancashire Fusiliers on the left.

At dawn on May the 30th, 11th Brigade on the right was relieved by battalions of 3rd Division, and withdrew into a reserve position on the sea at Oost-Dunkirk Bains. Lieutenant-General Brooke, commanding II Corps, was called home to help in organizing the defence of Great Britain; Major-General Montgomery of 3rd Division took over II Corps; Brigadier Anderson of 11th Brigade went off to command 3rd Division; and Lieutenant-Colonel Horrocks of the Middlesex Regiment assumed temporary command of 11th Brigade.

The German forces round the perimeter were gathering strength, and during the day began to press hard. The attacks along the beach on 12th Brigade's left, and on 12th Brigade's right at Nieuport, were particularly difficult to hold off. Lieutenant-Colonel Allen was shot dead by a sniper, and Major J. L. Lotinga took command of the Royal Fusiliers. German reconnaissance aircraft and an observation balloon in Nieuport directed heavy artillery fire on to the division's guns, which were still in action. German aircraft were overhead most of the day, on their way to bomb the ships carrying out the evacuation, or on their way back. The Germans kept up their pressure all day, but the point of most danger was more effectively guarded when the Black Watch arrived from the Lys and took over the left sector of 12th Brigade, next to the sea. The Royal Fusiliers were then able to concentrate on Nieuport bridge.

Before dawn on May the 31st, the enemy launched a powerful attack along the whole perimeter. His artillery smoke-screen, however, was blown into shreds by the high wind, and served only to blind his advancing troops. His medium and heavy guns switched from smoke shell to high explosive, and wave after wave of infantry came in to the attack. The Royal Fusiliers at Nieuport were pushed back but not broken through. The South Lancashires scattered attack after attack with their 3-inch mortars.

The German thrust against the right of 12th Brigade reached a brick factory on 10th Brigade's left. A party of the 1st/6th East Surreys, although surrounded, held out there until the 1st East Surreys could be brought up to keep the Germans out. The Germans confidently advanced into what they thought was a gap in the line, and were thrown back by the Surreys of both battalions.

During the afternoon, a squadron of Blenheim bombers attacked Nieuport bridge. These were almost the first RAF aircraft the BEF had seen for some time, and for miles along the perimeter the troops were cheering and waving.

That evening the German infantry came in once more in strength, supported by artillery, mortars and machine-guns. Although the attack was thrust home over and over again, the exhausted troops of the division held fast; weapons overheated and ammunition ran low, but the enemy could not get through. As the Germans were forming up for one of their biggest attacks the Blenheims arrived again and dropped their bombs in exactly the right place; the attackers were scattered, and did not come in again. If they had started earlier, they might well have got through, and all would have been lost. This was the climax of the battle. Somehow, the German armour, which had broken up the Allied defence on the frontiers of France, never reached the Dunkirk perimeter. It is believed that Hitler had intervened personally for the first time in the campaign, and ordered his tanks to pause and reorganize. The tanks may also have had difficulty in getting across northern Belgium in time. In any case, their failure to arrive saved the BEF. The nearest German tanks were six miles from Dunkirk.

At dusk, the division began to make a stealthy and gradual withdrawal towards the beach.

The troops had been on half rations for several days, and had had little or no rest since crossing the Lys. The withdrawal was only sketchily planned, but in spite of the exhaustion of the troops was carried out in perfect order.

The sappers had driven two columns of lorries into the sea at La Panne, and on top of them had built a causeway from which men were to embark into small boats. The boats were to take them out to five destroyers waiting about a mile out to sea. Seven or eight thousand men were to be taken off in this manner.

When embarkation began, as darkness began to fall, there were only fifteen small boats, and the journey to the destroyers was taking about an hour. Three squadrons of German bombers put in a furious attack on the piers at dusk, and a medium gun ranged accurately on the approaches. The embarkation began at nine at night; four hours later, not more than four hundred men of the division had been embarked.

Major-General Johnson had been able to ring up Admiral Sir Bertram Ramsey, Vice-Admiral Commanding at Dover, to ask for more boats, but meanwhile several of the fifteen boats had been lost or sunk. The position looked hopeless; La Panne was being bombarded with increasing fury, and the night was lurid with flames and acrid with smoke. Major-General Johnson rang up the War Office and asked for ships to take six thousand to be at the docks and Mole at Bray Dunes and Dunkirk by daylight. These were promised, and he sent out his staff officers to gather up the scattered men of the division and get them moving along the sands to Bray Dunes and Dunkirk, three and ten miles away.

Small columns of weary men set out to trudge along the beach in the glare of burning houses and vehicles and of bomb explosions. As soon as the ships came alongside the Mole at Dunkirk or the dock at Bray Dunes, the men swarmed aboard until there was not even standing room. Then the ships sailed away for home, under almost continuous air attack. Not all the troops who embarked arrived safe home; they were sunk, and rescued, and sunk again—or killed as they crowded together on the narrow decks.

By two-thirty in the morning of June the 1st, the last defenders of the rear-guard withdrew from their positions, covered by carriers, and made their way back. Enemy guns were pounding the roads and beaches, and units were scattered among the shell-bursts. As daylight broke, some twenty Messerschmitt fighters raced over the beaches, hammering away with their machine-guns; bullets flicked up clouds of sand and spray among the men waiting on the beaches and in the water. A constant irregular crackle of musketry followed the wheeling aircraft. The few boats that were still coming inshore were swamped by the crowds of men who tried to climb aboard. A few strong swimmers swam out to the waiting steamers. Most of 12th Brigade walked along the shore, dodging shell-bursts, bombs and machine-gun bullets, to Bray Dunes, where two jetties had been built. The place was full of wounded men and ambulances, and the jetties were fully occupied in embarking them. Wearily the remnants of 12th Brigade began plodding onwards through the soft sand under the burning sun, while German aircraft swarmed like flies over Dunkirk ahead.

By three in the afternoon, in spite of constant attack from the air, most of the division had been embarked. Major-General Johnson remained, with officers of his staff, and about five hundred stragglers and walking wounded. There were no ships for some time, but at half-past five the destroyer *Worcester* came alongside the Mole at Dunkirk. The deck was much below the level of the Mole, and enemy aircraft attacked the destroyer while men were going aboard, but the whole party was embarked.

The destroyer put to sea, and was at once attacked by two or three squadrons of bombers. The captain manœuvred with great skill, but many of the exposed men on the deck were killed or wounded. Among the wounded were Colonel Evelyn Smith, the AA & QMG; Colonel Dening, a brilliant staff officer, was killed. There were three doctors on board, but so great was the crowd on deck that they had great difficulty in reaching and treating the wounded; there was no room between decks for wounded or anyone else. Even when the destroyer reached Dover at dusk, its troubles were not over, for it collided with another ship there. The damage, however, was slight, and both ships reached the quay. The last survivors of 4th Division were disembarked.

3. Home Forces

Battered and listing, some in tow, others only just under control, the ships of the Dunkirk rescue fleet berthed at the first English harbours they could reach. The dead and the wounded were carried down the gangways, and after them stumbled the uninjured—exhausted, filthy and hungry, most of their equipment left behind. This was a strange return for the fighting force which had sailed for France eight months before.

Trains took the men to various hurriedly prepared reception camps all over the country, where the most urgent needs were attended to—wash and shave, food, and, above all, sleep.

Within a few days, the scattered survivors of the division were on the move again, this time to re-form. Major-General Johnson's headquarters—staffed at first only by three officers—was set up in the George Hotel, Crewkerne, Somerset, sixty miles west of Southampton. 10th Brigade Headquarters was at Hymerford House, East Coker, six miles from Crewkerne towards Yeovil; 11th Brigade Headquarters at the Pine Crest Hotel, Lyme Regis, on the coast twelve miles south-west of Crewkerne; and 12th Brigade Headquarters at Wraxall Manor, a charming country house ten miles from Crewkerne towards Dorchester. Round each brigade headquarters the units of the brigade group—including gunners, sappers and medical units—occupied villages and farms.

Officers and men went on arriving from reception camps for several days. At first there were no vehicles, except a few hired civilian cars and lorries, no weapons, no ammunition and no accommodation stores. Almost as soon as they had arrived in their new areas, men who had returned from France were sent off on forty-eight hours leave. The division—and indeed most of the

British Army—was still in a state of disorganization on June the 10th, when Italy declared war on Great Britain.

There followed a series of changes in command throughout the units and formations of the division. Brigadier Hawkesworth was appointed BGS Scottish Command and reluctantly said good-bye to 12th Brigade; he was, however, eventually to return to command the division. The 1st South Lancashires left 12th Brigade to join 3rd Division; Lieutenant-Colonel D. M. W. Beak VC DSO MC, who had been commanding the battalion, was promoted to the command of 12th Brigade. Lieutenant-Colonel R. K. Arbuthnott DSO MC arrived to take command of the Black Watch, since Lieutenant-Colonel Carthew Yorstoun had been wounded. Lieutenant-Colonel F. J. Mitchell took over command of the Royal Fusiliers. In due course, the 1st Queens Own Royal West Kents joined 12th Brigade, replacing the South Lancashires.

Brigadier Anderson returned to the division, but was promoted to command 1st Division, and Brigadier T. M. L. Grover MC took over command of 11th Brigade. Major-General Johnson left the division to command Aldershot Command, and Major-General T. R. Eastwood DSO MC took his place.

Reinforcements began to arrive in huge numbers, for the division had suffered heavily—particularly the infantry battalions. Even after the arrival of officer reinforcements, the Northamptons were two officers and three hundred other ranks under strength; the 1st Surreys, four officers and three hundred and fifty-one other ranks; the Lancashire Fusiliers, five officers and three hundred and forty-nine other ranks. The division had lost almost half its fighting troops.

Commanders discussed changes in organization for which the disastrous campaign had shown the need, and summarized the lessons learned in France. Vehicles, weapons and new clothes were issued, and the division began to look itself again. Battalions spread out as reinforcements arrived, and before long some were occupying several villages.

On June the 20th, 4th Division came under the command of V Corps, and was ordered to take over the defence of the coastal region round Southampton. V Corps, with 50th Division on the right, 4th Division in the centre and 3rd Division on the left, was responsible for the defence of the coast from Lyme Regis to Bognor Regis. 4th Division's area contained Southampton, Portsmouth, Gosport and the Isle of Wight, and included more than fifty miles of coastline, and the country behind to a depth of some twenty miles. In addition to this, the Isle of Wight, defended by 12th Brigade, is more than twenty miles across its widest part, and more than half as deep.

Meanwhile, the Germans had been driving across France to Paris, and beyond to the Atlantic coast. As their advance spread along the Channel coast, swallowing up ports and air-fields, they became more and more conveniently placed for an attack on the south coast of England. This attack seemed almost sure to come; the German *blitzkrieg*, in which armour, aircraft, mobile infantry, infantry guns, flame-throwers and assault engineers flung themselves with apparently irresistible force on the weakest point in the Allied defences, had succeeded well enough in France and the Low Countries to encourage Hitler to make the attempt. The British Army had extricated most of its men from France, but had suffered grave losses in men and crippling losses in equipment. The RAF was locally outnumbered by the Luftwaffe. The British troops manning the defences of the south coast had every reason to expect that they would before long have to fight a deadly battle in the fields and among the farms and villages of the southern counties.

Along the whole of its part of the coast, therefore, V Corps dug trenches and laid belts of wire, prepared strong-points for all-round defence farther inland, and manned the positions night and day.

The hot summer weeks went by, and the enemy never came. The war in the air over the southern counties became more and more furious; the men of the division grew more and more bored with keeping their rifles with them even in cinemas, and with standing to at dawn and dusk. From time to time there was a 'flap' to enliven the long wait for the invaders. The most notable of these was on September the 7th, when just before ten at night the long expected code-word *Cromwell* was passed, to indicate that the Germans were on the way. The division stood by for nearly a fortnight before the immediate danger receded. For months afterwards, rumours were circulated, through the channels usual for army rumours, of the enemy landing force caught and destroyed at sea by the RAF, and of German corpses washed up on the British coast.

All three field regiments of the divisional artillery were reorganized. Each had consisted of two batteries, each of twelve guns organized as three troops. Now, in order to improve the speed and flexibility of command, the six troops of each regiment were divided between three batteries.

By the end of July, the corps commander was satisfied with the defences, and V Corps was able to relax a little. Only half the available strength was now to be employed on the construction and manning of defences; a quarter was to set to work on training, while the remaining quarter could leave the unit areas on recreational training, pass or leave.

During October, Major-General Eastwood handed over command of the division to Major-General J. G. des R. Swayne CBE. In mid-October, the division was relieved of its operational responsibilities, and began to move into winter quarters. The intention behind this relief was to give the division more time for training. Operationally, the division was in reserve; if the invasion were to come after all—in spite of the squalls and rain-storms that whipped the Channel as winter came on—the division's role would be that of counter-attack and of artillery support. The winter quarters were chosen for comfort; billets in the towns near the coast were far apart, and careful plans had to be laid for rapid concentration if the enemy were to land.

In January 1941 a new unit was formed. It began its life as the Divisional Reconnaissance Unit, and became first the 4th Reconnaissance Battalion and finally the 4th Reconnaissance Regiment. This regiment's role was to be to skirmish in front of the division's advance, and to act as a light mobile striking force. The regiment was equipped with armoured cars and carriers and with all the supporting weapons of an infantry battalion. Eventually it was even to be armed with a battery of light field-guns mounted on armoured cars. The regiment, which soon had its own distinctive cap-badge, quickly began to earn a distinctive reputation for speed of movement; and on active service it was to show its versatility and tenacity by holding the line when infantry battalions were withdrawn, and by fighting more or less as an infantry battalion.

The ensuing months were filled with exercises organized at all levels—War Office, Command, Corps, Division, Brigade and unit—with courses of immense diversity and with training of every kind. The division was up to strength in men, and was fully armed and equipped. The period of defensive waiting was over; the division still had its operational duties, but training had become the centre of its life.

In June 1941 4th Division's new role in the event of invasion became in particular the protection of fighter air-fields in Hampshire, and in general the formation of a counter-attacking force for attack in any direction. Aerodrome guards, consisting of infantry and guns, took up their positions overlooking the airfields, and manned observation posts day and night. The summer was hot, and life under canvas was far from unpleasant. Some of the troops helped neighbouring farmers on the land, while others showed a valuable talent for poaching. Exercise succeeded exercise—Locust, Bombard, Stampede and the mighty Bumper. Bumper was in fact described as 'army manœuvres'; it was a tremendous mock battle, lasting a full week, in which many formations took part. In the course of this exercise, units of the division advanced north-eastwards through two counties and deep into Hertfordshire, where they became almost inextricably entangled with the 'enemy'.

In October 1941 began a long period of intensive training punctuated by equally intensive 'flaps'. On October the 12th, the division was ordered to send cadres from each brigade group in turn to Inveraray, in Argyllshire, for training in sea-borne landing, or combined operations, on Loch Fyne. 12th Brigade's cadre left for Scotland a week later. A week later still the division was ordered to mobilize at once for a move overseas, and the brigade cadre came back again. The rumour—a particularly strong one—was that the division was bound for Russia, which was now at war with Germany, and one or two officers began to appear in magnificent fur coats. Nobody felt particularly cheerful about soldiering in a ruthless campaign in a cruel climate.

By November the 11th the mobilization orders had been cancelled; the division was to move to Aldershot Command, and to go ahead with training in combined operations. The move to Aldershot began at the end of the month and 12th Brigade's cadre went off to Inveraray again.

The second 'flap' began on January the 9th 1942, when the division was ordered to prepare to move to Northern Ireland; advance-parties were sent off, but combined training at Inveraray went on. This move, however, turned out to be a feint to cover the move of American troops from the USA to Ulster, and the advance-parties returned after plastering Northern Ireland with divisional signs.

In March 1942 Major-General Swayne handed over command of the division to Major-General J. L. I. Hawkesworth CBE, who had commanded 12th Brigade in France. The division had made great strides under Major-General Swayne, to whom many of its future successes in battle were due.

Towards the end of the month, the division began to move to Scotland in order to join the Expeditionary Force, which was being prepared for a sea-borne assault. The units of the division were spread out in the counties of Kircudbright, Dumfries and Roxburgh, with Divisional Headquarters first at Melrose and then at Dumfries. Scotland was a relief to the eye after the military architecture of Aldershot, and Scottish baking was a delight to palates hardened by army rations and war-time bread. Above all, the people were extremely friendly and hospitable.

In May 1942, the division was ordered to reorganize as a 'mixed division', consisting of two infantry brigades and a brigade of infantry tanks. 11th Brigade left the division to join 78th Division, and was replaced by 21st Army Tank Brigade. The tank brigade was commanded by Brigadier T. Ivor-Moore MC, and its battalions were the 12th and 48th Royal Tanks and 145th RAC.

As soon as the tanks joined the division, infantry and tank co-operation became a feature of the 'combined ops' training which was being intensified at Inveraray and elsewhere. A series of divisional exercises prepared the division for an Expeditionary Force exercise called Dryshod, in which embarkation and assault landing were practised on land. The division's biggest exercise since Bumper, Dryshod went on for ten days, and covered much of the Western Lowlands of Scotland in that time.

Senior staff officers of the division spent several weeks at First Army headquarters in London, planning an assault landing on the North African coast. First Army was to go off eventually to make its landing, but 4th Division was to be left behind, not to follow for several months.

In mid-November certain units of the division were warned for service overseas as part of Force 125; vehicles were to move a month or even six weeks later. In December everyone had fourteen days embarkation leave—people at home were growing sceptical about these repeated embarkation leaves, and civilians in comfortably reserved occupations would say to the soldier, 'What, you still here?' On February the 8th 1943, Scottish Command informed the division that Force 125 would not after all be needed.

By this time most of the division was beginning to feel a certain exasperation. After more than two years of training, officers and men had reached a high state of technical skill and of confidence in their own powers. The arrival of the tank brigade and the long training for sea-borne assault had encouraged them to feel themselves members of an élite formation, chosen for a special task. The mighty battles of El Alamein and Stalingrad had put a stop to the run of German victories; indeed, the Germans in North Africa seemed vulnerable to a crushing blow, had it not been for the apparently unaccountable slowness of First Army in Tunisia. A long succession of exercises had served the double purpose of preparing the division for war and of whetting everyone's appetite for the real thing; after a while, practice of any kind becomes wearisome, and the man in training longs to use his hard-won skill.

A week later the situation changed abruptly. Major-General Hawkesworth received from the Director of Military Operations at the War Office a message to this effect—'I have certain documents and instructions for you, but feel it is essential to inform you personally; you will also wish to discuss them. Please arrange to come to the War Office during the next few days.' Major-General Hawkesworth left for London on February the 17th, and came back five days later, with the news that the division was to depart for a tropical climate a fortnight later. All formation badges were to be obliterated, and serial numbers and bands of colour were to be painted on vehicles and equipment. Vehicles were to be prepared for use in the desert, and canopies lowered to facilitate compact loading. Yellow stars nearly two feet across were to be painted on horizontal surfaces on vehicles, for air recognition. The voyage was to last about three weeks.

In preparation for the move and for the handing over of billets, the last days before departure went by in a rush of work. His Majesty the King paid a farewell visit to the division. Before the end of February, the vehicles were off to embark at ports on the west coast between Penarth and Barrow-in-Furness. In the second week of March, the men of the division went by train to Glasgow, and there embarked into a variety of troopships. The biggest of these was the well-known Orient Liner *Orion*, now converted for trooping. This ship of 22,500 tons took aboard more than 5,500 troops, including the whole of 10th Brigade Group and Divisional Headquarters. Major-General Hawkesworth, with his GSO 1, Lieutenant-Colonel S. N. Shoosmith, and his AA & QMG, Lieutenant-Colonel Kinna, travelled by air. The convoy included the troopships *Ormonde, Cuba, Nea Hellas, Banfora* and *Windsor Castle*.

The order of battle of the division at this time is given at Appendix B, and with it a list of commanders and divisional staff officers. The 2nd Northumberland Fusiliers, who in 1940 had been under command of the division, had become the divisional machine-gun battalion in 1941, but in 1943 were left behind. The 91st Light Anti-aircraft Regiment RA, once a South Staffordshire infantry battalion, had joined the divisional artillery; this regiment was equipped with the quick-firing Bofors gun. The Brigade Ordnance Companies RAOC had become Brigade Workshop Companies REME, each with an Ordnance Field Park Section, and DADME had been promoted to CREME.

The troopships formed up in the Firth of Clyde, where a great fleet of transports, cargo-ships and warships of many types was already at anchor. The presence of five aircraft carriers and some battle-cruisers encouraged the optimists to expect a powerful escort. When the convoy sailed, early in the morning of March the 16th, it was guarded adequately enough by a squadron of destroyers. By noon the convoy of twenty-six ships had formed up in the open sea, and was moving south-west; by evening the ships were swinging in the Atlantic swell, and sea-sickness had set in.

The Bay of Biscay was as unpleasant as its reputation. After five days at sea, the convoy was approaching the Straits of Gibraltar; seventeen ships went on to the south, and 4th Division's ships were among the nine that turned towards the Straits.

The ships passed Gibraltar in darkness, but the lights of neutral Algeciras and Tangier marked the shore on each side, and the Rock itself, though blacked-out, was plainly to be seen. The Sierra de Nevada, the brown and white mountains that rise to a tremendous height along the south coast of Spain, were an impressive sight in the next morning's sunlight. The weather had improved as the ships steamed farther southwards, and the Mediterranean had the warmth of an English summer day.

During the night of March the 23rd, 'action stations' was sounded, not for the first time, and all officers and men stood by in the stuffy troop-decks. Enemy aircraft attacked the convoy, and torpedoed the *Windsor Castle*, on which there were no troops of 4th Division. Next morning the ships steamed into Algiers harbour. There was an end to the long uncertainty about the division's role, for it was to join First Army in Tunisia.

4. The Tunisian Campaign: Béjà

The troopships and transport ships unloaded at ports along the Algerian coast, from Algiers itself to Bône, two hundred and sixty miles nearer the Tunisian front. The division had not arrived unscathed, for the slow convoy carrying the vehicles had been attacked on the way. Scores of vehicles were sunk or delayed.

The March days were already warm enough for swimming, and the Mediterranean lacked the numbing chill of home waters. The nights, however, were bitterly cold. The troops camped, in varying degrees of discomfort, under canvas already provided, eagerly collected rumours from the distant fighting, and watched for German aircraft. They wrote home, began to pick up a smattering of French, accustomed themselves to insects of astonishing size and gruesome appearance—ants an inch long, six-inch centipedes, and scorpions of various colours—and became acquainted with the cheap, sour wines of the country and the potent, sticky, sweet apéritifs. The transport, guns and tanks arrived, and the waterproofing and protective wrappings and mineral oil had to be stripped off. Units shook off the lethargy of a long sea-voyage with gun-drill, weapon-training, route-marches and wireless practices; ammunition vehicles were loaded, officers and men were briefed, and the battalions and regiments and all the subsidiary units which made up a Mixed Division began to move eastwards through Algeria.

Most of the country along this part of the North African coast is fertile enough, though mountainous. From the neatly tended fields and vineyards which run down to the sea, the roads make their way inland by zig-zagging up the face of towering hills or by threading along the sheer sides of enormous gorges. Most of the hill-sides are covered with trees or bushes, or at least with scrub; and sometimes a small field can be seen, far up on the hill, with an Arab and an ox struggling across it with a primitive plough. The roads had been planned with skill and care, and most of them had been adequately surfaced. Neglect and the passage of heavy vehicles, however, had broken them up until every motor-cyclist had to watch for potholes six inches deep or more, which might throw him over the handlebars; and the driver of every heavy lorry had to steer away from the crumbling verges which might tilt the vehicle into the ditch.

Beside the road, Arab boys with ingratiating smiles would hold up a handful of eggs or even flowers as each vehicle went by; and soon after any unit camped for the night near the road, often miles from the nearest village, men and boys would appear with chickens and eggs and donkey-loads of fruit for sale. Towns were few, and far between; several of them were pleasant enough, with a tree-shaded square and a few inviting cafés, from which French civilians watched without much interest the lorries full of staring troops.

As the long columns of the division's assorted transport moved steadily eastwards—staff cars with swaying wireless masts, Bren carriers with roaring engines and grinding tracks, ponderously bouncing field-guns, lorries of every shape and size (the tanks went most of the way by rail)—a man stood on the seat beside every driver, with his head outside the vehicle's roof, and searched the sky for enemy aircraft. Experience had proved that heroism was useless against the multiple guns of Focke-Wulf and Messerschmitt fighter aircraft, which would fly low among the hills and valleys, and appear suddenly round the shoulder of a ridge. When the air sentry warned the driver—with a yell or a bang on the roof—of imminent air attack, the vehicle would halt with a screech of brakes, and the men inside would scurry into the fields away from the road.

The men now on their way to the front knew little more about the fighting than did the newspaper-readers at home—indeed, there was little more to be known. In November 1942, American forces had landed at Casablanca, Oran and Algiers, and the British First Army, commanded by Lieutenant-General K. A. N. Anderson CB MC, who had commanded 11th Brigade in France, had landed nearer the Tunisian border and headed for Tunis and Bizerta. There were at this time no Axis forces in French North Africa. In spite of its imposing title, the First Army was weaker on landing than was the 4th Division, for the 'army' consisted only of two infantry brigades and a battalion of tanks. Half the infantry was provided by 11th Brigade, which with 10th and 12th Brigade had made up 4th Division in France from 1914 to 1918 and in 1939 and 1940.

The Germans and Italians threw tank and infantry forces into Tunisia, in order to hold open their line of withdrawal. First Army was only thirteen miles from Tunis when it was halted, and was pressed back some fifteen to twenty miles.

So, in December 1942, ended the first phase of the campaign—the race for Tunis and Bizerta, won by the Germans and Italians.

Division by division the First Army grew in strength, but the equally growing strength of the enemy, the difficulty of the country and of the weather, the strength of the German positions and the great length of the British lines of communications prevented Lieutenant-General Anderson from mounting a decisive attack which would push the Axis forces into the sea. The First Army's power had, however, grown to such an extent that there could no longer be doubt of the result. The first rush had been carried out by two brigades of 78th Division, which as a formation was not complete until early December. 6th Armoured Division arrived a fortnight later, 46th Infantry Division reached the front early in February 1943, and 1st Infantry Division took its place in the line late in March.

The period of reinforcement on both sides, between December 1942 and March 1943, was the second phase of the campaign.

In March 1943, the front was where the last German attacks had left it. The Germans held commanding heights among the mountains from Tamera in the north to Hunt's Gap in the centre, and from Hunt's Gap to Longstop Hill, which rises from and commands the valley of the River Medjerda. From Longstop Hill, the front crossed the Medjerda to the Djebel Bou Aoukaz, and then ran eight miles southwards to Peter's Corner, eight miles east of Medjez on the Tunis road, and went on southwards to the Goubellat Plain.

At the end of March the third phase of the campaign was about to begin. The First Army was preparing the ground for its final assault; and during the first week of April it had begun to push back the Germans on the left. Lieutenant-General Anderson's next move would be to force the enemy back in the centre from the position overlooking the road from Béjà, ten miles south-west of Hunt's Gap, to Medjez el Bab. This task was to be carried out by

V Corps, commanded by Lieutenant-General Charles Allfrey, with 4th Division on the left and 78th Division on the right.

Meanwhile the first troops of 4th Division were arriving in Béjà, ready to take over the Hunt's Gap sector from the weary battalions of 128th Brigade. 4th Division, therefore, reached the battlefield just in time for the opening of the campaign's third phase, when the First Army was about to begin its final assault.

Béjà was an unhappy little town of white houses and narrow streets; it was important to the First Army because it stood at the junction of three main roads—one leading north to Tamera, a second going north-east through Hunt's Gap to Mateur and a third leading west towards Medjez el Bab and Tunis—and for this reason had been heavily bombed by the Germans. The first seventeen miles of the Bizerta road from Béjà run through a rich valley whose rocky walls open out widely on each side of Hunt's Gap, but at the Gap itself close in to a couple of miles.

10th Brigade began to take over Hunt's Gap itself from 128th Brigade before dawn on April the 4th. The Bedfords, commanded by Lieutenant-Colonel D. S. W. Johnson, were the first battalion in the line, taking up positions covering the Gap itself.

The sector was a mountainous one; the troops of both sides were comparatively thin on the ground, and comparatively inactive. The enemy's positions looked down on the valley between Béjà and Hunt's Gap, and no transport could move in that area in daylight. The Germans had few field-guns, but their infantry-guns and mortars were fast and accurate in shooting at vehicles on the move. All supplies and reinforcements had to be brought up at night; and the companies of the battalions in the hills to left and right of the Gap could be supplied only by mule.

During the night of April the 4th, the East Surreys, commanded by Lieutenant-Colonel H. A. B. Bruno MBE, relieved the 5th Sherwood Foresters in the mountains on the left, and the DCLI took over the positions of the Hampshires on the whale-backed Djebel Munchar, four miles south of the Gap. The East Surreys were on the Djebel Zebia, some two and a half miles to the left of the Bedfords. From the forward slopes of this mountain—nearly two thousand five hundred feet high—they looked across a pass at the German-held face of the equally lofty Djebel ben Drar. On the left of the East Surreys were the 2nd/5th Leicesters, under Major-General Hawkesworth's command.

The brigade settled down and began to get the feel of real operations, after nearly three years of exercises. Enemy guns and mortars fired occasional rounds into company areas; Messerschmitts and Spitfires tumbled fighting among the clouds overhead. Germans and Arabs were sometimes to be seen moving about on distant hill-sides; sometimes vehicles and mules appeared. For the time being, Brigadier Hogshaw intended only to dominate No-man's-land, to make sure of the exact position of enemy posts and to identify the enemy's units. The Germans did not seem to be reinforcing the sector, and appeared to be content with sitting in their positions, without aggressive action unless they were molested.

During the evening of April the 5th, Major-General Hawkesworth took over command of the Béjà sector from the commander of 46th Division.

V Corps' thrust in the centre of the First Army front was to begin in the darkness of the morning of April the 7th. 78th Division was to clear the strong German positions among the mountains which look down from the north on the road from Béjà to Medjez el Bab.

10th Brigade's part was to be a deception attack on Guessa el Ald farm, nearly a mile in front of the right-hand company of the Bedfords, and on another group of buildings at Point 303, three-quarters of a mile to the left front of the same company. The Surreys were to send two sections of carriers, under Captain Brown, to make as much noise as possible on the road a mile and a half short of Guessa and Point 303, in the area held by the Bedfords. Churchill tanks of 25th Army Tank Brigade were to clatter about behind 10th Brigade's positions. Field-guns, medium machine-guns and mortars were to open fire on various tasks, and battalions were to fire off Verey lights from time to time.

When, during the night of April the 6th, 10th Brigade began to raise its martial uproar, the Germans must almost certainly have started to move forces across their front to the Hunt's Gap sector. But in the small hours of the morning the noise died away; the Germans stared into the darkness, and no attack came in; and, before the German troops could get back into place, 78th Division's attack burst like a storm on the weakened positions three and four miles south-east of Hunt's Gap. The attack went in on a front of five battalions; all broke through successive German positions, and 78th Division took a hundred prisoners in the first twelve hours of the battle.

All through the next two days, the advance of 78th Division rolled forward, and the division took five hundred more prisoners during April the 9th. In addition to the hundreds of enemy soldiers who had been captured, an unknown number had, of course, been killed and wounded.

By late afternoon of April the 9th, it was clear that the enemy had withdrawn from the front of 10th Brigade, and during the night Major-General Hawkesworth ordered the brigade to advance on Sidi Nsir, ten miles north-east of Hunt's Gap. The brigade's advance was to be supported by 172nd Field Regiment (since 4th Division's own field guns had not yet arrived), 451st Light Battery (equipped with 25-pounders), a section of heavy mortars from 68th Chemical Warfare Mortar Company, 59th Field Company (less one section) under Major Daniels, and 'B' Company of 10th Field Ambulance. The remaining section of 59th Field Company, guarded by the 2nd/5th Leicesters, was clearing mines from the road running across the division's left flank. A battery of 91st Light Anti-aircraft Regiment was to move into action at Hunt's Gap during the morning of April the 11th.

Brigadier Hogshaw gave orders that 10th Brigade would go forward from its positions with the Bedfords on the right, the East Surreys on the left, and the DCLI following up in reserve. The brigade's front was to cover some four miles; its left wing was to cross the southern end of the Djebel ben Drar, while the right travelled through the rolling country on the other side of the Béjà-Mateur road. In effect, the brigade would be moving up the valley through which the road runs, and clearing in its advance not only the whole valley but the high ground which commands it from each side.

On April the 10th, 12th Brigade went into action to the southeast of 10th Brigade. The two brigades advanced in different directions and with different roles; in fact 4th Division was fighting two separate brigade actions.

At dawn on April the 11th, 10th Brigade began to move on foot up the valley towards Sidi Nsir. A rapid advance was prevented by booby traps, which were scattered all over the valley, and which killed and wounded men of the East Surreys and the Bedfords. Sappers of 59th Field Company, moving with the leading troops, cut a gap through the mine-fields, destroyed the booby traps by the roadside, and cleared away the gigantic wreckage of two Tiger tanks—a road-block of nearly a hundred and twenty tons of scrap-iron—less than a mile beyond Hunt's Gap. These were the first Tiger tanks recovered by the Allied forces in Tunisia.

The enemy at first put up little resistance, and the infantry had to contend only with the fire of guns and mortars. The Bedfords were advancing along the road when a heavy concentration of artillery fire burst among the advancing troops, and Lieutenant-Colonel D. S. W. Johnson was killed; Major Whittaker took command of the battalion. By the time the battalion had been advancing on foot for twelve hours, wheeled vehicles could reach the leading troops only with difficulty. Major Whittaker decided to halt for the night, and to form a close leaguer on the hillside just beyond Sidi ben Hedirich, five and a half miles beyond Hunt's Gap.

On the left of 10th Brigade, the Surreys, three and a half miles north of the Bedfords, reached the Djebel Grembil, but were halted there by intense machine-gun fire. The Surreys renewed their attacks at dawn of April the 12th, but were again repulsed.

The country through which the infantry had been moving on foot was rough enough to make supply extremely difficult. No trucks or even motor-cycles could reach the headquarters of the East Surreys, and the Bedfords were in a position only slightly better. Carriers had to be used to carry rations and petrol, and even they could not reach the battalions until late at night. The night was quiet, and no further advance was made, nor did the enemy make any move.

To the west of the valley through which 10th Brigade was advancing, 4th Reconnaissance Regiment, in action for the first time since it was formed, had taken over the road and the neighbourhood between Chemical Corner and Zouave's Bend, to the left of the positions from which the Surreys had moved forward. The Reconnaissance Regiment was to guard 4th Division's left flank, and to keep in touch with 46th Division on the left.

April the 12th was a difficult day for 10th Brigade. German fighter-bombers were continually attacking the Sidi Nsir road, interrupting the process of supply though doing little damage. The enemy's 81-mm mortars and his mine-fields were a constant trouble. The rocky escarpments which command most of the valley enabled the defenders to hold up attacking troops with no more than a few mortars and cleverly placed machine-guns. Supply was growing more and more difficult, and only carriers could be used for the routine administration of the battalions.

The Bedfords on the right resumed their advance at dawn of April the 12th, when Major D. T. Yate-Lee took the advance guard ('D' Company) forward along the left side of Djebel Aoud, some three miles to the right of the point from which the East Surreys were moving off. The company was halted near the hillside village of Haroun by heavy concentrations of fire from German guns and mortars.

Seeing that there would be no getting forward on the left, Major Whittaker sent 'A' Company round the right of the hill, to cross the crest and join the advance-guard at Haroun if possible. 'A' Company came under mortar fire on the way, but by noon was within a thousand yards of Haroun, on the other side of the ridge. An hour later, a patrol from the company went through the pass which cuts into the crest and leads to Haroun; on the other side, however, the way towards the village was barred by a wall of mortar fire.

Brigade Headquarters could give Major Whittaker no information about enemy or Allied troops on his right flank, which was now uncomfortably exposed. In order to secure this flank, he sent 'B' Company out, at three in the morning of April the 13th, to make sure of the hill at Bateun el Kram which overlooked the right-hand slopes of the Djebel Aoud. At the same time, 'C' Company attacked north-eastwards along Aoud towards Point 583.

Two hours later, all seemed to be going well; 'C' Company had met fierce opposition, but both companies had reached—though they had not cleared or consolidated—their objectives, and 'B' Company sent back twenty-six prisoners who had been glad to give themselves up.

At eight-thirty in the morning, the radio link with both 'B' and 'C' Companies broke down. Major Whittaker had no choice but to go on with his preparations for the advance by 'A' and 'D' Companies in front of Haroun, and himself crossed to the left side of the Djebel Aoud with the gunner representative, ready to support the attack.

At ten o'clock, bad news began to come in. 'C' Company, after enduring a great deal of shelling and mortaring, had been violently counter-attacked and over-run by enemy infantry supported by heavy mortars, artillery fire which included air-bursts, and the fire of light machine-guns from three sides.

'B' Company, too, was under fire from the right. At eleven in the morning, enemy counter-attacks over-ran most of the company on Bateun el Kram; the Germans followed up, and before long were menacing the rest of the battalion. Major Whittaker gathered his companies in round the crest of the Djebel Aoud, where they took up defensive positions. The battalion had lost two hundred and thirty-four men during the day; all but ten of these were missing—there was no news of Major L. C. Young or of seven subaltern officers.

Since the Bedfords had been so badly knocked about, and were now in a fairly precarious position, Brigadier Hogshaw, who was watching the battle, decided that it was time to bring up the reserve battalion. At four in the afternoon, three companies of the DCLI moved into positions on the right of Djebel Aoud, and the Bedfords crossed the crest to take up positions on the other side, looking down on Haroun. In these positions the right wing of 10th Brigade held firm.

On the brigade's left wing, the Surreys attacked once more at three in the afternoon of April the 13th. Enemy aircraft strafed the gun positions behind the brigade, but the artillery fire never slackened. The Surreys were only partly successful; after hard fighting, 'C' Company reached the Djebel ben Touil, in front of Grembil, but the position was precarious, the rest of the battalion could get forward only slowly, and dusk was gathering. The forward troops withdrew again.

April the 13th had been another bad day for 10th Brigade. The advancing battalions had run up against two strong and determined German battalions, which had had time to choose the ground on which they would make a stand, and had been able to find defensive positions which were naturally formidable. On the left, however, the brigade had won a foothold on the Djebel Grembil, among the enemy's defences; on the right, the Bedfords (weakened by heavy losses) and three companies of the DCLI were hard up against the enemy's positions among the hills.

At ten-fifteen in the morning of April the 14th, 'A' Company of the East Surreys was to attack the Djebel el Hara in front of 'D' Company on Grembil. The company was delayed on the way to the start-line by heavy artillery fire, and when the troops were near the hill-top they were halted by the fire of machine-guns and mortars, from positions almost impossible to see in the rocky faces of the surrounding hills. By eleven o'clock the company had suffered discouraging losses, and had no hope of reaching the top of the hill.

The company began to withdraw. Lieutenant-Colonel Bruno sent 'D' Company forward from Grembil to divert the enemy's attention from 'A' Company. 'D' Company too was halted, after a short advance, by machine-guns and mortars. The men of 'A' Company had to get off the hill as best they could, leaving behind those of their wounded who could be seen by the enemy. 'D' Company withdrew again to their positions on Grembil.

The DCLI and the Bedfords stayed in their positions all day, for Brigadier Hogshaw had decided to attempt no further advance on the right for the time being, and had given orders for consolidation.

Soon after dusk, 30th Field Regiment, which had already been in action behind 12th Brigade, took over from 172nd Field Regiment, which had been supporting 10th Brigade, and Lieutenant-Colonel R. B. Rice took over command of the artillery group. During the night, the Durhams arrived from 12th Brigade's front to relieve the East Surreys.

The advance was over for the time being. 10th Brigade was to prepare defensive positions from the Djebel Aoud on the right to the Djebel Grembil on the left, in order to prevent the enemy from filtering back to Hunt's Gap. Positions were dug and wired, mines were laid, and the road was blocked by a platoon of Bedfords and a troop of anti-tank guns, under Captain Adams, commander of 38th (New Zealand) Anti-tank Battery.

April the 15th was a comparatively quiet day for 10th Brigade, but while orders were being given out concerning the defensive positions, the area occupied by 'C' Company of the Surreys was shelled by a heavy gun. One shell burst in the mouth of a cave in which one of the platoons was sheltering; eight men were killed and sixteen wounded. The Surreys returned to their positions, relieving the Durhams. The Durhams left the sector and went back to their own brigade. All three battalions of 10th Brigade spent most of the day digging, erecting barbed wire and laying mines.

Meanwhile, during the evening of April the 9th, Major-General Hawkesworth had ordered the battalions of 12th Brigade forward on to the Djebel Sidi bel Mahdi, five miles south-east of Hunt's Gap and to the right front of 10th Brigade. 12th Brigade's role was to follow up behind 78th Division's attack, and the positions to be occupied were held by battalions of 78th Division which were taking part in the attack. Before dawn on April the 10th, the battalions of 12th Brigade began to move on to the Mahdi.

At five o'clock in the evening, the Black Watch, commanded by Lieutenant-Colonel W. P. Barclay, moved forward across the valley to the north-west, towards the Djebel Rmel, a long narrow hill four miles away, from which the enemy had withdrawn. On arriving there after dark, the battalion began to dig in.

During the morning of April the 11th, Major-General Hawkesworth gave orders that 12th Brigade was to take over from troops of 78th Division the south-western entrance to the valley of the River Tine. From its source in the hills nearby, the Tine flows north-eastwards past the southern end of the Djebel Rmel, which was held by the Black Watch. Beyond the hill, the valley opens out to a width of four miles, with mountains on each side. The river flows roughly parallel with, and roughly equidistant between, the Sidi Nsir road up which 10th Brigade was then about to advance, and the Medjez-Tebourba road towards which 78th Division was fighting. Some nine miles of mountains divide the valley from each of these roads.

The Black Watch, therefore, already commanded the entrance to the valley from their positions on the Djebel Rmel. The battalion had had an uncomfortable day. The arrival of four enemy deserters in the lines of 'D' Company before seven in the morning had been a good beginning, but an hour later German guns had begun to shell the battalion area. During the afternoon enemy mortar-fire knocked out two of the battalion's anti-tank portees, and during the evening Stukas came screaming down on the hill to drop their bombs among the slit trenches, though without doing any harm.

Four miles farther west, troops of 38th Brigade were edging through the hills towards the north-western wall of the valley, and, beyond 38th Brigade, 10th Brigade was about to move up on the left. Four miles south-west of Rmel, troops of 46th Division held the Mahdi; two battalions of these were to come under Brigadier Callaghan's command during the evening of April the 11th. Immediately to the east of the Mahdi rises the Mergueb Chaouach, which commands the entrance to the Tine valley from the south; Chaouach was held by 78th Division.

All Brigadier Callaghan had to do, to secure the valley's entrance, was to bring up the Royal Fusiliers and the 1st Royal West Kents to take over on Chaouach. By nightfall on April the 11th, 12th Brigade was in position.

78th Division's attack was still going well. The division had taken more than a thousand prisoners since the fighting began, and had reached the Djebel el Ang, well over two thousand feet high, the highest peak between the valley of the Tine and the Medjerda. 1st Infantry Division, which had arrived a little over a fortnight before, was already clearing the Medjerda valley on the right of 78th Division.

April the 12th was another unlucky day for the Black Watch. Troops engaged in the relief of the forward company during the morning were caught in the open by the fire of enemy guns and mortars. The battalion lost two officers and six others killed during the day; Major R. W. Fulton and Captain I. D. Rankin of 77th Field Regiment, the battalion's FOOs, were also killed. Lieutenant-Colonel W. P. Barclay, Major C. N. M. Blair, Captain A. R. B. Brett (the adjutant) and the chaplain, the Reverend J. Grant, Lieutenants D. M. Irons and T. D. Cunningham and fifty-one others were wounded.

This shell-fire prevented the Black Watch from getting fresh troops into the positions of the forward company, which had withdrawn. Meanwhile, enemy troops moved up into the company's position. Soon after eight in the evening, the battalion sent in a counter-attack behind a screen of artillery fire to take back the positions, but enemy machine-gunners on the flank halted the attack with heavy fire. Very early in the morning of April the 13th, however, the Black Watch (now commanded by Lieutenant-Colonel B. J. G. Madden, who had just been promoted) swept the enemy off the position.

Brigadier Callaghan at once sent the 2nd Hampshires, who had been placed under his command, across the valley from the Mahdi to occupy the hill at el Kerma, facing Rmel across the valley from two miles to the west. The Hampshires made a silent approach to the hill, and by early afternoon were in occupation.

Later in the afternoon, Brigadier Callaghan sent off the 16th Durhams, also temporarily under his command, to help 10th Brigade, who were at that time in difficulties which have already been described.

From time to time during the day, enemy mortars and guns fired bombs and shells into the positions held by the Black Watch and the West Kents. Of the hundred and fifty shells which landed among the West Kents, no less than forty were duds. The low quality of the enemy's heavier ammunition was often noticeable in North Africa.

12th Brigade's patrols saw nothing of the enemy during the night. The troops made no move during April the 14th, except to duck when the enemy's guns or aircraft made themselves unpleasant. Brigadier Callaghan was taken ill and had to be taken to hospital; Lieutenant-Colonel J. M. Haycraft of the West Kents took command of the brigade.

Five miles beyond Chaouach, 78th Division was driving forward at the summit of the Djebel el Ang. Another three miles of fighting through the hills would bring them to the Medjerda valley, and to Longstop Hill which commands it. The summit of Ang was taken, but the growing force of the enemy's opposition prevented the division from advancing much farther during the day.

The whole front of 4th Division settled down to a routine of patrols, shelling and local reliefs. More important activities, however, were going on behind the front, in headquarters where staff officers were already planning the division's next battle.

On April the 14th, Major-General Hawkesworth had sent out to eight senior officers of the division an Operation Instruction marked *Most Secret and Personal*. The eight officers who were to supervise the planning required by this Instruction were the CRA, Brigadier M. A. B. Johnson DSO MC; the Commanders of 21st Tank Brigade and of 10th and 12th Infantry Brigades, Brigadiers T. Ivor-Moore MC, J. H. Hogshaw MC and R. G. W. Callaghan; the CRE, Lieutenant-Colonel P. F. Foley; the OC Divisional Signals, Lieutenant-Colonel F. W. P. Bradford; the AA & QMG, Lieutenant-Colonel C. J. Kinna; and the GSO 1, Lieutenant-Colonel S. N. Shoosmith.

The situation which had led up to the drafting of the Instruction was afterwards clearly described by the Army Commander in his dispatch of November the 6th 1946. 'On 12th April I was ordered by General Alexander to prepare a large-scale offensive to capture Tunis . . . the target date being 22nd April . . . Enemy resistance was still formidable and he held strong positions. These had to be overcome and his strength exhausted before a real breakthrough could be effected . . . There are three entrances into the

Tunis plain: In the south (etc., etc.). In the centre (etc., etc.). In the north—along the axis Medjez-Massicault. This is the most direct way and the best tank country. But it was protected by very strong enemy positions which barred the way and prevented deployment of large forces across the River Medjerda. I expected very heavy fighting here before I could break through. None the less, I decided my plan as follows: V Corps to make the main attack from Medjez and to break into the enemy's main defensive system between Peter's Corner and Longstop . . .'

For its attack in front of Medjez, V Corps was to consist of 1st (British) Infantry Division, 4th Division, 78th Division and 25th Tank Brigade. Each division in turn was to strike its blow at the buttresses of the enemy's defence. First of all, 78th Division on the left was to complete its long mountain battle by taking the sinister Longstop; 1st Division in the centre was to cross the river and clear the rolling ground to the east and south-east, known as the Inner Circle; and 4th Division on the right was to force its way along the Tunis road from Medjez, round Peter's Corner to the hills beyond Massicault, from which the city of Tunis may be seen.

One paragraph of the Operation Instruction gave a significant warning: 'It is appreciated that as soon as the offensive is launched the enemy may re-act with a violent counter-attack with available tanks; 4th Division must be prepared to meet it.'

A number of units already under Major-General Hawkesworth's command were to remain so for this operation. These were 102nd Field Regiment (twelve wheeled 25-pounders and eight 'Sexton' 25-pounders on tank chassis), 456th Light Battery (six 25-pounders), 5th Medium Regiment (4·5-inch guns and 5·5-inch gun-howitzers), 12th/54th Heavy Battery (7-inch howitzers), a detachment of 5th Survey Regiment, Royal Artillery, 'A' Flight of 651st Air OP Squadron, the heavy mortars of 68th Chemical Warfare Company and the 2nd Hampshires. The Hampshires had suffered crippling losses when the Germans had flung Bladeforce back from Tebourba, and were by no means up to strength. Later on, 93rd Anti-tank Regiment and a battery of 54th Heavy Regiment were to come under Major-General Hawkesworth's command. 145th RAC was to join 1st Division in the attack on the Inner Circle. The rest of 21st Tank Brigade would be with 4th Division.

4th Division was to begin moving into its new sector during the night of April the 17th, when 10th Brigade was to hand over its positions on the Sidi Nsir road to a Combat Team of the 1st American Division. The brigade was to rest on April the 18th, and during the following night was to relieve 2nd Brigade of 1st British Division south-east of Medjez. During the 18th, Major-General Hawkesworth was to hand over the Béjà sector to the commander of the American division, and on the following day was to assume command of the Medjez sector. 12th Brigade would be relieved by 18th Combat Team on the night of April the 19th, and was to rest in divisional reserve. The Hampshires were to move into positions covering 10th Brigade's right flank from behind the Djebel Djaffa, seven miles south-east of Medjez.

While 78th Division still hammered away at the enemy's obstinate defences in the hills north-west of Medjez, and gathered its strength for the assault on Longstop, 10th and 12th Brigades handed over their positions on the Sidi Nsir road and at the entrance to the Tine valley, and prepared to move into the new sector. Nearly a fortnight of experience in action had done much to prepare the infantry of the division for the formidable tasks before it.

5. Operation Lilac Blossom

The new sector was to be taken over from 1st British Infantry Division. During the night of April the 19th, 10th Brigade (including the 2nd Hampshires) took over from 2nd Brigade. By four in the morning of April the 20th, the four battalions were in position. The DCLI on the left relieved the 1st Loyals in the Basin, a valley in front of the Medjez-Goubellat road and five miles south-east of Medjez. The Bedfords, now commanded by Lieutenant-Colonel K. J. G. Garner Smith, took over from the 6th Gordons on the Djebel el Mourhra, two and a half miles south-west of the Basin. The Hampshires, at Mansour on the Medjez-El Aroussa road, nine miles south-west of Medjez, guarded the brigade's right flank against counter-attack through the Mahmoud Gap, at the near end of the Goubellat Plain. The East Surreys, in reserve, were in a hide near Handley Cross, two and a half miles north of the Hampshires. From Mansour to the Basin, the four battalions held a line of four miles of hilly country. The companies were naturally thin on the ground, and there were gaps between battalions, but, while 2nd Brigade was still in the neighbourhood, each battalion area was occupied by a force of double strength.

In front of the brigade's positions were some two or three miles of stony and scrubby hills, and beyond the hills opened the Goubellat Plain on the right and the valley of the Hamar on the left. The German line ran across this more open country, from Peter's Corner, on the Medjez-Tunis road, to Delaney's Corner, six miles south of Peter's Corner. This front was held by two battalions of the Hermann Goering Jaeger Regiment, almost the best German infantry in Tunisia.

Between the Hermann Goering battalions and those of 10th

Brigade, therefore, lay a stretch of country occupied by no troops, since the low ground to the east was overlooked from the westward hills.

During April the 19th, 48th Royal Tanks, commanded by Lieutenant-Colonel G. H. Brooks, had moved into harbour at the village of Testour, six miles behind Mansour. 12th Royal Tanks, commanded by Lieutenant-Colonel J. C. E. Harding MC, had arrived the same day, but most of this battalion's wheeled vehicles, with its light aid detachment and fitters, were either being unloaded at Bône or were on their way to the front. 145th RAC, commanded by Lieutenant-Colonel A. C. Jackson, was already under the command of 1st Division, and was waiting for orders in harbour a mile north of the Surreys. Brigadier Ivor-Moore's headquarters were behind the Djebel el Mourhra, held by the Bedfords.

During the night of April the 20th, 12th Brigade, now commanded by Brigadier R. A. Hull, began to move into a concentration area south of Medjez, where it was to remain in divisional reserve. Advance parties from the artillery regiments were digging and camouflaging gun positions in and round the Basin—some of these positions were actually in No-man's-land; and the lorries of the RASC were working hard on a dumping programme that was to leave in the gun area five hundred rounds for every gun. Guns and infantry of 1st Division were still in the sector, most of them on the point of moving out. Divisional Headquarters had settled down in a wadi behind the Djebel el Mourhra, near the headquarters of 21st Tank Brigade. The night was one of the first to lack the bitter chill of winter; it was cool, and extremely dark.

At eight-fifteen in the evening of April the 20th, the division was warned that the Germans were likely to put in an attack that night, either on the left against Medjez or on the right through the Mahmoud Gap. 10th Brigade stood to, and 48th Royal Tanks prepared to move. At eleven-thirty-five the 1st Duke of Wellington's, a battalion of 1st Division which was holding Banana Ridge, three miles to the left front of the DCLI, was attacked by a force of some sixty German infantrymen, and had to put in a local counter-attack in order to regain lost positions on the ridge. At the same time, an enemy force attacked Fort MacGregor, a mile to the right of the DCLI, and about a hundred and fifty Germans advanced on the left companies of the DCLI. Before long, both the left companies of the DCLI were fighting hard; and soon afterwards

'D' Company on the right was attacked while it was handing over to 'D' Company of the Surreys, which for the time being was under Lieutenant-Colonel Goldsmith's command. The Germans pushed through on the left, and reached the Basin, but were held there by infantry of 2nd Brigade which had not yet left the area.

Soon after midnight, the DCLI found that the direction of the German attack on the left was across their left front towards Banana Ridge, and that on the right the enemy was pushing past the two 'D' Companies towards the Bedfords to the right rear. Between half-past twelve and one in the morning, the Bedfords heard tanks moving across their front and advancing past their right flank, between the Djebel el Mourhra and the Djebel Djaffa farther south. German infantry, moving with the tanks, reached and occupied the advanced dressing station of 10th Field Ambulance. Major P. L. O'Neill, Captains H. E. Smith and I. E. W. Gilmour, the Reverend H. C. Wood and thirteen others were missing when the Germans eventually withdrew.

On the right, therefore, German infantry, with armour which included the formidable Tiger tank, were within half a mile of Divisional Headquarters; mortar-bombs were bursting in the gully among the headquarters vehicles, and the staff officers and clerks stood to. At two in the morning, the leading Germans reached a farm four hundred yards from Brigadier Ivor-Moore's headquarters, and were halted by fire from the headquarters and from the guns of a nearby battery of 30th Field Regiment.

Major Loveday, brigade major of the Tank Brigade, left Brigade Headquarters with a staff-sergeant to find out what was happening at the dressing station nearby. While on their way, the two men were ambushed and captured by a group of heavily armed Germans, who were shouting, cursing and waving their arms about in a manner that suggested drugs or drunkenness. Without any ceremony the Germans stood the two men against a wall and fired off at them a wild fusillade. Both the victims fell—but Major Loveday was unhurt. As soon as the coast seemed clear, he crept back to the headquarters. The body of the staff-sergeant was found next day where he had fallen.

The position was growing grave, and 145th RAC, which had been under the command of 1st Division, was placed under Major-General Hawkesworth's command again. 'B' squadron was immediately placed under the command of Brigadier Hogshaw; two troops went to protect Divisional Headquarters, and a third troop went to the headquarters of 21st Tank Brigade. An hour later Brigadier Ivor-Moore brought 'A' Squadron up to the headquarters area threatened by the German troops on the Djebel Djaffa.

Brigadier Hogshaw brought up two anti-tank guns from the Surreys to defend his headquarters. 'C' Company of the Surreys, with two more anti-tank guns, went to hold Handley Cross. 'B' Company, with the last two guns, advanced towards the dressing station. The rest of the battalion stood to, just to the north of Handley Cross. On Djebel Djaffa, 'D' Company and 4 Platoon of the Bedfords reported tanks in the pass between Djebels el Mourhra and Djaffa. Ten minutes later, the rest of the battalion lost touch with both the company and the platoon. At two in the morning, 'B' Company on Djebel el Mourhra sent out a patrol to see what had become of 4 Platoon; a small-arms battle was raging on the platoon's position, and the patrol was driven back by the fire of automatic weapons. At three-fifteen, a second patrol from 'B' Company went towards 12 Platoon, on the southern slopes of Mourhra, and this patrol too was fired on from the position it was approaching. At four in the morning, a company from the 6th Gordons, of 1st Division, joined the Bedfords and prepared to launch a counterattack from 'B' Company's positions if necessary. Shells and mortarbombs were bursting on 4 Platoon's position, and to the right rear of 'B' Company, towards the headquarters area and the dressing station.

In fact, 'D' Company on Djebel Djaffa had held out, though 4 and 17 Platoons had been overrun and taken prisoner. This resistance on Djaffa, with the increased strength of British infantry on Mourhra and the violent resistance of the headquarters and the field-guns behind the two hills, brought the Hermann Goering Jaegers to a halt. Their thrust had in fact already lost its chance of deeper penetration, for another mile or two would have placed them between 12th Brigade to the south and 145th RAC to the north. Darkness, the confusion usual in large-scale reliefs, and the wide gaps between 10th Brigade's positions had favoured them, but morning was breaking, another brigade of British infantry had arrived and Churchill tanks were on the way.

12th Brigade, meanwhile, had moved into the neighbourhood from the west, with Brigade Headquarters leading. When the headquarters arrived at its new location, four miles south-west of

Djebel Djaffa, and heard the news, it stood to at once. The battalions were still on the road in their lorries, and Brigadier Hull ordered them to deploy in defensive positions along the track west of his headquarters. The enemy did not reach these positions, however, and the brigade's only losses during the night were Lieutenant-Colonel H. Mannington, Lieutenant-Quartermaster C. H. Campbell and four others, who were missing after the advanced dressing station of 12th Field Ambulance had been overrun.

When their thrust lost its impetus, the German tanks and the infantry of the 2nd Battalion of the Hermann Goering Regiment withdrew to the long slopes of Djaffa. From this hill the Germans could overlook all the surrounding country; the roads from Medjez to Bou Arada and El Aroussa, and the village of Goubellat, lay below it, and observers on the top of the hill could see nearly as far as Sloughia, six miles away.

The withdrawal to Djebel Djaffa, and by part of the raiding force to Goubellat beyond it, was covered by skirmishes behind 4th Division's forward positions. Gunners crouched in their gun-pits while machine-gun tracer streaked and crackled overhead; staff officers and batmen, armed with tommy-guns, lay among the bushes round Divisional Headquarters, waiting for an attack which never arrived; the infantry of 10th Brigade and of 1st Division stalked the German tanks which loomed on the dark hillsides; and the Hermann Goering Jaegers bustled their machine-guns and mortars into position, shouting quite openly to each other, let fly with a few rounds and bustled away again.

To the left front of 10th Brigade, the German attack, supported by at least six Mark Four tanks, reached Banana Ridge, overran two companies of 2nd Brigade and some guns, and penetrated between Banana Ridge and Grenadier Hill, farther south-east. 1st Division, however, mounted a powerful counter-attack; and by day-break the 2nd North Staffords had taken two hundred and forty-one prisoners from the 1st Battalion of the Hermann Goerings.

As day broke the Churchill tanks began to appear. At five-thirty in the morning, 'A' Squadron of 145th RAC arrived to defend the headquarters area, and 'B' Squadron reached 10th Brigade.

'B' Company of the Surreys reached the dressing station at five-thirty, and, after a fight lasting half an hour, drove the enemy off. The company held the positions it had won while troops of 1st Division took up the pursuit.

Six tanks of 'A' Squadron, commanded by Captain C. Newton-Thompson, advanced at six-thirty towards the saddle between Mourhra and Djaffa, which was held by German tanks and infantry, and engaged a Tiger tank and two Mark Fours. The rest of 'A' Squadron came up soon afterwards, and the Churchills knocked out the Tiger and one Mark Four, and damaged the third. Three of the Churchills were left damaged on the battlefield; and when an armoured recovery vehicle went out later to bring them back, it too was knocked out. The Tiger was later demolished by sappers who first searched it and found valuable papers inside.

The Germans had hoped that their tanks would be able to cut gaps in the British defence, and that the Hermann Goering infantry would be able to occupy the gaps. They had succeeded in seizing and holding the Pass, between Mourhra and Djaffa, but, as the strength of the opposition grew, the German infantry had to cover the withdrawal of the tanks.

At seven in the morning, 'B' Company of the Bedfords sent another contact patrol towards 12 Platoon; once more the patrol came under fire from the platoon's position, and it was clear that 12 Platoon had been overrun and that the Germans were in occupation.

At eight o'clock, 'B' Squadron of 48th Royal Tanks arrived, and took over from 'A' Squadron of 145th RAC, which was needed in its original role in support of 1st Division. All through the morning, 'B' Squadron lay in hull-down positions behind the Damrha ridge, covering the saddle from two miles to the west, while 'A' and 'C' Squadrons of the same battalion, in reserve, waited farther back.

All through the morning, British and German tanks were firing at each other over the whole front. A section of 17-pounders, the first of these powerful anti-tank guns to go into action in Tunisia, destroyed two Mark Fours at long range on the slopes above the Basin. 104th Field Battery, in its folds in the ground in the forward slopes of Mourhra, fired at targets all round the compass, although infantry were fighting on the ridges all round the guns. At ten in the morning, the Gordons were clearing the Germans from the ridge behind 'B' Troop of this battery, and some twenty Germans broke cover and ran across an open field on the left flank of the guns. The enthusiastic gunners, who for hours had been alert for a direct attack on the gun-position, promptly let fly at the enemy with every type of weapon from a Boys anti-tank rifle to a Verey pistol.

Lieutenant S. J. Cobb, however, with a sequence of highly unorthodox fire orders, reminded them of their proper weapons, and they wheeled their 25-pounders round and opened fire over open sights at less than two hundred yards range. The Germans who survived at once dropped to cover in the deep corn, and stayed there until the Gordons came up to take them prisoner. This was the only recorded occasion on which field-guns of 4th Division engaged enemy infantry over open sights.

'D' Company of the Bedfords, of which there had been no news all night, at last got in touch with the Hampshires on the right. 17 Platoon had been overrun, but the company was holding out on Djaffa, although completely surrounded by Germans most of the time. Soon afterwards, 'A' Company saw enemy infantry withdrawing from Djaffa towards Goubellat, and engaged them with Vickers machine-guns. Another attempt by 'B' Company to reach 4 Platoon was beaten off by the fire of guns and mortars. Between ten and twelve in the morning, 'A' and 'B' Companies and Battalion Headquarters were both under almost continuous fire from German guns and mortars on Djaffa. Reports came back from the battalion observation post on Mourhra that German tanks were still in the Pass, and, between the artillery salvoes which were bursting all round them, were firing at the Churchills lying hull-down a few hundred yards farther west.

'B' Company of the Surreys left the dressing station and rejoined the rest of the battalion. 'D' Company was still with the DCLI near the Basin. Meanwhile, Brigadier Hogshaw and Lieutenant-Colonel Bruno were planning a battalion attack on Djebel Djaffa.

At one-thirty in the afternoon, 'A' Company of the Surreys began to climb the long south-western slopes of the Djebel Djaffa, followed by the rest of the battalion. For the first mile and a quarter, the troops were in dead ground, but at two-thirty the enemy opened fire on the leading platoons. At the same time the tanks of 'A' Squadron of 48th Royal Tanks, farther to the left, moved forward across the wadis which run down north-westwards from the hilltop. The tanks of 'B' Squadron also moved forward into hull-down positions, and opened fire with all their weapons at any enemy movement they saw, in support of 'A' Squadron's advance.

Soon after three o'clock, the leading platoon of 'A' Company reached the crest of the Djebel el Mehirigar, a mile south-west of Djaffa and about two hundred feet lower. As the men began to toil up the last slopes before the summit, the fighting became savage; the infantry were halted and pinned down by fire, and could get no farther than two hundred yards up the hill. The Churchills of 3 Troop, 'A' Squadron, reached a crest over on the left and saw German tanks in front of them. Captain Lott fired and hit the first at short range with his 6-pounder; a Mark Four, two hundred yards away, fired back, and the shot burst in through the turret ring under the gun mounting and set the Churchill on fire. Captain Lott and the wireless operator baled out, but the other three could not get out, and died in the tank. The other two Churchills of 3 Troop hit the first tank and a third, and the German crews leaped out.

To the left of 3 Troop, Lieutenant Gudgin's tank, of 4 Troop, was hit at close range by a shot which knocked back the front machine-gun and its mounting, broke through and set the engine on fire; Lieutenant Gudgin and his crew escaped. A second Churchill of 4 Troop was halted when a shot smashed a bogey; a second shot hit the side of the hull and cut the tow-rope, but struck at too sharp an angle to penetrate, and bounced off. These shots were fired by a dug-in anti-tank gun which was afterwards knocked out by the third tank of 4 Troop.

Farther to the left still, a Mark Six a hundred and fifty yards away fired its 88-mm gun and hit the tank of Lieutenant E. A. A. Harvey, 'A' Squadron's reconnaissance officer. The shell broke through the turret armour above the gun, failed to explode, but broke up and set fire to the wireless and some small kit. The crew baled out under fire. Lieutenant Harvey and the wireless operator, Trooper N. Watts, both slightly wounded, went back to the tank a few minutes later and squirted hand extinguishers into the flames until the fumes drove them out of the turret. Lieutenant Harvey got into the driver's seat and released the hand-brake, so that the tank rolled backwards into cover behind the ridge. The two men left the tank then, since the fire seemed likely to break out again if the engine were started. Later on, the driver, Trooper Amos, who had been cool and determined all through the battle, went back to the tank with the gunner, Corporal Muchmore, found that the fire had gone out, and drove the tank back.

The advance of 'A' Squadron was stopped by German tanks and anti-tank guns, and the Churchills were unable to see and so to support the Surreys on the right because of the scrub.

'A' Company, higher up on the hillside, was losing men, and

ammunition was running low. The enemy was fighting back hard, with tanks and heavy machine-guns joining in. The company had to withdraw a hundred yards down the hill to reorganize.

At five in the evening, four Messerschmitts bombed 'B' Squadron from six hundred feet, but inflicted neither damage nor casualties.

Lieutenant-Colonel Bruno brought 'C' Company up to attack round the left flank of 'A', supported by the fire of 'B' from Djebel Mehirigar, and himself led the attack. The company stormed up the hill, in the face of a withering fire, and men of the East Surreys were within twenty yards of the top when they were finally stopped. Lieutenant-Colonel Bruno ordered the company commander, Major R. C. Guy, to withdraw, and soon afterwards was himself killed, with Lieutenant H. N. Marlow, in the heart of the enemy's positions. The guns of 30th Field Regiment put down a smoke screen, and 'B' Company gave covering fire; and with this help Major Guy, himself wounded, got his company back behind Djebel Mehirigar, where it was joined by 'A' Company. Major R. O. V. Thompson, the second-in-command of the battalion, took command, helped the leading companies to withdraw, and organized the evacuation of wounded by carriers.

Brigadier Hogshaw brought 'A' and 'C' Companies and Battalion Headquarters down from the hill to reorganize near Brigade Headquarters; 'B' Company stayed on Djebel Mehirigar for the night. The companies took up their night positions, and prepared to meet any counter-attacks down the hill. The battalion had lost in the Djebel Djaffa action two officers and five others killed, one officer and twenty-six others wounded and thirty-five missing. The tanks also withdrew from the hill at dusk; for the loss of three Churchills and one armoured recovery vehicle, they had knocked out a Tiger, a Mark Four and three Mark Threes.

The Bedfords during the day had lost only one killed and two wounded, but a hundred and nineteen were missing—the men of the platoons which had been overrun.

During the night the Black Watch came forward to the foot of Djebel Djaffa, ready to attack it in the morning.

The DCLI meanwhile had been engaged in heavy fighting round the Basin. During the afternoon, 2nd Brigade mounted a vigorous counter-attack, with the help of the DCLI, cleared the Germans out of the Basin, took a considerable number of prisoners and destroyed about twenty tanks. During the action, the DCLI had lost, in all, fourteen killed, twenty-two wounded and seventy missing.

The German thrusts past Grenadier Hill and into the Basin had both come to nothing—or, for most of the Germans, to captivity, wounds or death. Whatever their losses on Djebel Djaffa, however, they had not apparently loosed their hold on it under the assault of 4th Division's infantry and tanks.

Early in the morning of April the 22nd, Major G. G. Maggs MC, commanding 'B' Company of the Surreys on Djebel Mehirigar, moved cautiously up the slope down which 'A' and 'C' Companies had been forced to retire during the day before. He climbed nearer and nearer to the crest, and all was still; no shot broke the comparative peace of the morning. At last he reached the crest and stood erect on it; Djebel Djaffa was no longer defended.

Among the dead British and German soldiers lying round the hilltop he found a wounded German. This man had a curious story to tell. The German force on the hilltop had suffered severe losses during the fierce attacks by the Surreys, and the nerve of the survivors had been shaken. They had withstood the charge first of 'A' Company and then of 'C'; but when the artillery's smoke began to eddy across the hillside in front of them, they believed a third charge was coming through it, and they turned and made their way down the steep back of the hill at the same time as the Surreys on the other side were retreating to Mehirigar. Patrols of the Reconnaissance Regiment, who with sappers searched the other parts of the hill for mines, found only wounded Germans.

That evening the bodies of Lieutenant-Colonel Bruno, Lieutenant Marlow and five other men of the East Surreys were buried where they had fallen, near the crest of Djebel Djaffa.

The battle was over, and the division's intelligence officers began to piece together the story of the German attack. Hoping to delay and disorganize the First Army's preparations for the final thrust towards Tunis, General von Arnim had flung against 10th Brigade's new sector a force of about seventy tanks, three battalions of infantry and a company of sappers fighting as infantry. (At this time he had only some hundred tanks in action.) This assault was known as Operation Lilac Blossom; the toughest German soldiers were given to the use of perfume and even of cosmetics, and this fragrant name was curiously suitable.

The first phase of the attack was a pincer movement round

Banana Ridge, by the 1st Battalion, 754th Grenadier Brigade to the north, and to the south by a company of the Hermann Goering Engineers, with tanks of the 10th Armoured Division.

The northern thrust reached the Djebel Hoka, which looks down on Medjez from only three miles to the east. From Hoka the Grenadiers made a half-hearted attempt to surround Grenadier Hill to the south-west. They surrounded, but failed to overrun, some of the British positions on the hill, and no frontal attack followed the initial skirmishing. Early in the afternoon, 1st Division counter-attacked and drove the Grenadiers back towards their own lines.

The tanks with the Hermann Goering sappers penetrated some way round the south of Banana Ridge before being halted by the DCLI and troops of 1st Division. During the afternoon they too were driven back from the foot of Banana Ridge.

Meanwhile, the second phase had begun, when a more powerful force thrust north and north-west from the village of Goubellat. 1st Battalion of the Hermann Goering Jaeger Regiment, riding on tanks, went northwards up the road towards Grenadier Hill, and reached the north-eastern slopes of the Djebel el Mourhra. There, at dawn, the force was counter-attacked by 1st Division; two companies were surrounded and all but wiped out—a hundred and eighty Germans were captured.

2nd Battalion of the same regiment, supported by tanks, found their way through the British lines in front of Djebel Djaffa, broke through the Pass and probed towards the headquarters beyond. This force was pushed back on to the hill, from which it began to withdraw after the attacks by the East Surreys during the afternoon and evening.

Operation Lilac Blossom achieved no tactical advantage for the enemy. The attack was launched with a force which might well have done very serious harm to the troops of a single infantry division, thin on the ground. But the same force was quite inadequate to deal with two divisions, one of which included a brigade of tanks. The two British divisions, neither of which had seen a great deal of fighting since France, gained experience and confidence, though at the cost of considerable losses. The Germans lost thirty-three tanks and more than four hundred and fifty prisoners, apart from killed and wounded; 4th Division lost five tanks, thirty-six men killed, eighty-one wounded and two hundred and forty-nine missing; and V Corps went on pushing outwards from Medjez.

6. Peter's Corner

The final battle in Tunisia was now about to begin. To the right of 4th Division, 6th Armoured Division of IX Corps was pressing the enemy hard in the Goubellat Plain. On the left flank of V Corps, 78th Division had a footing on Longstop Hill. In the centre of V Corps, 1st Infantry Division was fighting for the high ground at Gueriat el Atach, between Peter's Corner in front of 4th Division and Longstop Hill in 78th Division's sector.

4th Division's task was to secure the right flank of V Corps, partly by aggressive reconnaissance of the Goubellat Plain, and of the Hamar Valley which stretches from Peter's Corner to Delaney's Corner; and partly by an attack on the positions from which the Germans dominated the Tunis road at Peter's Corner.

Patrols of the Reconnaissance Regiment, the Bedfords and the DCLI began to search the Goubellat Plain and to probe the Wadi Hamar even before the Germans were known to have left the Djebel Djaffa. To the south of Delaney's Corner and beyond it, the armour of IX Corps was engaged in a mobile battle—clouds of dust were pierced by the bright flash of tank guns, and aircraft wheeled and soared continually overhead. Patrols searching the Wadi Hamar for a southern approach to Peter's Corner were halted by German mortars half-way between Peter's Corner and Delaney's Corner.

Since, by April the 24th, 1st Division was firmly in position on Gueriat el Atach, and so overlooked most of the neighbourhood of Peter's Corner, 4th Division could make a beginning on the second part of its task. Major-General Hawkesworth decided to bring 12th Brigade in on the left of 10th Brigade, in order to clear first the positions immediately round Peter's Corner, then the Argoub el

Hania, the long ridge two miles beyond, and finally the village of Ksar Tyr—a mile and a half farther on still—and the high ground to the south. Peter's Corner itself was the gateway to a stretch of perfect tank country which extended as far as Tunis, twenty-seven miles away.

The hills round Peter's Corner were to be attacked by the Royal Fusiliers, supported by all the division's field-guns, two troops of 81st Anti-tank Battery and a section of 225th Field Company. The battalion was to advance south-westerly at midnight across two and a half miles of rolling fields of grass and corn, and to take the Peter's Corner positions from the flank. Four low hills—El Azabi, Sidi Abdallah, Sidi Salem and Sidi Médiene—surround Peter's Corner, and each of these was a company objective.

Trouble began for the Royal Fusiliers when during the afternoon of April the 23rd the commanders of companies and specialist platoons were on El Atach, looking over the country through which they were to advance. German aircraft bombed and machine-gunned the party; Major H. I. N. Hope Johnstone, commanding 'Y' Company, Sergeant Powell, commanding the Mortar Platoon, and Captain J. C. D. Jarrod, commanding 'X' Company, were wounded. Captain Jarrod was able to carry on, but 'Y' Company had to be led into the attack by Captain J. H. Gibson-Horrocks, who had no time for reconnaissance.

At midnight, Captain A. C. O'Brien led 'W' Company forward, and 'X', 'Y' and 'Z' Companies followed in turn. The troops were in cardigans and shirt-sleeves in the warm night. The first enemy positions, in the Oued Milah, were not a serious obstacle, and thirty-five prisoners were taken from the Hermann Goerings. The division's guns meanwhile were hammering away at the objectives and at the high ground beyond.

The fire of machine-guns on the left flank began to give trouble. Since these machine-guns might well prevent the rest of the battalion from crossing the Oued Milah, Captain O'Brien wheeled his company left to deal with them. They were not, however, easy to deal with, and 'D' Company was considerably delayed.

'X' Company meanwhile was crossing the Oued and climbing the slopes of El Azabi, on to which 'W' Company should have led the way. Since there was some opposition and no sign of 'W' Company, Captain Jarrod halted his company and sent out patrols to search for 'W' Company, rather than spend his company's strength before reaching his objective, Sidi Abdallah. But as darkness began to give way to the dim light of dawn, Captain Jarrod found that his company was hopelessly exposed on the bare slopes of El Azabi, and withdrew it into the Oued Milah behind. There he found 'W' Company, which was still trying to silence the obstinate machine-guns.

To the right of 'X' Company, 'Z' Company, commanded by Captain R. C. Henderson, was quite unable to reach Sidi Salem; the company was halted by barbed wire and eventually driven back to its start line by machine-gun fire. Farther to the right still, 'Y' Company had at first made good headway towards Sidi Médiene; but after a while there was no further news of the company, and by daylight it had completely disappeared.

If all had gone well, Battalion Headquarters would have moved forward at dawn to Sidi Médiene. As it was, dawn found the headquarters at Zraouina Farm, on the forward slope in full view of the enemy. At eight in the morning, Lieutenant-Colonel Brandon was in a slit trench, talking by wireless to Brigade Headquarters, when a mortar bomb burst behind him; several men were wounded, the signal truck was wrecked and Lieutenant-Colonel Brandon was killed.

He had been one of the personalities of the division. After many years of service in the ranks of the Royal Fusiliers, he had been promoted in May 1939 from Regimental Sergeant-Major of the 1st Battalion to Lieutenant-Quartermaster of the 2nd. He greatly distinguished himself in the retreat to Dunkirk, and soon afterwards exchanged his quarter-master's commission for that of a combatant officer. His promotion was deservedly rapid, and in August 1942 he was appointed to the command of his battalion. He was a fine leader of men, being gifted with the rare combination of force of personality and great courage with friendliness of manner.

At midday the situation was no better. There was still no news of 'Y' Company, and 'X' and 'Z' were still trapped and losing men in the wadi. Captains O'Brien and Jarrod agreed that they would have to break out, and were reconnoitring the ground for an attack when they walked into a mine-field. Both company commanders and Captain T. V. Lightfoot of 'X' Company were wounded. Captain J. M. Spooner of 'W' Company took command. He rallied the men of both companies, showing himself in order to draw the enemy's fire and show his own Bren-gunners their targets, and heartening the men in their unpleasant predicament. Lieutenant P. M. Mellish of 'X' Company volunteered to go back to Battalion Headquarters for help. The Germans spotted him on the way, and machine-gun bullets hit him in the legs and back.

Early in the afternoon, Major W. T. Llewellyn Jones, who as second-in-command had taken over command of the battalion, sent 'Z' Company forward again, to help 'X' and 'W' with a flanking attack round to the right. The company worked some way round, but was eventually halted by machine-gun fire from dominating positions.

Brigadier Hull meanwhile had brought up 'B' Company of the Black Watch and 'C' Squadron of 12th Royal Tanks, to attack first Sidi Médiene and then Sidi Salem from the west, while on the left the three companies of the Royal Fusiliers were attacking. The Black Watch reached Point 103, the last crest before Sidi Médiene, but could go no farther because of mines, which destroyed three of the carriers, and the furious fire of the enemy. The tanks too were halted by mines which broke the tracks of four of them; two more were knocked out by anti-tank guns. The company commander and fourteen others actually reached Sidi Médiene, and found it covered with dead and dying Germans; but they ran out of ammunition and were unable to hold it.

Screened by the fire of tanks and artillery, the remnants of the Black Watch withdrew; seven men of the company had been killed, and fifty-six wounded, including all four officers. 'C' Squadron also came back, having lost six tanks; three officers and twelve others were wounded.

At dusk, Brigadier Hull ordered the Royal Fusiliers back to the shelter of Banana Ridge. 'W', 'X' and 'Z' Companies returned, but there was still no sign of 'Y'. The battalion had taken some seventy-five prisoners from the 1st Battalion 754th Grenadier Brigade, which had been one of the attacking battalions in Operation Lilac Blossom. The Black Watch had taken a prisoner, from whom they learned that Sidi Médiene was held by the 1st Battalion of the Hermann Goering Jaegers, which had also taken part in Lilac Blossom. The German troops had been ordered to stand to the last man and the last round; and strong reserves of tanks waited behind them in case 4th Division were to break through.

The enemy had clearly chosen their ground for a stand. 78th Division was having to fight like tigers for Longstop; 1st Division was being fiercely counter-attacked on Gueriat el Atach; 12th Brigade had been driven back from Peter's Corner, and 10th Brigade's patrols could not approach it from the south. 10th Brigade's aggressive patrolling in No-man's-land, however, had had its effect; the Germans had prepared another counter-attack through Goubellat, but had been discouraged by the constant come-and-go across the plain of strong mobile patrols.

Major-General Hawkesworth decided to modify his plans for 12th Brigade's attacks battalion by battalion, and gave Brigadier Hull orders for a brigade attack, supported by 12th Royal Tanks, two troops of Scorpions (tanks equipped with chain flails for detonating mines), and all the guns and all the sappers of the division. A mine-field task force was to deal with the mine-fields in front of Sidi Médiene and behind Sidi Salem. The attack was to go in soon after dark on April the 25th.

At ten o'clock that night a confused uproar broke out to the north of Peter's Corner; the fire of small-arms and mortars punctuated the unsteady roaring of carrier engines, and tracer flashed across the corn-fields. All this was started by a detachment of the DCLI, sent to divert the enemy's attention, and to draw fire which would reveal his weapon sites.

At the same time, the mine-field task force, consisting of a company of the Black Watch and detachments of 7th Field Company and the Divisional Provost Company, was advancing behind an artillery barrage on Sidi Médiene, followed by the rest of the Black Watch. The task force cut a lane through the mine-field, and the infantry pressed forward through the fire of machine-guns and mortars towards the Sidi Médiene ridge, from which German flares rose from time to time through the tracer-bullets into the dark sky. At ten-forty the battalion reached the ridge and went in with the bayonet. After some ferocious hand-to-hand fighting, the Black Watch cleared the Germans off the ridge, and at once began to dig in, preparing for the counter-attack which was sure to come. Both sides had lost a number of men.

The expected counter-attack came in at dawn and was beaten off, though the Black Watch suffered considerable losses. A troop of Churchills from 'B' Squadron also arrived at dawn, but after a while all the tanks were stopped by mines.

Farther to the left, meanwhile, the Royal Fusiliers had attacked El Azabi from the direction of Snake Ridge instead of from Gueriat el Atach. 'W' and 'X' Companies crossed the Oued Milah and reached El Azabi without meeting opposition, though the mortars and machine-guns had some trouble in getting across the wadi. The low hill was scattered with the debris of a hurried retreat by the Germans. Digging in such rocky ground was far from easy, and apart from a small gully there was no natural cover. 'B' Squadron 12th Royal Tanks set out to support the Royal Fusiliers, but lost ten tanks in the mine-fields in front of Sidi Médiene, and was unable to give decisive help.

The main Tunis road crossed the wadi in the battalion area by means of a stone and an iron bridge side by side. The sappers of 225th Field Company found that both the bridges were wired and booby-trapped. They started work on the iron bridge, but very soon a booby-trap exploded and wounded Lieutenant J. W. McKay. A few minutes later, part of the stone bridge blew up.

The sappers found another way across the wadi, and did their best to clear it of mines in the dark. As day was about to break, some mortar carriers and machine-gun carriers were brought up to make the crossing. As soon as the leading carrier left the road it blew up on a mine; several men were wounded, including Sergeant Bristier of the Mortar Platoon, who lost an arm.

Daylight revealed to the German machine-gunners the troops and vehicles gathered by the crossing, and the vehicles had to be withdrawn to cover. The rifle companies of the Royal Fusiliers meanwhile were crouching uncomfortably on the open sides of El Azabi, completely overlooked by the Germans on the higher ground across the main road. The men kept as low as they could, and very few of them came to grief in the subsequent shelling and machine-gunning. Any further advance across the open ground would have been through mine-fields.

The sappers worked hard all morning on the iron bridge, and by midday it was clear. Some of the anti-tank portees came racing forward in an effort to run the gauntlet into the dead ground on the other side. The vehicles were damaged and halted by accurate mortar fire. It was not until after dark that Battalion Headquarters of the Royal Fusiliers and the supporting weapons were able at last to cross the bridge and to reach positions beyond the wadi.

Both the Black Watch and the Royal Fusiliers spent April the 26th digging-in, wiring, clearing mine-fields for the next advance and patrolling. The sappers cleared a crossing over the Oued Milah by which tanks could join the Royal Fusiliers. At about midday, seventy-two Boston bombers boomed overhead in formations of twelve, and dropped a thunderous load of bombs on and around Ksar Tyr. Two large fires went on burning there for some hours.

Brigadier Hull now brought forward his reserve battalion, the West Kents, to break into the ring of German positions which looked down on Peter's Corner.

After dark, two companies of the West Kents, led by Major E. Dann, formed up behind El Azabi. At ten o'clock they went silently forward across El Azabi to the Tunis road, one company making southwards for Sidi Salem, and the other directed on Sidi Abdallah.

While the West Kents were still working their way forward, the Germans confused the situation by mounting an attack on Sidi Médiene. At one in the morning, intense mortar fire began to burst among the Black Watch's positions, and two anti-tank gun portees and a carrier loaded with ammunition were set ablaze. The mortar fire even exploded German mines in the ground behind the ridge. Half an hour later the main attack came in on the right flank, supported by flame-throwers, and was beaten off with the help of heavy defensive fire from the guns behind Banana Ridge.

Part of one company of the West Kents, meanwhile, had reached Sidi Salem, cleared it and had begun to consolidate. The rest of the force could not reach Sidi Abdallah. A mine-field task force, commanded by Major Richardson of 7th Field Company, began to clear up the mine-fields to the south-east of the Tunis road, between el Azabi and the two objectives of the West Kents.

At dawn of April the 27th, 'A' Squadron of 12th Royal Tanks came up, passed through the gaps cut in the mine-field by the sappers, and with part of Major Dann's force made for Sidi Abdallah. Fierce machine-gun fire held back the infantry, and Major Dann was among the killed, but the tanks went on in spite of losses and reached the crest of the rise, before withdrawing behind it again to take up hull-down positions.

There the tanks stayed, enduring the fire of a variety of weapons, and firing back at every possible target. At one in the afternoon, German aircraft bombed them, but they held on. At two-thirty, 'A' Company of the Black Watch, with the help of guns and of Hurricane fighter-bombers, struggled forward behind a thick smoke screen to tighten the grip on Sidi Abdallah.

While the tanks waited nearby in case they were needed to beat off a counter-attack, 'A' Company held Sidi Abdallah against all comers for two hours, with the help of the gunners behind Snake Ridge and in the Basin. But the Hermann Goerings had orders to attack and hold the ridge 'regardless of cost'; and the Black Watch were driven off by a powerful force which included Tiger tanks. At six in the evening, three Churchills—all that was left of 'A' Squadron —came back across the Tunis road. The squadron had lost fifteen tanks, though eight were afterwards recovered. By nightfall the Germans were firmly back on Sidi Abdallah, though very few of their infantry had survived the assault.

April the 28th was a comparatively quiet day for 12th Brigade. A flight of the stubby Focke-Wulf fighters appeared suddenly in the sky, machine-gunned the road towards Medjez and wheeled away over Grenadier Hill; one was shot down, and crashed near Banana Ridge.

10th Brigade meanwhile had been waiting to make for Tunis the moment the Germans showed signs of withdrawal from Peter's Corner. Such a withdrawal might well have been expected, since the tanks of IX Corps on the right were beginning to get round behind Ksar Tyr, and on the left of V Corps the survivors of the German garrison of Longstop Hill were in full flight, with 78th Division after them. The Hermann Goering Division, however, in spite of the crippling losses inflicted on it by 4th Division, held out and clearly intended to go on holding out; and, eight miles to the north, the Germans were still counter-attacking 1st Division. Major-General Hawkesworth therefore began to bring 10th Brigade into the Peter's Corner battle. Late in the afternoon of April the 28th, the DCLI took over El Azabi from the Royal Fusiliers, who were to rest before making another attack.

The Royal Fusiliers were to advance at dawn from El Azabi across the Tunis road to Sidi Abdallah and to Cactus Farm, a cluster of ruined white buildings and cactus hedges on the lower and left-hand end of the half-mile long ridge. The battalion's left flank was to be covered by the West Kents, who during the night were to attack and hold Point 133, a scrub-covered ridge three-quarters of a mile to the left of Cactus Farm.

The West Kents attacked just after seven in the evening, and by one in the morning of April the 29th they were on the ridge. Three hours later, however, the Germans came back with a purposeful counter-attack and swept them out of their positions. Soon after dawn, the West Kents went in again with a rush, and took Point 133 once more. They spent the rest of the day consolidating, and the position was further strengthened by anti-tank guns.

The Royal Fusiliers attacked at six the same morning. 'Z' Company on the right made for Sidi Abdallah, and 'W' Company on the left was directed on Cactus Farm. The two companies were supported by 'B' and 'C' Squadrons of 12th Royal Tanks. The advance was preceded by an artillery barrage and accompanied by harassing fire and a smoke screen.

Heavy German defensive fire came down almost at once, but the infantry were well dispersed and losses were not severe. However, Captain R. C. Henderson, commanding 'Z' Company, was wounded, and Lieutenant P. Lowy took charge. Two Churchill tanks blew up on mines when they left the lane cleared of mines by the sappers.

As the Fusiliers approached the low ridges which were their objectives, the enemy's fire grew more and more intense. Anti-tank guns were firing at short range at the vehicles moving through the mine-field, and the fire of machine-guns was added to that of mortars and guns. The Carrier Platoon, commanded by Captain J. A. Savill, managed to get through the mine-field, and advanced behind the tanks to support 'W' Company. The anti-tank guns followed the carriers, but the portees were halted and destroyed before the guns could get into action.

'Z' Company was coming under increasingly heavy fire, but with the help of the tanks pressed forward, and at last reached the crest of Sidi Abdallah. There the Fusiliers joined in a savage hand-to-hand fight with German infantry, whose positions on the crest and behind it were covered by fire from positions on the higher ground beyond. The Germans had to be winkled one by one out of their slit trenches and dug-outs; the enemy's supporting fire was accurate enough to make this a costly business. Lance-Corporal W. McQuoid led the way, closing in on the enemy and finishing them with grenades; he attacked again and again, going back to collect grenades from dead and wounded men, and going in once more. When the fight was over, he was nowhere to be found; and later his dead body was found on the battle-field.

On the crest they had taken, the Fusiliers found twelve enemy machine-guns and light machine-guns, a smashed 88-mm anti-tank gun, two 4·2-inch mortars and a number of dead Germans.

Only about thirty men of 'Z' Company remained. Lieutenant Lowy was among the killed, and the survivors were rallied by Second-Lieutenant J. E. Edmundson, himself slightly wounded in the shoulder. A single anti-tank gun had somehow survived the journey, and went into action on Sidi Abdallah. The men were very tired, but Second-Lieutenant Edmundson set about reorganizing them and consolidating the newly-won position. Most of the hill was under enemy observation; the part which was not was under continuous shell-fire. There was no news of 'W' Company on the left. A strong German counter-attack came in, with tanks which included at least one Tiger; and it was beaten off by Churchills and Fusiliers, and four of the German tanks were destroyed.

'W' Company was in trouble. All had gone well at first, but as the leading platoon approached Cactus Farm the enemy's fire became intense. There was no deep corn to give cover here; open grassland lay between the company and its objective. The farm was surrounded by mine-fields and garrisoned by resolute machine-gunners who were extremely well dug in. Captain J. M. Spooner therefore called a halt, to give the tanks time to come into action. But the tanks had come to grief; a mine-field near Cactus Farm and the close-range fire of German anti-tank guns had accounted for nearly the whole squadron.

The Carrier Platoon had been trapped in the mine-field, and four carriers were destroyed. Looking for a good position for his Bren guns, Captain Savill crawled forward along a low wall leading towards the farm; Germans in a trench on the other side of the wall saw him and killed him with a grenade. Lieutenant S. C. Gardner, the platoon's other officer, was making his way round to the left behind a knocked-out tank when he was killed by a burst of short-range machine-gun fire.

A platoon commanded by Lieutenant D. B. R. Johns attempted a right flanking attack, but was stopped, and Lieutenant Johns was killed.

A few tanks were still in action, and were firing at the farm, but they were separated from the infantry by a rise in the ground which could be crossed or seen over by neither tanks nor infantry. Captain Spooner realized the infantry would have to attack without the tanks, and gave the order to charge the farm. He picked up a Bren gun and himself led the charge, firing from the hip. He made straight for the nearest German machine-gun, and in spite of its fire killed the whole crew; then a second machine-gun only a few yards away fired a burst which struck him full in the body. Even as he fell, he swung round and fired a last burst at the crew of the second gun.

All the fighting was fierce in the extreme, and both sides were suffering heavy losses. The blazing sun made metal too hot to touch, and steel helmets became almost intolerable; men had to exert themselves for hours in the pitiless heat, refreshed only by a few gulps of warm water.

A few German positions were captured, but there were many more. The last few men of 'W' Company were pinned to the ground within a stone's throw of Cactus Farm.

Back at Battalion Headquarters, Major Llewellyn Jones was in touch with 'Z' Company but not with 'W'. He could see, however, that all was not well on the left, and decided to put in 'X' Company. The company was to move on to Sidi Abdallah behind 'Z' Company and then swing left to take Cactus Farm from the rear.

As in the initial assault, 'X' Company moved from the first through heavy defensive fire without losing many men. Lieutenant C. G. Port's platoon on the right reached 'Z' Company; Lieutenant Port himself was killed by a shell immediately afterwards.

'X' Company swung left and moved in to the assault. Captain A. A. Lee, commanding the company, sent back a radio message—'Everything OK, we're going in now to give them hell.' This was the last message from the company. Once more the German machine-guns were too many and too accurate. Captain Lee's body was afterwards found twenty yards from the cactus surrounding the farm; the bodies of Second-Lieutenant A. N. H. Sykes and Company Sergeant-Major R. West lay beside him.

Since Major Llewellyn Jones could not find out what was happening to 'W' and 'X' Companies, he decided to go up to Cactus Farm in his carrier with the adjutant, Captain T. C. Howes. A German anti-tank gun fired at the carrier as it drove through the mine-field, showing that the Germans were not far away. Nearer the farm, the litter of burnt-out gun-tractors and blown-up tanks and carriers told their own story. Major Llewellyn Jones found Sergeants Cooper and Petley of the Carrier Platoon nearby, and heard what had happened to the platoon.

One of the Churchills was still firing at the farm from short range. There were not enough survivors to mount an assault on the farm.

At 'Z' Company, the remaining men were consolidating. An officer of 22nd Field Regiment was directing fire as fast as he could talk into his wireless set, and Bren-gunners were engaging German troops who could be seen from time to time a few hundred yards away.

Early in the evening, a company of the West Kents was placed under command of the Royal Fusiliers, and with Churchills from 12th Royal Tanks made yet another attack on Cactus Farm. They were beaten off, and the German counter-attacks were so formidable that the West Kents lost Point 133 again. During the fighting round Point 133 and Cactus Farm, the West Kents had lost thirty killed, fifty-six wounded and a hundred and eighty-seven missing.

Brigadier Hull arranged that 'Z' Company on Sidi Abdallah should be relieved at nightfall by the West Kents, and the spirits of the Fusiliers rose at the prospect of some rest. At dusk, however, Major Llewellyn Jones was warned that the relief could not take place until the following night. All the available Fusiliers round Battalion Headquarters were hurriedly gathered into a party of some thirty men, and, loaded with food, ammunition and digging tools, went off to reinforce Sidi Abdallah, led by Captain Howes and the Intelligence Officer, Lieutenant M. J. Venning.

It was a pitch-black night with no moon. There was no clear path to Sidi Abdallah; the only guides were the Churchills still burning round Cactus Farm. A rendezvous had been arranged, at which the relief party was to meet a guide from 'Z' Company. The journey to the rendezvous was a long one through mine-fields; and, when at last the party arrived, there was no sign of the guide. Sidi Abdallah was all but impossible to find in the dark; the neighbourhood was bewildering with false crests. Captain Howes made a prolonged search, but could not find 'Z' Company. He took the party back to the road, and there met the survivors of 'Z', who had been counter-attacked and forced off the ridge. Two attempts to get back into the positions came to nothing, and 'Z' Company and the adjutant's party took up a new position for the night between Sidi Salem and Sidi Abdallah.

All through the night, the 7·2-inch howitzers of 54th Heavy Regiment, now under Brigadier Shoosmith's[1] command, shelled Cactus Farm at intervals of five minutes. Yet another attack on the farm went in before dawn and was beaten off; the Germans were clearly dug in very deeply.

[1] Brigadier Johnson had left the division, and Lieutenant-Colonel Shoosmith had been promoted to take his place. Lieutenant-Colonel G. A. Thomas took over as GSO 1.

During the night, 'A' and 'D' Companies of the DCLI, commanded by Major A. E. Harding, had put in a silent attack on Point 133. They captured the ridge, but the Germans came flooding back and surrounded it; ammunition ran low and the DCLI had to withdraw. Early in the morning of April the 30th, Major Harding's force went in once more, and once more took the ridge; and when at twelve-thirty in the afternoon the force was driven back again, the ridge had changed hands eight times in forty-eight hours.

The German soldiers manning mortars and machine-guns were fighting with such determination that they were never entirely dislodged. Whenever troops of 12th Brigade reached the crest of Point 133 or Sidi Abdallah, the German weapons remained in action on the downwards slope beyond, deeply dug in. The position at Sidi Abdallah was particularly difficult because the enemy never withdrew from Cactus Farm; and German observation posts to the north could direct the fire of mortars on to both Point 133 and Sidi Abdallah.

The tenacity of the German resistance at Peter's Corner was calculated. To the north-west, the difficult country allowed the Germans a comparatively easy and gradual withdrawal in front of 78th Division; and without heavy loss the Germans were able to hold against 1st Division the precipitous Djebel Bou Aoukaz, known as the Bou. To the south-east of Peter's Corner, a screen of German anti-tank guns among the hills was holding off the tanks of 1st and 6th Armoured Divisions. But the Tunis road, running through perfect tank country, could be held only by men and weapons; and there General von Arnim flung into the gap a mixed force, the hard core of which were the Hermann Goering Grenadiers and the surviving tanks of two armoured divisions and two heavy tank battalions, reinforced by sappers fighting as infantry, anti-aircraft gunners and even clerks and storemen from 'B' Echelon. By April the 30th, after a week's battering by 12th Brigade, this force had dwindled to less than fifteen hundred infantry and sixty tanks, but it still held Sidi Abdallah, Cactus Farm and Point 133. German prisoners from different units said they had fought in Russia and that they had never known such ferocious fighting there. 4th Division was never to see a battle much more deadly.

The determined and skilful resistance of General von Arnim's troops across the whole front of V Corps and in front of the left wing of IX Corps showed that successive blows against different buttresses of the defence were unlikely to knock the Germans out. The attacks of 1st and 78th Divisions, however, had given the First Army room to deploy its armour in force on the Tunis side of the Medjerda; and the fighting at Peter's Corner had greatly weakened the German reserves of tanks and infantry. The enemy was staggering, but still fighting back; a knock-out blow was needed. General Anderson began to regroup his forces.

4th Division's attacks on the ridges beyond Peter's Corner ceased. Apart from the DCLI's battle round Point 133, April the 30th was a comparatively quiet day; German infantry and tanks formed up behind Point 133 as though for yet another attack, but nothing further happened.

During the night of April the 30th, 12th Brigade handed over its positions on Sidi Médiene, Sidi Salem and El Azabi to 11th Brigade of 78th Division, and the DCLI withdrew to join the rest of 10th Brigade. 11th Brigade came temporarily under Major-General Hawkesworth's command, so that for a short time 4th Division consisted once more of the three brigades which had fought under Major-General Johnson in France three years before. The 1st East Surreys took over El Azabi from the DCLI, the 2nd Lancashire Fusiliers relieved the Black Watch on Sidi Salem and Sidi Médiene, and the 5th Northamptons were held in brigade reserve.

The 1st/6th East Surreys, meanwhile, commanded by Lieutenant-Colonel R. O. V. Thompson, had taken up positions round Zraouina Farm during the night of April the 28th, and were patrolling on the left flank of 11th Brigade.

12th Brigade had suffered grievously in the Peter's Corner battle; losses in officers had been particularly severe, including two commanding officers, a second-in-command and ten company commanders. The brigade had taken a hundred and seventeen prisoners since going into action early in April. 12th Royal Tanks had lost thirty-eight of its Churchills.

The whole division had been gravely weakened. After three weeks of fighting, the six infantry battalions had lost, in killed, wounded and missing, ninety officers and more than sixteen hundred other ranks—more than a third of their strength. Other units had lost some four hundred men. But the Germans opposing the division had suffered losses which weakened them even more seriously, and had been led to hold their reserve in the wrong place. The climax of the campaign was approaching.

7. Dunkirk avenged

On April the 30th, General Alexander had told Lieutenant-General Anderson that the country in front of Eighth Army was too difficult for a break-through without severe losses; First Army was therefore to be strengthened by the transfer of troops from Eighth Army, and was to deliver the knock-out blow. 7th Armoured Division, 4th Indian Division and 201st Guards Brigade, with all the necessary divisional and administrative troops, came up from the south to join First Army.

Lieutenant-General Anderson decided to break into the Tunis plain along the Massicault road, which 4th Division had been struggling to open. V Corps was to hold its present front from the west to the south-west of Tunis. IX Corps, advancing through the centre of V Corps, was to break open with two infantry divisions a narrow breach in the enemy's defences, and was to put two armoured divisions through the breach. One of the armoured divisions was to be the 6th, which was already in IX Corps, and the other was to be the 7th, from Eighth Army. The initial assault was to be carried out by 4th Indian Division from Eighth Army and by 4th British Division from V Corps.

At three in the morning of May the 6th, 4th Division on the right and 4th Indian Division on the left were to attack on a front of less than two miles. The assault was to be delivered across a start-line on the open, rolling hills four miles to the north of Peter's Corner; the division's final objective was to be the hamlet of Frendj, three and a half miles farther west, and a mile short of the Tunis road. When Frendj was taken, 6th Armoured Division was to go through and make for Tunis, just over twenty miles up the main road.

The division was to be supported by the guns of 78th Division (17th, 132nd and 138th Field Regiments), a field regiment from 7th Armoured Division, 473rd (Self-propelled) Battery, 5th Medium Regiment and a battery from 54th Heavy Regiment, in addition to 4th Division's own artillery; a total of some two hundred and fifty guns. There were to be gunner officers at the headquarters of brigades and infantry battalions, and advancing on foot with the infantry and in tanks. Also under Major-General Hawkesworth's command were to be a squadron (ten Grant tanks) from the Scorpion Regiment, two Air OP aircraft, the mortars of 68th Chemical Warfare Company (less one section) and the Carrier Company of the 1st Northumberland Fusiliers. 145th RAC was to support 4th Indian Division.

Five hundred and fifty shells were to be dumped within reach of every 25-pounder, four hundred shells for every medium gun, and a hundred and fifty shells for each of the heavy howitzers. 4th Division's own guns were to fire concentrations during the barrage, and afterwards were to be free for defensive and observed fire. The barrage was to be fired by five field regiments on the front of the two assaulting divisions.

At dawn on May the 3rd, command of the Medjez sector passed to 78th Division. The troops of 4th Division rested and had baths; there was time for Church Parade and for letters home. Units received reinforcements of officers and men, and reorganized. Vast movements of troops were going on all round, and the battered yellow trucks of Eighth Army began to appear among the olive-green First Army transport. The uniforms of the Eighth Army troops were also battered and yellow, and those of the officers showed an often decorative disregard of convention. The Eighth Army custom of wearing suède boots, gaudy scarves and corduroys soon spread to First Army, and never quite died out.

The gunners moved into their new positions behind the Gueriat el Atach, and found that the corn-fields for miles round were already crowded with guns and vehicles and command-posts. The tracks leading into the gun area and towards the infantry start-line were inches deep in powdery grey dust. A few vehicles would send up a towering grey cloud that could be seen for miles.

General Anderson, meanwhile, had arranged for a dummy concentration of tanks far to the south, so that the enemy would believe First Army's armour to be divided and so would feel safe for the time being, in spite of the obvious movement round Medjez. The RAF kept the Luftwaffe out of the sky over the gun area.

At night the tracks were as busy as a London street, with more guns coming into their new positions, tanks and infantry moving up, and supply lorries with ammunition and rations crawling nose to tail. Somehow it seemed unfair that the choking dust should rise from every wheel to blacken the already dark night.

During May the 5th, while the infantry were still moving up, the divisions of V Corps to the left and right attacked, to safeguard the flanks of the main attack and to prevent the enemy from concentrating his reserves.

The battalions moved up, and the West Kents took up their positions along the start-line, which they were to guard. Major-General Hawkesworth liked to have his headquarters well forward, and in preparation for the attack he placed it in front of his foremost infantry, covered only by the West Kents on the start-line, and hidden only by a single ridge.

At three in the morning of May the 6th, the six hundred guns in the area opened fire with the barrage and concentrations, breaking up the stillness and darkness of the night with flickering light and with concussions that shook the air. 10th Brigade went forward first, with two battalions up, behind the barrage and through the defensive fire on fixed lines of all the machine-guns the Germans could bring to bear. The Surreys on the right, with 'A' and 'C' Companies forward, were supported by 'C' Squadron of 48th Royal Tanks and two troops of 38th Anti-tank Battery; the DCLI on the left, with 'B' and 'C' Companies forward, were supported by 'B' Squadron of 48th Royal Tanks. Each battalion had under its command two sub-sections of 59th Field Company. The Bedfords, the rest of 38th Anti-tank Battery, and six Scorpions followed up.

The infantry's chief trouble at first was from the clouds of acrid dust kicked up by the shells bursting ahead. Visibility was so bad, in fact, that Battalion Headquarters of the East Surreys soon found itself in front of the companies. Soon after the East Surreys had sorted themselves out, 'C' Company reached and took Point 156, just over a mile from the start-line. The DCLI were checked, but the Churchills of 48th Royal Tanks came up and dealt with the opposition. The right-hand troop of 'B' Squadron, having fired a single 6-pounder shell at some dug-outs on the ridge near Point 156, took thirty prisoners and sent them back to the infantry.

'B' Company of the Bedfords took over Point 156, in order to allow the Surreys to go forward again. Battalion Headquarters and 'C' Company of the Bedfords stopped short of the crest, a little way in front of Montarnaud Farm. Germans on the right flank opened fire on 'C' Company with machine-guns and 88-mm guns; the company fired back and silenced the opposition.

Soon after five in the morning of May the 6th, the Surreys reached the crest, a mile and three quarters from their start-line, and took Point 175, their final objective. The DCLI reached the same crest farther to the left some twenty minutes later, having been delayed by enemy fire. One of the Churchills, on its way to help, was knocked out by an 88-mm gun, but the other tanks fired back, knocking out the gun and killing all its crew but one, who was captured by the infantry. By six o'clock both battalions were digging in, with the help of sappers equipped for blasting. The tanks of 'C' Squadron took up hull-down positions behind the ridge. Overhead, as day broke, the sky was filled with the steady roar of squadron after squadron of bombers, and the grinding thunder of continuously bursting bombs was close enough in front to shake the ground. The enemy positions were hidden behind a curtain of brown dust and black smoke. By this time, the guns had fired nearly seventeen thousand shells into the enemy positions on the division's front.

In the corn-fields, there were shell craters every few feet, showing the intensity of the barrage. There were plenty of abandoned German guns and equipment, but the absence of dead Germans showed how few of the enemy had stayed to stem the attack. Indeed, as the attack went on, German infantrymen, dazed by the barrage, had flung their weapons down and run away.

'A' and 'D' Companies of the Bedfords, meanwhile, had formed up behind the Surreys and attacked south-eastwards towards Point 151, seven hundred yards away on the right flank. By ten to six, in spite of German machine-guns, both companies were on the objective; the fire of mortars and guns inflicted some loss on the infantry as they dug in. Twenty minutes later, Lieutenant-Colonel K. J. G. Garner Smith, commanding the battalion, reinforced the two companies with 'B' Company, anti-tank guns and Vickers machine-guns.

12th Brigade and 12th Royal Tanks, meanwhile, had been following up behind the left wing of the DCLI. The Black Watch led the way, followed by the West Kents and the Royal Fusiliers. At ten to five, having met no opposition, the Black Watch caught up the DCLI, a mile short of 10th Brigade's objective. Going ahead on the left of the DCLI, the Black Watch reached the ridge at the same time. The Germans there were still fighting back with machine-guns and anti-tank guns, but with the help of 'C' Squadron of 12th Royal Tanks the infantry finished off this opposition and took several prisoners.

At a quarter to six, 'A' and 'C' Companies of the Black Watch went forward towards the next crest, half a mile away. Half an hour later, the two companies had reached the foot of the slope, and lay there while the guns pounded their objective. The artillery concentration stopped, the Churchills put down a smoke screen and the infantry went up the slope to the top. The tanks lay up in the valley behind Point 161, while the infantry dug in, helped by sappers who blew holes in the ground with Beehives. Soon afterwards Lieutenant-Colonel Madden was wounded, and the second-in-command, Major C. N. M. Blair, took command of the battalion.

On the right of the main assault, the Reconnaissance Regiment had moved off at half-past four, attempting to reach the Tunis road through 78th Division's area. The regiment met strong opposition, lost a number of men and made only slow progress. By eight in the morning, however, the left-hand squadron was within striking distance of its objective, Point 141, half-a mile south of the Bedfords on Point 151. With the help of tanks, the Reconnaissance squadron forced its way on to Point 141, but patrols were still prevented from venturing along the Tunis road by fire from a commanding point on the other side.

At twenty past seven in the morning, 12th Brigade began to complete its task when Lieutenant Hall took a fighting patrol of the Black Watch towards Frendj. Ten minutes later, German vehicles began to drive out of Frendj on the far side, while shells from the 25-pounders burst all round. At a quarter to eight, Lieutenant Hall's patrol came back and reported that Frendj was deserted and that carriers and wheeled vehicles would be able to get through the wadis that seamed the neighbourhood. By this time the Black Watch were forward in strength, and their anti-tank guns were in position. The troops could see the right-hand battalion of 4th Indian Division crossing the sky-line nearly a mile to the left rear.

Before eight in the morning, the first tanks of 6th Armoured

Division were on their way through the infantry positions. About half an hour later, 7th Armoured Division began to pass through 4th Indian Division.

4th Indian Division pushed on, and early in the afternoon was able to hand over to the Royal Fusiliers Point 165, half a mile to the left front of the Black Watch. By five in the afternoon, the West Kents had occupied Frendj, and the Black Watch, relieved on Point 161 by the Bedfords, moved up on the left. 4th Division had completed its first task, and settled down in its positions.

Since the division had reached the crests from which it could dominate the Argoub bou Rhabrhouba, German resistance had been sporadic. A few fighter aircraft bombed a group of Churchills without doing any damage; there was a certain amount of dive-bombing and shelling; and 10th Brigade was mopping up all day, skirmishing with small groups of German infantry, gunners and a few tanks. No unit, however, lost heavily during the day's fighting; and the division had taken nearly two hundred prisoners, as well as important maps and documents.

6th and 7th Armoured Divisions, having got away to a flying start, swiftly dealt with the enemy's comparatively feeble resistance, and thrust up the main road towards Tunis. By dusk, the tanks were in harbour round Massicault, eighteen miles from the city. The Germans had been throwing every man they could find into the gap—even single 20-mm anti-aircraft cannon were rushed up from Tunis to reinforce the anti-tank screen—but all without effect.

Early in the morning of May the 7th, the armoured divisions went forward again, followed by reconnaissance parties from 4th Division's field regiments, which were to support the tanks. Soon afterwards the guns began to move forward past the infantry they had been supporting, and up the Tunis road. They turned to the left off the main road at Saint Cyprien, and took up positions behind the last high ground before Tunis, twelve miles away. The guns were still moving up through a cold drizzle of rain when men of 6th Armoured Division standing beside the road shouted that armoured cars of the Derbyshire Yeomanry were in Tunis. They were right—and the Americans were in Bizerta, the second city of Tunisia.

The Tunis road was an astonishing sight to troops who for weeks had been observing the rigid march discipline imposed by the danger of air attack. Guns, tanks, jeeps, trucks and staff cars were crawling along, nose to tail and two or three lines abreast. The most advanced of the German airfields had been overrun by the swift thrust of the tanks; the Allied air forces in North Africa were stronger than they had ever been before; and for the first time since the war began the Allies had not merely air superiority but air supremacy—British and American fighters had been able to keep almost every German aircraft out of the sky over the attack since it began. During May the 6th, Allied aircraft had flown two thousand five hundred sorties, the greatest number in one day ever reported.

Tunis and Bizerta had been the only Tunisian ports from which the Axis forces might have been evacuated. The loss of Tunis to the British and of Bizerta to the Americans put an end to the enemy's hopes of getting any significant proportion of his men and equipment out of North Africa. The two Allied thrusts to the coast, moreover, had cut his armies into three; part remained north of Bizerta, part was between Bizerta and Tunis, and the greater part, still ready to resist, was between the First Army round Tunis and the Eighth Army far to the south.

This third group had still a chance of prolonging the campaign, and had every intention of doing so. It began to withdraw, in front of both the Allied armies, into the peninsula of Cape Bon, to the east of Tunis. The entrances into the cape could be defended from the sides of mountains which rise steeply in places to more than two thousand five hundred feet. The rugged hilly ground of the cape would also lend itself to defence; and it contained airfields, one small port, and railway lines.

On May the 8th, 7th Armoured Division passed through Tunis and turned left on its way towards Bizerta. 6th Armoured Division drove through the city and turned right towards the base of Cape Bon. At the coastal spa of Hammam Lif, ten miles beyond Tunis, German guns and infantry brought the tanks to a halt. The enemy's position was a strong one, for the solid houses of the town filled the narrow gap between the sea on the left and a sixteen-hundred-foot mountain on the right. On the other side of the same mountain, 1st Armoured Division, which had come up on the right from Army reserve, was also halted at Créteville, five miles south of Hammam Lif.

4th Division, which was to follow up behind the tanks of 1st or 6th Armoured Division, was brought forward to wait on the bare, dry downs round La Mohammedia, ten miles short of Créteville.

These were curious days of waiting for the men who had broken open the gap in the German defences; the battle had left them behind, though they had moved forward nearly twenty-five miles. They had to be ready to move in any direction at any moment; there were no Germans within reach, but German shells would burst from time to time among the vehicles and tents, fired by guns among the hills far to the south. There was little news, and what there was seemed improbable. The speed of the German retreat was such that every attack that was ordered had to be cancelled. The approach of victory found the division puzzled rather than jubilant.

When the tanks were halted at Hammam Lif and Créteville, 10th Brigade prepared an attack through Créteville. Brigadier Hogshaw went forward to reconnoitre, with Lieutenant-Colonel Garner Smith of the Bedfords, Lieutenant-Colonel Kinnersley of the DCLI, and Lieutenant-Colonel R. B. Rice of 30th Field Regiment. Brigadier Hogshaw had gone for orders to Divisional Headquarters when a shell burst near the jeep in which the rest of the party was travelling. Lieutenant-Colonel Rice was killed and the other two officers were wounded.

The Royal Fusiliers, on the other hand, were in the best of heart. Lieutenant-Colonel A. F. P. Evans was holding a conference on May the 7th, when a battered German truck drew up nearby and out stepped Captain J. H. Gibson-Horrocks, who with most of 'Y' Company had disappeared on April the 24th. The company had worked its way deeply into the enemy positions at Peter's Corner during the night, and had lost touch with the rest of the battalion. Daylight found the company isolated and surrounded by strong enemy positions. Ammunition ran low, and more and more men were lost. Lieutenant B. G. Sexton led a gallant bayonet charge against Sidi Médiene, but the fire of German machine-guns killed him and killed or wounded all his men. When ammunition ran out, Captain Gibson-Horrocks and those of his men who survived were taken prisoner, and sent to Tunis.

When the prison camp there had been overrun by the British advance, Captain Gibson-Horrocks had commandeered the nearest vehicle and had driven round until he found his battalion. Most of 'Y' Company had been in the prison camp when it was liberated, but several men had been sent away.

The main body of the battalion, moving in lorries towards La Mohammedia next day, passed most of the men of 'Y' Company, who were recuperating in a dressing station; they were thin and drawn but extremely cheerful. There was no news of the rest for several weeks, when the battalion heard that they had been put on board an Italian ship at Tunis, and had been on their way to Sicily when aircraft of the RAF had turned the ship back to Tunis.

During the moonlit night of May the 9th, the tanks and infantry of 6th Armoured Division flung themselves into the streets of Hammam Lif, regardless of loss, cleared the Germans out of the town house by house, and broke through into the base of Cape Bon. Then, in daylight of May the 10th, the tanks began to move across the base towards the coast on the other side. The German forces in the cape would soon be cut off, but they might still fight on among the difficult hills. Elsewhere in Tunisia, huge numbers of Germans were already surrendering; but in Cape Bon, and farther southwest where the 90th Light Division was trapped between the two Allied armies, there might still be fighting to do.

In the hope of breaking up the German forces in the cape before they could organize their defences, Lieutenant-General B. G. Horrocks MC, commanding IX Corps, pushed 4th Division through the gap at Hamman Lif. By midday, troops of 6th Armoured Division were six miles beyond the town, and 12th Brigade began to follow up. 'B' Squadron of the Reconnaissance Regiment led the way, followed by the West Kents and 'B' Squadron of 12th Royal Tanks. The rest of the infantry brigade, with the remaining tanks, 77th Field Regiment and other supporting arms, followed close behind, a packed mass of vehicles of every kind crawling slowly forward by every available road and track under a cloud of white dust. 10th Brigade, with 48th Royal Tanks, 30th Field Regiment, 'A' Reconnaissance Squadron and other supporting troops, followed 12th Brigade on the same road. In places where a track ran beside the main road, five lines of traffic were advancing nose to tail on a front of fifty yards.

By three in the afternoon, 12th Brigade was well into the plain which lies across the base of Cape Bon; the leading troops were past the village of Soliman, nine miles beyond Hammam Lif. A mile farther on, 4th Division's axis, which since Hammam Lif had been a single road, divided into two, and 12th Brigade took the right-hand prong of the fork. 6th Armoured Division had led the way as far as Soliman, but there the tanks turned south and made for the coastal resort of Hammamet, on the other side of the cape.

As soon as 12th Brigade began to advance along roads not previously travelled by the tanks, the infantry began to meet a certain amount of disorganized local resistance. By this time, prisoners were beginning to arrive in groups of twenty and thirty. By seven in the evening, the West Kents and their tanks had reached and cleared Beni Khalled, six miles south-west of Soliman, and the West Kents halted there to garrison the village. In spite of darkness, a pursuit group, consisting of the Black Watch, 'B' Reconnaissance Squadron and a squadron of tanks, pushed on towards the coast. At three in the morning the group had reached the coast, at the village of Korba, fifteen miles beyond Beni Khalled. There it captured a hospital ship, intact, and took the enemy garrison completely by surprise.

10th Brigade followed 12th Brigade as far as the parting of the ways just beyond Soliman, and there took the left fork. After brushing aside some fairly feeble resistance, the brigade settled down for the night between Soliman and Menzel bou Zelfa, nine miles farther east. The Surreys and the DCLI were beyond Menzel.

Before dawn next morning, May the 11th, prisoners began to arrive in vastly increased numbers. No longer were there groups of dejected men, guarded and on foot; instead they began to drive into the division's positions in their own great yellow Diesel lorries and trailers, fifty or sixty men with their baggage in each, with German drivers, unguarded, festooned with white cloths to advertise their surrender. Senior German officers, gazing blandly ahead through the wind-screens of their staff cars, drove by with their batmen and aides-de-camp; they might have been on their way to an early lunch in Tunis, for all the concern they showed. One lorry carried a brass band complete. Sometimes convoys of German lorries were followed by a line of German military police or dispatch riders on their own motor-cycles; once or twice the Germans or Italians were even riding—though not for long—on British or American trucks they had captured. The procession even included an 88-mm gun, with its crew and ammunition. The enemy soldier was extremely eager to carry with him into captivity as many comforts as he could, but this item of equipment was a curious choice. There were men of the 4th Division standing beside the road who remembered the German photographs of comrades captured at Dunkirk—British soldiers who had been driven back to the edge of the sea, where they fought to the end of their ammunition and their strength, and who appeared in the photographs trudging back towards Germany, filthy, exhausted and unshaven, grim-faced, heavily guarded. The contrast between the beaten British Expeditionary Force and the beaten Afrika Korps gave point to the question German officers were apt to ask their prisoners—'Why do you go on fighting when you know you are beaten?' The question was not a taunt, but a genuine request for information. In this Tunisian May, the Germans were showing that they knew when they were beaten, and what they should do about it; and they showed, too, a curious lack of concern.

By seven-thirty in the morning, 10th Brigade had collected about a thousand prisoners and a field bakery near Menzel bou Zelfa; 12th Brigade's captures included a German brigadier and his medical staff, who were allowed to treat the wounded on the hospital ship off Korba. 12th Brigade sent a guard on board to make sure that the ship remained off Korba.

In spite of the mass surrenders, the Germans still had a chance of defending the cape while they attempted to evacuate towards Pantelleria and Sicily. The division's next task was, therefore, to get in amongst them before they could reorganize.

Major-General Hawkesworth organized two columns, one for each of the main roads running into the cape. 10th Brigade Group was to advance up the road which runs near the north-western coast, while 12th Brigade moved up the south-eastern coast.

10th Brigade moved off at ten in the morning; 'A' Reconnaissance Squadron led the way, followed by the carriers of the DCLI, the rest of the DCLI in lorries, the guns of 104th Field Battery, the tanks of 'C' Squadron, 48th Royal Tanks and the rest of the brigade and its supporting troops.

At first the traffic was dense, but soon after Menzel bou Zelfa it thinned out. Before long, every vehicle in the convoy was racing down a road empty of all but surrendering enemy troops—the next British vehicle in front or behind might be half a mile or more away, and the enemy, on foot or in vehicles, was everywhere. The only unpleasant incident was when American Kittyhawks machine-gunned and bombed the brigade column, in spite of a conspicuous show of yellow Celanese air-recognition triangles. Eight of the DCLI were wounded in these attacks.

By one in the afternoon, the DCLI had reached and occupied the village of El Haouaria, in the tip of the cape, and thirty-four miles in a straight line from the starting-point at Menzel bou Zelfa.

The boasted map-reading abilities of the gunners were unable to cope with the inaccuracy of their small-scale maps, on which the roads were not marked, and with the eccentricity of their compasses, caused by some metallic deposit in the ground. A sergeant-major had to be sent into the village to find out its name. The brigade had taken about five thousand prisoners by this time.

Brigadier Hogshaw, who was with the Reconnaissance squadron, took it down the south-eastern coast to Kelibia, fifteen miles away. The squadron drove as fast as it could past crowds of surrendering Germans and Italians, and reached Kelibia at three in the afternoon. Leaving most of the squadron in the village, Brigadier Hogshaw went on with a patrol to meet 12th Brigade.

12th Brigade too had begun to collect prisoners early in the morning. The Royal Fusiliers, a couple of miles beyond Beni Khalled, were surrounded by thousands of gleefully surrendering Italians; the officers were dressed up for the occasion, with swords and gold braid. The Germans were more glum, but sometimes grotesquely confident. Captain H. J. Witheridge told a group of German officers that Tunis and Bizerta had fallen; the senior officer replied that he did not believe it—and remarked to the others that, even if it were true, the British would never capture Algiers.

By noon, 4th Division had taken twenty thousand prisoners, and tens of thousands more were on the way.

At one in the afternoon, 12th Brigade began to move northeastwards from Korba. 'B' Reconnaissance Squadron led the way, followed by 'B' Squadron, 12th Royal Tanks, the Royal Fusiliers and a 25-pounder battery from 77th Field Regiment. The Reconnaissance squadron suffered some loss from the fire of Italian antitank guns, and occasional road-blocks delayed the advance. At Menzel Heurr, eleven miles from Korba and half-way to Kelibia, the bridge was blocked by a blazing tank, and the column came to a halt. One of the Churchills grappled the German tank and dragged it away, and the leading troops began to form up on the other side. At that moment, an armoured car appeared on the road ahead, speeding towards the bridge; a few moments later, the Reconnaissance troops recognized it as 'one of ours', and when it arrived Brigadier Hogshaw stepped out. The encirclement of Cape Bon was complete.

The enemy who remained inside the cordon were for the most part waiting for a chance to surrender. During the evening, however, a gunner officer told the 48th Royal Tanks that a group of enemy was holding out at Mraissa Farm, ten miles north of Menzel bou Zelfa. The enemy had twice sent out a man with a white flag, but had opened fire each time when British troops moved up to occupy the farm.

Lieutenant-Colonel Brooks sent off a section of three carriers from his Reconnaissance Troop. They reached the drive leading up to the farm at seven in the evening, and were met by a German soldier waving a white flag; he said there was nobody else there. The troopers suspected a trick, and opened fire on the farm and on the eucalyptus trees that surrounded it. Enemy machine-guns on the ridge behind the farm fired back. In the gathering dusk, two of the carriers circled round to the right and drove towards the farm, firing continuously. Nine Germans surrendered, including a general. After a few more bursts of fire from the carriers, thirty-one more Germans came out; soon afterwards nearly a hundred and fifty more appeared, led by Captain Meisstier, commanding the German naval forces in Tunisia; and during the next two hours thirty more came out.

During the evening of May the 12th, while the rest of the division was collecting prisoners, arms, vehicles and a certain amount of enemy food and 'souvenirs', Lieutenant-Colonel Kinnersley sent a DCLI patrol to investigate reports of enemy coastal guns firing at British shipping from Rass el Fortass, fourteen miles north of Menzel bou Zelfa. A platoon of 'D' Company and a section of carriers went off, and in the small hours of the morning were fired on by enemy infantry strongly dug in. Lieutenant-Colonel Kinnersley went up himself next morning, followed by the rest of 'D' Company. The enemy were by now ready to surrender, and the DCLI organized their departure for Divisional Headquarters. The force consisted of a battalion of Germans, two companies of Italians, and Major-General Koechy, commander of the Luftwaffe in Tunisia. The surrender of German and Italian troops was often enlivened by a cheerfulness and even a frivolity not often seen in their senior officers. Major-General Koechy was wearing full-dress uniform, glittering with medals and braid. He surrendered with a traditional flourish to an officer of equal rank, presenting his sword to Major-General Hawkesworth. The surrender of this commander marked the end of organized fighting in Cape Bon.

The surrender to 4th Indian Division on May the 12th of

Colonel-General J. von Arnim, commander of the German Afrika Army Group, completed the ruin of the enemy's armies.

Parts of 4th Division had covered a hundred and fifteen miles in twenty-seven hours. The fast-moving columns racing up the roads of Cape Bon had appeared among enemy troops who believed the nearest British units were fifty miles away, and had prevented the organization of any resistance. Since that great fire-plan of May the 6th, few of the division's guns had fired a single round.

In five weeks, the division had learned more about fighting than in two and a half years at home. The cost had been heavy, for the division had lost three hundred men during May, so that the total for the campaign had risen to nearly two thousand four hundred—about one man in seven. The proportion of senior officers lost had been particularly high; the division's establishment in Lieutenant-Colonels commanding units was seventeen, and six of these had been killed, four had been wounded and one had been captured.

4th Division had taken some fifty-one thousand prisoners. The total number of Axis prisoners taken in Tunisia was nearly a quarter of a million. The German losses in Tunisia before this mighty defeat were estimated as fifty thousand; the British First and Eighth Armies had lost nearly thirty-five thousand men. Very few enemy troops had escaped, and vast quantities of material were captured with them. General Anderson was able to write, 'Dunkirk was amply avenged.'

8. Algeria and Egypt

The holiday atmosphere of the pursuit gave way to maintenance parades and training programmes; the German helmets and minefield flags, with which almost every driver had decorated his vehicle, and the curious hats were thrown away; enough enemy small-arms to equip an infantry brigade were collected from the reluctant troops. For many weeks the division had German and Italian food with almost every meal, and every unit area was rank with the smell of ersatz cigars. Some units solved the housing problem by scouring the countryside for enemy tents, and added to their war establishment of transport recaptured British or American vehicles, or enemy cars and lorries ranging in size from a minute Opel saloon to a colossal Diesel lorry with an equally enormous trailer.

For the next few weeks, the division was occupied mainly with the guarding of prisoners of war in hurriedly improvised camps, and in taking part in the celebrations which followed the great North African victory. A contingent of fifteen hundred officers and men from all arms marched behind Major-General Hawkesworth in the Victory March in Tunis, at which General Alexander took the salute. In June the Prime Minister, Mr Winston Churchill, reviewed the division; and later in the month the men of the division lined a stretch of road between Nabeul and Grombalia to greet His Majesty the King.

During this blazing North African summer, the division's Concert Party was formed. The first Concert Party Officer was Lieutenant J. F. Brooking, who before the war had had considerable experience in repertory theatre; his Stage Manager was Lance-Bombardier Murdoch. The Concert Party was one of the most successful Welfare ventures arranged within the division, and its great popularity was fairly earned. Nobody could have known, during the early rehearsals in the sweltering heat of North Africa, what success the Party was to achieve, or the variety of places in which it was to perform—on tour in Africa, with a captured Italian trailer for a stage; up Monte Ornito in Italy, where German gunfire inflicted losses on the Party; in the Anzio bridge-head, into which it was invited to entertain the weary garrison; in the magnificent Opera House at Cesena; and, finally, in a theatre in Athens.

At the end of June 1943, the division left Tunisia, and moved to the neighbourhood of Bougie, on the Algerian coast. Operation Goblet was now being prepared, in which the division was to join in an assault landing on the south-east coast of Italy, near Crotone. Reinforcements arrived to bring every unit up to full strength; Landing Craft (Infantry) were allotted to the brigades for training; and divisional and brigade planning staffs left for Algiers. On August the 7th, the two infantry brigade groups were warned that they were to move four days later to the Combined Training Centre at Djidjelli.

Just after this move had begun, the division suffered a blow more grievous than the enemy was able to inflict on it at any time during the war. Operation Goblet, and all the preparations for it, were given up; and this fighting formation, with experience of two campaigns, with a rapidly growing confidence in its own powers and knowledge of its job, and with every reasonable expectation that it was to lead the assault on what Mr Churchill called 'the soft under-belly of Europe'—from this proud position, the division sank to that of an administrative unit, filling the gaps in other divisions and engaged on fatigues and other unskilled work. Major-General J. L. I. Hawkesworth CB CBE was posted to command 46th Division, which was preparing for the Sicilian campaign; and, on the same day, each infantry battalion was ordered to send eight officers and two hundred and fifty other ranks to the Reinforcement Training Depot at Philippeville, from which they would be posted to other divisions. The division's support battalion, the 2nd Royal Northumberland Fusiliers, arrived from England; and, instead of rejoining the division, it was placed under the command of 46th Division. The drain on 4th Division's man-power went on, and before long few infantry companies could muster a platoon without difficulty. The reasons for this abrupt change of policy—the fact that a Mixed Division, with only two infantry brigades, could not hold a sector in a satisfactory manner—could not at the time be explained to the remnants of the division; and, when the division was ordered to send a thousand men to work as labourers on the docks and in the dumps of equipment and ammunition at Bône, the division seemed to most of its members to be on the point of being disbanded. The work was vital enough; but to gunners and tank crews, highly trained in the use of intricate and powerful weapons, such clumsy employment was utterly discouraging.

While the division was sending out drafts, there were many changes among the senior officers. Major-General H. J. Hayman Joyce DSO arrived from England in early September, and took command of the division. The AA & QMG, Lieutenant-Colonel C. J. Kinna, went to Allied Force Headquarters in Algiers, and was replaced by Lieutenant-Colonel H. P. Mackley. The ADMS, Colonel C. H. K. Smith, had already been promoted to be DDMS, Tunis Area, and had been replaced by Colonel P. F. Palmer. Lieutenant-Colonel F. W. P. Bradford MBE, commanding the Divisional Signals, went to 1st Armoured Division and was succeeded by Lieutenant-Colonel P. A. Duke. Brigadier P. Scott, of 12th Brigade, and Lieutenant-Colonel Moberley, the CRE, left for 46th Division, and were replaced by Brigadier F. M. Elliott MC and Lieutenant-Colonel J. E. Nelson. The CRA, Brigadier S. N. Shoosmith, took over 10th Brigade when Brigadier Hogshaw fell ill, and Lieutenant-Colonel I. V. R. Smith, who had commanded 14th Anti-tank Regiment for three years, became CRA. Brigadier Shoosmith, Colonel Palmer and Lieutenant-Colonel Duke were to stay with the division through all its fighting; Brigadier Smith was killed in the following March.

Early in December, the division began to return to normal; a first draft of two thousand five hundred reinforcements arrived, and shortly afterwards the division was warned to be ready for a move at short notice. 21st Tank Brigade, with its Brigade Signals, Light Aid Detachment and Workshops, 6th Light Field Ambulance and 107th Tank Brigade Company RASC, left the division and became Army troops. By November the 11th, another great draft of reinforcements had made the division up to its full strength, except for first-line reinforcements. The division dumped all its guns, vehicles, accommodation stores and other heavy equipment; this was an unhappy moment for the gunners, who were parting with the first 25-pounders they had had, and which they had kept in perfect condition for three years. On November the 15th, taking only personal weapons and equipment, the division began to move in RASC lorries across the hills to the badly-equipped staging-camps near Algiers. After celebrating a wet Christmas in the dripping pinewoods of the Forêt de Ferdinand, west of Algiers—cheered only by the optimists who calculated that the division was bound for England ('Left-hand-down out of Algiers') and by a remarkable supply of beer and spirits (the ration had been a pint of beer a month, and Algerian wine, even at one-and-six a bottle, was no adequate substitute)—the division embarked in several ships which included the liner *Orontes*. The ships turned right-hand-down out of Algiers, passed into a warmer climate and steamed through the Suez canal (where troops on the bank advised those on the ships not to worry too much about the hardships of the campaign in Burma); and off the squalid town of Suez, they anchored and unloaded the troops by lighters on the shore at Ataqa, where advance-parties were waiting to meet them.

The division was camped by New Year's Day 1944 on the sandy waste between Suez and the jagged heights of the Djebel Ataqa; compared with the tree-shaded fields round Bougie, a dreary neighbourhood. Every unit had some Nissen huts for offices and so on, but nearly all the division lived under canvas. Frequent duststorms and whirlwinds continually menaced tents of every size. The climate was, however, a great deal milder than that of Algeria, and even in January the troops were often able to parade in shirt-sleeves. Almost everyone had the chance of a short leave in Cairo, and there were cinemas—Shafto's Shuftis—and a few clubs; but nothing could make life in the desert very enjoyable.

The arrival of 28th Infantry Brigade from Gibraltar now made the division up to full strength as an Infantry instead of a Mixed Division. The brigade consisted of two battalions, the 2nd King's (Liverpool) Regiment and the 2nd Somerset Light Infantry; at the same time, the 1st Argyll and Sutherland Highlanders arrived to join the brigade as its third battalion. The division was re-equipped with rather a mixed collection of equipment, some of which seemed to have seen long service in the desert, and some of which was almost new, and under the command of III Corps began training in combined operations.

Soon after the division's arrival in Egypt, the plans for an assault on Rhodes, which had caused the move, were abandoned. Various units which had joined the division began to leave it, and the Argylls were withdrawn for service elsewhere. Training, however, continued, and in various exercises at the Combined Training Centre, Kabrit, the brigade groups were worked vigorously into the teams that were to serve together in action. 10th and 12th Brigades had already fought in France and Tunisia, and had spent several years training in England; but the King's and the Somersets, who had been stationed in Gibraltar since the war began, had still to gain experience of active service conditions.

Early in February, the division's future was at last decided; under the cover of a pretended move to Palestine for further training, it was to go to Italy, where since early winter the Fifth and Eighth Armies had been halted among the mountains between Naples and Rome. Major-General Hayman Joyce, with a small party, left for Italy by air, and the division began to gather all its transport and guns together into dumps, since all the heavy equipment was to be left behind for the use of other troops in Egypt. For the second time in three months, the division was to travel without its equipment.

9. Italy: The Garigliano salient

On February the 15th 1944, the advance Echelon of Divisional Headquarters and 10th Brigade Group left Alexandria in HMT *Ascania*; and on the 21st, after an uncomfortable voyage in the teeth of a gale, the ship docked in Naples harbour. Next morning, Major-General Hayman Joyce held a conference at General McReery's Corps Headquarters at Sessa Aurunca, and outlined the plan for the immediate future.

The front at this time stretched across Italy from Minturno to Ortona; the Eighth Army, commanded by General Sir Oliver Leese, held the right sector, and the Fifth Army, under General Mark Clark, held the left. The Fifth Army's line met the Mediterranean coast near the mouth of the River Garigliano, crossed the river into a mountainous bridge-head farther north, and receded again to the east of the river across the entrance to the wide Liri Valley, which runs away north-westerly towards Rome. The entrance to this corridor between the mountains was guarded by the famous Benedictine Monastery of Monte Cassino; high on its towering base of rock, the ancient building looked across the wide valley towards the Garigliano bridge-head, and looked down on Route Six, which runs from Naples to Rome. To the north of Cassino, the Fifth Army held another bridge-head, this time across the Rivers Rapido and Secco, beyond which the front turned east to cross the lower slopes of Monte Cifalco near Valleluce.

The Garigliano bridge-head was in the left-centre part of this front; from the northern approaches to the bridge-head the Monastery could be seen, and from the southern approaches the traveller could see the Mediterranean. 4th Division was to take over the bridge-head from 46th Division, and to come under the command of X Corps. 10th Brigade was to begin the relief on the night of February the 24th, coming temporarily under the command of 46th Division, and taking over the sector nearest to the coastal plain. The brigade's front was then to be extended to Monte Ornito, the two thousand five hundred foot height north of the village of Sujo. Sujo lies at the foot of the mountains, near the point where the Garigliano flows out into the coastal plain. 12th Brigade, which at that time had not reached Italy, was to take over its sector on the night of March the 9th, and 4th Division would take command of the bridge-head next day.

Meanwhile, 4th Division was to take over all 46th Division's equipment except personal weapons and stores. To take over battle-worn equipment, part of which had already seen hard wear in Tunisia, and nearly all of which had been in continuous use since being driven through the sea in an assault landing on the shores of Italy, was a depressing business for troops who had already regretfully handed over two excellent sets of transport and guns at Bougie and Ataqa. Some of the guns were rumoured to have fired seventeen thousand rounds; certainly some of the 3-inch mortars, which were taken over in the mortar positions, were very worn, having been used in heavy fighting ever since the Salerno landings. Age alone, however, is not a prime cause of unserviceability; much of the same veteran equipment was to be used effectively in Greece at the end of the year.

On the relief of 46th Division, certain units were to join 4th Division. These included the 2nd Royal Northumberland Fusiliers, so the division and its support battalion joined up for the first time since the division left England. Another most welcome addition was the 2nd/4th Hampshires. This battalion had fought with the Hampshire Brigade in Tunisia, and then had left 46th Division to provide Beach Groups for the Sicily and Salerno landings; at Salerno, the Hampshires' Beach Group had joined in particularly heavy fighting. After a period of uncertainty (like that endured by 4th Division), during which it was compelled to send drafts to other Hampshire battalions, the battalion had reassembled at Pontecagnano for vigorous training. Fit and efficient, it went into the line at the end of February as the vanguard of 4th Division, and was some weeks later to complete 28th Brigade. The division still had only two field ambulances; 185th Field Ambulance from 128th Brigade therefore joined 28th Brigade, so that from the outset each brigade was served by a first-class medical unit.

A section of the Military Air Interpretation Unit (West), commanded by Captain Martyr, joined Divisional Headquarters. All arms of the division were to benefit from the use of air photographs of much of the ground covered in the Italian campaign, and the value of these photographs was greatly enhanced by the able interpretation by Captain Martyr's 'Mae West' section. Lieutenant Van Rijn joined the division to interrogate prisoners of war, and stayed with it until it left Italy. This officer is a Dutchman, in spite of his English appearance, and his family lived under the German occupation; truculent Nazis were often startled into obedience by the latent force of his personality.

The relief of 46th Division went according to plan, although 12th Brigade had to take over its equipment in a great hurry. Major-General Hawkesworth and many former members of the division then serving with 46th Division visited the relieving units and headquarters on their way back.

The first sector held by the division was ten miles long, extending from Sujo in the south through the Garigliano bridge-head, and across the mountains and part of the valley beyond, to Rocca d'Evandro station, six thousand yards south-east of Cassino. The northern part of the line was held at first by Hermonforce, consisting of the King's Dragoon Guards and three companies of the Hampshires. This force was later relieved by Prestonforce, made up of 4th and 44th Reconnaissance Regiments under the command of Lieutenant-Colonel Preston. The southern, or bridge-head, part of the front was held by 1st Guards Brigade on the right, 12th Brigade and the DCLI in the centre and 10th Brigade on the left. The valley of the Garigliano at the north-eastern foot of Monte Ornito, and on the edge of the Liri Valley, was held by 'C' Company of the Hampshires, who were placed under the command of 1st Guards Brigade for the purpose. Reinforced by carrier and anti-tank platoons from the Guards Brigade, and with representatives from the gunners and the support group, 'C' Company blossomed into Wayforce (after its commander, Major W. C. T. N. Way), which became Morganforce when 'A' Company relieved 'C'. Finally, 'A' Company of the Surreys relieved 'A' Company of the Hampshires, the second-in-command of the DCLI, Major A. E. Harding, relieved Major Morgan, and the group became Hardingforce.

The Italian climate was very different from that of North Africa or Egypt. The worst of the winter was over, but the weather was still bitterly cold and wet; there was rain in the Garigliano valley, and on the heights above it the troops had to put up with icy winds and with snow and sleet. Supply parties, groping their way up the slippery tracks towards the heights beyond the river, knew that a stumble might send a laden man or mule slithering down a steep mountain-side.

The positions on the right of the bridge-head were extremely close to those of the Germans; the garrison on Monte Ornito could look across to Monte Cerasola and see German troops moving on one side of the crest and British on the other. There was a story current at the time that a Guards battalion, which wanted to identify the enemy units opposite, shot a German and hooked his body into their lines with a large steel fishing-rod made for that purpose.

Life in these forward positions was particularly uncomfortable, as the men were confined most of the time to their sangars— enclosures walled with rocks and earth, water-proofed with old bivouac tents, and roofed with wooden beams buried in boulders as a protection against mortar-bombs. Although the troops had just arrived from a warm climate, they came to little harm from the weather. Every man went up the mountain with a leather jerkin, thick underwear, at least four pairs of socks and two blankets; this protection was increased by odd blankets left in the sangars by previous occupants and by men who had been killed or wounded. The rather limited use of tommy-cookers was possible, and the water ration of two pints a day could be increased by melted snow or rain water. Boots wore out quickly on the rough tracks, and rotted in the wet, and some battalions kept cobblers in the forward areas.

The supply system was complicated but successful. The Corps organization was a good one, and the drill for supplying the bridge-head had been brought to a pitch of efficiency. 4th Division quickly became used to moving supplies by mule and porter. Traffic control had to be strict, as many of the roads and tracks in the forward area could be seen by the Germans; and nearly all these roads and tracks were narrow, winding and unmetalled, and but for the restriction of traffic and constant work by the sappers they would have become unfit for use. Jeeps and trailers were used as much as possible, and some of the tracks would not take any other kind of vehicle. A jeep convoy, consisting of most of the division's jeeps, ran nightly from the 'B' Echelon area at Roccamonfina, and its marshalling before dusk was a picturesque sight, as the square of the little town was filled with small warlike vehicles, occupied by muffled passengers and weighed down with bulky loads.

The right sector of the division's front was supplied by a bumpy track, little wider than a jeep, which branched from the main road at Gallucio, and then twisted and turned its rocky way round the southern spur of Monte Camino, through Calabritto and Cocuruzzo, and down to the road close to the east bank of the river—and within reach of German patrols, which sometimes laid mines on it. No driver ever loitered on this route, and many a passenger who crouched in the back of a bounding and lurching jeep, clutching a tommy-gun, all the way to Rocca d'Evandro, felt that only Providence could bring him safely home.

The division's main supply route was from behind the left flank. A rough track led down to the river, crossed by a pontoon bridge known as Skipton Bridge, and joined the Minturno road. The rank smell which hung round this place was due not to the foulness of the battle-field but to a hot sulphur spring that welled up close to the advance dressing station, and in which troops were able to take a welcome bath. On the left of the road were dense orange groves, with many trees laden with fruit; these rich orchards were sown with 'S' mines, which took a steady toll of the foolhardy, the unwary and the wary. Not all were detonated by humans; dead donkeys and horses, gaseously distended, lay among the trees, and the branches were draped with shreds of dog. On the right of the road, overshadowed by mountain crags, was Skipton Dump, stacked with supplies—bales of fodder, oil-drums, petrol and water-cans. A little farther on were the lines of the mule-pack companies; and then the road was brightened by a display of unit signs marking jeep-heads for the battalions in the line. Skipton was always a busy place; mule trains were constantly arriving or departing, led by Arabs in steel helmets or red skull-caps, or by soldiers of an Italian mountain regiment, wearing Alpine plumes, dark green battle-dress and impressive mountain boots. British escorts or reconnaissance parties, with the least possible equipment, soft hats, rifles or tommy-guns slung, and hiker's long thumb-sticks, gave the place a holiday atmosphere; and now and then little groups of Basuto Pioneers went by, as cheerful as Christy Minstrels. But occasionally the rushing sigh of a heavy shell would stir the air for a moment, and there would be the resounding crash of an explosion near Sun Track beyond the river; or the sharp crack of another 'S' mine would be heard from among the orange trees.

From Skipton, good mule tracks, known as Vine Street, Bond Street and Downing Street, all clearly marked with tapes, led up to the great green bowl of the Valle di Sujo, or Harrogate. This valley was the staging area for troops moving into or out of the line; they usually rested there for twenty-four hours, for the bowl was so big that three infantry brigades could probably have been hidden in it. There was a smaller supply dump there, and additional mule lines. Small parties of unit representatives lived in the bowl, to meet the mule trains coming up from jeep-head and to lead them on. The supply system was kept going by the Staff Captain 'Q', Captain W. J. F. Weller, who acted as the custodian of an information centre at Harrogate as well as co-ordinating the activities of great numbers of supply parties.

From Harrogate, large parties of men and mules climbed between Monte Rotondo and Monte Turlito, and turned right to Cheshire, a large terraced valley between the grey rocky masses of Monte Tuga and Monte Turlito. The valley contained a forward supply dump and ammunition point, a brigade headquarters, and unit and Basuto porter parties. Here the mules were unloaded and returned to Harrogate; and everything—rations, ammunition, 'comforts' and water—was carried on men's backs to troops holding the line. The farthest away were on Cerasola, a mile and a quarter in a straight line from Cheshire—but no path followed a straight line for long in those mountains.

Rations were good, and the ten-man ration-packs were convenient for mule and porter transport; the packs included tinned bacon, steak and kidney pudding, treacle roll, tea, chocolate, sweets, cheese, jam, margarine, cigarettes, biscuits and toilet paper. These were supplemented by such 'comforts' as cakes baked at 'B' Echelon. To make up for the lack of fresh fruit and vegetables, many of the jeep-head parties swept lanes into the mine-fields near Sujo to gather oranges, accepting the risk because they felt it was a point of honour that the men in the line should have the best of whatever was available. Some parties collected as many as a thousand oranges in one day.

4th Division had little time in which to prepare for its entry into this maze of communications and of static positions near mountain tops. During the damp and cloudy afternoon of March the 6th,

12th Brigade disembarked on the upturned bottom-plates of capsized ships in Naples harbour; and three days later, the brigade had taken over its equipment, and Brigade Headquarters and the Royal West Kents had relieved 128th (Hampshire) Brigade Headquarters at Sujo and the Hampshire battalion on Monte Rotondo. The DCLI, who had just relieved another Hampshire battalion round Sujo, came under the command of Brigadier F. M. Elliott MC. The Royal Fusiliers and the Black Watch, who had farther to go than the West Kents, spent an uncomfortable night in the mountains after climbing for several hours on March the 9th; they went on climbing next day, and the Black Watch, under the command of 10th Brigade, went into action that night on Monte Ornito. The Royal Fusiliers had to spend two more nights on the side of Monte Turlito, as their relief of the 3rd Grenadier Guards had been postponed on account of plans for an attack by the Grenadiers over the crest; the attack was eventually cancelled. On March the 12th, Advanced Brigade Headquarters, carrying a maximum of portable equipment, on a minimum number of mules, went up into the mountains to relieve 10th Brigade Headquarters at Cheshire.

The Garigliano sector at this time was what was known as 'quiet' —there was no large-scale fighting, or much likelihood of it. Each side's artillery fired daily at the other side's supply routes and infantry positions; observation-post parties could have excellent training if they could put up with the cold wind that swept into their open sangars; and every night, patrols crept about in a No-man's-land, the width of which varied on the front of each battalion, and tried to find out whether the Germans still occupied positions which had already been spotted. The whole division was new to the Italian country-side, and many of the younger soldiers were reinforcements from England who had seen no fighting at all; this kind of warfare was an initiation which cured inexperience and lack of physical toughness, and damaged a minimum number of men in the process.

The Royal Fusiliers, on Cerasola, the right flank of 12th Brigade, were closest to the Germans, and were opposed by Reconnaissance troops of the 15th Tank Grenadier Division. The positions of the two forces did not directly face each other, since the crest of the mountain rose between them; each side had built sangars a few yards from the top. Open movement was possible in the battalion area—soldiers might be cooking or changing their clothes all over the mountain-side, and, just beyond the jumbled rocks above them, Germans were living in the same fashion, guarded, as were the Fusiliers, by a few machine-guns laid on the sky-line. 'W' Company's sniper, after spending many hours flat on his stomach scraping, picking and digging, completed a shallow crawl-trench to a point overlooking a German observation post; and on his arrival there, eliminated one of the familiar faces that constantly peered through its square loop-hole.

In the centre of 12th Brigade's front, the Black Watch held most of Monte Ornito, and had some positions in front of the peak, which is about two thousand five hundred feet high. The Germans were not far away, however, on the western slopes.

In these conditions, the enemy's positions and habits were so closely watched that there would be discussions over air photographs about the likelihood of a particular sangar being occupied or unoccupied; and when, after a snow-storm, an aircraft photographed the enemy's forward area, and the tracks followed by German supply trains showed up clearly, there was enthusiasm among the Intelligence experts and hard work for the gunners. The maps of the neighbourhood—even the 1 in 25,000—were of little use to soldiers engaged in such detailed warfare, and air photographs took their place; photograph 'mosaics' were always used for briefing and interrogating the nightly patrols.

While the division was holding this mountainous salient, the New Zealanders made the second Allied attack on Cassino, which could be seen from Monte Ornito on a clear day. The American 36th Division had attacked the town in January and had been beaten off and badly knocked about. The second assault, on March the 15th, was known as Operation Spadger; 4th Division's part in it was to be a deception scheme during the night of the 15th. A heavy rainstorm in the valleys and a fall of snow, together with intense darkness, prevented the scheme from being completed; movement was difficult, even in the most familiar surroundings, and in the Guards' sector a man and two mules went over a precipice. The German defences, shaken by the enormous air attack in which more than a thousand tons of bombs were dropped, wavered for several days under the powerful assault of the New Zealanders, and then held; and the New Zealanders had to build among the ruins of Cassino the defences which men of the 4th Division were later to occupy.

Before Operation Spadger came to an end, the division entered into a complex series of reliefs; 4th Division was to be relieved by 4th Moroccan Mountain Division, and was to move across Italy to the Adriatic coast. On the night of March the 18th, the Hampshires took over Monte Ornito from the Black Watch, and 28th Brigade, which had just arrived from Egypt, relieved 10th Brigade in the left sector, round Sujo. On the right of the bridge-head, the French relieved the Guards Brigade on the Pietrafosca spur, and on March the 22nd took over Cerasola from the Royal Fusiliers.

Mule trains were now returning heavily laden from Skipton, as all stores and salvage were to be cleared from the mountain before the division left. On the night of March the 23rd, French troops took over Monte Ornito from the Hampshires, who in turn relieved the West Kents on Monte Tuga and Monte Turlito, to which they had moved earlier on from Monte Rotondo. Next night, the Hampshires handed over their new sector to the French, and went down to Harrogate. The relief of 28th Brigade on the left and 4th Reconnaissance Regiment on the right was arranged for the nights of March the 26th and 27th, and command of the division's sector passed to 4th Moroccan Mountain Division on March the 25th.

Meanwhile there had been a change of plan. 4th Division was not after all to move to V Corps in eastern Italy, but was to come on March the 26th under the command of XIII Corps, so moving from the Fifth to the Eighth Army. 10th Brigade, which had already moved to a staging area at Giugliano, camped at Alvignano, and the rest of the division went back to the Volturno valley, between Venafro and Pietravairano.

Everyone set to work at once on badly needed maintenance, for which there had been little enough time since the equipment had been taken over. The Army Commander, General Sir Oliver Leese, visited the division several times, bringing gifts of cigarettes, and met representatives of all arms and many units. The weather was already warmer; the division thought over its first experience of Italian warfare and prepared for its next.

10. Sant' Elia

The division was not allowed to rest for long; its next task was to relieve 3rd Algerian Division in the mountains north of Cassino. On March the 26th, Major-General Hayman Joyce took a small party to reconnoitre the new sector. During this reconnaissance, the CRA, Brigadier I.V.R.Smith, was killed by shell-fire.

On March the 27th the Bedfords, who were to go into the line on the night of the 28th, entered the mountains north-west of Venafro, and moved to a lying-up area. By March the 31st the DCLI and the Surreys had followed, and command of the division's left sector had passed to 10th Brigade. On the following night, 12th Brigade arrived to take over the centre sector. Divisional Headquarters was established on April the 2nd, and the relief of the Algerian Division was complete when Prestonforce took over the right sector on the night of April the 3rd. Prestonforce was commanded by Lieutenant-Colonel P. Preston, and consisted of 4th Reconnaissance Regiment, the Somersets and a detachment of Number 2 Support Group.

The task of Divisional Headquarters in taking over from the Algerian Division was not quite so straightforward as if the headquarters to be relieved had been British. The French commander, General Monsabert, and his staff spent never less than three hours on a ceremonious—and enjoyable—lunch. After lunch, the General and his senior staff officers withdrew for a further three hours, after which the war was resumed. Most business had therefore to be carried on with General Monsabert's American Liaison Officer, a gaunt and very helpful giant called Colonel Sweat. Co-operation between the two headquarters was smoothed by the fact that 4th Division's GSO 2, Major Lord Wynford, had been on General Monsabert's staff in North Africa.

The Sant' Elia sector had no future as a battle-field. It represented the high-water mark of an Allied attack which had broken against the impregnable mountains, and receded to surge forward elsewhere, leaving, under the eyes of the defenders, troops who could advance no farther. The Germans were too strongly placed to withdraw up the valley to Belmonte and Atina until compelled to do so by withdrawals on other fronts; but even so, plans had to be made for pursuit in case of such a withdrawal. There was also the possibility of a thrust by German tanks into the Rapido plain to the south. In order to support either the pursuit or the defence, 12th Canadian Armoured Regiment came under Major-General Hayman Joyce's command, and 6-pounder and 17-pounder anti-tank guns of the 14th Anti-tank Regiment were deployed in carefully dug and camouflaged positions. Eventually the sector was to be handed over to a holding force made up of miscellaneous units, while the main attacks went in elsewhere, and, for experience in mountain warfare, flights of 2771st and 2778th Squadrons of the RAF Regiment joined 4th Division's infantry battalions in their sangars and ravines. Later on the Italian Bafile Battalion joined Prestonforce for experience.

The new front extended for about eight miles across the wild and mountainous country of the Upper Rapido. Prestonforce was in positions north and north-west of Vallerotonda, covering the Ancina and the mountain village of Valvori. 12th Brigade, north and north-west of Sant' Elia, blocked the Secco valley and the road from Belmonte. 10th Brigade held the heights covering the Colle Belvedere and the southern part of the road which twists up the mountainside from Cairo to Terelle. Almost all the division's forward positions could be overlooked from mountains in the country held by the Germans; from the bare grey cliffs of Monte Cifalco, two miles north of Sant' Elia and three thousand feet high, Germans of the 5th Mountain Division looked down into the valleys; five and a half miles west of the same village, the tremendous peak of Monte Cairo, more than five thousand feet high, dominated the whole scene; and, the same distance away to the south-west, the Monastery of Monte Cassino, less high but equally commanding, lowered over the valley of the Rapido. Directed from such observation posts, the German guns could adjust their fire accurately on to most parts of the division's forward area. Shelling and mortaring were more frequent and more accurate than on the Garigliano front, and the division lost more men.

The period during which the division held the Sant' Elia sector was marked by no particular activity either there or elsewhere in Italy. This was the last quiet interlude of static warfare before the third assault on Cassino; the Germans in the mountains to the north were to be stirred up as little as possible. If German guns and mortars made a nuisance of themselves, the division's heavy weapons replied, and it was at this time that counter-mortar organizations were first tried out; but company raids on enemy positions were undertaken only by permission of the divisional commander, and patrols went out in search of information rather than for a fight.

The Germans, on the other hand, were more aggressive than they had been in front of the Garigliano salient, possibly because here it was their turn to hold the dominating positions. The ground was wooded, covered with scrub and seamed with deep ravines; enemy patrols sometimes moved through battalion positions at night without a shot being fired by either side. The infantry had orders to fire only at Germans within twenty-five yards; but ambushes were organized to wait for unwary enemy patrols. Often the Germans would shout a few words in English, to gain time in a surprise encounter. Sometimes they would carry out a full-scale raid: during the day they would bring down prolonged harassing fire on a company position, perhaps make some sort of demonstration, and then after dark put in the raiding party, covered by a box barrage, on one of the more isolated platoons.

A mile and a quarter south of Sant' Elia, the Inferno stream emerges from among the mountains into the plain, on its way to join the Rapido near Cassino. The water-course was dry, and along part of it a track fit for light lorries had been blasted and bulldozed by French engineers. The ravine through which the track ran was the main base for the Sant' Elia sector; Hove Dump was opened by the RASC a mile short of the valley's mouth, and other parts of its length were used by Rear Brigade Headquarters and transport sections. On the lower slopes were the little camps of the administrative parties which served units in the line; and higher up were the bivouacs of battalions in transit, for the place was also a staging area. A battalion was always held in reserve there, in case of a counter-attack which might turn the division's left flank, and farther up the valley was main Divisional Headquarters.

A little way below Hove, near the mouth of the valley, there was a wide open space where the troops of battalions going out of the line climbed into their lorries, sometimes interrupted by a spasm of German shelling; more often, the infantry marched along the Inferno tracks, and met the transport in the valley behind Aquafondata. The jeep train which travelled every night to the Colle Belvedere with supplies drove down Inferno and entered the Rapido plain, travelling westwards towards Cairo village. The quiet country road was lined with orchards or olive-groves, and from time to time the jeeps would pass a wayside shrine or farm; but there was no sound or movement in all the country-side. No civilian life persisted here as on other battle-fields; whether the Italians had fled or been evacuated, or had died on their torn fields or in their ruined homes, none stayed behind to tend their farms or breathe the polluted air. Occasionally the eyes of a half-wild cat would gleam in the shadows or a famished dog would shrink away from the swollen flanks of a dead horse or ox. As the column approached the Rapido, the charnel stink of the battle-field thickened round it; the cultivated groves thinned away, and the road crossed a sodden plain, passing more dead cattle, a tank on its side in the ditch, and, farther from the road, the listing bulk of Shermans bogged in the fields. Some of the trees had been smashed to splinters, others had been so torn that every twig hung limp and broken. Water gleamed in the many shell holes, and the rubble of shattered houses showed white in the gloom. Cairo village lies at the foot of the range of which Monte Cairo is the peak and Monte Cassino the south-western corner. Beyond the village the road turns to the north and begins its zig-zag climb—more than twelve hundred feet in less than a thousand yards—up the side of the Colle Belvedere. The road here passed near the German positions, and was guarded by troops of the Northumberland Fusiliers and a squadron of the RAF Regiment. At the end of that part of the road which could be used—the rest was held by the Germans—the jeeps unloaded their supplies on to mule trains, while German shells burst in showers of brilliant sparks above and below and sometimes in the jeep-head. As soon as the mules were loaded they moved off to the forward positions; the most exposed of these had to be supplied by porters, as the clattering hooves of mules would have drawn fire at once. The jeep-head, known as Beefsteak, was constantly harassed anyway; there were frequent losses among the supply parties, and shells often started fires among the ammunition in the jeep-head dump, or in the mortar positions on the ridge above. Beefsteak always stank of dead mules, for the mule lines were in the line of the enemy's harassing fire, and the Arab muleteers buried the animals so hurriedly that a hoof or more was often left out.

The division had not only to hold its sector but to train for its next task; a training programme for all three brigades and for certain of the divisional troops was to be completed in little more than a month. To make this possible, the battalions had to relieve each other in turn. There was tank and infantry training at Viticuso with 1st Canadian Armoured Brigade, and at Alife with 26th Armoured Brigade; and river-crossing practice on the Volturno at Barracone and near San Giorgio Dragoni, with a Canadian river-crossing training team.

At first the battalions of 4th Division relieved each other; and then Canadian battalions began to take their turn in the rota of reliefs.

Eventually the relief of 4th Division by 2nd New Zealand Division began; Divisional Headquarters handed over on April the 15th, and went back to Pietravairano. The Hampshires were replaced by a Maori battalion three nights later. The Somersets and Bedfords were relieved by the New Zealanders during the next two nights, and 4th Division's second spell of action in Italy was over.

Not a minute of the division's second brief rest in the valley of the Volturno was wasted. The first needs of men back from the line were a hearty breakfast, a good sleep, a hot bath, clean clothes, and in the evening a visit from the mobile cinema. Such small comforts were luxuries to men who for ten days or a fortnight had lived under intermittent harassing fire, unable to move in daylight out of their cramped positions, and at night straining their eyes in the darkness for movement among the bushes and boulders in front. But as soon as the units had settled down in their new areas, they began intensive training again, for there was much to do and little time. The weather was already growing milder, though from time to time the rain fell in torrents, flooding bivouacs and reducing the fields to mud; then the troops engaged in Exercise Quack would curse the weather again, as they staggered through the slush towards the Volturno, heavily equipped and carrying eighteen-man assault-boats on their shoulders.

The division was striking roots into Italy. The divisional baggage dump, which held all personal possessions not needed for operations, was set up at Venafro, where it was to stay for two months before moving to Rome; its last move in Italy was to Cesena, six months later. The division's first cemetery was established, also at Venafro; Corporal Taylor of the King's took charge of it, with Corporal Shipley as his assistant. When the division began its northwards advance a few weeks later, the Senior Chaplain and the DAAG, the Reverend B. D. M. Price and Major R. G. Collett, chose new sites, at which Corporal Taylor opened the cemetery while Corporal Shipley finished the work at the site left behind. Both British and Italian working parties helped at the cemeteries.

In March the division was able to appoint a staff captain for Welfare. This appointment was reinforced in April when Lieutenant-Colonel R. D. Judd MC arrived to take over the duties of AA&QMG from Lieutenant-Colonel H. P. Mackley, as Lieutenant-Colonel Judd was particularly keen on an efficient and comprehensive Welfare organization. He at once began the first of his Welfare experiments, and arranged that REME should build five mobile canteens. These took the road early in May, and served snacks to the division's troops until October. Until the division reached Rome, an army cookery school at Venafro supplied the canteens with cakes and so on.

Among the other Welfare arrangements made at this time were two ENSA shows and a welcome tour of the division by Caroll Levis, his wife and an accompanist. A number of vacancies was allotted to the division at the Eighth Army Rest Camp near Mundorff Bridge, a long and imposing Bailey bridge which crossed the Volturno at Ponte di Raviscanina. The camp had a dreary look, as it consisted entirely of Nissen huts, but the service and the amenities were excellent; all who stayed there spoke well of it, and wished their forty-eight hours had been longer. A few members of the division—generally those whose turn had come to be left out of battle at 'B' Echelon—were able to spend seven days' leave at Bari or the Sorrento Peninsula. Finally, before returning to the line, everyone had a day off in Naples; everything worth sending home which could be found in the Neapolitan shops cost a formidable price, but there were plenty of ways of passing time, and the San Carlo Opera House was immensely popular with the troops.

As training went on, the division began to shape itself into the team which was to show the highest fighting qualities in the long advance to come. On April the 11th, the new CRA, Brigadier R. C. H. Kirwan OBE, arrived from the Anzio bridge-head, and Brigadier C. A. Montagu-Douglas Scott, Irish Guards, came to command 28th Brigade. On April the 20th, command of the division was handed over by Major-General Hayman Joyce to Major-General A. D. Ward DSO (The King's Regiment) who had commanded a brigade of 5th Division at Anzio. The new commander took over the division at a critical moment in its career; the few weeks of fighting it had seen in Tunisia and Italy had given the last touches to its long training in Home Forces, and now, tough, able and self-confident, probably as efficient as any division in Italy, it was ready for any task. Major-General Ward was to command the division in its greatest assault, and was thereafter to lead it to success in all its duties, directing all its greatest achievements. Five days later, Brigadier A. G. W. Heber-Percy DSO came from the 4th Grenadier Guards to take over 12th Brigade from Brigadier Elliott. By this time, 12th Brigade had relieved 1st Guards Brigade in Cassino.

11. Garrison in Cassino

Cassino had been a legend even before the division left North Africa. The town and the great crag behind it comprised the most important position held at this time by the Germans in Italy. Across almost the whole width of Italy, the Fifth and Eighth Armies faced mountainous country into which they could not hope to penetrate with any speed. But in front of the centre of the Fifth Army, the valley of the Liri ran away, parallel with the coast, to within a few miles of Rome. The entrance to this valley is so strong in natural defences that before the war the Italian General Staff used to use it as an exercise example of an impregnable position.

The first few miles of the valley lie between two ranges of mountains; on the left Monte Majo, and on the right Monte Cairo, each surrounded by lesser heights, and each about five thousand feet high. The entrance to the valley is barred by a swift-flowing river—the northern two-thirds of its course across the mouth of the valley are called the Rapido, and the southern third the Gari—which joins the Liri at the left-hand end of the valley's entrance, where the two rivers become the Garigliano. The Liri flows away along the left-hand side of the valley. At the right-hand end of the entrance to the valley, Monte Cassino, topped by the great Monastery which had been ruined in the air attack on March the 15th, looked down on the whole valley and on the approaches to the Rapido, from a height of fifteen hundred feet above the plain. At the foot of this great height lies the town of Cassino; on March the 15th it had been smashed into mounded heaps of rubble, among which stood tottering walls and archways; under the crumbled ruins were cellars, in which soldiers of several nations lived an unhealthy, exhausting and deadly life. To the right of the town and beyond it rises Castle Hill, four hundred and fifty feet above the plain, topped by the ruins of a castle which had been built in the Middle Ages and had withstood every assault until that of March the 15th. To the right of Castle Hill, the Rapido runs northwards towards Colle Belvedere, and beyond the river rise in turn the steep sides of Colle San Comeo, Colle Majala, and Monte Castellone. From within the Fifth Army's lines, the whole valley could be seen from the great whale-back of Monte Trocchio, which is nearly as high as Monte Cassino, and faces it across the Rapido. The Via Casilina, now known as Route Six, one of the two great main roads that join Naples and Rome, runs into Cassino from the right of Trocchio, turns sharp left in the town, swings round the foot of Monte Cassino and runs along the right-hand side of the Liri valley.

The Fifth Army had crossed the upper reaches of the Rapido, and Polish troops had a foothold on the mountain-side between the Canadians on the Colle Belvedere and the Guards on Castle Hill. The western part of Cassino town was held by the Germans, and the eastern part by the Guards; but to the south of the town the Fifth Army had not been able to cross the river to attack the Gustav Line beyond. The Monastery was the key to the valley, and Cassino was considered to be the key to the Monastery; and, for the time being, there was stalemate in Cassino.

The town was like another world. The conditions in which the garrison had to live were so bad that troops were allowed to stay there only for eight days, and the foremost positions were so bad that they could be occupied without relief for only half that time. The place could be reached only at night, and even then the approach had to be covered by a heavy smoke screen, known as Cigarette. The period during which Cigarette was laid by the 25-pounders— from ten at night until the supply parties were back under cover— was an anxious one for all concerned, and particularly for the gunner FOO in the town, who had to adjust the points on which the smoke canisters fell according to the wind blowing at the time. The passage of his orders might be interrupted by bad wireless reception, so that he had to repeat his corrections over and over again; and some canisters would always fall short, in company areas, and others would fail to clear Castle Hill, covering the infantry with acrid smoke. Cigarette was the most unpopular task the gunners had to undertake. The majority of the field batteries had to remain silent, so that the Germans would be unaware of the great number of guns gathering round the entrance to the Liri valley. Cigarette was therefore fired by very few batteries, and a huge weight of smoke-shell had to be fired by each; this ammunition had to be dragged out of its trenches to the guns, and replaced next night. The rate of fire was often high, and lasted for some time, and the strain and wear on the guns—which had recently been carefully calibrated—was a constant worry. As soon as the fuse-length was given out, gunners would adjust the fuses as fast as possible; and after a while there would be half a dozen shells ready for the gun. Then the FOO in Cassino would send back a correction, and every fuse would have to be readjusted with hair-line accuracy, by the dim light of an electric hand-lamp, with a worn and slippery fuse-key. Perhaps worse than all this, Cigarette was not a screen which could be explained in terms of ordinary artillery smoke screens; and the gunners were compelled to fire smoke at intense rates, and with several guns concentrated on a single point of origin, without understanding why.

12th Brigade began to relieve the Guards in the town on the night of April the 22nd, when 'A' and 'B' Companies of the Black Watch took over the central strong-points on Route Six. On the following night, 'W', 'X' and 'Y' Companies of the Royal Fusiliers relieved the 3rd Welsh Guards in the northern part of the town, and 'A', 'B' and 'C' Companies of the West Kents took over from the 3rd Grenadier Guards the more open southern sector.

In the closely built-up northern and central sectors of the town, very few of the positions had a field of view of more than fifty yards or so. From loop-holes scooped in the rubble at the base of tottering walls, from the former basement windows of strongly reinforced cellars, and from open slit-trenches in the wilderness of debris, the brigade's machine-guns covered the larger open spaces which had once been the squares and public gardens of the town. As far as possible, every section or sub-section post could be seen and covered by fire from its neighbours; but many a small garrison under the command of a corporal spent its days in virtual isolation, never quite certain from what distance or what direction in the surrounding desolation the Germans were looking at them. South of Route Six, the more open part of the town allowed the positions held by the West Kents to be more widely spaced. The left-hand company of the brigade, occupying Mary, Helen and Jane—three ruins still recognizable as large houses—faced the lateral stretch of Route

Six on which were the Hotel des Roses and the Baron's Palace, and were separated from the Germans by the Rapido. The Baron's Palace, like the Colosseum and the Amphitheatre, had endured for several centuries, and still provided protection to its garrison against the bombardment of modern weapons. The river had formerly passed under the town through underground culverts, but had been opened up by the explosion of bombs and now flowed, clear and clean, near the German positions.

All three battalion headquarters were right forward in the town, in quarters so cramped that headquarters staffs had to be reduced to a minimum. The headquarters of the Royal Fusiliers were housed in the cellars of the Jail, which were comparatively spacious. The crumbling tower of the Jail provided as good an observation post as any to be found, but—perhaps for this reason—it was singled out as a target for heavy long-range German guns. The Black Watch and the West Kents shared the Crypt under the Church, not because it was roomy but because nobody could find anywhere else. The Crypt still had the shell of its church standing over it; from the roofless nave, a hole in a pile of rubble led down into a sort of brick-lined chute, closed by blankets at each end. The two battalion headquarters shared a completely subterranean room which would have been anything but spacious for one of them. The only sub-division of the available space was into cubicles with low vaulted ceilings. All the members of the headquarters, from commanding officers to orderlies, worked, ate and slept there; the wireless sets on battalion, brigade and artillery frequencies were continuously, and noisily, working; the wounded were brought in for treatment, and waited there until night-fall, when they could be evacuated; whatever cooking was possible, including the essential brew-ups, went on in all odd corners at odd hours of the day and night; and the sanitary system—buckets carried out and emptied at night—was unavoidably more public than in normal conditions. But the hundreds of tons of rubble on top of the Crypt made it capable of withstanding even a direct hit from the 21-centimetre shells which burst on it from time to time. The ventilation was strangely good, but all light was artificial. The men there used fresh rations for the most part—meals were cooked at 'A' Echelon and sent up cold, to be reheated if necessary. One of the worst anxieties of those in the Crypt was over communications, since the telephone lines were constantly being cut by the enemy's fire, and could not be mended until after dark. Often the muffled uproar and concussion of a heavy concentration would suggest that the forward troops might be in difficulties without any means of calling for support.

Nobody could find his way through the remains of the town by following a map or air photograph of the town as it had been before the great air-raid. Small beaten paths twisted in all directions among the dunes of rubble, skirting craters which were sometimes forty feet across and which held enough water to drown a man. Some of the craters were used as latrines, others provided water for washing; in either case a careful choice was necessary. Corpses lay everywhere among the ruins, some partly buried in debris, others completely exposed, but the town was comparatively free of the stink of decay. Some of the dead lying beside the porters' tracks were already skeletons. Parts of the town were flooded into dismal swamps where mosquitoes were about to breed by the million.

The western part of the town was held by German soldiers of the 1st Parachute Division, one of the toughest formations of the German army. In the series of rear-guard battles this division was to fight during the enemy's long retreat up Italy—battles often fought for the benefit of the less heroic infantry and tank grenadiers of other divisions—it was to prove that it was by far the best German division in Italy. The men were all volunteers, and most had been chosen for the physical toughness needed for airborne fighting. The division had fought in Crete, and had begun there to build up within itself a tradition of superiority and of 'kameraderie' which was proudly accepted by nearly every recruit. The divisional commander made every effort to maintain this high morale during the long unhappy weeks of withdrawal; and his success was such that the division was put into the line at every point that became important, even if it had to cross Italy to reach its new sector. Wherever the division appeared, a fierce defence was imminent, even though the divisions on each flank might be withdrawing. General Heydrich, the division's able commander, supplemented his propaganda within the division by giving every parachutist's wife a special chain, so that women honoured by marriage to these warriors might recognize each other. These men were the Nazi ideal of the soldier, tough, disciplined and unreasoning; they clung to an incongruous code of right and wrong, fair and unfair, in the game of fighting which was their life. At Cassino they respected both the Red Cross and the wounded man; ambulances on both sides drove about openly, though the German ones may not always have carried wounded.

A day never passed at Cassino without one or two periods of shelling and mortaring, varied with salvoes from nebelwerfers dug in behind Monastery Hill in the valley to the south. Much of the shooting was unpleasantly accurate; the surviving buildings were so battered and rickety that a near miss would often bring some of the walls or roof crashing down. Many of the posts were in cellars which the Germans had shored up and strengthened, but a direct hit on one of the weaker positions would always cause losses.

The Castle was one of the most unpleasant strong-points at Cassino. It was actually behind and above the German part of the town; at night, when the porters scrambled up to it with supplies, they passed within a few yards of German posts in the towers of the long wall which climbs the hillside between the town and the Castle. In spite of its commanding position, observation forward from the Castle was almost impossible, as the western rampart was five feet thick, and observation posts outside it were exposed to German snipers. Observation northwards was possible only because the keep walls on either side had been completely smashed. The Germans, on the other hand, could look down into the Castle court-yard from Monastery Hill, so that no movement was possible in daylight, except in the keep itself. So much of the keep was taken up by sangars and reserve stores of water, food and ammunition, that there was room to move only a few feet at a time in any direction.

The plan of defence was based on interior lines of fire from light machine-guns in sangars at the foot of the walls, supplemented by positions from which one or two men could throw grenades or fire tommy-guns at any enemy trying to climb the cliff or get into the Castle. The breaches in the ramparts were mined, and some were wired as well. The Germans had tried to storm the Castle during the March fighting, and had suffered terrible losses; and in April they confined themselves to shelling the place from time to time. This did little serious damage to the building, but brought down chunks of the masonry on the heads of the garrison.

When the Guards Brigade returned to take over Cassino for the second time, everybody knew that the town would not have to be occupied much longer. The regrouping that was going on—the arrival of the Poles on the right, the arrival near Cervaro and behind Mount Trocchio of all the division's guns and of hundreds more—

and the dumping of supplies alongside Route Six and elsewhere, showed that the Spring offensive was not far away. 12th Brigade left Cassino with a feeling of relief that the shut-in, seemingly pointless days of waiting were over; a week and a half underground and without exercise had left the men pallid, though still healthy.

The relief of the Cassino garrison was spread over two nights, those of May the 4th and 5th. Both nights were clear and bright, and only the constantly drifting smoke of Cigarette hid from watchers in the Monastery the long processions of men in gym-shoes moving up and back along Route Six. Fifteen minutes before the agreed time limit on the second night the relief was complete, and 12th Brigade returned to its old billets at Baia e Latina.

To hold the ruins of Cassino for eleven days during the pause between battles for the town gave the brigade little valuable experience, except for the self-confidence earned in the endurance of trying conditions. The brigade had been prevented from aggressive action by the necessity of concealing positions as far as possible, and because patrolling among the cratered roads and tangled debris would have provided little or no information about the enemy.

The German Parachute Division, however, had been fiercely aggressive all the time, undeterred by the losses usually suffered by their raiding parties. Their only gain had been to force the brigade to abandon a minor position in the centre of the town. The object of these raids was partly to get information about the impending offensive, and partly to maintain the parachutist custom of aggressiveness and bravado; their attitude was also shown by the jeering, contemptuous tone of the leaflets printed by the parachutists for the benefit of their opponents. They had maintained the original strong-points in which they had sheltered during the air attacks and the fighting of mid-March; and every night they had come forward to the banks of the Gari to build additional defences. In general, they had shown every intention of holding on to the end.

12. The Gustav Line: preparations

The Liri valley is the gateway to Rome—the classical route for an army marching on the city from the south, and the only practicable one for a large force.[1] The gateway, however, was firmly shut, and was held shut by very strong hands indeed; two vigorous attacks, by the Americans in January and by the New Zealanders in March, had been beaten off. Only an immensely powerful assault could open the valley. It was well worth opening, for it led not only towards Rome but towards the Anzio bridge-head.

The River Rapido, which crosses the mouth of the valley from Cassino to Sant' Angelo, is some sixty feet wide. By moonlight, its dark silent waters seem to slide by as swiftly as a mill-race—in fact the rate of flow is about seven knots. The country on the near bank of the river is exposed; that on the far side is difficult for both infantry and armour. Hillocks and low ridges provide ideal defensive positions, and many of the streams and ditches between them are wide and deep enough to stop a tank.

The Germans had had months in which to prepare their positions, which though simple were very skilfully placed and constructed. All positions were covered by defensive fire, admirably planned and co-ordinated, and accurately registered by guns and mortars which held large reserves of ammunition. Seventeen hundred feet above the entrance to the valley rises Monte Cassino, from which German observers could direct the fire of their heavy weapons; and German commanders up there could move their forces about the battle-field spread out like a chess-board below. No smoke screen could blind the watchers on so steep a crag; and there could be no hope in May of an adequate mist or fog.

[1] Quoted from Field-Marshal Alexander's dispatch.

The mouth of the valley was so strong a position that the Germans were holding it with comparatively light forces. In any case, Field-Marshal Alexander had deceived the enemy into expecting the main attack on the coast at Civitavecchia, nearer to Rome than Anzio, and the German reserves were therefore not within easy reach of the Gustav Line, as the first line of German defences in the Liri valley were called. Half-a-dozen battalions of infantry held the Gustav Line; but the garrison was by no means inadequate.

With all possible secrecy, Field-Marshal Alexander began to regroup the Fifth and Eighth Armies, shifting the full weight of the Eighth to the mouth of the Liri valley, while Fifth Army took up its positions along the Garigliano from the Liri to the Mediterranean coast. From the Apennines, the great mountain spine of Italy, to the Adriatic, V Corps was to go forward as opportunity offered.

Fifth Army was to attack with two corps—on the left, along the coast, would be II American Corps; on the right, the French Expeditionary Corps, with its ferocious Goumiers, the Algerian and Moroccan mountaineers.

Eighth Army held the mountains in the centre of Italy with X Corps. The Polish Corps was to attack the Monastery from the north-east. XIII Corps was to break into the Gustav Line, and I Canadian Corps was to pass through and break the Adolf Hitler Line behind it.

XIII Corps for this attack consisted of 6th Armoured Division, 8th Indian Division and 4th and 78th Infantry Divisions. The corps commander, Lieutenant-General Kirkman, intended to send 4th Division across the river on the right and 8th Indian Division across on the left. At eleven o'clock on the night of May the 11th, all the guns of XIII Corps—more than six hundred of them—were to open fire on the positions of the German guns and mortars. Since on the right and left the guns of the Poles and of the French would be opening fire at the same time, the weight of artillery deployed on a front of some ten miles would be greater than at any battle since the Great War of thirty years before.

At a quarter to twelve, the infantry of the two divisions was to cross the river and advance into the Gustav Line behind a slow, rolling barrage fired by nearly five hundred guns. 4th Division on the right was to seize a bridge-head between Sant' Angelo and Cassino, expand it by thrusting straight ahead, and swing right to meet the Poles on Route Six, two miles behind Cassino. Having isolated Cassino, the division was to destroy the German garrison in the town. 8th Indian Division on the left was to cross the river at and south of Sant' Angelo, clear the 'Liri Appendix', the tongue of land between the Liri and the Gari, which would be to the left rear of the bridge-head, and push straight forward to the Adolf Hitler Line. 78th Division was to be ready to pass through either of the assaulting divisions. The tanks of 6th Armoured Division and of 1st Canadian Armoured Brigade were shared out between the three infantry divisions, to join them in the bridge-head as soon as the sappers had been able to get their bridges across the river.

To strengthen 4th Division for the battle, a considerable extra force was placed under its command. This force consisted of 26th Armoured Brigade Group, 1st Guards Brigade Group, an artillery group, a field survey detachment, an Air OP flight and two Advanced Air Support Tentacles. A massive artillery group, under various commanders, was to support the division. This was to include three field regiments, two medium regiments and a medium battery, a battery of heavy anti-aircraft guns and two batteries of American heavy howitzers.

On April the 20th, the new divisional commander, Major-General A. D. Ward, on his way to Divisional Headquarters for the first time, spent the morning on Monte Trocchio, looking down on the sector into which 4th Division was to attack. That evening, with the GSO 1, Lieutenant-Colonel G. A. Thomas, and the CRA, Brigadier R. C. H. Kirwan, Major-General Ward framed the plan on which the division was to fight its battle.

Next day, he held his first conference on Operation Honker, as the attack was to be called, described his plan, and set all arms and services of the division to work out their own special problems with great thoroughness. In brief, the plan was that 10th Brigade on the right and 28th Brigade on the left should make the assault crossing of the river between the confluence of the Rapido and the Gari, a mile and a half south-east of Cassino, and a point a mile and a quarter farther down-stream. The Cassino sector on the extreme right was to be held by 1st Guards Brigade Group, which was not to attack but was to guard the right flank of 10th Brigade.

The group which was to assault on the right was to consist of 10th Brigade, commanded by Brigadier S. N. Shoosmith, under whose command were to be the 17th/21st Lancers (less one squadron) as well as supporting arms and services of 4th Division. Brigadier

Shoosmith chose his crossing-places at the point where the Ascensione brook runs into the Gari, and at a point six hundred yards farther down-stream. These crossings were to be known as Rhine and Orinoco respectively.

The group which was to assault on the left was to consist of 28th Brigade, commanded by Brigadier Montagu-Douglas Scott, and this group was to include one squadron of 17th/21st Lancers. Brigadier Montagu-Douglas Scott chose 'X' Crossing at a point five hundred and fifty yards below Orinoco, and 'Y' Crossing two hundred and fifty yards farther down-stream still.

Forty-two assault boats were to be allotted to 10th Brigade, and thirty to 28th Brigade.

The assaulting troops were to advance as quickly as possible to a depth of some three thousand yards beyond the river. When this was done, Major-General Ward intended to send forward 12th Brigade, preferably on the right through 10th Brigade; so that, while 12th and 28th Brigades pushed forward, 10th Brigade could swing right to take Cassino.

The division was to carry out this plan by advancing to four successive objectives. The first of these, Brown Line, was about a thousand yards beyond and parallel with the river, and so, once taken, would provide protection against counter-attack to the crossing-places. Blue Line was a thousand to fifteen hundred yards farther on, and since it followed the line of the first high ground beyond the river it would shield the crossing-places from observation from within the Liri valley. Red Line was a bulge nearly two thousand yards deep beyond Blue, and Green Line, some fifteen hundred yards farther on still, extended into a deep salient on the right and pointed towards the back of Monte Cassino, and to the point at which XIII Corps was to join hands with the Poles.

The timing of the attack provided for Blue Line to be reached by three-thirty in the morning of May the 12th. Since Field-Marshal Alexander expected three weeks of fighting before the enemy would give way, timings were generally on the optimistic side, and failure to adhere to them was unlikely to prove disastrous.

Brigadier Shoosmith intended to send first the Surreys and then the Bedfords across the Gari at Rhine. The Surreys were to swing right and to advance beside the river first to Brown and then to Blue. The Bedfords were to follow up and to draw level with the Surreys on the left. 'D' Company of the DCLI was to cross at

Orinoco, and to spread out in order to guard working parties at the crossing. Once the Surreys and the Bedfords were across the river, the rest of the DCLI was to follow, either to pass through to Red or to deal with counter-attacks.

Brigadier Montagu-Douglas Scott intended to send first the King's and then the Somersets across the river at 'X' and 'Y' Crossings. The King's were to take Brown, and the Somersets were to pass through to Blue. As soon as the Somersets were across the river, the Hampshires were to follow and to be ready to take up the advance to Red and Green Lines.

The artillery plan was precisely synchronized with each stage of the infantry's advance. If the infantry were to fall behind schedule, they would lose the advantage of the barrage, which was too elaborate to be altered once it had been begun.

The first task of the guns was to silence all the German guns and mortars before the infantry launched their assault boats, and to soften the German defences which covered the crossing-places. While the infantry advanced behind the barrage, those guns not engaged on the barrage were to provide defensive fire in front of them if necessary. Every line of the barrage was to be marked for the infantry by one smoke shell on every hundred yards of front, and Bofors guns were to fire bursts of tracer along the axis of advance, so that in the darkness and confusion the infantry would not lose direction.

A diversion scheme, intended to draw the enemy's attention from his front to his left flank, was to be provided by Bofors guns, tanks and medium machine-guns firing across the river north of 10th Brigade's crossing-places.

Each brigade was to set up three ferries in its sector, as near as possible to the infantry crossing-places, for supplies, wounded, reinforcements and vehicles. These were to be worked with cableways and with rafts capable of 5-ton and 11-ton loads. As early as possible, the division's sappers were to build their Bailey bridges across the river. 225th Field Company was to build Amazon Bridge, capable of carrying tanks, in 10th Brigade's sector between Rhine and Orinoco. 59th Field Company was to build Blackwater Bridge, capable of a 9-ton load, across the river loop in 28th Brigade's sector, below 'Y' Crossing. 7th Field Company was to build Congo Bridge, capable of a 30-ton load, in 28th Brigade's sector, three hundred yards down-stream of Blackwater.

Elaborate precautions were taken to conceal from the enemy the concentration of so great a striking force in front of the Gustav Line. The movement of civilians, the use of wireless sets, the marking of routes, the dumping of material, the movement of vehicles and the density of tents and vehicles were all kept under careful control. The division's training in the assault crossing of rivers had been too extensive to be concealed, but its duration could be disguised, and orders and documents were all prepared as though intensive training was to continue until May the 21st.

At the end of April, the division began to take over its sector, which was being held by 8th Indian Division, with 12th Brigade in Cassino under its command. 1st Guards Brigade returned to Cassino and relieved 12th Brigade, and battalion after battalion of 4th Division took up position within reach of the river.

The May weather was hot, still and clear. Troops who would not be seen by the enemy packed away their battle-dress and put on khaki drill; the infantry and other arms which worked right forward wore olive drab shirts and denim slacks.

The whole division was active during the last week before the battle. Patrols went out every night to screen preparations from German patrols. Pioneers from the forward battalions and sappers lifted mines from the approaches to all the bridge and ferry sites. Reconnaissance parties had a final look at the river. Assault boats were brought forward by starlight and camouflaged against the watchers in the Monastery. Gunners and mortar detachments dug pits for their weapons, and covered them with camouflage. There was some danger that the preparations in 28th Brigade's sector might give the show away, and defensive barbed wire had to be put up as a deception; this task was unpopular with the fatigue parties, who had to work on ground which was dangerous with uncharted and unswept mines.

The hard-working RASC and gunners went on dumping ammunition. Farther back, infantry battalions and cableway and rafting parties worked to a steady routine of day and night exercises which brought them to a high pitch of efficiency. The assault ferry companies, which did not move forward with their battalions, practised on the swiftest reaches of the Volturno, where conditions were most like those on the Gari.

All this time the enemy remained inscrutable. Sometimes one of his guns would slowly range on a point of little obvious importance; or a shattering concentration of shells or nebelwerfer salvoes, bursting on one of the division's forward positions, would interrupt the warm peace of a spring day. The echoes would die, the dust settle and the smoke drift away; quiet would return to the whole front.

There was no apparent change in the German routine in Cassino. There was a good deal of movement on the night of May the 6th, and a group of about seventy Germans was spotted and shelled. The Guards, however, who knew the sector well, thought there was no evidence of a major relief.

Farther south, enemy patrols crossed the river from time to time, and there was some danger that they might discover the preparations going on. In spite of these alarms, the division's reconnaissance and working parties went out and came back without trouble.

On the night of May the 8th and 9th, small convoys began to filter forward. On the night of the 10th, the roads were packed with traffic, as infantry, tanks and essential transport moved up. By dawn on May the 11th the whole division was in position, and every unnecessary vehicle had gone back to the rear. So far as the Germans could see, the countryside was as tranquil and as empty as before.

During May the 11th, commanders gave out their final orders. During the afternoon special Orders of the Day by Field-Marshal Alexander and General Sir Oliver Leese were read out to all the troops. These Orders revealed the vast extent of the attack; the Allied Armies in Italy were to strike the first blow—the second and third were to be huge attacks by the Russians and the launching from England of the invasion of western Europe.

Commanding officers visited as many of their men as they could reach, and wished them good luck. Chaplains went quietly round to say a few words of encouragement, and to hold simple services where they could. Every man rested who could. A few made their wills at the last moment.

A few hours later, most of the men of the division were to undergo their first ordeal by battle since the fight for Tunis, just over a year before; for many of them, it was their first battle of all. The battle would put to a severe and searching test the physical fitness, the mental and moral fibre and the individual efficiency of every man, the determination of every unit and its ability to fight as a team. At this grave moment of self-questioning, commanders and their men were able to put their confidence in their own training and experience, and in the completeness of the plans and preparations for the assault.

13. The assault on the Gustav Line

At dusk on May the 11th, the front was comparatively quiet. The moon would not rise until half-past eleven, but the lofty crests of the mountains could be seen against the clear sky full of stars.

As the troops of the division moved stealthily forward, nightingales were singing in river-side meadows as tranquil as an English park. Clouds of fire-flies, a dancing haze of lights, shimmered above fields sown with mines. Farther back, the gunners began to cut down the trees which they had left standing like a screen in front of their guns.

At ten o'clock, the guns of 104th Field Battery began slowly to fire smoke screen Cigarette. The smoke screen had been fired at ten o'clock almost every night for weeks, and silence at ten might have meant the arrival of German reinforcements at eleven. But no ration parties moved through Cassino behind the smoke screen. From time to time a machine-gun would burst into a sharp chattering, or, with a concussion like the thump of a far-off door in an empty house, a gun would fire; the enemy was being harassed neither more nor less than usual.

At a quarter to eleven, Cigarette came to an end, and the smoke round Cassino drifted away. If this event suggested anything to the Germans, they showed no sign of it. The gunners hurriedly prepared for the real work of the night.

And at exactly eleven o'clock, along a front of many miles, the massed guns of the Eighth Army opened fire. The whole horizon seemed to burst into flame, with light that leaped for an instant from the dark sky-line into the star-lit sky, dancing from hill to hill and revealing the whole country-side for a photographic moment, blinking open in the darkness a huge eye of noonday—each flame was vivid with chemical green or blue, or tinged with orange. The flash of each discharge was followed by the impact of its sound, which made the air flap like washing on a line; the noise ranged the whole scale of percussion from the high-pitched crack of the heavy anti-aircraft gun to the thunderous reverberation of the great American howitzer. Between the concussions, the echoes could be heard rushing and crackling against the hill-sides, so that there was never a moment of silence. The gunners could hear the ferocious rush of shells from batteries close behind them and the protesting screech of steel violently driven through the air. The infantry on the banks of the river heard the shells tearing the sky far above them, and heard them choiring down into the Gustav Line, to burst in a chain of crashing detonations like a giant fire-cracker.

The German line stayed strangely dark and silent. Bright points of red and yellow light winked up and down Monastery Hill where the shells were bursting, and the occasional glare of explosions showed where ammunition dumps were hit.

Lieutenant-Colonel R. O. V. Thompson, commanding the Surreys, who were to lead 10th Brigade's assault across the river, intended the battalion to advance from the far bank with 'D' Company, commanded by Major C. E. Byrne, on the right, and, on the left, 'A' Company, commanded by Major M. Plastow. 'C' Company, commanded by Major A. H. Newton, was to guard the crossing-places and Battalion Headquarters; a platoon commanded by Lieutenant Davis was to get a simple assault-boat ferry working at each crossing-place. 'B' Company, commanded by Major G. G. Maggs MC, and the Carrier Platoon were to form the battalion's reserve.

The battalion was to land in a stretch of flat, overgrown fields, crossed by drainage ditches. On the left was the River Pioppeto, on the far bank of which stood Square Wood, a hundred yards from the Gari; the wood concealed powerful German positions. On the right was Point 36, a small rocky bluff a hundred yards south of the point where the Rapido flows into the Gari. The bluff was honeycombed with caves, which made it a strong defensive position. To the west, the fields were bounded by Queen Street, the road from Cassino to Sant' Angelo. The flatness of the fields had prevented the Germans from siting many positions from which they could cover the river; but the fields were sown with mines, and snipers were perched in every tree that grew there.

At a quarter to twelve, the battalion launched its boats, and at once the Germans opened up with a storm of fire from machine-guns and mortars. Two of 'A' Company's boats were sunk by an exploding bomb. The rest of the first wave got across, but as soon as the infantry scrambled ashore the empty boats were carried downstream by the swift current. 'D' Company's beach-master, Captain W. G. Spencer, immediately launched his reserve boats, and Lieutenant Davis's ferry helped 'A' Company across. By midnight both companies were on the other side.

Forming up on the far side was difficult. In the confusion, the troops had crossed out of turn according to the carefully planned order of priority, and platoons were mixed up. A river mist was forming, and this, mingled with smoke and dust, thickened into a fog through which the directional tracer of the Bofors guns could not be seen. 'A' and 'D' Companies found themselves in a mine-field, and suffered severe losses. Blinded and confused, their comrades falling around them and the battle going against them, officers and men rallied into groups and fought their way towards their objectives.

'A' and 'D' Companies separately reached the edge of the bluff at Point 36, but were halted there by machine-gun fire, and before long both companies had fallen far behind the barrage. 'B' Company crossed the river, using only one assault boat and the ferry, and without losing a single man; but the company was unable to advance much more than two hundred yards from the river bank. 'C' Company followed, and went on to Point 36, where it joined 'D' Company. Battalion Headquarters reached the farther side of the river, but had to keep close to the bank in order to avoid the mine-field; the headquarters was sprayed from time to time by machine-gun fire and ceaselessly mortared, and had to move three times during the night.

'B' Company got on the move again, advancing slowly through the thick fog and darkness, under fire from all sides. A little while before dawn, the company reached Queen Street, and joined up with troops of the Bedfords, who had followed the Surreys across the river. The two companies made for Point 63, the second objective of the Surreys, but were driven back by the Germans there.

The fog was as thick as ever, but the confusion in which the Surreys had been fighting began to clear. The main body of the battalion fought hard for Point 36, and at five-forty in the morning of May the 12th 'C' and 'D' Companies together went in with the bayonet. By half-past six, the hillock was clear, though intimidated Germans were still hiding in the caves. The Surreys found thirteen machine-guns on the hillock, and took twenty-four prisoners.

Repulsed from Point 63, 'B' Company rejoined the rest of the battalion, and Lieutenant-Colonel Thompson placed all his companies on and around the hillock. He brought up the Carrier Platoon, on foot, to reinforce the position, and distributed the survivors of 'D' Company, which had suffered worst in the minefield, among the other rifle companies. For the rest of the day, and all through the night of May the 12th, the Surreys held fast to their hillock, constantly expecting a counter-attack, shelled and mortared, machine-gunned from time to time, and often sniped at by the tenacious Germans.

At five to two in the morning of May the 12th, as soon as the ferry had been brought back after landing the last boat-load of Surreys, the Bedfords had begun to cross.

Lieutenant-Colonel W. A. Whittaker had planned an assault by three companies—'D' Company on the right, commanded by Major E. Charkham; 'C' Company, commanded by Major G. V. Martin, in the centre; and, on the left, 'B' Company, commanded by Major A. S. Jenkins. 'A' Company, commanded by Major S. F. Rayner, was to follow and mop up. The battalion was to advance to Queen Street, reorganize there and push on at once to Blue Line.

Ferrying was slow, for the ferry would take only twelve men at a time; the enemy's fire was still bursting along both banks of the river; the fog was thickening, and wounded men of the Surreys, waiting to be evacuated, were gathering on the far bank. Good luck, hard work and a great deal of courage kept the ferry going, and all four companies were able to get across.

They formed up on the far bank, and made for Queen Street. Almost at once, the compasses on which they relied for their direction became erratic; and 'B' and 'C' Companies walked into the mine-fields and began to lose men. The barrage rolled away into the fog and darkness, far ahead of the infantry, and when it reached Blue Line Major-General Ward had it stopped.

The Bedfords, however, fought their way forward towards Queen Street. The Germans along the road resisted fiercely, and the

THE ASSAULT ON THE GUSTAV LINE   133

fighting grew confused. By dawn of May the 12th, all four companies were on or near Queen Street.

Major-General Ward decided that 10th Brigade must tighten its grip on its shallow bridge-head before advancing towards Blue Line, and Brigadier Shoosmith therefore ordered the Bedfords to dig in where they were. At the same time, Brigadier Shoosmith ordered the DCLI, commanded by Lieutenant-Colonel G. R. D. Musson, to cross the river and to secure the left flank of the bridgehead. 'D' Company of the DCLI, commanded by Major C. S. Gill, had already crossed at Orinoco, and held a lonely bridge-head of its own there. The company was cut off from 28th Brigade on the left by the sinister Square Wood.

At seven-thirty in the morning of May the 12th, therefore, 'A' Company of the DCLI, commanded by Major G. Rork, made its way down to Rhine. Only two platoons and company headquarters were able to cross the river before the intensity of the enemy's defensive fire prevented further ferrying; squalls of machine-gun bullets menaced anyone who stood up. Thickening the fog with smoke-bombs from their 2-inch mortars, the platoons made a short advance before being compelled to dig in.

It was indeed fortunate for the assaulting troops that well into the morning of May the 12th thick fog filled the valley, and helped to hide the crossing-places and the consolidating troops. When the fog lifted, all the ferrying and bridge-building had to stop at once, for the line of the river was swept by machine-gun fire.

The Germans began a series of counter-attacks on the positions held by the Bedfords, and 'B' Company in particular had some close fighting. Private L. R. E. Savage, finding that the Germans were creeping close up in the long grass, repeatedly stood up in his slit-trench to get a better shot. All went well until a burst of automatic fire broke his rifle; but he crawled to a wounded man, collected another rifle and went on bobbing up and down in a hail of bullets. A German tank appeared, but took no part in the fighting, possibly discouraged by the shower of mortar bombs that burst on and round it as long as it was within range. All the German counter-attacks were broken up.

10th Brigade had a firm hold on its shallow bridge-head, but there were still no bridges across the river, and ferrying was not going well. The cableway parties of 14th Anti-tank Regiment had lost four officers and sixty other ranks already. The officer in charge at

Orinoco, Captain Norton, had been killed. Gunner W. L. Moorley, himself wounded, had plunged three times into the swiftly flowing river to rescue men of the bridge construction party who had been wounded on the banks and had fallen in.

Conditions in 10th Brigade's sector, therefore, were difficult and trying. In 28th Brigade's sector the situation was very much worse.

Early on the night of the assault, 28th Brigade's ferry company had moved up to the river. The control post, check-points and launching-points had been manned. Tapes and telephone wires had been laid from the control post and boat assembly area to the launching-points. Strong swimmers crossed the river with cables to haul the assault boats across the swift current. Naked, they waited on the far bank for their clothes, which were to be delivered by the first boats. Soon after eleven at night, the files of infantry carrying the assault boats should have reached the launching-points.

But the leading battalion, the King's, had had trouble in making its way to the launching-points, and reached the river some thirty-five minutes late.

This naturally dislocated the timed programme of events, and the marshalling of boat-loads and the launching of boats was hurried and disorderly. Worse than this, however, was that within a few minutes of the arrival at the river of the first boats, the corps artillery switched from counter-battery concentrations, which had kept most of the German heavy weapons quiet, to the barrage, and a storm of fire from machine-guns, mortars and artillery began to burst on both banks of the river and along the approaches to the launching-points. But for the shelter of the flood-banks, and of old slit-trenches dug by the Americans in January, 28th Brigade would have suffered crippling losses before crossing.

Many of the German posts covering the river had escaped destruction in the artillery bombardment, and their machine-guns began firing as soon as the detachments guessed that British troops were crossing the river.

Some of the assault boats were holed while they were still on the bank; others were hit as they slid into the water or were pushed out into the stream. One at least capsized when a machine-gun was loaded into it. The marshalling of boat-loads became difficult as the men began to scatter to escape the defensive fire.

In these moments of confusion and disaster, there were still men whose only thought was of how best the battalion could get across the river. Company Sergeant-Major W. H. Palin rallied the men round him, formed them up into boat-loads and checked them into their boats; the success of his company's crossing was largely due to his singleness of purpose.

Urgent requests for the reserve boats were passed to the control points, and the men of two companies were slowly ferried across at 'X' and 'Y' crossings. As they landed on the other side, they found themselves under fire from three sides. Whichever way they turned on the enemy posts, their attacks were frontal and their flanks were enfiladed.

The German positions had been less battered by the artillery preparation than could have been expected; small-arms fire was accurately co-ordinated with the defensive fire from guns and mortars; the proportion of automatic weapons to German infantrymen was high, and there was plenty of ammunition for every weapon. In spite of this, the King's gained a foot-hold on the far bank. They saw nothing of the barrage, which was moving on through the darkness beyond the German defences. Scattered men, who had lost touch with the rest of their sections, were left in a state of uncertainty on the near bank at 'X' crossing.

The Somersets, meanwhile, had caught up with the last of the King's, and had to wait in the taped lanes through the mine-field, under increasingly heavy fire. Rafting vehicles and a bulldozer added to the congestion when they began to come down the slope to 'Y' crossing; they were held up by the crowd of waiting and wounded men, and could not reach the river. The ferry company was losing men, and every loss was serious, for every man had been trained for a special task and was needed. Mist, fumes and smoke combined into a thick fog that filled the valley and crept up the slope leading down to the river. Telephone wires were cut by fire; the ferry company's Number 38 wireless sets were not receiving well, and orders and information could not be passed quickly. Other wireless sets either broke down or were smashed by the enemy's fire. Communications with the bridge-head on the far side of the river were tenuous. The only link between the launching-points and Brigade Headquarters was the Number 22 set of Major A. R. Babington, of 104th Field Battery, who shared with his signallers a shallow slit-trench at the foot of the slopes on the near side of the river. In this exposed position, Major Babington went on calling for neutralizing fire until the fog cleared next morning; then the Germans saw his aerial, and brought down such heavy concentrations of fire all round that the aerial had to be dismantled.

Every difficulty, therefore, faced the Somersets as they approached the river. At 'X' crossing, the stragglers were repeating a wild rumour that all but a dozen men of the two companies of King's which had crossed the river had been wiped out. When for a short period a wireless set got in touch with Battalion Headquarters, Major H. Platt, commanding 'A' Company, reported the situation to his brother and commanding officer. Lieutenant-Colonel J. R. I. Platt told him to go ahead with the crossing and to report progress.

Major Platt embarked at 'X' crossing with a small reconnaissance party. On the far bank he came up against a group of Germans, and both he and his batman were severely wounded and taken prisoner. On May the 13th, the Hampshires found them both in a German dressing station; they had been given no medical attention, and Major Platt lost a leg as a result.

Lieutenant A. E. Sutton-Pryce, also of 'A' Company, was the next to cross the river, with his platoon. He was followed by another platoon of 'A' Company, only fifteen strong, led by Lieutenant Lyons of 'B' Company, but the remaining thirty or forty men of 'A' Company stayed on the near bank.

Ferrying had come to a stop. Until traffic across the river could be resumed, Lieutenant-Colonel J. R. I. Platt brought 'B' Company, commanded by Captain R. E. Fox, up to the near bank on the left of 'A' Company, and spread out the men of the two companies in order to give fire support to the troops in the bridge-head on the other side.

The company of the Hampshires working the ferry—under fire, many of the boats sunk or smashed, a strong current running and cables being carried away from time to time—were having a bad time but were doing extremely well. One of them, Lance-Corporal H. Grainger, swam the river three times with ropes to tow the assault boat over. Between these ventures, he stood naked on the bank of the river for some four hours, under intense fire from artillery, mortars and machine-guns, guiding the assaulting troops into their boats. Two days later, after showing great bravery, he was killed in the bridge-head.

Having sorted out the men of his own battalion at 'X' crossing, Lieutenant-Colonel Platt went to see how things were going at 'Y' crossing, and found that all the assault boats there had been smashed before all the King's could get across. He therefore told Major T. P. Lucock, commanding 'C' Company of the Somersets, to bring forward his company with one of the reserve assault boats. When the boat arrived and ferrying began again, he sent across the rest of the King's—one company and Battalion Headquarters —followed by Major Lucock's company and a platoon of 'D' Company.

A hundred and fifty yards down-stream from 'Y' crossing, Lieutenant-Colonel Platt found an abandoned cable across the river. He called forward to this point the rest of 'D' Company of the Somersets, commanded by Major P. Nation, with a second reserve boat, and sent them across the river. Lieutenant-Colonel Platt next crossed the river himself and visited 'C' Company of the Somersets. The company had pushed forward from 'Y' crossing, until heavy fire halted it on the edge of a mine-field. There the company held firm, maintaining contact with the bridge-head at 'X' crossing.

Lieutenant-Colonel Platt returned across the river to the east bank, and there met Lieutenant-Colonel Garnons Williams, commanding officer of the King's. With Battalion Headquarters of the Somersets, the two commanding officers then re-crossed the river together into the bridge-head. Lieutenant-Colonel Platt was already suffering from wounds in the head and face.

While they were reconnoitring the bridge-head from the positions held by 'C' Company of the Somersets, Lieutenant-Colonel Garnons Williams was mortally wounded. Lieutenant-Colonel Platt was crawling back towards his headquarters when he was wounded again, this time severely. For thirty hours, until discovered by Lieutenant A. G. Morgan, he lay helpless in the open; but at the end of that time, his spirits were so high that he encouraged all who saw him before he was evacuated.

As the sun rose and began to shine through the mist, a grey light revealed along the approaches to the river a litter of broken and trampled tapes, scattered webbing equipment, craters, tumbled clods of earth and listing and battered vehicles. The enemy's retaliation grew in fury; machine-guns raked the flood-banks with a storm of bullets, and close patterns of shells and bombs of all sizes burst in the bridge-head, along the river banks and along the approaches. The ferry company's control post was smashed in by a direct hit, and Majors E. C. Henley and W. C. T. N. Way of the Hampshires were among the killed.

Work had begun on the bridges almost as soon as the infantry had launched their boats. At midnight, columns of vehicles had begun to move slowly down to the river, led by lorries carrying bridging equipment. By one in the morning, the sappers were at work on Amazon, Blackwater and Congo Bridges, in spite of the shells bursting on and round the bridging sites. By three-fifteen in the morning, however, the sappers had been driven to cover by furious shelling, and all work came to a stop. When daylight came, and the mist began to thin out, all the men working on the river banks had to withdraw. The sappers, the surviving bridging and rafting vehicles, the foremost traffic control posts and the Hampshire ferry company all went back to cover.

The evacuation of wounded was not going at all well. Many of the stretcher-bearers had themselves been wounded, and their stretchers were lost; there were more wounded men than could be aided. Many of them were gathered in under the shelter of the near flood-bank for such attention as could be given with a dwindling supply of dressings. The regimental aid post of the Somersets had been destroyed, and the medical officer wounded. Lance-Corporal Vallard, a stretcher-bearer of the Somersets, carried back a number of wounded men by himself, repeatedly crawling back to cover with a man on his back.

A jeep drove openly down to the river, and halted only when machine-gun bullets began to kick up the dust round its wheels. The passenger got out, and quite leisurely raised a Red Cross flag. He was the Reverend R. Edwards, chaplain of the Hampshires, who had come with a load of dressings and a stretcher to help the wounded. With the help of a stretcher-bearer, he began carrying back wounded men, cheerfully disregarding the enemy's fire; he also swam across the river to help the wounded in the bridge-head.

The battalions in the bridge-head spent nearly the whole of May the 12th pinned down, deafened by the constant explosion of shells and mortar bombs, and by crackling streams of machine-gun bullets. From time to time, the Germans would put in counter-attacks of platoon strength. Little was gained by either side during the day. The German commander still felt that there was a possibility that the attack on the Gustav Line was a diversion to draw his attention away from the main assault on the coast near Rome. Keeping his reserves well back in order to meet this threat, he did his best to over-run the XIII Corps bridge-head with the garrison of the Gustav Line.

Work on the bridges was held up all day; but at five in the evening the guns laid a thick smoke screen in front of the Amazon site, and behind it the sappers of 225th Field Company once more moved their equipment down to the river and began work. The fire of the enemy, however, prevented them from getting on very quickly, and the situation in the bridge-head was growing desperate.

At eight in the evening of May the 12th, Major-General Ward decided that the battalions in the bridge-head were too tired and weakened to get much farther by themselves. It was time to bring up the reserve brigade; but the battle could not wait for another laborious crossing in boats. Amazon Bridge, therefore, was to be finished at all costs.

Work on the bridge went on all evening and most of the night, interrupted and delayed by artillery and snipers. By a quarter to four in the morning of May the 13th, the bridge could be crossed by men on foot; and an hour and a quarter later the first squadron of the 17th/21st Lancers was crossing into the bridge-head. By eight in the morning the tanks had deployed, and were helping the Bedfords to clear up the left flank of the bridge-head, in the angle between the River Pioppeto and Queen Street. The infantry of 12th Brigade were beginning to march across the bridge; more tanks were following up. The battle was at last beginning to turn against the enemy.

As soon as the Royal Fusiliers and the Black Watch were across the river, they met and dealt with small groups of German machine-guns and of snipers. The morning mist had cleared, and the enemy's guns, mortars and nebelwerfers pounded away at the infantry as they formed up for their attack.

'D' Company of the Black Watch reached Queen Street and turned left towards the Pioppeto, intending to cross the stream into 28th Brigade's sector. The bridge across this stream, however, had been destroyed, and the steep banks could not be crossed by the tanks. The traffic jam was complete after the scissors bridge, coming up to deal with the obstacle, was halted by a direct hit, and blocked the road. Brigadier Heber-Percy, commanding 12th Brigade, therefore made a quick change of plan; instead of breaking into 28th Brigade's sector, the two battalions, preceded by an artillery barrage and accompanied by two squadrons of the Lothians, were to attack within 10th Brigade's sector. The start-line was to be Queen Street, from Point 31 on the right to Point 33 on the left, a front of six hundred yards.

By nine o'clock in the morning of May the 13th, the Black Watch had reached Point 33, in spite of resistance. At ten o'clock the artillery barrage began, and down came the enemy's defensive fire, which took toll of the advancing infantry. Some shells of the barrage fell short and burst among the infantry; some of the infantry were too eager, and ran into the barrage. The companies of both battalions, however, steadied themselves, and went forward with a rush.

'W' Company of the Royal Fusiliers, commanded by Major W. I. Thomas, swung out to the right to deal with a group of small fortified buildings at Point 37, six hundred yards north-west of Point 36. Fire from these buildings was already raking the battalion, and might have caught the advancing troops in enfilade. The company was halted by the fire of two machine-guns. Lance-Corporal Denis Corke called for volunteers to help him, and, with Fusiliers Hunt and Ashley, charged first one and then the other, killing the crews and silencing the guns. The company reached and cleared the houses, and consolidated there.

'Z' Company, commanded by Major T. C. Howes, went in on the left of 'W', and in spite of losses advanced steadily. Lieutenant-Colonel Evans, striding along with his long stick among the leading platoons, encouraged his men as they went forward.

By noon, the leading companies of the Royal Fusiliers were on Point 41, between Brown and Blue Lines, and fifteen hundred yards beyond Amazon. The Black Watch were on the left-hand Massa de Vivo (Point 69), a thousand yards farther south-west, and actually on Blue Line. Both battalions had taken a number of prisoners, and had crushed all the opposition they had met.

The two battalions spent the rest of May the 13th digging in, and in getting their supporting weapons across the river and into action.

The West Kents and the DCLI were by this time completely across the river, and ready to attack in their turn. Both battalions were to attack at two in the afternoon, the DCLI out to the right of 12th Brigade and the West Kents out to the left.

The DCLI's first objective was to have been the group of buildings already taken by 'W' Company of the Royal Fusiliers.

THE ASSAULT ON THE GUSTAV LINE

Unfortunately Lieutenant-Colonel G. R. D. Musson of the DCLI had not been told that the Fusiliers were there already, and the bombardment which preceded his battalion's attack inflicted further loss on the Fusiliers. Once this had been sorted out the attack was able to go on.

'B' and 'C' Companies of the DCLI, commanded by Major E. P. Banfield and Captain J. T. B. Notley, led the way, keeping very close to the barrage and advancing steadily through the enemy's defensive fire. Soon after two-thirty, both companies were on Point 63, and were on top of the Germans emerging from the dug-outs there. During the initial attack, the battalion took about a hundred prisoners from the Machine-gun Battalion of 1st Parachute Division, and afterwards caught several more groups of Germans in the caves and dug-outs which honeycombed the hillock. A curious feature of the German positions on Point 63 was that they faced north, towards Cassino, so that the DCLI attack had taken them in the rear.

'D' Company of the DCLI, meanwhile, had been attacking Square Wood, where some snipers were holding out within rifle shot of Amazon Bridge. Lieutenant-Colonel Musson sent three tanks to help the infantry; the tanks blazed away with their machine-guns and 75-mm guns into the wood, and some twenty Germans came out and surrendered.

The West Kents had ridden up to their start-line on the tanks of 'B' Squadron of the Lothians, and had begun their attack on the left of the Black Watch. The West Kents advanced from Point 33 along the northern bank of the Pioppeto, and after an advance of a mile 'B' Company crossed the stream and reached the Casa Petrarcone, just inside 28th Brigade's sector. The company commander suspected the presence of a German machine-gun in front of the house, and sent Private C. Gridgeman off to investigate. The machine-gun was there all right, for it opened fire as Private Gridgeman crept towards it, sniping at it from time to time; forty yards from the machine-gun he leapt to his feet and rushed the post; the startled Germans surrendered, and Private Gridgeman took seven prisoners back to the house. The company withdrew before dusk, since it was in a salient which would have been precarious during the hours of darkness.

The Hampshires, under the command of 12th Brigade, had begun to cross Amazon Bridge early in the afternoon, before the DCLI and the West Kents began their attack. As the infantry crossed the bridge in bright sunshine, the enemy brought down among and all around them the usual concentration of shells and mortar bombs. About three hundred yards beyond the bridge, however, they were able to take cover in shell craters and small ditches. The enemy's harassing fire was still heavy, but the men's spirits were high.

At two-thirty in the afternoon, the Sherman tanks with the Hampshires began to move off south-westwards, sweeping the low hills with machine-gun fire, and blasting every possible strongpoint with their 75-mm guns. The Hampshires stood up, formed into extended line with fixed bayonets and walked grimly forward beside the Pioppeto on the left.

Machine-guns in Square Wood opened fire; the tanks swung their guns round and blazed away, and 8 Platoon stormed into the wood and emerged with more than seventy prisoners.

The scissors bridge was still blocking the tank crossing over the Pioppeto, and the tanks came to a halt short of the bridge. From there they opened fire on the crest on the other side, while the Hampshires waded the stream and pressed on.

The enemy troops caught between this southwards thrust and the River Gari now began to surrender, and long lines of Germans were to be seen running forward from the left with their hands up.

The enemy in front were fighting back, but 'B' and 'D' Companies went on up the slope beyond the Pioppeto, mopping up as they went. Having topped the ridge, they had reached their first objective. Lieutenant-Colonel Fowler-Esson decided to take advantage of his battalion's success, and to strike deeper into 28th Brigade's sector. He chose Point 38, half a mile beyond the Pioppeto bridge, as the next objective, and 'B' and 'D' Companies were very soon there. Captain R. Wakeford, leading 'B' Company on the right, was accompanied only by an orderly, and armed only with an automatic pistol. He killed a number of Germans, and when his company caught up with him he handed over no less than twenty prisoners.

'A' and 'C' Companies on the left were following the line of the Gari, winkling snipers out of the wheat along the river bank, and having trouble with mines.

Prisoners by now were surrendering in a continuous stream; the Hampshires had left their objectives behind, and after such successes there was no stopping them. Lieutenant-Colonel Fowler-Esson, who had been with the leading companies throughout, kept them going, and before long 'B' Company was on Point 50, half a mile beyond the previous objective, and actually outside the divisional sector. A strong-point in the house on the top of the rise was vigorously defended, but 'B' Company went in with grenades and tommy-guns and silenced it. Captain Wakeford once more led the assault. He was twice driven back by grenades, but with a final rush he reached a window and flung in his grenades. Five Germans surrendered at once; a sixth emerged from a dug-out in a posture of surrender and suddenly shot one of the Hampshires. The German was disposed of.

'C' Company on the left went still farther, and actually reached Point 46, nearly half a mile inside 8th Indian Division's sector. The company later withdrew to consolidate within reach of the rest of the battalion.

The whole attack had been a perfect example of a set-piece operation; tanks, guns and infantry had co-operated with a precision hardly to be expected even of a carefully rehearsed exercise at a battle school. The battalion had lost eleven men wounded and one killed. Its flanking thrust had cleared Brown Line across the whole front of 28th Brigade's sector and beyond.

The enemy was clearly thrown off balance by the speed and force of the thrust, and it was some time before his guns and mortars started work on the new positions. He did little damage then; but 'D' Company was unfortunate when the house in which company headquarters was established collapsed on several men, who were dug out very bruised and shaken.

The Hampshires were, however, generally in even better heart than when they began, and were further cheered to hear that they had taken some two hundred prisoners. The battle-field was scattered with German corpses and equipment.

The Hampshires were in touch with the survivors of the King's and the Somersets who remained in the bridge-head, and 'C' and 'D' Companies of the Somersets were able to take advantage of the Hampshire attack by coming forward to Brown Line. During the evening, Lieutenant-Colonel Fowler-Esson sent the King's and Somersets back across the river, and sent some of the prisoners with them. A few days later the Somersets and the King's were withdrawn to rest areas.

During May the 12th, four weakened infantry battalions had taken a bridge-head which on the right was only a few hundred yards deep, and on the left was shallower still and extremely precarious. The crossing-places were under direct fire, and there was no bridge. By dusk of Saturday, May the 13th, the situation had changed; there were five fresh battalions of infantry and two battalions of tanks in the bridge-head, and there was a bridge across the river. The bridge-head was between half a mile and a mile deep, and sappers could work freely at the bridging sites. Two platoons of 4·2-inch mortars from 12th Support Group, 329th Anti-tank Battery's 17-pounder troop, a troop of 6-pounders and all the anti-tank guns of the infantry battalions were across the river and in action. More and more traffic was crossing Amazon Bridge, and the enemy's harassing fire was growing weaker and weaker.

The Germans were beginning to panic as the battle turned against them, and were feverishly bringing up reserves. They had not been able to co-ordinate their defence against 4th Division's repeated blows in different directions. Pounded by the division's guns and intimidated by its tanks, many German troops gave up the struggle. By nine in the evening, four hundred of them were already in the divisional prisoner-of-war cage, and many more were on their way. Whole platoons of prisoners in grey-green uniforms were marching back along the dusty road behind Monte Trocchio.

In most places, however, Germans had fought back fiercely and courageously. The Royal Fusiliers, for instance, had captured a company sergeant-major of 1st Parachute Regiment near Point 63; he was just sallying out alone, armed with a bazooka, to give battle to the advancing tanks.

To the right of 4th Division, the Germans on and beyond Monastery Hill were resisting the Poles with determination and often with ferocity, beating off attack after attack, and driving the attackers back to their start-line. On the 4th Division's left, 8th Indian Division had cleared Sant' Angelo, seized a bridge-head of about the same depth as the 4th Division's, though narrower, and had two bridges across the Gari. The best news, however, was from the French Expeditionary Corps, for the Goumiers were sweeping through the mountains which faced the Garigliano bridge-head and had captured Monte Majo, the highest peak of all.

During May the 13th, the Hampshires had cleared Brown Line in 28th Brigade's sector. At half-past nine in the evening, Brigadier Heber-Percy gave the battalion its task for the night—to advance to Blue Line, a thousand yards to the west.

THE ASSAULT ON THE GUSTAV LINE 145

At two-forty-five in the morning of May the 14th, the Hampshires began to cross the start-line in silence. The companies went forward in extended order, guided by tracer bullets fired down the line of advance. The night was dark, and filled with heavy mist thickened by cordite smoke.

Losing a few men on the way, the battalion pushed on, and by daylight had reached Blue Line. The Germans seemed to have withdrawn a little before the attack began; certainly their positions had been uncomfortable since the Black Watch took the left-hand Massa de Vivo, some three-quarters of a mile away to their left rear. The Hampshires' new position was along the track between the Casa Petrarcone on the right and the Casa Pegazzani on the left. In front of the track, an easy slope descends to the Pioppeto three hundred yards away. Five hundred yards beyond the Pioppeto rises the knoll topped by the Massa Vertechi.

12th Brigade's next task was to go forward to Red Line. Brigadier Heber-Percy ordered an early start, at five in the morning of May the 14th.

Supported by the tanks of the Lothians, 12th Brigade went forward at dawn. 'W' Company of the Royal Fusiliers put in an attack on the right of the Black Watch, and, in spite of stiff opposition, advanced north-westwards from Point 41 to the Cassino-Pignatoro road, half a mile away. The defensive fire of German guns and mortars was once more the chief means of resistance, and there was some machine-gun fire and sniping.

Soon after the Royal Fusiliers reached their objective, a fierce counter-attack came in from the north. It was beaten off, and was followed by confused fighting throughout the morning, during which the Germans were at times very close to the battalion's positions. One German tank only a hundred yards away was extremely troublesome until it was knocked out by a direct hit from one of the medium guns firing from behind Monte Trocchio. All the German counter-attacks were broken up, and the tanks of the Lothians were knocking out German self-propelled guns at the rate of one an hour.

'A' and 'B' Companies of the Black Watch moved forward from the Massa de Vivo (Point 69) well spread out, in the brightening daylight; each company was followed by a troop of tanks. Five or ten minutes later, a blinding mist shut down on the battle-field, thickened by the smoke fired by the division's guns to hide the advance from the Germans on Monastery Hill. Before long, nobody could see more than a yard or two, and the attack was in confusion. The tanks, blinded, could not choose their ground, and some were bogged. They could only follow the infantry, who were advancing on a compass bearing and so could not pick a route suitable for tanks.

Lieutenant-Colonel Madden took the situation in hand, speaking to his company commanders over the wireless. The whole battalion rallied to the roar of tank engines, and formed up round the five tanks which had not got lost or bogged. There was neither time nor visibility for a search for the rest. 'C' Company, however, which found itself behind the rest of the battalion, announced that it too had a tank.

The mass of infantry and tanks moved off, advancing slowly and steadily on a compass bearing. When the tanks came up against an obstacle, the infantry halted and guided them round.

The force reached the wood five hundred yards north-west of the Massa de Vivo (Point 69). Rather than find the way round it, and risk losing direction, Lieutenant-Colonel Madden asked the tanks to thrust their way through. This they did, and tanks and infantry came out the other side and found themselves on the main road between Cassino and Pignatoro.

The bank on the other side of the road was too steep for the tanks, but a gap was found, and they were led through it one by one. When the force formed up again and moved on, the enemy began to resist.

The steam-roller advance went on, while the Germans fired wildly into the mist. When the fire was too heavy, the infantry lay down and fired back, while the tanks blazed away with all their guns. The infantry would stand up again and advance a few yards more before getting down again. The tanks were more or less blind in the mist and smoke, and the infantry had to guide them forward. Corporal G. Grant walked in front of one of them, waving a white handkerchief to show the direction. When he spotted an enemy position, he pointed it out to the tank, and then led the tank on again. The very heavy machine-gun and mortar fire failed to persuade him to take cover at any time during the attack.

In this manner, the force reached the top of the low rise a hundred and fifty yards beyond the road. Lieutenant-Colonel Madden found that from this rise the battalion could dominate, though it had not reached, Red Line, and set the companies to digging in. 'C'

Company garrisoned the road, in case the Germans were able to rally there; snipers were already making a nuisance of themselves behind the main body of the battalion.

The Black Watch soon found that they had forced their way through the enemy outposts on to a very strong German position indeed. Machine-guns and mortars had been left abandoned along the ridge; and a German anti-tank gun, with a round in the breech, pointed towards the tanks its detachment had not seen in time.

The mist did not lift until an hour later. During that time, the infantry dug in, and gathered the wounded into a house. Major D. E. F. Coates, who had been commanding 'D' Company, was found dead with five of his men. The mist made things difficult, but it had given the battalion inestimable help in reaching and assaulting the Point 76 ridge.

When the mist finally melted away, the Black Watch were able to look around and take stock of their position. The tanks hurriedly moved to hull-down positions, and the infantry prepared for the inevitable counter-attack.

Nobody counted the counter-attacks that broke against the position during the rest of the day. 'B' Company on the right had a good field of fire, and could not be shaken. 'A' Company could see the Germans forming up, but the Germans could approach the company's position through dead ground most of the way. Fortunately, the Germans could not avoid crossing one open stretch of ground, and there 'A' Company's fire did great execution. 'C' Company too was fighting hard in the wood behind.

Battalion Headquarters was not defended in strength, and the surrounding hedges and trees gave the Germans a chance of stalking the position. Seven German prisoners held there were set to digging slit-trenches for the headquarters and for themselves. Soon afterwards a stream of machine-gun bullets crackled into the position from the wood behind. One of the German prisoners, digging away in his tin hat behind a hedge, had been spotted by one of 'C' Company's Bren-gunners, who was not 'in the tactical picture' and at once opened fire. Battalion Headquarters passed its comment to 'C' Company through the usual channels.

The tanks meanwhile were firing at every German movement they saw, and Lieutenant-Colonel Madden called forward the reserve tank from 'C' Company to help Battalion Headquarters. The tank was on the other side of the road from the headquarters and, since a German machine-gun was firing down the road, direct communication was impossible. The Number 18 set at the headquarters had to speak to the rear-link tank, which had gone back to the Massa de Vivo, and the rear-link tank would then relay the orders to 'C' Company's tank—the gap was forty yards between the tank and the infantry, but the communications to it were nearly a mile long. The tank would cruise down the road to shoot up the Germans trying to get at Battalion Headquarters, and then would move back to its hide until called out again.

Meanwhile, German anti-tank guns had arrived, and immediately knocked out two of the tanks. After a pause, two more of the tanks were set on fire, and eventually the fifth came to the same end. Only the reserve tank remained in action, trundling up and down the road behind Battalion Headquarters; and finally it too was hit, and the infantry were defenceless against enemy tanks.

Help, however, was on the way, for the West Kents too were taking part in 12th Brigade's advance, on the left of the Black Watch. Supported by a squadron of the Lothians, the battalion moved forward through the mist at five in the morning. The machine-guns of the Hampshires, to the left rear behind the Pioppeto, gave support, and artillery concentrations on possible forming-up places probably prevented a number of counter-attacks.

In spite of fierce opposition, the West Kents and the tanks reached and took Point 62, seven hundred yards to the left rear of the Black Watch on Point 76.

On their way to Point 62, the West Kents had been halted for several hours by strong German positions on the northern and western slopes of Massa Vertechi. Powerful counter-attacks from the same neighbourhood were averted only by artillery fire directed at probable German forming-up places. It was clear that 4th Division's left flank was exposed and must be strengthened.

Major-General Ward, therefore, ordered the Hampshires forward across the Pioppeto to seize Massa Vertechi, a thousand yards to the north-west. The West Kents at the same time were to attack from Point 62 towards the Pignatoro road.

The Hampshires had now reverted to the command of Brigadier Montagu-Douglas Scott, who visited the battalion in the early afternoon to give his orders for the attack on Vertechi.

At a quarter to six in the evening of May the 14th, the barrage began, and at six o'clock the companies moved forward. The pioneers rushed a carrier, loaded with light bridging equipment, downhill to the Pioppeto in order to build a tank crossing. Before reaching the stream, the companies ran into the heavy defensive fire of the enemy, and lost more than a hundred men in two minutes. The pioneers' bridge sank in the soft mud beside the banks of the Pioppeto, so that the tanks could not cross; and as a result the attack began to lose its momentum.

Lieutenant-Colonel Fowler-Esson got out of the tank from which he was directing the battle, and with Major Mitchell and Regimental Sergeant-Major Newsome rallied the companies and led them forward across the stream in the teeth of fierce opposition. Every kind of German gun seemed to be dropping concentrations of shells among the advancing infantry; Captain Dent, commanding 'D' Company, was among the wounded.

Captain Wakeford was wounded in the face and both arms, but led 'B' Company up the slope on the left of the battalion, and kept his company under perfect control in spite of the withering fire. Half-way up the hill the company was halted by heavy machine-gun fire, and he organized and led a party which charged and silenced the machine-guns. As the company went forward again, mortar bombs were bursting among the men, and Captain Wakeford was wounded in both legs. But he still led on, reached the crest, reorganized his company, directed its consolidation and reported to Lieutenant-Colonel Fowler-Esson before stopping to have his wounds attended to. During the seven hours that passed before the stretcher-bearers could reach him, his unwavering high spirits continued to encourage the men of his company. For his conduct in this action and during the fighting of the day before, he was awarded the Victoria Cross. The closing words of his citation read: 'His selfless devotion to duty, leadership, determination, courage and disregard for his own serious injuries were beyond all praise.'

Captain Wakeford's batman, Private J. C. Baxter, also fought with conspicuous gallantry. When NCOs were falling in the defensive fire, Private Baxter rallied a group of leaderless men round him, and gathered up a small force of Bren-gunners and riflemen. He kept them together and urged them on, led them on to their objective and allotted their positions. When the enemy's shells and mortar bombs began to burst on the position, he organized stretcher-bearers to carry away the wounded.

The West Kents also attacked again during the evening. By this time the battalion mustered only three rifle companies, one of which was only twenty or thirty strong. The objective was a wide one, being the thousand yards of the road between the Black Watch on the right and Point 86 on the left. In view of the extent of the objective and the weakness of his battalion, Lieutenant-Colonel H. P. Braithwaite decided to aim first at cutting the road at a single point in the thousand-yard stretch.

The fighting was confused, and the infantry suffered a steady drain of casualties. In spite of this, they reached the road on the left of the Black Watch. The tanks accompanying the West Kents were actually firing into the Black Watch's positions until Lieutenant-Colonel Madden sallied out with a white flag.

The arrival of the West Kents made life very much easier for the Black Watch. The dangerous counter-attacks from the left flank came to an end; and a guide party led by Lieutenant Lamond, which had been fired on behind 'C' Company's wood, was able to make a detour through the country cleared by the West Kents and to bring forward the ambulances. 'C' Company was also able to clear the last Germans out of the wood during the night.

By dusk on May the 14th, therefore, the Black Watch and the West Kents were both on Red Line, but very little of Red Line was held within what had been 28th Brigade's sector. After three days of hard and continuous fighting, 4th Division had extended its bridge-head to a depth of three thousand yards—a firm base for further advances.

The enemy had been desperately making temporary reorganizations all day; not one of his manœuvres had been a voluntary one. He had to decide whether to pull out or to try to slow up the advance of XIII Corps long enough to allow the reorganization of his defences. He was bringing up units from far away, and flinging them piece-meal into the battle, but whatever advantage he might have gained was neutralized by the growing strength of XIII Corps west of the river.

By half-past eight in the morning of May the 14th, Congo Bridge was ready for infantry. During the night of May the 14th, the sappers also completed Blackwater Bridge, which crossed the Gari into the divisional sector south of the Pioppeto.

The Sherman tanks of 19th New Zealand Armoured Regiment had arrived to relieve the Lothians during May the 14th, but German counter-attacks, particularly on the left, were so determined and powerful that both tank battalions stayed with 12th Brigade for the rest of the day. The Lothians withdrew during the evening into reserve.

At ten-thirty in the morning of May the 15th, the West Kents and the New Zealand tanks attacked down the road to the left in an attempt to reach Point 86, which overlooks most of the sector on the left. The enemy put up a stiff opposition, and the battalion's attack failed, though it reached Point 66, six hundred yards south of the Black Watch positions on Point 76.

By this time, the repeated attacks of the Poles from the north had all but cut off the Monastery; one more ridge, the steep and cruel Colle Sant' Angelo, and the garrison and its observers would have to give in. But the Poles were weakened by casualties and desperately tired, and there was no hope of taking that last ridge until XIII Corps from the south could join in the attack.

It was towards this ridge that 78th Division was to thrust, battering its way, as 4th British and 8th Indian Divisions had done, through the defences of the Gustav Line and through the observed fire of German guns. 78th Division was to come up on the left of 12th Brigade, pivot round the brigade to the right and strike northwards towards Route Six behind the Monastery. This division had four report lines; the first corresponded with the 4th Division's Red Line, and was renamed Grafton; the fourth corresponded roughly with Green Line, extending farther to the west, and was called Bedale. From Bedale, 78th Division would be able to support the Polish attack on Colle Sant' Angelo, and with a final thrust cut off the escape of the garrisons of the Monastery and of Cassino itself.

Apart from the morning attack by the West Kents, May the 15th was a comparatively static though not a quiet day for the 4th Division. Counter-attacks still had to be beaten off by infantry and tanks, and shells and mortar bombs had to be endured, but no major advance or withdrawal took place. 38th Brigade had begun its advance at three in the morning with an attack on Massa de Vendettis, five hundred yards to the south of the Hampshires on Vertechi. The brigade reached this objective without meeting opposition, but had to fight hard for Massa Tamburrine, half a mile farther on and seven hundred yards south-east of Point 86. Having taken the second objective, the leading battalion of 38th Brigade pushed on to the third, immediately to the south of Point 86, and after fierce fighting took it just after midday, and with it sixty prisoners and four anti-tank guns.

An hour later, the 5th Northamptons of 11th Brigade attacked towards Point 86 from the features taken by 38th Brigade. After hard fighting, this battalion reached its objective, and came up on the left of the West Kents. Before dusk the Northamptons relieved the West Kents, who moved back a mile into brigade reserve.

(The records of the fighting on the Grafton Line are confusing and contradictory, and the accuracy of the above account can by no means be guaranteed. The draft record of the British Historical Section, Central Mediterranean, suggests that 12th Brigade should have been holding the Grafton Line as far as Point 86 before 11th and 38th Brigade reached it. The record comments, of the action by the Northamptons, 'Altogether the battalion collected a hundred and twenty-six prisoners from an area which was supposed to have been the start-line for the main attack.' Grafton, however, had already been described as a *report line*, which suggests that 78th Division had no reason to expect that the whole of it would be clear. The commanding officer of the 17th/21st Lancers, who supported the Northamptons in their attack, stated afterwards that the intention was to clear Grafton as quickly as possible before pushing on. The issue is confused by the fact that the West Kents were reported on Point 86 during the morning of May the 15th, having been reported just short of it at dusk the day before. The account given above is based on a subsequent inquiry by 4th Division's Historical Officer.)

The final battle of the Gustav Line was now about to begin. At nine in the morning of May the 16th, 78th Division began to cross the front of 4th Division on its way to Route Six. The jaws of the pincers were beginning to close behind the Monastery and Cassino. General Sir Oliver Leese had already put the Canadian Corps into the Liri valley through 8th Indian Division. With the appearance of this fresh corps on the battle-field, the Germans realized at last that they had been deceived and that the main attack was about to fall on the Hitler Line.

78th Division's advance at last began to distract the enemy's attention from the forward positions of 4th Division on the left. Major-General Ward decided to take the opportunity of straightening out the line between the Black Watch on Point 76 and the DCLI on Point 63; at that time the Germans were holding a salient five hundred yards deep between the two positions.

Brigadier Shoosmith brought the Bedfords out of reserve to

attack the eastern flank of this salient. Reorganized as three companies, the battalion, supported by tanks, began its attack at six-thirty in the evening of May the 16th. 'D' Company was halted almost at once on the start-line by machine-gun fire, but 'A' Company was able to get forward. Just before eight in the evening, Major Rayner, commanding 'A' Company, was wounded, and Captain Hollick, although he too had been wounded, led the company on. 'D' Company was digging in on the start-line, under Second-Lieutenant Wiggins; all the other officers of the two companies had been killed or wounded. By nine-forty 'A' Company, now reduced to one officer and twenty-nine others, had reached Point 50 and taken it at the point of the bayonet, with five tanks still in close support. One of the platoons, commanded by Sergeant Snape, was on the road three hundred yards to the north.

The enemy had resisted the advance stubbornly, making telling use of machine-guns and mortars; the Bedfords lost ten officers and ninety-two other ranks during the attack.

On the left of the Bedfords, the West Kents, also from reserve, came up to attack at the same time, also supported by New Zealand tanks. They too met fierce resistance from the Machine-gun Battalion of 1st Parachute Division, and by dusk were consolidating short of their objective on Point 58, five hundred yards west of Point 50.

The German Machine-gun Battalion suffered heavily as well as inflicting heavy losses in this action. The tenacity of the Parachutists was illustrated by the admission of prisoners that no food had reached them for forty-eight hours and that many of them had run out of ammunition.

The West Kents were now on the right of 12th Brigade instead of on the left, and the salient which had divided the right flank of 12th Brigade from the left of the 10th was reversed to protrude into the German positions. Sergeant Snape's platoon was less than half a mile from Route Six by this time.

Patrols during the night saw little of the enemy, but forty prisoners were gathered up. In fact, the Germans were withdrawing from the fields between the railway line and that part of the XIII Corps front which faced north. At the same time, they were bringing up in lorries a regiment of Panzer Grenadiers to hold open a gap through which at least the more valuable of their troops could escape. This was the last of the reserve they could get into the Liri valley, but the garrison of the Gustav Line had already lost the battle; the Germans were hopelessly beaten.

During the night of May the 16th, General Leese gave orders for a concerted attack by XIII Corps and the Polish Corps at seven the next morning. The jaws of the pincers were to close still farther behind Cassino and the Monastery.

At seven in the morning of May the 17th, 78th Division and the Polish Corps began their simultaneous attack. Carrier patrols of the Black Watch went out towards Route Six and found no Germans.

As 78th Division's attack on the left ploughed forward, Major-General Ward sent 12th Brigade forward towards Route Six. The companies of the Royal Fusiliers had dwindled to some thirty men each, and the battalion was reorganized as two companies. 'WX' Company, commanded by Major W. I. Thomas, and a company of the West Kents went forward at once to Route Six, opposed only by snipers, and before noon they had reached it. Any parachutists who were going to get out of Cassino would have to scramble across the side of the mountain. The rest of the Royal Fusiliers and the West Kents, supported by tanks of the 19th New Zealand Armoured Regiment, followed up, and by night-fall were astride Route Six, waiting for German visitors. At dusk 'WX' Company moved forward on to the lower slopes of Monastery Hill, in order to narrow the escape gap still further.

The Black Watch on the left also moved up to Route Six, and during the afternoon made contact with 11th Brigade, on the left flank of 12th Brigade. Until now, German snipers had maintained a precarious but disconcerting existence behind 4th Division's lines, and remained active for many days after the main German positions had been overrun. As though these isolated sharpshooters were in close touch with the progress of the battle, they now began to give themselves up, and came out of ruined houses and deep dug-outs to surrender.

On the right of 10th Brigade's positions, a New Zealand tank rolled forward through the trees, halted, fired its gun into the Baron's Palace and swept the railway line with machine-gun bullets. No reply. The crew got out, brewed up and had lunch, watching the heavy howitzers' shells bursting on Monastery Hill, where the Poles were attacking once more.

The battalions dug in, and waited. Anti-tank guns, mortars and medium machine-guns were brought right forward. To the left of 12th Brigade, 78th Division too moved up to the road.

Soon after eleven at night, figures approached the positions of the West Kents, and were challenged by sentries; a roar of automatic fire went up, and twelve Germans were found dead. Soon afterwards, more of the parachutists came clambering over the rocks towards the Royal Fusiliers on the mountain-side, and the West Kents on the railway line gathered more prisoners in. The 25-pounders meanwhile were monotonously dropping shells along the mountain tracks by which the enemy might try to escape. There was no attempt at an organized break-through, but rather a general stealthy approach by small parties of men who would fight only if they were compelled to do so. The Bedfords sent out patrols to intercept them; one of these, led by Lieutenant D. G. Calvert, reached Route Six and waited in ambush; the Germans walked into the trap, and the Bedfords opened fire at five yards range. The surviving parachutists scattered, reorganized and came in with Schmeissers and grenades, only to be beaten back again with loss. Lieutenant Cox took a patrol across Route Six to search buildings at Point 80, at the foot of Monastery Hill. The buildings were clear, and 'C' Company of the Bedfords moved up to Point 80.

Shortly afterwards, the Bedfords were finally withdrawn. The battalion had lost a major, three lieutenants and fifty-seven other ranks killed, and two majors, three captains, six lieutenants and a hundred and forty-seven other ranks wounded.

Throughout the night, Verey lights were going off, and sudden bursts of small-arms fire, hoarse shouts and the scuffling of hob-nailed boots on the rocky slopes, punctuated the arrival of the Germans. The reiterated cry, 'Another couple coming down, sir', marked their disposal, as the prisoners were led back to Battalion in the darkness. By dawn, 12th Brigade had taken seventy prisoners, who were being shepherded back to Brigade Headquarters, the uninjured helping those who had been wounded before surrendering. XIII Corps had, however, been unable to seal completely the exit from the town, and a large proportion of the German garrison escaped, to fight again another day.

Early in the morning of May the 18th, Major Thomas decided to investigate, and, with his batman, Fusilier Barden, began the long steep climb towards the Monastery. The first catch was a Parachutist sergeant-major, fast asleep behind a rock; he was rudely awakened and ordered down to company headquarters. Farther on, and a good deal higher up, Fusilier Barden surprised a party of six Germans, who surrendered at once, and accompanied him down the hill. Major Thomas went on alone; he was only a hundred yards from the Monastery when he saw a steel helmet in the mouth of a cave, and with a hoarse roar summoned its wearer to come out. The steel helmet disappeared, to be replaced by a white table-cloth on the end of a pole.[1] When Major Thomas repeated his summons, the standard-bearer emerged with caution and with no less than nineteen comrades, just as Lance-Corporal Frost, breathless from the climb, joined Major Thomas. 'Only two?' asked the Germans with some embarrassment, as they were formed up. Taking one of them as a guide, and leaving the rest to Lance-Corporal Frost, Major Thomas climbed up to the Monastery, and there met a Polish patrol which had just arrived. Their meeting marked the link-up between the XIII and the Polish Corps, and sealed the enemy's defeat.

Brigadier Shoosmith sent the Surreys forward into Cassino at nine in the morning—the order was 'Push on like mad'. 'C' Company reached the Colosseum at nine-thirty-five. By midday, the battalion had occupied the whole town, and detachments were climbing the hill to the Monastery. From cellars and dug-outs, small parties of Germans came out to give themselves up; one of them threw a grenade from behind the white flag and killed one of the Surreys.

Even in the moment of triumph there were tragedies; Lieutenant G. Sloan was killed and another man wounded by an exploding mine, and early in the afternoon a powerful booby-trap killed Major G. G. Maggs MC, Lieutenant S. T. Hawkins and two others.

That afternoon the Surreys were withdrawn. Six officers and thirty-one others had been killed since May the 11th, eight officers and a hundred and two were wounded, and five were missing.

The DCLI followed the Surreys into Cassino, and collected thirty Parachutists there. At three in the afternoon the battalion was withdrawn.

Cassino began to fill up with sightseers—staff officers from Divisional Headquarters, press photographers, even a couple of gunner subalterns who had walked down from the gun positions three miles back. The troops were more than willing to pose for

---

[1] The table-cloth now hangs in the regimental museum of the Royal Fusiliers, in the Tower of London.

highly unrealistic shots of 'Our men entering Cassino'—four of 'our men' as grim as any newspaper reader could wish, and the fifth grinning all over his face. But posing and sightseeing came to an abrupt end when three of the photographers were killed by a booby-trap. The Cassino Task Force began to clear the town, and traffic began to pass through at last, on its way towards the next job—the Hitler Line.

The battle-field in the bridge-head was as grim in its way as the ruins of Cassino. The fields and orchards were torn with craters and scattered with clods of earth, the lanes and tracks were littered with smashed branches and discarded equipment. Every farmstead, which from its little hillock had looked down on the surrounding fields, was battered into rubble. Here and there along the tracks lay the discoloured and rusting hull of a Sherman, where the German anti-tank gunners had got in a shot before themselves being overrun and killed. The bodies of British and German soldiers still lay in the long grass and in the ditches, sometimes near the crater of the shell that had killed them, sometimes half hidden by the scarlet poppies among which they had fallen.

4th Division's task was finished, though 12th Brigade and the Reconnaissance Regiment remained in the line until May the 20th, under the command first of 78th and then of 8th Indian Division, advancing beside Route Six between 78th Division on the left and the Poles on the right. The division's guns came forward across the river, and stayed in action until May the 27th. The eventual withdrawal of the Royal Fusiliers took place under persistent and accurate shelling; Lieutenant-Colonel A. F. P. Evans, always on the spot when things were difficult, stayed behind to look after the wounded, and was killed just as he was about to drive back. Lieutenant-Colonel C. A. L. Shipley took command of the battalion.

Through the gap opened by 4th Division and 8th Indian Division, other troops went on to break the Hitler Line and to pursue the enemy beyond it. The men of 4th Division turned their backs on the Monastery, on the ruined fields in which they had fought, in their greatest battle, to outflank it, and on the graves of many of their comrades. For a short time there would be rest, baths, hot meals, quiet nights and shelter; and then the division would go forward again to join in the pursuit that was soon to be launched along Route Six—forward across the river, through Cassino and past the Monastery, the three great bastions of the German defence.

14. The pursuit: Palombara

The strength of the division's infantry, terribly diminished in the fierce battles in the bridge-head, rose again as reinforcements arrived. There was leave to Naples, Sorrento and other places; some of the units organized sports meetings, men of many units went off to see a show in which Miss Marlene Dietrich was appearing in person. Infantry officers returned to the battle-field to discuss and to learn from the battle they had fought. The sun blazed down all day. The drab denims in which the infantry had crossed the river gave way to khaki drill, and the whitened belts and gaiters of 'peacetime' reappeared.

Everyone followed with deep interest the news of the pursuit of the German forces, as they fell back in confusion from the broken Hitler Line towards Rome. Across the whole width of Italy, the Fifth and Eighth Armies were on the move, and from far-off England there were tales of tremendously powerful forces gathering along the south coast for the invasion of Europe. These sunny weeks of May were no less momentous than those of 1940, when 4th Division had gone forward into Belgium to meet the Germans, or of 1943, when the division had broken through the German defences in Tunisia.

By June the 1st, the few short days of rest and reorganization were over; the division was to follow up behind XIII Corps, which was leading the pursuit in Eighth Army's sector. During the week that followed, units and brigade groups took to the road again. This time the journey up Route Six was undisturbed by shelling, and the Mad Mile—the stretch of straight road leading down to Cassino—was quiet at last. The ruins of Cassino were tidy, and sappers were at work on the road through the town. Beyond Cassino, the fields on the left of the road, which less than three weeks before had seen such bloody fighting, were peaceful in the sunlight, and a few Italians moved cautiously among the ruins that had been their homes. After a long slow march, the division settled down for the time being in corps reserve near Ceprano, in the Liri valley sixteen miles beyond Cassino.

During the morning of June the 6th, listeners-in to the BBC heard the great news that General Eisenhower's armies were landing on the north coast of France, and that the leading troops of Fifth Army had taken Rome. Fifth and Eighth Armies between them had taken twenty-five thousand prisoners since May the 11th.

That morning, the division moved forward again, and during the evening concentrated in the rolling country fifteen miles east of Rome. XIII Corps was pursuing the enemy astride the Tiber, with one armoured division on each side of the river. 6th British Armoured Division was advancing along Route Four, which follows the east bank of the river. 4th Division, with 25th Tank Brigade, was to advance into the rolling country on the right of Route Four, and was to open the country road that runs northwards from Tivoli, on Route Five seventeen miles east of Rome, to join Route Four some fourteen miles away. 4th Division was to pass to the right of Rome, as it had passed to the right of Tunis thirteen months before.

With the DCLI on the right and the Surreys on the left, 10th Brigade went into action at dawn on June the 7th, advancing behind patrols of the Reconnaissance Regiment. The brigade group crossed Route Five some five miles west of Tivoli, and took the narrow road that leads northwards into the hills.

There was no resistance, but crumbling road-surfaces, demolished bridges and cleverly placed mines delayed the advance. The Surreys suffered an unhappy loss when the commanding officer's jeep blew up on a mine; Lieutenant-Colonel R. O. V. Thompson, Lieutenant G. H. Gudgeon and Corporal Efford were killed, and the driver, Private Kinnard, was wounded. Lieutenant-Colonel C. G. S. McAlester MC arrived two hours later to take over command of the battalion.

During the afternoon, Brigadier Shoosmith brought forward the Bedfords and a squadron of Sherman tanks of 51st Royal Tanks, and by nightfall the whole brigade was in the line. The Surreys on the left had reached the hamlet of Castelchiodato, seven miles beyond Route Five; the Bedfords were a mile farther to the right; and the

DCLI were on Poggio Cesi, a hill two miles to the south-east of the Bedfords.

Early in the morning of June the 8th, 12th Brigade on the right began to move forward through Tivoli. The Black Watch, riding on tanks of 142nd RAC, led the way. There were no delays at first, and the Black Watch did not dismount until they reached the village of Palombara Sabina, seven miles beyond Tivoli and only two miles to the right of the Bedfords. The inhabitants of the village came streaming out to greet the British troops; the infantry went in on foot to search the place, while the tanks went through.

Half a mile beyond Palombara, the tanks were halted by a blown culvert, and could not find a way round; the country on both sides of the road was too steep for a diversion. The sappers brought up a bulldozer, but it was hit by shell-fire, and nothing more could be done about the demolition. The Black Watch resumed the advance on foot, with 'B' Company on the right of the road and 'C' on the left.

Almost at once the infantry came up against strongly placed German positions. On the right of the road, 'B' Company clambered up the mountain-side until halted by a company position a thousand feet higher than the blown culvert. On the left of the road, 'C' Company found the going extremely difficult, for the countryside was a tangle of little hillocks and valleys, over-grown with bushes and orchards, among which the German positions were cunningly concealed.

Lieutenant-Colonel Madden brought 'A' Company up on the left of 'C'; and, when 'A' Company in its turn was halted, sent 'C' Company across behind 'A' to make a wide swing to the left. The country facing 'C' Company was still very difficult indeed, but the company was fortunate enough to meet Sergeant Dickson, a South African who had been captured by the Germans some months earlier, had escaped and had been in hiding ever since. Sergeant Dickson not only knew the country perfectly but he knew how to find his way through the German positions. Skilfully guided, 'C' Company threaded its way through the difficult country.

When Brigadier Heber-Percy wirelessed his orders to the Black Watch to halt and consolidate, 'C' Company, hot, tired and thirsty, was three miles beyond the blown culvert, and a mile to the west of the village of Moricone, on the Palombara road. The company reported its position to Brigade Headquarters, and was at first flatly

THE PURSUIT: PALOMBARA

disbelieved, for there were—or had been—strong German defences between the culvert and Moricone. The company found a good position in a cherry orchard, and dug in there before making the most of a magnificent crop of cherries. Sergeant Dickson volunteered to go back to Palombara in order to bring up the ration parties—nobody else could hope to find the way from Palombara to the cherry orchard in the dark, since the country was far too difficult for a compass march. The sergeant went off, and at three in the morning returned with the ration party, himself carrying a load. The Black Watch had found a friend indeed. During the small hours of the morning, 'A' Company moved up on the right of 'C', and both companies could hear 10th Brigade coming up on the left.

The Surreys had moved forward again at dawn of June the 8th, and by noon were two miles due west of Moricone. Tanks of 51st Royal Tanks, having swung widely to the left in order to avoid the more difficult part of the country, joined them there. The Bedfords, also with a squadron of tanks, came up between the Surreys and the Black Watch on the right, and pressed slowly forward during the night. By ten in the morning of June the 9th they were a mile and a half north-west of Moricone, from which the Germans had withdrawn during the night. During the afternoon, the Bedfords reached Route Four, three and a half miles beyond Moricone. The Royal Fusiliers also moved up to Route Four during the day, and sent patrols along the main road to the right, while the Bedfords patrolled to the left.

The country ahead of the division was even more difficult than that through which it had already passed, and there were signs that the enemy intended to make every use of the hills and streams to delay the advance along the east bank of the Tiber. On the west of the Tiber, however, 6th South African Armoured Division was moving fast through easier country. Field-Marshal Alexander, decided to strengthen the more promising thrust on the left, and 4th Division was ordered to cross the Tiber into XIII Corps reserve.

The division handed over its positions to 8th Indian Division, and during the next few days returned to Route Five. After a short pause, the brigade groups travelled along Route Five into Rome—where the soldiers and the newly liberated Italians eyed each other curiously but undemonstratively, and where every man in the back of a three-tonner was able to whistle at a girl again—and thence to a concentration area on the west bank of the Tiber and some fifteen miles north of the city. There was some bitterness because although the division spent some days in this area, and although Rome was already full of American troops, the city was out of bounds to all troops of the Eighth Army.

25th Tank Brigade had stayed behind, east of the river, and 4th Division was now to be joined by 1st Canadian Armoured Brigade. Representatives of this brigade began to arrive to live with the infantry battalions they were to support, and to join in discussions and exercises intended to give the division further training in co-operation with tanks.

The battle, meanwhile, was receding into the distance, and the division was to follow up. On June the 16th, the division began to move to an area beyond Viterbo, fifty miles north-west of Rome; and on the same day, ironically enough, permission to visit the city was granted.

The midsummer weather broke into torrential rain-storms, which so soaked the ground that complete units were thoroughly bogged. Officers and men were, however, able to visit Rome, and life between showers was pleasant enough.

The pursuit was being maintained by the South African tanks on the left and 78th Division on the right. 4th Division, still comfortably in reserve, was promised on June the 21st a stay of ten days in its present area. Training programmes and leave rosters were at once prepared; Major-General Ward and most of his senior staff officers left Divisional Headquarters to call on units or to attend brigade exercises.

At this moment, XIII Corps found itself firmly checked, for the first time since the Hitler Line. Kesselring had got his troops under control again, and needed time to prepare his main line of defence in Italy—the Gothic Line, far away beyond Florence. The line on which the Germans now made their stand ran through Lake Trasimene, and took its name from the lake. The troops of XIII Corps which had carried on the pursuit were not strong enough to break this line, and the reserve was needed.

Training had already begun when later on June the 21st 4th Division was ordered to go into action on the following day. The Reconnaissance Regiment, which was almost completely immobile, being up to the axles in mud, was to move that same night.

15. The Trasimene Line

Before dawn on June the 22nd 1944, the division began to move out of its concentration area north of Viterbo. The fighting advance that began with this move was to continue until the troops were sixty-five miles from the point where they first went into action; and because of the complications of fighting in the difficult country before them, they were to cover more than a hundred miles of Italy before withdrawing into reserve on August the 10th. By that date, they were to have reached the suburbs of Florence, and to have driven across the Arno all the German troops opposing them.

The first twenty-five miles, from Strada to Tuori and Monte San Savino, were across undulating country, dotted with small farms and covered by vine-yards and fields of growing corn. The larger rivers, such as the Chiana, flowed through flat valleys crossed by irrigation canals; sometimes one mile of this kind of country would be so like the next that map-reading became extremely difficult.

Wheeled vehicles were rarely able to leave the road for more than short distances. The narrow, untarred country roads, overlooked from the hills around them, threaded their way from saddle to saddle and from ridge to valley, rising and falling, winding to left and right, crossing bridges and culverts. The German sappers had made clever use of these complications; many of the bridges and culverts were blown up or mined or both, many of the biggest trees were felled across the road. Before the division's wheeled traffic could advance, there was much heavy work to be done—bridges to be built, craters to be filled in, mines cleared, diversions to be constructed; and the work was done quickly and well by the division's sappers, helped by working parties drawn usually from the Anti-tank and Light Anti-aircraft Regiments and the Northumberland Fusiliers. The roads were made for nothing heavier than the occasional hay-wain or market cart; only an elaborate control system could keep the massive traffic of the division moving through such a series of difficulties. The Provost Company and traffic control parties from the Light Anti-aircraft Regiment and other units worked hard and well to keep the wheeled vehicles on the move.

The surface of the roads soon broke up into drifts of fine dust, sometimes a foot or more deep. Every wheel that churned through the dust raised it in dense clouds, which settled more and more thickly on clothes and skin, and hung like a fog around every convoy, choking and blinding drivers, passengers and motor-cyclists. In the forward areas, these dust-clouds could be seen for miles, and the German gunners were quick to fire into them; the most rigid march-discipline had to be maintained. A short rain-storm was enough to turn most of the roads into something between a morass and an ice-rink, and even in the hot Italian summer there would usually be a rain-storm once every ten days.

The division's advance was opposed at various times by several German divisions, including the 1st Parachute Division—the old enemy of Cassino days—the Hermann Goering Division, the 15th Tank Grenadier Division, and the 334th, 356th and 715th Infantry Divisions. They were most of them made up of good troops and they fought hard. They were, however, feeling the strain of their long retreat since the fall of Cassino, always under pressure, harassed by artillery and threatened by tanks, their communications always under fire from the RAF, and rarely helped or defended by their own aircraft. Their losses were often heavy, and some of their battalions were very thin on the ground; their only remedy was to bring to Italy drafts of troops trained for other theatres of war. But the German formations were led by skilful and determined generals; they opposed the steady advance of the Allied forces stubbornly and often with ferocity. They made full use of every helpful feature of the ground, placing observation posts in commanding though inconspicuous positions on the heights, and covering likely approaches with machine-guns and anti-tank guns. The German infantry often came back at 4th Division in local attacks and counter-attacks; they were sometimes supported by tanks, though these were not often to be had nor lightly to be expended. The Germans withdrew reluctantly, usually at night; they left rear-guards behind, cut the roads as they went, and covered their withdrawal with heavy artillery and mortar fire on the infantry's forward positions. As they moved out of their positions, they left behind them a widely scattered debris of tanks and guns, with which they had fought until they were destroyed in action or had to be spiked or burnt by their detachments.

At the end of the third week in June, XIII Corps had been brought to a halt south-west of Lake Trasimene by strong German delaying positions between Lakes Trasimene and Chiusi. 78th Division, on the right, was held up on the south-western shore of Trasimene, and 6th South African Armoured Division, on the left, faced stiff opposition near Lake Chiusi. The intention of the corps commander, Lieutenant-General S. C. Kirkman, was to push 78th Division through the German defence, and to move the rest of the corps forward after the initial attack. In order to narrow the front for the assault, 4th Division was to take over 78th Division's left sector.

On June the 22nd, therefore, 28th Brigade Group, with 12th Canadian Armoured Regiment, 4th Reconnaissance Regiment and Divisional Headquarters, moved from the concentration area north of Viterbo to a forward concentration area north of Citta di Pieve, ready to take over the allotted sector that evening. That afternoon a torrential rain-storm soaked the concentration area into a morass, and many vehicles were bogged until the following day. Before dawn, however, 28th Brigade and the Reconnaissance Regiment had taken over their part of the sector.

Brigadier Montagu-Douglas Scott had all three battalions of his brigade in action; the Somersets on the right were near Strada, the Hampshires in the centre were south of Vaiano, and on the left the King's were south-east of the marshes bordering Lake Chiusi. The brigade's left flank was guarded by the Reconnaissance Regiment, which from positions south-west of Lake Chiusi faced along the lake's western shore. The rest of the division was already under orders to move to a forward concentration area during the next two days.

On June the 24th, 78th Division on the right began to attack towards the River Pescia, which flows into Trasimene from the west. After breakfast that morning, the Somersets, supported by a squadron of the Canadian tanks and by artillery fire, began to advance to the right of Vaiano and towards Poggio del Papa, which lies a thousand yards north of Vaiano. The enemy had hidden machine-guns and snipers in the unreaped crops; north of Vaiano, German infantrymen of 1st Parachute Division would lie low in the standing corn until the tanks had passed by, and then delay the Somersets with machine-gun fire. The tanks reached Poggio and severely damaged the enemy there, but had to withdraw before dark as the infantry were held up at a bridge five hundred yards to the south-west.

More rain during the afternoon of June the 24th slowed down the brigade's advance, and Brigadier Montagu-Douglas Scott decided to give up the attack with tanks. Instead, he told the Somersets to consolidate the positions their advance had reached, and ordered the Hampshires on their left to send forward fighting patrols. These patrols reached a cluster of houses a quarter of a mile east of Vaiano, and houses on the southern outskirts of Vaiano itself, and found them all clear. From Vaiano, however, they could hear sounds of digging, firing and occasional explosions.

During the morning of June the 25th, the Somersets heard from civilians that the Germans had left Vaiano. A patrol reported that this was true, and Lieutenant-Colonel McKechnie sent a company forward to Poggio. During the rest of the day, the Somersets advanced a thousand yards to the north-east from Poggio and towards Badia.

The Hampshires, meanwhile, moved into Vaiano and searched it, before pushing on towards La Villa, a village two miles to the north-west. They came under machine-gun fire from a hill on the left which had also caused the Somersets some trouble, but Lieutenant-Colonel Mitchell sent 'D' Company with some of the Canadian tanks to clear it, and they captured the hill soon after midday.

The Hampshires' next objective was the ridge running east from La Villa. 'C' and 'D' Companies led this attack, accompanied by a troop of tanks; 'A' and 'B' Companies followed up, and the remaining tanks gave supporting fire from the hill they had just helped to capture. The Germans resisted the attack with furious machine-gun fire, and shelled and mortared Vaiano, where Battalion Headquarters had been set up. Major-General Ward and Brigadier Montagu-Douglas Scott, who were visiting the battalion, were both slightly wounded, and had to report to the regimental aid post for treatment.

During the afternoon, 'A' and 'C' Companies, on the right and in the centre, reached the ridge, but there was still resistance on the left. A platoon of 'C' Company was halted and lost its platoon commander on the way to clear a house on the left flank; 'D' Company could not move forward at all.

Lieutenant-Colonel Mitchell decided to push 'B' Company forward, with the help of tanks and artillery, to a hill south of La Villa. Early in the evening, Major Blaker took 'B' Company across its start-line to attack in the face of determined resistance. Each side lost a number of men, but the Germans lost their position as well.

Late that night, as the battalion battle-patrol was going out through 'C' Company's positions, German infantry crept up through the deep corn and fiercely attacked the company. The farm-house in which company headquarters was set up was smashed in by bazooka shells and over-run by the enemy; signallers, stretcher bearers, the company clerk and the colour-sergeant—who had cheerfully reported with the rations during the fighting—were all taken prisoner. The fighting was close and confused, and ammunition began to run low. The tide turned at last; the company commander, Captain Bichard, gathered up and launched a last counter-attack, and by three the next morning had brought his company back to its original positions. Captain Bichard was the only officer left, as all his platoon commanders had been hit during the day's fighting and the battle-patrol officer had been killed.

At dawn on June the 26th, patrols found La Villa empty of the enemy. Later on, the Hampshires occupied the village, before advancing, against slight resistance, a thousand yards farther to the neighbourhood of Lopi. The Somersets then sent a strong patrol and some tanks to Badia, a mile and a half east of Lopi. They found Badia empty, and soon afterwards met the 2nd Lancashire Fusiliers of 78th Division. This battalion was moving up to occupy the high ground east and north of Badia; Lieutenant-Colonel McKechnie accordingly placed the forward companies of Somersets south of Badia, between the Lancashire Fusiliers on the right and the Hampshires on the left.

On the same day, after the Hampshires had occupied La Villa, Reconnaissance patrols moved towards Porto, a small village two thousand yards west of La Villa. The road had been deeply cratered, but early that afternoon the patrol reached the village and found it clear. 'A' Squadron moved into the village, and sent a patrol towards Gioiella, two and a half miles to the north-east, and the next town after Lopi on the divisional axis. The patrol moved slowly, clashing occasionally with the retreating Germans, and by nightfall it was still some way from Gioiella.

During the afternoon the King's, with a squadron of Canadian tanks, passed through the Hampshires round Lopi to attack Gioiella. The Germans opened fire on their advance with machine-guns, inflicting casualties, and the fighting became fierce. In a series of checks and advances the battalion pushed on towards a hill five hundred yards south of the town. Here the Germans fought back so stubbornly that the leading companies could move no farther; a fresh fire-plan had to be made, and a new attack mounted. After another hour and a half of hot fighting, the tanks got into the town, with the infantry a little way behind; and after still more fighting the town was taken, and positions in it were consolidated by eleven o'clock that night.

Now that Gioiella was captured, Major-General Ward was ready to pass 10th Brigade through 28th Brigade and towards Casamaggiore. 10th Brigade was then to lead the advance along the divisional axis. The brigade had already moved forward to a concentration area near Strada, and during the morning of June the 27th Brigadier Shoosmith sent forward the DCLI with a squadron of Canadian tanks to pass through the Hampshires at Lopi. The DCLI were strongly opposed in difficult country, and spent two and a half hours forcing their way three or four hundred yards to the floor of the valley beyond Lopi; but during the rest of the day they gained the ridge east of Gioiella, and the cemetery on the next ridge a thousand yards east of Casamaggiore. Around this cemetery the two forward companies and some tanks were firmly in position by nightfall, with a standing patrol between the main positions and Casamaggiore.

Every yard over which the division had advanced since breaking through the Trasimene positions had been fought for, and the Germans clearly meant to put up the stiffest resistance against any further advance. Moreover, the German 1st Parachute Division had been reinforced by 334th Infantry Division, and had narrowed its front accordingly.

June the 28th was a day of hard fighting against fierce opposition and local counter-attacks; there were times when the issue might have been in doubt, but the determination showed by all ranks won the day for 10th Brigade. At dawn the DCLI attacked eastwards from the cemetery towards Casamaggiore, but were held up by heavy machine-gun fire from the town. More tanks of 12th Canadian Armoured Regiment were called up to help, but early in the afternoon the assaulting companies were still held up outside the town.

On the right of 10th Brigade, the Bedfords had attacked before dawn, in bright moonlight. With 'A' and 'B' Companies forward, the battalion moved up to its start-line, the road which ran along the cemetery ridge between Casamaggiore and Fratavecchia. Before reaching the start-line, the leading companies came under heavy fire from artillery and nebelwerfers, and lost a number of men; these included 'A' Company commander, Major Lord Wynford (who had only just arrived from being G S O 2 at Divisional Headquarters and who was severely wounded), and Lieutenant Cox took command of the company. At half-past six in the morning, the leading companies, each with a troop of Sherman tanks, moved north from the start-line towards a ridge midway between the start-line and the road between I Nardelli and Pozzuolo. They met scattered parties of Germans on the way, and occasional snipers and machine-gun detachments; 'A' Company had to clear several small strong-points, including a farm-house garrisoned by a full platoon, the men of which were either killed or captured. 'B' Company suffered severe losses in a sudden clash with enemy infantry, but pushed on to the ridge, and reached it rather to the right of their objective. Major Jenkins then wheeled the company to the left, and approached his objective up the track which ran along the ridge. As the leading platoons moved forward, German machine-guns hidden in buildings nearby opened up with a storm of fire, and a skilfully concealed Tiger tank opened fire from the left. In the confused fighting which followed, two platoons were separated from the rest of the company, and did not reappear until next day; 'B' Company had shrunk to less than thirty men. Major Jenkins therefore decided to join forces with 'A' Company and to hold a farm on the ridge, and visited 'A' Company himself to tell Lieutenant Cox of this decision. Shortly afterwards, the Tiger tank, which had destroyed two of the Shermans, swept the road with machine-gun fire and killed Lieutenant Cox. 'A' Company was now reduced to two officers and forty other ranks. Before the two companies could amalgamate, Germans on the left advanced to counter-attack; they were scattered by artillery fire and disappeared among the gullies in the side of the ridge. The Tiger moved westwards towards the road leading to Pozzuolo, and found a position from which it could fire at the Sherman tanks moving up to support the Bedfords.

All through the day's fighting, artillery observation posts, including those of the 78th Medium Regiment, saw a good deal of enemy infantry and tanks moving about round Pozzuolo and I Nardelli, a mile farther east. 78th Medium Regiment in particular spoilt several attempts by the Germans to destroy the small force of Bedfords in their isolated position. The Germans skilfully outflanked the farm held by the composite company, and assaulted it from only seventy yards away; but the attack was beaten off by fire from every available weapon, and 78th Medium Regiment again brought down defensive fire.

The critical moment in the day's fighting came at about half-past one in the afternoon. The DCLI were held up outside Casamaggiore, pinned down by heavy fire, and needed reinforcement before assaulting the town again. The two forward companies of the Bedfords, reduced to seventy men between them, were on their objective but threatened by counter-attack from I Nardelli, a thousand yards north of their farm. At this moment, however, the 2nd Lancashire Fusiliers of 78th Division, who were advancing on the right, moved forward to a hill a thousand yards south-east of the farm, and engaged the Germans east of it, preventing the attack from I Nardelli from developing. Shortly afterwards, fighter-bombers several times attacked Pozzuolo, in reply to 10th Brigade's request for close air support, while 78th Medium Regiment fired at Germans near the village and south of I Nardelli. This treatment blunted the enemy's enthusiasm, and the situation became comparatively quiet. On the left, Brigadier Shoosmith strengthened the DCLI's positions between the cemetery and Casamaggiore with the remainder of the Bedfords and the reserve company of the DCLI; reinforced their left flank with two companies of the Surreys; and, to the left again, on the outskirts of the town, brought up the fourth company of the DCLI.

Early in the evening of the 28th, the rest of 10th Brigade—two companies of Surreys—attacked Casamaggiore from the south-east, supported by tanks and by an artillery programme which included counter-mortar shooting. The attack went well, and the enemy's opposition slackened and dwindled to sniping. After little more than an hour's fighting, the Surreys entered the town.

During the late evening and the night, the Surreys cleared Casamaggiore of the remaining Germans, and advanced a mile northwards along the Pozzuolo road to a cross-roads half a mile west of the Bedfords' farm. The most difficult part of this operation was clearing the town, which was full of mines and booby-traps. By dawn on June the 29th, a platoon of the Surreys had reached the cross-roads; the DCLI had gathered and consolidated between the cemetery and Casamaggiore; and the rest of the Bedfords joined 'A' and 'B' Companies at the farm.

June the 28th ended badly for the King's. During the night, a strong patrol went out to search a hill north-west of Gioiella. As the patrol approached the hill through a ravine, German machine-gunners on the hill itself and in a farmstead near it opened fire; and at the same time, the company position from which the patrol had come was swept by heavy machine-gun fire. Trapped and cut off from support, the patrol suffered heavy losses; only a sergeant and one man came back. By three in the morning firing had ceased, and further patrols went out to reconnoitre and to bring in the wounded. They drew no fire, and found that five men of the first patrol had been killed, six wounded, and an officer and twelve other ranks were missing. At dawn the patrols moved on to the hill from which most of the fire had come, and found no Germans there.

During the day, Lieutenant-General Kirkman had decided that the 4th Division was not after all to relieve any units of 78th Division, and 4th Division was therefore free to advance on a two-brigade front within its existing boundaries. On June the 29th Major-General Ward brought 12th Brigade up on the left.

From the first, progress on June the 29th was much more rapid than it had been during the sharply contested advances and fierce battalion fights of the day before. On the right, the Bedfords found I Nardelli unoccupied, and pushed on a further two miles before finding the enemy. The battalion then wheeled left and covered a mile more towards the north-west in order to come up on the right of the Surreys.

The Surreys reached Pozzuolo without meeting the enemy, and found the town extensively mined and cratered; the battalion cleared the town, and went on towards Petrignano—slowly, because of the many craters and demolitions on the road. After a mile, they met the Germans again.

In the centre, the West Kents moved off soon after dawn, going north-west from Gioiella. By three in the afternoon, the battalion had advanced seven thousand yards to the north-west of Gioiella, and reached and cleared Laviano, a village a mile east of Pozzuolo. After Laviano the advance became very much more difficult, but the battalion was able to move another two miles to the north before consolidating for the night; meanwhile, the Royal Fusiliers had moved up on the right of the West Kents.

During the night, a few German aircraft machine-gunned roads in the divisional area. The sight of German tracer bullets slanting down in coloured streaks from the dark sky had become unusual; but the German air force was not entering a new phase of activity, and the air attacks continued only for three nights.

10th Brigade on the right, and 12th Brigade on the left, now faced the enemy's delaying positions between Valiano and Petrignano. Major-General Ward decided to see whether the Reconnaissance Regiment alone could break through these positions. In case this was impossible, he ordered 10th and 12th Brigades, each supported by Canadian tanks, to be ready to take over the assault.

At dawn on June the 30th, Lieutenant-Colonel Preston sent two Reconnaissance squadrons through the Surreys towards Petrignano. The patrol on the right was first halted by machine-gun fire a thousand yards south-east of the town, and then, when it tried to press forward, was shelled and mortared. The patrol then turned right, and reached a high point a mile east of the town; it was prevented from going farther by German artillery and machine-guns. The patrol on the left drew fire a thousand yards south-west of Petrignano, wheeled left towards Valiano and was again fired on thirteen hundred yards south-east of this village. Turning left once more, it moved closer to the village until mortar-bombs and machine-gun fire brought it to a halt. For the time being, the Reconnaissance Regiment had done its work, but had yet to suffer a disaster that afternoon. A time-bomb exploded in the house occupied by the regiment's forward headquarters, killing eighteen soldiers and civilians and injuring eight others. Several officers, including Lieutenant-Colonel Preston, had very narrow escapes.

At ten in the morning, the DCLI advanced to attack Petrignano from the east. By noon they had taken a ridge a mile east of the town, but were held up by machine-guns, mortars and a self-propelled gun; a fresh attack arranged for the evening was delayed by heavy fire from mortars and artillery. An hour later, 'A' Company, on their way up to their start-line, met a party of Germans, and after a fight took twenty-six of them prisoner.

By this time, the division had been engaged for more than twelve hours in heavy and confused fighting, and the enemy still showed no signs of withdrawing. Panther and Tiger tanks were moving to the north and west of Petrignano; on the left, the Royal Fusiliers were pinned down a thousand yards south of the town; and on the right the DCLI were faced by a strong force of Germans.

Forty minutes later, the DCLI began their attack, and after a while the enemy in front of them began to thin out. All the available guns fired at retreating vehicles and running men, and shelled the roads leading out of Petrignano. Farther to the left, the Canadian tanks were firing at long range at German lorries. The Germans, however, had left a rear-guard in the town, and machine-gun and mortar fire kept the DCLI back. By nine in the evening, two companies were a few hundred yards away to the east, a third was on a ridge behind these two and the fourth was half a mile farther south.

As night fell, the artillery and mortar fire falling in the DCLI's positions slackened and finally ceased. Just before midnight, patrols reported that numbers of Germans were moving out to the north, and a company moved up to close the exits from the town. Farther to the north, a German ammunition dump blazed all night. At dawn next day the DCLI entered the town unopposed, and found the main street cratered and blocked with debris. During the battle for the town, they had taken seventy-four prisoners, and the Surreys and Bedfords twenty-four between them.

On the left of the DCLI, the Royal Fusiliers had started their attack an hour and a half earlier, and were halted by fierce fire from the ridge six hundred yards south of Petrignano. With the help of a squadron of tanks, the Fusiliers cleared the ridge, but were halted again by fire from the ridge extending westwards from the town, where tanks and anti-tank guns were in position. They were unable to advance farther during the day.

On the left of the Royal Fusiliers, the West Kents were not to move until the Fusiliers had passed Valiano. As the Fusiliers were halted three thousand yards from the village, the West Kents were generally limited to firing mortars and artillery at Germans near Petrignano and Valiano. They were, however, able to push a company forward to the left flank of the Royal Fusiliers.

During the night, patrols reported that the Germans were beginning to withdraw, and lorries could be heard moving away to the north. Early in the morning of July the 1st, a patrol of West Kents entered Valiano, and although the men loosed off a *feu de joie* in the streets the noise drew no reply.

The formations on each flank of the division had kept pace with the advance from Strada. 78th Division on the right was north-east of Petrignano. On the left, 6th South African Armoured Division had come into line with 4th Division, and, after a hard day's fighting on June the 30th, its leading troops had crossed the road running east from Valiano.

In a little more than eight days of fighting, the division had forced its way for more than eight miles through the strong German delaying positions west of Lake Trasimene. The country across which the division had advanced was difficult, the enemy determined, skilful and well armed; the division had lost many men, but gained valuable experience of mobile fighting and equally valuable confidence in its own power to beat the Germans in this kind of warfare.

16. The Arezzo Line

Having pierced the Trasimene Line, XIII Corps took up the pursuit again. For the first days of July, 4th Division was engaged in a running fight, in which most units spent more time in travelling than in fighting. The Germans, falling back as steadily as they could, did their best to delay the advance, leaving behind them obstinate rear-guards of snipers, machine-gunners, anti-tank guns and sometimes tanks. Every defile of any kind—cross-roads, bridges, embankments, narrow streets—was prepared for demolition or cratering by the ingenious German sappers, and every obstacle was sown with mines. Often, however, the speed of the division's advance was such that the Germans had no time to complete their destructive work, and bridges and other vulnerable points were captured intact; or, if the demolition was completed, the Germans were often unable to organize the defence without which no obstacle is much use.

The only really hard fighting on July the 1st took place at Gabbiano, a hamlet on a low hill two and a half miles beyond Petrignano. The Royal Fusiliers found the place strongly defended by machine-guns, mortars and artillery. By nine in the evening, however, the battalion had taken the place and consolidated there. During the approach to the hill, Major Tyndall, commanding 'Z' Company, with Captain P. Hesketh and several other wounded men, were prisoners for a short time when two ambulances missed a turning and drove into the German lines. Fortunately, the German Parachutists were confused by an attack by the Somersets, and the wounded men managed to escape.

Less than a mile to the left of Gabbiano, the West Kents mounted a battalion attack on Fasciano. Lieutenant-Colonel Braithwaite organized a model assault by tanks and infantry, and the village was taken.

The north-westerly direction of the division's advance now led across the canal and the various rivers which run through the Val di Chiana. The nearest bridge, five miles beyond Gabbiano, was blown up by the Germans on July the 2nd as the leading platoons of the West Kents approached it, but the infantry had no trouble in crossing the water-courses, which had little water in them. The town of Foiano, beyond the bridge, might have been made into a strong defensive position if the Germans had been given time to organize a defence of any strength, but by noon the West Kents had cleared the town. The direction of the advance now turned northwards, running parallel with the Val di Chiana, and fanned out to the north-west from Foiano.

Six miles beyond Foiano, the advancing troops found on July the 3rd many half-finished deep gun-emplacements, heaped round with a litter of empty shell-cases and burnt cordite bags. The piles of abandoned material—bricks and mortar, steel girders, heavy timber, rolls of roofing felt, wire fences and notices ordering civilians to keep out—showed that the division had advanced far more quickly than the Germans had expected, and that the arrival of the leading battalions had interrupted the preparation of a formidable defensive position.

The enemy's resistance was beginning to stiffen again, and both the Black Watch and the West Kents had hard fighting short of Badicorte and beyond Marciano, two hamlets four and six miles beyond Foiano. During the night of July the 3rd, however, the Germans withdrew again.

The infantry were now passing through the last of the flat country west of the Val di Chiana and south-west of the town of Arezzo. A few miles farther on, six miles of steep and complicated hills barred the way to the River Arno. Not far away to the right front, the jagged crest which hid the town of Arezzo could already be seen.

The Royal Fusiliers, with a squadron of 14th Canadian Armoured Regiment, passed through the West Kents early in the morning of July the 4th, and soon had reached the foothills beyond the Arezzo-Sansavino road. They climbed some three hundred feet to the hillside village of Oliveto, and there the Germans brought both infantry and tanks to a halt.

The Black Watch also crossed the Arezzo-Sansavino road, and

penetrated rather farther into the hills than the Royal Fusiliers had done. They reached a point not far short of the mountain village of Montealtuzzo, four miles to the south-west of the Fusiliers at Oliveto, before halting for the night. The two battalions were separated by a wide stretch of hilly and wooded country. The Black Watch were not in touch with the troops of 6th South African Armoured Division, who were somewhere on the left, but Major-General Ward had used his liaison officers to maintain contact with the South Africans, and, although the leading battalions were isolated, their advance was being carefully co-ordinated.

During the afternoon of July the 4th, patrols from the Reconnaissance Regiment reached Dorna, down in the valley two miles to the right of the Royal Fusiliers, and early in the evening the patrols handed the hamlet over to the Somersets. To the right of the Somersets, the Hampshires had also crossed the Arezzo-Sansavino road.

Major-General Ward's plan for July the 5th was to send 12th Brigade forward into the hills to the left of Civitella, which stands two miles farther up the spur on which the Fusiliers at Oliveto already had a footing. 28th Brigade was to move into the hills to the right of Civitella. The village, which from a strong natural position looks down on its approaches, would then be cut off.

The Germans, however, had chosen the hills that now faced the division as their next delaying position, and had organized a strong defence there. The division's task was rendered the more formidable by the height and steepness of the hills, and by the lack of adequate roads through them.

At dawn on July the 5th, the King's, with 'A' Squadron, 11th Canadian Armoured Regiment, moved off towards the hills northeast of Dorna, making for the village of Tuori, which like Oliveto stands on the end of a spur jutting out into the plain. Tuori was defended by the Germans, and a sharp fight began; snipers and machine-gunners inflicted losses on the King's, and the German infantry counter-attacked repeatedly. By noon, however, the King's had taken the village, and had a firm hold on it, which almost continual shelling did nothing to loosen.

During the afternoon, Brigadier Montagu-Douglas Scott sent forward a company of the Hampshires with three tanks to take over Tuori from the King's. The King's moved on again, but could not get much farther in daylight because of the enemy's fierce defensive fire. After dark, in spite of counter-attacks, the battalion pushed on; 'A' and 'B' Companies moved up the ridge on which Tuori stands, and 'C' Company advanced along the next ridge to the left, separated from the rest of the battalion by a deep valley.

At dawn on July the 6th, the Somersets, with the three tanks from Tuori, passed through the King's, with 'B' Company on the right-hand ridge and 'A' Company on the left.

The valley which divides the two ridges up which the Somersets were advancing is closed at its farther end by a ridge, along which runs one of the few roads in the neighbourhood. To reach the end of the valley and to close this road were the first objectives of 28th Brigade.

Both companies of the Somersets were fighting hard all day, and by evening 'B' Company on the right-hand ridge was within a short distance of the road. There, however, the company was halted by the intense fire of German guns and mortars. During the evening, 'C' Company of the Somersets, commanded by Major G. G. Blackler, passed through 'B' Company to resume the attack with a new fire-plan. The Germans fought back hard; a self-propelled gun opened fire from the left flank, destroyed a tank and was silenced by the guns of 30th Field Regiment. By ten at night, the Somersets had reached the crest and the road.

'C' Company had some difficulty in holding on to its gains that night. The men were very thin on the ground, and the Germans were both strong and aggressive. Two counter-attacks came in and were beaten off; the first actually reached company headquarters, where it was halted by Major Blackler and his staff at the point of the bayonet.

On the left-hand side of the valley, 'A' Company of the Somersets, commanded by Major Lord Darling, had achieved a similarly pre-carious success. The company had reached the ridge across the end of the valley, and held a hill which looked down on the road beyond. The shelling and mortaring, which had made the winning of this hill a heavy task, disorganized the ration parties, and the company had very little to eat for thirty-six hours. In spite of this, and of the company's weakness and the enemy's fire, the position was held by frequent and active patrolling.

12th Brigade too had begun to advance early in the morning of July the 5th. On the left, the Black Watch moved into Montealtuzzo soon after dawn, and held it for the rest of the day. Since there were frequent reports that there were Germans moving about near Ciggiano, three miles to the east, Lieutenant-Colonel Madden sent some men and tanks to keep the neighbourhood quiet for the next twenty-four hours, while 12th Brigade's attack was being developed.

In the centre of 12th Brigade, the West Kents advanced on San Pancrazio, two miles to the north of Montealtuzzo. The advance was slowed by the steepness and roughness of the going, across which the tanks of 14th Canadian Armoured Regiment could not always keep up with the infantry, and by shelling, machine-gun fire, mortaring and demolitions. By night-fall the battalion had cleared some three miles of country between Montealtuzzo and San Pancrazio, but had not reached the latter village. During the night, both infantry and tanks pushed on a little farther, and next day were able to advance a further thousand yards to Poggio al'Olmo, west of San Pancrazio, before the enemy, who was now fighting hard, made further progress impossible.

On the right of 12th Brigade, the Royal Fusiliers also began to advance at dawn on July the 5th. Two hours later, the leading companies were halted by German infantry and artillery. They tried to get past to the left, but found the Germans strong enough to withstand a battalion attack. When the leading platoons were checked, they were compelled to leave four wounded men lying in the open; small-arms fire prevented the stretcher-bearers from bringing them in. The battalion's chaplain, however, the Reverend P. R. Wansey, openly drove the ambulance jeep up to the men, got them aboard and brought them safely back. While the rest of the battalion dug in under intense fire from mortars and guns, the chaplain walked about among the wounded, dressing wounds, encouraging and comforting the injured men, and organizing their evacuation.

On July the 6th, the battalion tried to push ahead again, and once more the Germans brought the infantry to a halt with the fire of machine-guns, mortars and artillery; they also laid 'S' mines in front of the positions held by the Royal Fusiliers. For the next three days, the battalion could make no further move.

During July the 6th, six RAF Kittyhawks, which had been asked to strafe nebelwerfers west of San Pancrazio, missed their target by six miles, and attacked guns of 77th Field Regiment with machine-guns, cannons and bombs. There were no casualties, which was a relief for the gunners but showed that the destructive effect of air attack on well dug-in positions in difficult country—a form of attack of which 4th Division was making liberal use—should not be rated too highly.

The Black Watch moved forward on July the 7th, dealing with a succession of German defensive positions, sometimes without the help of tanks, and came up on the right of the West Kents to positions seven hundred yards short of San Pancrazio. All three battalions of 12th Brigade were now up against the main German defensive positions in the hills.

The Germans had halted the battalions as it were in mid-stride. As a result, the Royal Fusiliers on the right were separated from the Black Watch in the centre by three miles of wooded and hilly country. The Partisans—who had recently appeared for the first time—and other Italians were constantly reporting the movement of Germans in this gap, where infiltration would have threatened the division's supply routes and gun areas. Major-General Ward therefore placed the Reconnaissance Regiment under the command of Brigadier Heber-Percy, who placed it in the gap.

In the Tuori sector, meanwhile, Major-General Ward had decided to pass 10th Brigade through the Somersets on the ridge at the end of the valley. The Germans, however, with typical tenacity, had hung on between 'A' and 'C' Companies, and, as the Surreys approached the crest just before dawn on July the 7th, they were halted by fierce fire from the front and left front.

The Surreys were to have passed through the Somersets and the King's on the heights round Tuori, and to have pushed on into the hills beyond. Stiff German resistance, however, penned the Surreys in the valley, and for a while the three battalions were mixed up there. During the night of July the 7th, the King's withdrew into reserve, the Surreys regrouped on the right and the Somersets regrouped on the left.

During July the 7th, when the Germans were still expected to continue their withdrawal in front of the division, the guns of 22nd Field Regiment had been brought right forward to support the advance of the Surreys. But when the Germans made a stand on the hills, they could look down on the gun positions, and for twenty-four hours the guns had to be silent. During the night of July the 8th, by which time it was clear that rapid advances were over for the time being, 30th and 77th Field Regiments laid a smoke screen between the Germans and 22nd Field Regiment. Supposing this to be the prelude to an attack, the Germans brought down defensive fire, but 22nd Field Regiment was able to extricate itself, not without loss.

During the night, the DCLI relieved the Surreys, and the Bedfords relieved the Somersets. The Germans were very aggressive indeed all through the night, but the reliefs went off smoothly enough.

During the night of July the 9th, the Surreys took over the right flank of the division from the Hampshires, who had been guarding the flat country west and south-west of Tuori. The Hampshires reported that the road to Arezzo—the town was still firmly held by the Germans—seemed to attract casual traffic. A Canadian jeep had gone racing through towards the German lines before anyone could stop it, and was never seen again. A three-ton lorry, full of South African troops, was turned back just in time, and a British colonel in an Eighth Army Headquarters staff car was at first indignant when the sentries advised him not to drive into Arezzo.

Having been halted by the enemy's main defensive positions, the division settled down to a period of vigorous patrolling. Patrol reports were supplemented by reports from reconnaissance aircraft, escaped prisoners of war, Italian civilians and German prisoners. These reports showed that, behind a screen of small defensive posts which shifted from time to time, the Germans were improving their already strong positions across the whole of the division's sector. The Germans, moreover, were far from passive, and put in several well-organized but unsuccessful attacks.

There were occasional incidents, clashes in the dark, grenade-throwing and raids by both sides. The Black Watch, whose commanding officer had been wounded earlier on, had the additional bad luck of a direct hit on their battalion headquarters; the gunner officer and two signallers were killed, the adjutant was wounded and the wireless sets were wrecked.

The Bedfords caught a German anti-tank gunner, dead drunk. There were reports that German commanders were worried by the increase of drunkenness among their troops, and were threatening offenders with cancelled leave and confiscated 'NAAFI' issues.

The check to the division's advance lasted until early on July the 16th. During the whole of this period, the division's guns and close-support aircraft were continually attacking the enemy's gun areas. There was no certain way of finding out the cumulative effect of this on the German gunners, but the persistence and accuracy of the enemy's artillery fire showed that they were probably as resolute as their infantry, and determined to give them the best possible support.

The enemy's brave defence was sullied by an atrocious massacre in Civitella. The Germans alleged that the Italians had committed hostile acts near the town, and had sniped at two soldiers. During the celebration of the Feast of Saint Peter and Saint Paul, when all the people of the town were at mass, a detachment of SS Troops attached to 1st Parachute Division entered the little town and ordered the congregation to leave the church. The women and children were separated from the men, and sent away. Then the Germans divided the men into groups of five, stood them in front of the church and shot them down with machine-guns; they shot the priest as he came out of the church. They made a crude attempt at cremating the bodies in the market-place; some of the bodies were later found, burned beyond recognition, and others, including that of the priest, were later identified. The Germans then turned from murder to arson, throwing incendiary grenades through the windows of houses. They committed a similar massacre in San Pancrazio, where eighty civilians were killed.

Since all the useful roads of the Arezzo district run through Arezzo itself, the Arezzo Line was to be breached by the capture of the town itself. At one in the morning of July the 15th, 6th Armoured Division (on the right of 4th Division) and the New Zealand Division began their attack. 4th Division's part was diversionary only. By the morning of July the 16th, tanks of XIII Corps were entering the town, and all along the line the German defence began to crumble. The Arezzo Line was breached, and Eighth Army's next objective was Florence.

17. From Tuori to Montevarchi

XIII Corps was now to advance on Florence along the valley of the Arno. 6th Armoured Division would be on the right of the river, and 4th Infantry and 6th South African Armoured Divisions would be on the left. On the right bank, the wild mountains of the Pratomagno rise to more than five thousand feet above the river; the Monti di Chianti on the left are only half as high but are equally rugged.

On its way to the last straight stretch of the Arno that leads to Florence, 6th Armoured Division was to cut across 4th Division's right front, into the tangle of mountains beyond Tuori. 28th Brigade was, therefore, to withdraw from 4th Division's right flank, pass behind the rest of the division, and relieve 12th South African Motor Brigade on the left of 12th Brigade. 4th Division's sector would then be several miles farther to the left, as would that of 6th South African Armoured Division.

28th Brigade made its circuitous march without trouble, and before dawn on July the 15th had relieved the motor brigade. The King's on the right were near Palazzuolo, two miles to the southwest of the Black Watch at Montealtuzzo; the Somersets in the centre held a line through Rapale Birococcoli and Montalto, and the Hampshires on the left held Calsiolo and Villa d'Arceno. The brigade's front was seven miles wide, but there was only one promising road within the sector that led in the right direction—to the north.

The centre of the brigade's positions was eleven miles due south of the town of Montevarchi on Route Sixty-nine, which runs through the Arno valley beside the river. 28th Brigade from the south, and 10th Brigade from the south-east, were to converge on Montevarchi.

From Palazzuolo, a little country road winds its way north-westwards to Montevarchi, through a succession of steep hills and valleys and of dirty villages. Had it not been for the heat, the dust, the demolitions, the diversions and the rough going, the country might have appeared beautiful and the villages picturesque.

The Germans began to withdraw in front of 4th Division before the fall of Arezzo. By six-thirty in the morning of July the 16th, 10th Brigade had cleared the whole of the ridge across the end of the Tuori valley. A mile farther on, the Bedfords had to fight for the next ridge, but had taken it by early afternoon, and advanced another mile before night-fall.

To the north, however, the Germans had not withdrawn from the mountains in the angle between the Canale Maestro della Chiana and the Arno, and 6th Armoured Division, having taken one of the Arno bridges to the north, was not after all to cut across 4th Division's right front. Brigadier Shoosmith, therefore, had to send the Surreys into the hills to clear them. 'A' and 'B' Companies of the Surreys, skirting the foot-hills, made for Chiani, on the canal, three and a half miles north-east of Tuori; and 'C' and 'D' Companies advanced into the hills towards Poggio alle Forche, three and a half miles north of Tuori. By eight-thirty in the morning of July the 16th, both columns had reached their objectives; and since there seemed to be no Germans about, both were withdrawn. Later in the day, however, Germans north of Chiani began sniping at the XIII Corps sappers working on the road, and the Reconnaissance Regiment had to send out a patrol to clear the neighbourhood.

In the centre, meanwhile, the Royal Fusiliers had entered San Pancrazio at dawn on July the 16th, and had learned from the dazed and weary Italians there that the Germans had left during the night. Without much difficulty the battalion went on up the road to the north; two miles farther on, they had some trouble with German machine-guns, and the road was harassed by artillery fire. At Badia Agnano, the sappers had to build a causeway across the ravine for the tanks; the slope beyond was difficult going, but the tanks were still up with the infantry when they reached the hill three-quarters of a mile beyond. On the summit of this hill stands the village of Castiglione Alberti, 12th Brigade's last objective for the time being; and on the slopes behind this village the Royal Fusiliers consolidated undisturbed for the night.

On the left of the division, the King's led 28th Brigade's advance north-westwards from Palazzuolo early in the morning of July the 16th. During the afternoon they passed through Ambra, and on reaching Cennina, six and a half miles beyond Palazzuolo, they drew level with the Royal Fusiliers, who were at Badia Agnano, three miles to the right.

One of the FOOs of 104th Field Battery, Lieutenant B. D. Dudding, was travelling in a Sherman tank with Brigade Headquarters. A little way south of Cennina, the road is cut into the hill-side, and is bounded on the left by a drop of ten feet. The verge crumbled under the weight of the tank, which rolled over the edge and landed upside down, neatly balanced on its turret. Lieutenant Dudding, who had been standing up in the turret, drew his head in quickly enough, but not his fingers, which were firmly gripped between the turret and the soft ground. In this unhappy position, trapped by the fingers in the capsized tank, he stayed for nearly an hour; when at last he was dug out, he found that his fingers were unhurt.

Eventually the enemy appeared again—though not in force—at San Leolino, a mile and a half north of Cennina. 'D' Company of the King's had advanced behind a small patrol commanded by Sergeant C. A. Welsby. After searching miles of hilly and thickly wooded country, the patrol reached a strongly fortified house, occupied by a German observation post. The patrol was quite inadequate for an assault, and might reasonably have waited for the main body of the company before attacking so strong a position. In spite of the odds against them, however, and in spite of their long and exhausting march, the men of the patrol dashed at the house. The Germans inside held them off with small-arms fire; but Sergeant Welsby rushed alone at the front door and burst it in. The Germans surrendered immediately; they included a sergeant-major, a sergeant and two corporals of the Hermann Goerings, and they had about them many useful papers.

When the main body came nearer, two private soldiers of the King's, with Lance-Sergeant Brunt and Gunner Ransome of an FOO party which had been scattered on the way up the hill, walked into San Leolino for a wash at the village pump. They were enjoying their wash when a dirty and untidy individual, dressed in a rudimentary uniform, came up and made sinister gestures at them with a rifle. Surprised, they looked more closely at him, and realized that he was a German who was trying to persuade them that they were his prisoners. One of the privates flung a grenade—without taking out the pin—the German ducked for cover, and the party made briskly for the open country. On the outskirts of the village, they came up with a solitary German loafing along with his rifle slung round his back, and kidnapped him almost without stopping. Incidents of this kind happened from time to time in open, mobile warfare, but were not always brought to so satisfactory a conclusion.

The Germans were frightened out of San Leolino by an impressive display of fire-power, when the fire of a field regiment, a battery of self-propelled guns, several tanks and some medium guns came down in a fire-plan arranged in little more than a quarter of an hour by Lieutenant-Colonel Brocklehurst.

By midnight the King's had covered a further three-quarters of a mile, and consolidated on the high ground between San Leolino and Galatrona, a mile to the north-west.

Early in the morning of July the 17th, a patrol of the Bedfords reached Pergine, three miles to the right of the Royal Fusiliers at Castiglione Alberti. The rest of the Bedfords followed up, and, after being checked for a while three-quarters of a mile farther on by artillery and machine-guns, reached La Querce, three and a half miles beyond Pergine. There was some German opposition there, but with the help of tanks of 12th Canadian Armoured Regiment the battalion crushed it.

By late afternoon, the leading platoons were immediately east of Levane, three-quarters of a mile to the north-west, and the guns of 22nd Field Regiment were firing at opportunity targets round the village. The sappers, however, well forward as usual, had spotted a 'monster task' in a blown bridge on the north-western outskirts, and were eager to get on with it. The fire of the 25-pounders was in the way, and had to be stopped to let the sappers in. The Bedfords concentrated for the night round Levane.

During the morning of July the 17th, the Somersets had gone forward to make a circuit through the difficult country to the left of the positions held by the King's. Late in the afternoon, the leading platoons had reached Mercatale, a village a mile in front of the King's, beyond which the road had been so repeatedly cratered and was in such a state of collapse that no vehicles could pass along it. The battalion consolidated for the night a little way beyond the village.

The Bedfords at Levane were now only three miles from the King's near Galatrona. This convergence of 10th and 28th Brigades pinched out 12th Brigade, which was withdrawn into reserve. The day's advance had made possible the move forward of Divisional Headquarters to the neighbourhood of Dorna.

A move of Divisional Headquarters was not lightly to be undertaken. The headquarters was itself a unit of considerable size, with a long column of cumbersome but essential LCVs and other vehicles. For the purpose of mobile warfare, the headquarters was increased by a crowd of valuable oddments—liaison officers from the divisions on each flank and from 4th Division's own brigades, RAF liaison units, photo-interpretation teams, political warfare officers, 'Phantom' sections and many more. Some of these brought their own vehicles to increase the traffic problem; others relied on the 15-cwts or PUs already with the headquarters, so that there were always some vehicles which went grinding heavily along, piled high with passengers from hub to roof, like a Neapolitan omnibus. Once on the move, therefore, the headquarters took up a great stretch of road for a long time; and, on arrival at its new location, it spread out over a great deal of ground. Since both road space and concealed ground were needed by fighting and administrative units, the disadvantages of a move forward had to be weighed against the importance to the divisional commander of being in close touch with the battle.

Early in the North African campaign, the problem had been solved by the division of the headquarters into 'Main' and 'Rear'. This system remained in effect in Italy, but became more and more difficult to work as the pursuit gathered speed. The theory was that the divisional commander, in his Main Headquarters within easy reach of the fighting units, should have with him only the senior officers of his intelligence and operational staffs; at Rear Headquarters, several miles farther back and therefore out of the way of the fighting units, the administrative staffs continued to supply men and material. The administrative staff, however, felt the lack of that up-to-date information of the battle which is essential to effective administration. The result was that the senior officers of the administrative staff tended to filter forwards into Main Headquarters, leaving behind the Postal Section and the Mobile Bath Unit to be reconciled to each other by the Senior Chaplain.

After a few weeks of mobile warfare, during which Divisional eadquarters had to move sometimes as often as four or five times a week, the drill for movement was perfected. The headquarters was nearly always far enough forward to be 'on top of the battle', but not so far forward as to cumber the fighting troops. Moves took place at the greatest possible speed, and the headquarters occupied a minimum area. Combined with the intelligent use of liaison officers, this quick follow-up did much to maintain friendly relations between the staffs—at both Divisional and Brigade Headquarters— and units, and to dispel the ancient belief that the staff live in a world quite separate from that inhabited by the fighting soldier.

At dawn on July the 18th, the DCLI began to pass through the Bedfords on their way to Montevarchi, three miles beyond Levane. Montevarchi is an attractive town which stretches for more than a mile along Route Sixty-nine, with many pleasant villas and flowering gardens. It is less than a mile from the River Arno; and to the north-west of the town, Route Sixty-nine and the river run side by side towards Florence. 4th Division was not, however, to take the easy road to the city; the division's task was to clear the mountains that rise to the left of the road.

Soon after ten in the morning, the leading platoons reached the outskirts of the town. An hour later, they had made their entry, and were pushing on in spite of some machine-gun fire. The town was not badly damaged, and stood up remarkably well to subsequent shelling. At the southern end, there was a great gap in Route Sixty-nine, where, until a few days before, a bridge had crossed the stream which flows down to the Arno. The bridging of this gap was a heavy and difficult task for the South African sappers working for XIII Corps, and when at last the twenty-five-yard Bailey span was complete they called it—in a phrase which may have been meant to look like Bantu—Twazabuga Bridge.

By early afternoon, the DCLI had pushed the remaining Germans out of Montevarchi, and their patrols were ready to move into the hills to the east of the town. Any further advance, however, was prevented by the fire of artillery and machine-guns, and by salvoes of rockets from nebelwerfers. The Germans were firmly in position on Ricasoli hill, a mile and a half west of Montevarchi, and had plenty of support from heavy weapons. Progress for the time being came to a stop.

At the same time, the Somersets, with 'B' Squadron, 11th Canadian Armoured Regiment, had been approaching Ricasoli from the south. The battalion met German resistance which grew gradually stiffer as it came nearer to Ricasoli. At night-fall, the Somersets consolidated on the main road seven hundred yards south of the hill.

The night was a noisy one, with patrol clashes on the hill-side and defensive fire bursting along the main road. The pitch darkness of the night, and the activity of the German artillery, hampered the movement of essential transport and the vitally important task of making the roads and tracks fit for use. The road between Divisional Headquarters and 10th Brigade Headquarters was blocked by ditched vehicles. One liaison officer, Lieutenant W. G. Alexander, had to leave his motor-cycle and walk three miles—a most unusual event, as liaison officers were chosen rather for their skill on motor-cycles than for their enthusiasm for walking.

The German defences on Ricasoli remained firm until the night of July the 20th, when a patrol from the Somersets found the hill deserted. The Somersets moved on to Ricasoli at dawn on July the 21st, and the Hampshires occupied the next hill, three-quarters of a mile to the west. Two hours later, 10th Brigade, led by the Surreys, began the advance again.

18. From Ricasoli to Gaville

For a week after the capture of Ricasoli, the pace of the division's advance was conditioned by stubborn enemy opposition to 10th Brigade along Route Sixty-nine, and by the difficulties of opening 28th Brigade's main axis of advance through the hilly and difficult country three miles farther to the west. The division advanced slowly, but by July the 22nd had covered enough ground for Divisional Headquarters to come forward to Montevarchi.

During this week, 1st Canadian Armoured Brigade, which had been fighting beside the division's infantry since the first attack on the Trasimene Line, was withdrawn and placed under the command of 8th Indian Division. It was replaced by 25th Army Tank Brigade, which had fought with 4th Division in earlier battles. 51st Royal Tanks were affiliated to 10th Brigade, 142nd RAC to 12th Brigade, and the North Irish Horse to 28th Brigade. 98th (Self-propelled) Field Regiment was replaced by 142nd (Self-propelled) Field Regiment.

These were not the only departures from the division. Lieutenant-Colonel G. A. Thomas relinquished the appointment of GSO 1, which he had held for nearly fifteen months, on his appointment as BGS Eighth Army. Lieutenant-Colonel D. Peel Yates, who had been GSO 2 of 4th Division in Scotland, came to take his place. Not long afterwards, Brigadier Montagu-Douglas Scott left 28th Brigade to take over command of 1st Guards Brigade. He was replaced by Lieutenant-Colonel Preston, promoted from command of the Reconnaissance Regiment, which was taken over by Lieutenant-Colonel A. C. S. Delmege.

The Hampshires were withdrawn from the line to Monte Sansavino. As soon as they arrived, they began to smarten up their uniforms 'for a visit by the Commander-in-Chief'. Two days later, in the bright sunshine of the July morning, the battalion held a ceremonial parade, at which His Majesty the King decorated Captain Wakeford with the Victoria Cross he had won at the Gustav Line. His Majesty then drove down a road lined by detachments from all arms of the 4th Division. The same evening, the Hampshires concentrated in readiness to return to the line.

Early in the morning of July the 20th, the Surreys went forward to clear the rough country west of Route Sixty-nine. They deployed to cross Ricasoli hill, met the Germans on the other side, and three hours after starting had fought their way on to Passelli hill, a mile away to the north-west. There they swung right towards Montecarlo hill, a mile away. The Germans here fought back fiercely, but the Surreys mounted a battalion attack and took their objective during the afternoon.

The hill had been held by a rear party from the Hermann Goering Division. There was an infantry platoon under an experienced regular sergeant, whose orders were to cover the withdrawal of the main body by holding on as long as he could in safety; and there were two F O Os, one serving the divisional artillery and the other a mortar regiment. The sergeant saw the Canadian tanks coming, and very properly decided to withdraw his platoon. The German gunner officer, however, wanted to stay, and, needing the protection of the infantry, assured the sergeant that the position was safe for another twenty-four hours. Less than three hours later, the Surreys took the whole party by surprise, shooting two of the Germans and capturing the two officers and forty other ranks.

The Surreys cleared Montecarlo hill, and sent a company to take Castelvecchio hill, a thousand yards to the west. At the end of the day, the battalion had a firm hold on all three hills.

The stiff resistance which the division had just met had been on one of many delaying positions, along which the Germans hoped to delay the advance to Florence of XIII Corps. Each line of these positions was known by a girl's name; at Ricasoli, the division had passed through the Irmgard Line, and it was now approaching the Karin Line.

The next few miles of the advance, between lines, were not particularly hard going. During July the 21st, the Hampshires cleared three miles of road westwards from Ricasoli as far as Cavriglia, and reached Castelnuovo, two miles farther to the north-west.

At dawn on July the 21st, the Bedfords advanced up the main road from Montevarchi, with the leading company riding on tanks. A mile from San Giovanni, three and a half miles up the road, 'D' Company, which was in the lead, turned to the left off the main road to clear the high ground in front of the Surreys on Montecarlo and Castelvecchio hills. The fire of German guns and mortars began to fall near the infantry, and hastened their advance into the hills. The company had crossed the front of the Surreys before the German fire brought it to a halt. The country was difficult, and the infantry had been hurrying; the company commander was not sure of the map reference of his position. He chose from the map a hillock which he reckoned he should be able to see, and sent a radio message to 22nd Field Regiment to put down a few rounds on it. Within a few minutes the first shells whistled down and burst among his own men, fortunately without doing any harm. He was then able to report his position with some accuracy.

'A' and 'B' Companies meanwhile were advancing one on each side of the main road, while the supporting tanks drove down the middle of the road in case of mined verges. The two companies fought their way forward until they were halted by heavy fire at the stream which runs through the south-eastern outskirts of San Giovanni. The whole battalion had now come to a halt, and consolidated. 'D' Company in the hills could not be reached by supply parties, and had to make do with what they were carrying.

Early on July the 22nd, the Hampshires, with 'C' Squadron of the North Irish Horse, moved off from Castelnuovo, towards Meleto, a mile and a half to the north-east, and three miles to the west of San Giovanni on Route Sixty-nine. Meleto stands in the centre of a ridge, looking down on the wide shallow valley through which the Hampshires had to approach. The Germans had not neglected this promising defensive position, and machine-guns all along the ridge opened fire as soon as the Hampshires were within range. At one in the afternoon, the two leading companies of the Hampshires were about half-way up the ridge. One was near the road leading into Meleto; the other was half a mile to the left, advancing against German positions round a weed-grown cemetery and a farm in which a tank was emplaced.

In spite of extremely heavy fire from the enemy's guns and nebelwerfers, both companies reached the crest of the ridge during the afternoon. Private Alan Churchill of 13 Platoon, though a small man and weighed down by a heavy Bren gun, was well up in the leading wave of the assault. When the company had reached the crest of the ridge, a German counter-attack came in from the left flank, bringing with it a machine-gun which raked the Hampshires from only a hundred yards away. Private Churchill, still with his Bren gun, crept to within thirty yards of the machine-gun, then charged across the open, firing from the hip. When he rejoined his platoon, he was leading four large Germans.

The commander of 13 Platoon was wounded during the assault, and Sergeant John Savage took charge. He led the platoon with such fury, up the steep hill-side and through the fire of artillery and machine-guns, that he overran the German defenders, killing and capturing as he went. When he reached the crest, he saw beyond it a Mark Four tank and an 88-mm gun, and led his panting men on to capture both. By this time, 13 Platoon and the platoon on its flank were reduced to ten men each and had no officer between them. Sergeant Savage reorganized the little force, consolidated on the ridge, and five minutes later he and his twenty men scattered twice their number of counter-attacking Germans.

The Germans, however, still held Meleto itself, and Brigadier Preston brought up the King's to attack it next day if necessary. The attack was not needed, as the Germans retreated from the village during the night, maintaining their hold only on the ridge to the east of the village. A company of the King's tried to clear this part of the ridge during the night, but was driven back. The northern exits from the village were being closely watched by the German gunners, and the King's were unable to move beyond the village during July the 24th.

After dark, the Somersets relieved the Hampshires, and at dawn on July the 25th attacked north-westwards from the ridge to the left of the village. The Germans put up no serious opposition, but the country was extremely difficult for both infantry and tanks, and progress was slow. During the afternoon, however, the Somersets reached Gaville, another village on a ridge, two miles north-west of Meleto. There was some resistance in Gaville, and the battalion took fourteen prisoners and silenced several machine-guns.

The King's, meanwhile, had been covering the gun positions of 30th Field Regiment and guarding the sappers and working parties opening the road between Meleto and Gaville. This kind of protection was essential in rapid movement through close country, where a whole battalion of Germans might be hidden down a side-road by-passed by the pursuing infantry. During the day, the King's found that the Germans had withdrawn from the eastern end of the Meleto ridge.

Having pierced the Karin Line at Meleto, 28th Brigade was now moving comparatively easily, though the roads were narrow and tortuous, and the German demolitions and mines were everywhere.

To the right of 28th Brigade, 10th Brigade had meanwhile been in contact with the eastern flank of the Karin Line, where it rested on the Arno at San Giovanni. The north-western advance of 28th Brigade from Meleto had begun to widen the gap which already lay between the two brigades. Major-General Ward therefore placed the Reconnaissance Regiment under the command of 28th Brigade, and sent the regiment to Cavriglia to stop the gap. Armoured car patrols searched the country between Meleto on the left and San Giovanni on the right, and had some skirmishing at San Cipriano, between the two places.

On July the 21st, while 28th Brigade was advancing on Cavriglia, 10th Brigade had been pinned down in front of San Giovanni. There was still some shelling on July the 22nd, but the situation seemed less forbidding. To the right, beyond the Arno, 6th Armoured Division were well forward, and on the left the Hampshires were beginning to outflank San Giovanni by getting on to the Meleto ridge. The Bedfords had some fighting on the outskirts of the town during the evening, but during the night the usual flashes in the night sky and reverberating explosions showed that the Germans were blowing up bridges across which they had withdrawn.

At dawn of July the 23rd, 'A' and 'B' Companies of the Bedfords, commanded by Major Hollick DSO, of 'A' Company, went forward to occupy San Giovanni. All went well until the infantry began to emerge from the far end of the town, when they were halted by a storm of German shells fired at point-blank range. For the rest of the day, the two companies had to hold on under heavy fire from German guns and mortars.

July the 24th was quieter, since an early-morning counter-battery shoot by the divisional artillery had diminished the enthusiasm of the German gunners. The Germans, however, had blown the bridges on Route Sixty-nine just beyond the town, and were guarding the demolitions. The Bedfords made no move during the day, but

Battalion Headquarters moved up into one of the brick factories in the town.

At dusk, 'C' Company went out to hold the Vacchereccia ridge to the west, between San Giovanni and Meleto. 'D' Company, which had moved across the front of the Surreys three days earlier, had already moved into reserve behind San Giovanni, and the Surreys were also in reserve.

During the night of July the 25th, the Bedfords were warned that an enemy wireless message had been overheard, in which the Germans mentioned their intention to raid the brick factory during the night. Battalion Headquarters was in a brick factory; the Germans had seen the move in, and had shelled the place. The situation was particularly delicate because a hundred men were away from the battalion on the occasion of the royal visit to the division; and the Special Mission Patrol, which might otherwise have been used for local defence, had relieved a platoon of Major Hollick's force at the far end of the town. The factory was too big to be defended by the available force, but a defence of the rooms used as living quarters was organized, and the Carrier Platoon was brought in to reinforce the garrison. The defenders waited until dawn; nothing happened.

At dawn of July the 26th, a patrol led by Lieutenant Robson found that the Germans had moved into a brick factory at the northern end of the town, near where they had seen some of Major Hollick's men emerge from the town three days earlier. While Battalion Headquarters was tensely waiting for them at one brick factory, the Germans had put in a determined raid on the other, and had found it empty.

On the right of the division, the advance seemed to be over for the time being, though the enemy made small local withdrawals. Early in the afternoon of July the 27th, the Reconnaissance Regiment relieved the Bedfords, who withdrew to Montevarchi. The town was an ideal rest centre for a forward area; it was bigger and in better condition than any other town taken by the division on its way to Florence. Roses and many other bright flowers were blossoming in the neat gardens; and when German guns could no longer reach the place, attractive girls reappeared there with the rest of the townsfolk.

19. The Chianti mountains

Having pierced two lines of delaying positions at Ricasoli and Meleto, the division was now approaching a third and far more formidable task. The Germans were still withdrawing unhurriedly towards their main defensive position—the Gothic Line behind Florence; but they were always ready to fight hard if they were forced to withdraw too fast, or if the alignment of their battalions was threatened by a sudden thrust.

Early on July the 25th, the corps commander gave orders that 4th Division's front was to extend three miles farther to the left. This meant that the sector was to include a stretch of country completely dominated by the Chianti mountains, which rise to a height of more than two thousand five hundred feet. Gaville, which 28th Brigade had already reached, lies at the foot of the highest, steepest and most rugged of these mountains; between Pavelli and the Arno near Florence, twelve miles away, a chain of heights looks down on all the roads that approach the city from the south and south-east. From all parts of the mountains that form this range, innumerable streams and ravines run down towards the roads which thread their way through the valleys and among the foot-hills. Stream joins stream, tributary flows into tributary, and even from the western side of the great watershed the streams twist round the mountains to flow eastwards into the Arno.

Heavy fighting among these mountains was clearly to be expected. Major-General Ward therefore planned to exert the division's main effort on the left and to hold on the right, where the advance of 6th Armoured Division along the farther bank of the Arno would probably drive the Germans back along Route Sixty-nine. On the right, the Reconnaissance Regiment was to continue to hold San

Giovanni, and was to patrol along the main road as the enemy withdrew. With two troops of 51st Royal Tanks, the regiment was also to patrol the rough country between the main road and 28th Brigade's right flank. 28th Brigade was to advance along the country road that winds across the eastern foot-hills of the mountains, while on the far side of the mountain range, and between three and four miles away, 12th Brigade was to follow a parallel road. 28th Brigade's axis was to be known as Red Route, that of 12th Brigade as Blue Route. The direction of the advance would continue to be north-west, following the grain of the country.

During the evening of July the 25th, the Black Watch, the first battalion of 12th Brigade into action, dismounted from their lorries at the village of Lucolena, behind the new front. Next day, the battalion began its advance, for once without the tanks, which had been held up by traffic jams on the narrow country roads. The companies crossed the road between Ponte agli Stolli and Dudda which runs across the foot of the mountains. Beyond the road, the infantry began their long climb, against desultory opposition. By the end of the day, 'B' and 'D' Companies had cleared the Poggio del Piano ridge, and 'D' Company had reached its crest, a mile and a half beyond the road and a thousand feet higher. 'A' Company cleared the Castello ridge, north-west of Dudda, and nearly five hundred feet lower. During the day's fighting, the commanding officer, Lieutenant-Colonel B. J. G. Madden DSO, who had been wounded several times before, was wounded yet again. So far he had always managed to get back to his battalion, but this time he had to leave it permanently when he was sent home a few weeks later. Major G. McP. Smith, the second-in-command, took over command of the battalion.

Meanwhile, the rest of 12th Brigade had been moving up. The troops could reach the new sector only by an inadequate country road, which soon began to crumble under the weight of traffic. As the column approached Lucolena, which was already crowded with troops of 24th Guards Brigade, which 12th Brigade was to relieve, the amount of traffic and confusion on the road grew worse and worse. The last straw was added when German guns began to shell the village while the West Kents were dismounting from their lorries.

The movement of the brigade's ponderous armoured command vehicle in rough country was always difficult. On one advance it had to be dragged forward by a Sherman tank. This time it swerved up a road-side bank and turned a complete somersault off the road. The brigade major, Major Gordon Black, and the driver were the worst injured of the seven men inside, and both had to be evacuated immediately.

By early afternoon of July the 26th, however, the West Kents, commanded by Lieutenant-Colonel H. P. Braithwaite, were in action, and six of the tanks had been able to find their way through a series of traffic jams to join the infantry.

The West Kents were to advance along the road that runs north-west from Dudda, and to take the village of Cintoia Alta, two miles beyond. The road approaches Cintoia Alta through a deep gorge, and rises to the village which stands on a ridge at the end. The place was a miniature citadel, but the clever co-operation between infantry and tanks proved too much for the Germans, and by midnight the West Kents had cleared the village.

The West Kents and the Black Watch were now well forward among the heights that dominate the country-side. Major-General Ward therefore planned that on July the 27th the two battalions should clear the highest peaks in the area, which looked down on both Red and Blue Routes. Once these heights were clear, the division could advance round the mountains.

Early in the morning of July the 27th, the West Kents moved out of Cintoia Alta along the road that leads into the mountains to the north-east. The ground was difficult and strewn with mines, but at first there was no resistance. By mid-morning, tanks and infantry—some of the infantry had ridden up on the tanks—had reached the summit of the battalion's first objective, the hill on which stands the rambling, thick-walled Fattoria di Monte Scalari. The West Kents were now more than two hundred and fifty feet higher than the Black Watch on Poggio del Piano, a mile to the south-east.

'D' Company made a move towards Monte Moggio, an equally high point three-quarters of a mile to the north-west, but German defensive positions checked the company sharply four hundred yards short of the summit.

The battalion's next objective was to be the highest peak of all—that of Monte Scalari, or Point 788, two thousand yards to the north-east, and nearly three hundred feet higher than the Fattoria.

Early in the afternoon, 'A' and 'B' Companies began to move along the track leading up the mountain-side. Almost at once they came under heavy fire from Monte Moggio on the left flank and from La Beccheria (Point 770) straight ahead, and they lost a number of men in the fire of artillery, mortars and machine-guns. They had difficulty in getting forward, but by evening were well forward on the slopes of Point 770, and on the saddle that runs south-eastwards from it to Monte Scalari. They were actually within seven hundred yards of the summit, but there they were halted by the enemy's defensive fire.

During this attack, two tanks on a narrow mountain track crushed between them the carrier in which Captain John Chinery of 77th Field Regiment was riding with his party. Captain Chinery transferred his wireless set to a tank, but the set was dropped on the way and stopped working. Since he was out of touch with his guns, he left his party and went forward to join the commander of the infantry company with which he was working. The company commander was right forward under heavy fire, cheering his men forward and urging on a reluctant tank. When the company reached the ridge, its commander was wounded, and Captain Chinery got him back under cover of the tank. The crew could not hear him over the thunder of the engines, and the two men were nearly poisoned by the exhaust fumes. Eventually Captain Chinery was able to move the wounded man away and have him evacuated; and then, although he had been himself wounded while directing the fire of the tank from an exposed position, he took over command of the company while it consolidated, arranged the necessary defensive fire, and stayed there until an infantry officer came to relieve him. Before going back, he visited the other companies to tell them about the defensive fire tasks he had arranged, and was finally evacuated six hours after being wounded.

During the fighting round Point 770, Lieutenant Folkard of 'A' Company took a small reconnaissance patrol to investigate a gully, and was ambushed by the Germans. They shot his batman and took the officer prisoner, but forgot to search him before leading him back. Shortly afterwards, a concentration of 25-pounder shells came down all around them; in the confusion Lieutenant Folkard drew his pistol, shot one of the Germans and escaped. He made his way back to the company, and was able to give some information about the German forward positions.

Early in the morning of the same day, the Royal Fusiliers had ridden in lorries as far as Cintoia Alta. By noon the battalion was advancing along the road from Cintoia Alta towards Cintoia, which lies at the foot of the south-western slopes of Monte Moggio. By early evening the village was clear, and the Royal Fusiliers were passing through it.

Before the road which leads on towards Florence could be used, the battalion had to clear the Bosco di Fuoco ridge, which looks down on the road from three-quarters of a mile north of Cintoia. The troops climbed the hill-side to the crest without trouble, and at dusk a company was able to advance along the road towards Mugnana, a mile beyond Cintoia.

On the other side of the mountains, 28th Brigade had begun to advance at the same time in the morning of July the 27th as 12th Brigade. The Somersets on the left had advanced up Red Route without much trouble, and had reached San Andrea, a mile and a half to the north of Gaville, and just over two miles from the Black Watch on Poggio del Piano. The King's had patrolled as far as Pavelli, half a mile to the north-east of Gaville, and had searched the country on the right flank without finding any Germans. Farther to the right still, the Reconnaissance Regiment had sent patrols towards the flank of 28th Brigade, and had found one or two machine-guns near the farthest point reached by the patrols from the King's.

Although at dusk on July the 27th the West Kents had seemed likely to reach the peak of Monte Scalari, the enemy's defensive fire had inflicted heavy losses on the advancing companies, and had held them back. When during the night the battalion tried to move in the other direction from Point 770, towards the Casa Pian della Vite, fifteen hundred yards to the north-west, it met equally stiff resistance from German infantry, supported by machine-guns and mortars. The West Kents put in a second attack soon after dawn, and again were beaten off.

The Royal Fusiliers had been under fire for most of the night, and at dawn of July the 28th were still several hundred yards short of Mugnana. Every time they tried to move on, they were pinned down by the fire of the German guns and mortars. They managed to clear the last slopes of Monte Collegale, which from the south looks down on the village; but the Germans forced them back from the high ground on the other side, from which there was equally good observation.

6th South African Armoured Division on the left was also held up by a stubborn German defence.

Brigadier Heber-Percy decided that to end the deadlock he would have to bring up his reserve battalion. The West Kents were to attack Monte Scalari, and the Black Watch were then to come up from the south and pass through them and along the crest of the range to take Pian della Vite. The Royal Fusiliers were to advance half a mile farther north-east up the Bosco di Fuoco ridge. From their objective, they would be able to support the Black Watch's advance from Pian della Vite to the mountain village of Linari, which looks down on San Polo, more than five hundred feet below—on 28th Brigade's axis.

Soon after nine in the morning of July the 28th, the West Kents began to advance towards Monte Scalari, slowed down by mines and other difficulties. The enemy's defensive fire was still heavy and galling, and self-propelled Bofors guns of 91st Light Anti-aircraft Regiment were brought up the mountain-side to smash up a tower on Point 762, half a mile to the north-west, from which the enemy's fire was probably being directed. This shoot was highly spectacular, and very satisfactory to the gunners, who had too few opportunities of showing what their mobile, quick-firing guns could do.

As the afternoon drew on, the West Kents seemed to have less and less chance of taking the height. There appeared to be no Germans on the mountain-side, but the enemy's resistance from positions which had been hidden until then was growing stiffer, and heavy defensive fire was coming from Pian della Vite, behind the advancing infantry. Finally the infantry withdrew to defensive positions at the Casa al Monte, between Point 770 and Monte Scalari, on Point 770 itself and on Point 762.

The Royal Fusiliers meanwhile had started to advance farther up the Bosco di Fuoco ridge. The Italian words mean Forest of Fire; the steep, rocky hill-side was covered with scrubby bushes and trees. As the Fusiliers advanced, the name of the place became apt indeed, for fire broke out among the bushes, spread widely, fanned by breezes which favoured the enemy, and swept down on 'Y' Company. The two forward platoons were cut off by the fire and by the Germans following it up, and lost touch with the rest of the battalion. All four of 'Y' Company's stretcher-bearers were captured by the Germans, and other men had to be detailed to collect the wounded. One of the men detailed was Fusilier T. Memory, who, although himself severely wounded in two places, refused to leave a badly wounded comrade, and, in spite of constant small-arms fire, managed to get him back to the regimental aid post. 'Y' Company was compelled to withdraw, and the village of Cintoia, completely overlooked by the Germans who had advanced behind the flames, became untenable. The Royal Fusiliers withdrew from the village up the hill-side on the other side of the road, and took up defensive positions on the ridge north-west of Monte Collegale. Late that night, the two missing platoons of 'Y' Company rejoined the battalion, having fought their way out, bringing with them most of their wounded.

The West Kents were still making efforts to reach Monte Scalari, and on the other side of the peak 28th Brigade were fighting for Santa Lucia, a mile up the hill-side from San Andrea and a mile and a half south-east of the summit. Brigadier Heber-Percy was hoping that 28th Brigade would be able to push northwards from Santa Lucia, so that the German defenders round Monte Scalari would have to retreat from the closing jaws of the trap; and Brigadier Preston was hoping that the 12th Brigade would be able to capture Monte Scalari, since the summit overlooked 28th Brigade's axis almost as far back as Montevarchi.

To resolve this deadlock, Brigadier Heber-Percy brought the Black Watch into action in an attack on Point 731, a thousand yards west of Point 770. 'C' Company, commanded by Captain P. Hutchison, advanced into the valley below the Fattoria, and met fierce opposition from Germans of whom some appeared for the first time on Point 731 itself. The company could not reach the crest, but dug in three hundred yards farther down. Captain Hutchison was wounded and had to hand over to Captain W. A. B. Callander; by the end of the battle 'C' Company was still in position, though only two officers and forty men were left.

12th Brigade could advance no farther to the north-west until the mountains were cleared. The Germans clearly meant to defend every individual height; and the only way their defence could be shaken was to loosen its keystone, Monte Scalari. Brigadier Heber-Percy, therefore, ordered the Black Watch to sweep the Germans off the summit at once.

'A' and 'B' Companies prepared to make the new attack, under the command of Major Lord Douglas Gordon, the senior company commander, who had led the force of two companies since the attack on the Poggio del Piano. The force was to attack straight across the valley from the Fattoria.

The mountain slopes on which the battle was fought are covered for the most part by thick woods of oak and fir, and by a thick undergrowth of bushes and bracken which hides outcrops of rock. The outlines of the hills are rounded rather than jagged and precipitous; but the gullies and ravines which run down from every summit could not be crossed by tanks, and were difficult going for the infantry. German tanks were reported in the neighbourhood, but the Germans made no use of armour in such forbidding country. The tanks of 142nd R A C, on the other hand, were most effective in their attacks on German infantry who were unprepared for the appearance of tanks on mountain-tops.

The two companies advanced steadily across the valley towards the first height they could see, without meeting any opposition. A troop of Churchill tanks moved off with them, but was soon held up by mines on the track, and had to wait while Sergeant Bonella and his pioneers cleared a path for them. When the leading infantry were half-way up the hill-side, machine-guns in front and on both flanks suddenly opened fire, and pinned them to the ground. Throughout this mountain fighting, the Germans made good use of surprise, holding their fire until the last possible moment. Some of the Black Watch, however, got round the edge of a wood on the right flank, and the infantry reached the first height. This was not Monte Scalari, but a hillock half a mile to the south-west of it. Darkness had fallen, and the Black Watch consolidated for the night. There was some mortaring by the Germans during the hours of darkness, and some skirmishing with parties of Germans lurking among the trees, but otherwise the night was fairly quiet.

At dawn of July the 29th, Major Gordon's force went forward again towards the next crest, known as Ring Contour, half-way between the hillock and Monte Scalari. The fighting was close and confused; the Germans, as usual, had left the woods infested with small groups of snipers armed with light machine-guns. One platoon of the Black Watch set off for the right flank, to give covering fire, ran into a group of snipers and lost some men before killing five Germans and smashing their machine-gun; a second platoon was halted among the trees, and lost nine men. During this close and savage fighting, one platoon sergeant all but trod on a machine-gun and its German crew among the bushes; his tommy-gun jammed at the critical moment, and the three Germans were able to scurry away among the trees.

This kind of skirmishing was unlikely to achieve a decisive result. The country was close, the Germans were determined, and the Black Watch were weary and had had neither food nor sleep since the day before. Major Gordon had to decide whether to consolidate on the ground his force had already won, or to mount a fresh attack in spite of the difficulties. He decided to attack once more, and sent back a request for tanks.

Three Sherman tanks were sent off to give covering fire from hull-down positions on Point 762, a mile to the left. Three Churchill tanks, with supplies and a reinforcement platoon from 'D' Company, were sent to join the infantry, running the gauntlet of enemy fire and snipers. Two of the Churchill tanks broke down on the rough ground. The third was led up by the troop commander, Lieutenant Howe, who walked in front of it and guided it round the outcrops of rock. Having delivered the tank's load, he led it back and ferried forward the most essential supplies—ammunition and water—from the other two tanks.

Soon after noon, the attack on the crest went in. 'A' Company, commanded by Captain J. Macdonald, assaulted through a wood on the left, supported by the fire of the Churchill and of 'B' Company on the right, and by the troop of Shermans on the left flank. The startled Germans were driven back with loss, and Ring Contour was taken.

As the Black Watch consolidated on Ring Contour, they saw that only a quarter of a mile of broken ground lay between them and the summit of Monte Scalari. Yet once more the weary but determined infantry prepared to attack, and yet once more they went on—and with them went the Churchill tank. Captain Macdonald, perched high up on the tank's turret, directed its fire in support of his men; he was blown off by the blast of mortar bombs, but climbed back again to fight on. Exhausted, the Black Watch drove themselves forward, and at last staggered on to the hard-won summit. They had taken Monte Scalari, and loosened the keystone of the whole German defence.

The tank went back for essential maintenance. The evening drew in, and mist began to gather among the shadows. The tired men on the hill-side prepared for the German counter-attack that was sure to come. Since the gunner observation officer had been wounded the day before, Major Gordon arranged the defensive fire by wireless with Lieutenant-Colonel G. McP. Smith at the Fattoria.

The mist grew thicker, and light faded from the sky. Soon after dark the German infantry came suddenly racing in at the Black Watch. The defensive fire fell short; this was bad enough for the Black Watch, but far worse for the Germans, who were in the open. Many of the shells hit trees and burst above ground-level, showering splinters of steel on the attackers. The Germans penetrated the Black Watch's positions, but they were thrown out again.

An hour later, a second headlong counter-attack came in, and once more the Germans were beaten off. Under cover of these attacks, some enemy snipers tried to work round the flank and towards the rear of the defenders, but the main effort was a surge of charging infantrymen who tried to sweep over the positions. The fire of the Black Watch cut down scores of Germans making these frontal attacks.

During the night, a party of porters arrived with a hot meal and other supplies, having been sniped at on the way up. Major Gordon decided that the situation was too menacing for relaxation, kept every man alert all night and left the meal in its containers until it could be safely issued. Ammunition was getting low, and a sergeant went back from the positions on Monte Scalari to Ring Contour to bring up more. He rejoined the forward platoons at dawn on July the 30th. Five minutes later, just after the ammunition had been issued, the third and last counter-attack came in, and was thrown back.

A number of German snipers, however, still lurked among the trees, and shells and mortar bombs were bursting among the Black Watch's positions. The Germans had ranged their guns carefully on Ring Contour, and the platoon there suffered gravely. The Germans held their positions beyond the summit of Monte Scalari; after the battle, a tour of the mountain showed that the two Black Watch companies had held positions on one side of the summit, and on the other side were positions which had been occupied by two Grenadier Companies of the 356th Division, one of the best German infantry divisions in Italy.

Breakfast came up with the tanks early in the afternoon. One of the Churchills was knocked out on the way up by a German with a bazooka, but the other silenced the German snipers with occasional bursts of machine-gun fire into the woods.

At dusk, another porter-party came up with a hot meal, and the supply of Major Gordon's force became normal. Both sides had suffered severely in the hard-fought battle. Captain Fotheringham, second-in-command of 'A' Company, was killed on July the 30th, after having been wounded and staying in action; Lieutenants Spurell, Poynting and Drysdale were wounded and evacuated; one platoon of 'A' Company was eight private soldiers strong when it was relieved. This was only part of the price paid by 12th Brigade for Monte Scalari.

Three days earlier, Brigadier Preston had given orders that the Somersets were to hold firm in their position round San Andrea, while the Hampshires passed through and took the road that twists across the mountain-side to Poggio alla Croce, a mile north of Monte Scalari and more than seventeen hundred feet lower.

At dawn on July the 28th, the Hampshires, who had already concentrated near Gaville, moved forward. As the leading company began to pass through the positions held by the Somersets, mortar bombs began to burst among the infantry. The enemy fire was clearly being directed from Santa Lucia, a mile up the hill-side, and Lieutenant-Colonel Mitchell sent 'B' Company up the hill-side to clear the hillock. The company was met by intense fire from mortars and machine-guns; the company commander was killed, and the wrecking of the Number 18 wireless set cut off the only means of communication with Battalion Headquarters. The company pushed on, and forced a German platoon back, but was eventually halted four hundred yards short of the objective. The Germans facing the company had in fact been reinforced the night before by about a hundred fresh troops who had left Germany only two weeks earlier.

For some time, Battalion Headquarters could gather news of the attack only from the wounded men who were being brought in from the hill. Later on, however, communications were reopened through the wireless set of 111th Field Battery, and Lieutenant-Colonel Mitchell decided to add 'A' Company to the force attacking Santa Lucia.

'A' Company worked round to the left of 'B' Company, and was closing in on the objective when German machine-guns suddenly opened a fierce fire. The company, however, broke through the defence, and reached the hillock late in the afternoon, with the loss of one man wounded. The company was now a little more than a mile and a half south-east of the summit of Monte Scalari.

The rest of 28th Brigade made little move during the day. During the afternoon, a patrol found no Germans on the road between

Gaville and Figline Valdarno, the next town on Route Sixty-nine after San Giovanni; and late in the evening a patrol went up the main road and found Figline clear.

The Reconnaissance Regiment had no difficulty in occupying Figline next day, July the 29th. Opposite the Somersets, however, the Germans were holding San Martino, three-quarters of a mile to the right of Santa Lucia.

During the afternoon, 'D' Company of the Hampshires began to move up the ridge from Santa Lucia towards Point 531, six hundred yards nearer Monte Scalari. The Germans, however, were heavily armed and had a good field of fire, and Lieutenant-Colonel Mitchell had to postpone the attack.

At dawn of July the 30th, 'D' Company attacked again, and after a short fierce fight took Point 531.

Red Route was no use to 28th Brigade until the heights above it had been cleared. When the King's took up the advance, therefore, their first objective was the Pian d'Albero, the plateau between Santa Lucia and Monte Scalari.

The King's passed through the Hampshires at midday, and climbed slowly upwards against resistance from the Germans on the heights. By the end of the day they had reached the Pian d'Albero.

At dawn of July the 31st, Lieutenant-Colonel Robins sent a strong fighting patrol, later followed by two companies, to the Poggio Mezzo Tondo, the height looking down on Pian d'Albero from the north-west. Here the King's raised a white flag to show their position to Major Gordon's watchful men on Monte Scalari, half a mile farther to the north-west. This advance by the King's released the Hampshires, who returned to Red Route near San Martino.

The German withdrawal, which had already begun on Route Sixty-nine, now spread to 28th Brigade's axis, and the brigade began to advance steadily across the mountain-sides along and to the left of Red Route. The Germans made a stand on the saddle which joins the Monte Scalari range and the lesser Monte Muro range to the north, but the King's cleared the subsidiary range and the Hampshires followed Red Route over the saddle and down into San Polo—six miles north-west of San Martino—in the foot-hills beyond.

Farther to the right, the Reconnaissance Regiment on Route Sixty-nine was still keeping pace with the infantry brigades, and was only a mile to the south-west of Incisa, five miles to the east of

San Polo. Farther to the right still, on the far side of the Arno, 6th Armoured Division was also keeping pace.

On August the 1st, the Germans in front of 12th Brigade also began to thin out, and the brigade followed them up along Blue Route. The Black Watch and the West Kents cleared the remaining heights of the Monte Scalari range, and the Royal Fusiliers, after re-occupying Cintoia, from which they had been driven back by the flames, advanced three miles to the north-west and entered Strada, three miles to the left of San Polo.

Strada was heavily mined, and the roads leading out of it to the north were covered by German machine-guns. German guns and mortars also discouraged any further advance during August the 1st.

Next morning, two troops of tanks from 142nd RAC joined the Royal Fusiliers, and soon afterwards 'Z' Company began to advance with their support. Almost at once, two of the tanks blew up on mines, and 'Z' Company was stopped by the fire of machine-guns and mortars. Heavy mortar and artillery fire had been bursting in Strada since early morning—Lieutenant-Colonel C. A. L. Shipley was hit in the mouth and lost a tooth—and the Germans were obviously holding yet another strong delaying position north of the village. Lieutenant-Colonel Shipley therefore organized a night attack by 'Y' and 'Z' Companies, supported by guns, tanks and machine-guns.

The first objective was a low ridge north of Strada, at right-angles to the road which runs north-westwards. Closely followed by the tanks, the infantry advanced through tall scrub on the left of the road, which hid them more or less until they were nearly on the ridge. The Germans were in houses and slit trenches on the ridge, and in houses on each flank; their machine-guns were, as usual, cleverly hidden. The leading section of 10 Platoon was halted by automatic fire from the front and flanks. Under cover of this fire, seven or eight Germans charged the section. The other men of the section were on each side of the road, watching the flanks, and only Lance-Corporal D. E. Doyle, who was on the road, saw the charge. In spite of heavy machine-gun fire and bright moonlight, Lance-Corporal Doyle stood up to meet the charge, firing his Bren gun from the hip. Alone, he beat off the Germans, killing or wounding at least five of them. The two companies lost some sixty men killed and wounded, but took the ridge, and with it a 75-mm gun and its towing vehicle.

When 'Y' and 'Z' Companies had consolidated their positions, 'X' Company passed through, and without opposition reached Petigliolo, a group of houses five hundred yards farther on, up a road branching off to the right.

Brigadier Heber-Percy brought up the Black Watch to put in a moonlight attack along the road leading to the north, but the battalion was halted by machine-gun fire at Ulinello, a thousand yards farther on, and waited there for daylight.

Next morning, August the 3rd, the adjutant of the Royal Fusiliers came forward to set up Battalion Headquarters, followed by the provost sergeant and his regimental police on motor-cycles. The adjutant drove too fast for the motor-cyclists, who lost sight of him, missed a turning and raced straight on through the Black Watch. Two miles farther on, Sergeant Smith and Fusilier Hansell, who were in the lead, shot past a German sentry day-dreaming outside a house. The German was no less startled than the Fusiliers; he scuttled into the house, while the perspiring Fusiliers jammed on their brakes and began to turn round. The front wheel of Fusilier Hansell's motor-cycle dropped into a man-hole at the side of the road, and no amount of struggling and cursing would get it out. He dropped the machine and hopped up behind Sergeant Smith, who had been waiting with not unreasonable impatience. Lance-Corporal Morgan and Fusilier Perrins had seen what happened, had turned round and were already withdrawing at full throttle. The three motor-cycles with their four riders provided an interesting example of high-speed withdrawal as they raced back past the sappers picking mines out of the road.

In spite of lack of experience of mobile warfare in mountainous country, and in spite of determined and skilful resistance, the division had assaulted and broken a series of extremely strong positions. Every day the division had gained in forcing the enemy back from his defensive lines was a day lost to the Germans who farther back were feverishly preparing the Gothic Line which they hoped to hold all winter. 12th and 28th Brigades had destroyed the south-eastern buttresses of the entire German defence of Florence; and from the heights they had taken they could see in the distance the domes and spires of the famous city.

20. Incontro Monastery

Once more the division moved steadily forward, along both Red and Blue Routes. There was little to check the advance except mines, demolitions and the inadequacy of the roads. As usual, the Italians welcomed the British soldiers with vociferous joy and generous offers of food and wine, and bands of well-armed Partisans appeared with offers of help and information. From time to time small groups of Germans would fight a local rear-guard action, but there was no large-scale defence.

The Reconnaissance Regiment, hampered by mines and demolitions, was clearing the country between the mountains and Route Sixty-nine. One of the light reconnaissance cars was sent to look at a village which was known to be held by the Germans. The car drove slowly towards the village until two machine-guns, one on the right and one on the left, opened fire. The car's machine-gun silenced the fire from the right, but the Germans on the left could not be seen. Lance-Sergeant F. W. Titchmarsh, in command of the car, leaped out with a Bren gun and began to stalk the Germans. Two more German machine-guns opened fire from the village; he fired back but could not silence them. He went on stalking the post on the left, drew its fire and spotted its position; and having in a similar manner spotted the other two posts, he returned to his armoured car and reported back on the wireless. Two heavy armoured cars came up as a result of his report, and Lance-Sergeant Titchmarsh directed the fire of their powerful weapons with rounds of tracer from his own Bren gun. The three German machine-guns hammered away at his armoured car, and one of the crew was injured by a bullet which came in through a gap in the armour, but the sergeant kept his car in position until the two heavy armoured cars had silenced the German posts.

On the right of 28th Brigade, the Somersets advanced first along Red Route and then along the Poggio di Firenze range of hills which overlooks it. On August the 4th, the battalion reached and cleared Monte Pilli, five miles north of San Polo, but on attempting to clear the last height before the Arno was halted by a vigorous German defence. This last obstacle was a steep, wedge-shaped peak, some fifteen hundred feet higher than the river beyond it; on its summit, Incontro Monastery dominated all the country-side in the angle of the Arno's westward bend towards Florence. While the Germans held Incontro, no force could hope to cross the Arno on 4th Division's side of the city; and none of the roads approaching the river from the south could be used for supply.

To the left of the Somersets, the Hampshires reached Vicchio di Rimaggio, at the foot of Incontro hill, two miles to the west of the Monastery and only half a mile short of the Arno. The Hampshires were fired on from Point 437—known by the code-name Darwen— a spur that thrusts out to the west from Incontro hill. 'A' Company turned towards Darwen, and reached the stream five hundred yards south of it, but could not climb the hill because of the strength of the German positions there.

On the left of 28th Brigade, 12th Brigade had some fighting along Blue Route, but by dusk on August the 4th had drawn level with 28th Brigade. The Royal Fusiliers were a mile and a half to the left of the Hampshires, between Bagno a Ripoli and Badia la Pieve; and the West Kents, a mile and a half farther to the left still, at Paradiso, were only half a mile short of one of the bridges which cross the Arno into Florence. From Paradiso to Vicchio di Rimaggio, therefore, the division held a front of three miles parallel with and just short of the river; at Vicchio, the line turned sharply to the southeast, behind Incontro, towards Incisa on Route Sixty-nine.

The division now entered into a period of active patrolling, reconnaissance of the Arno and elimination of the few Germans remaining between its most northerly positions and the river. The civilians, many of whom were refugees from Florence, were all eager to give information and help; the Partisans were sometimes disconcertingly eager. One group, however, led by a man named Il Potente, stood out above the rest, both for its efficiency and for the ability and personality of its leader. Il Potente was killed by a mortar bomb in one of the city's streets, and his death was a loss to the Allied cause.

The Germans had blown all the bridges leading into Florence, except for the narrow, ancient Ponte Vecchio, and had blocked the southern approaches with demolitions. The northern water-front was apparently guarded by a number of machine-gun posts. An endless stream of Italian Partisans and non-combatants and escaped British prisoners of war crossed the Arno and entered the division's lines. All had different accounts of the Germans in Florence; some said the city was powerfully garrisoned by the 'Tedeschi', others said there were only a few snipers there. The truth was probably that the main defence line lay in the hills behind the city, and came down to the Arno farther east, and that the city was not so much held as haunted by German military police and SS detachments and by the Italian Fascists. Occasional bursts of fire from automatic weapons were the only sounds of life from a city in which half a million people waited to be freed of the Germans.

Florence was an open city, and there was to be no fighting there which could be avoided. In spite of accusations and counter-accusations, neither side was intentionally shelling the main part of the city. The Germans had doubtless registered a belt of defensive fire along the river, but had no intention of fighting for the town itself. XIII Corps stood to gain nothing by forcing so formidable a river as the Arno, when farther to the east 6th Armoured Division was already on the other side, moving steadily northwards along the foot-hills of the Pratomagno. Beyond the river, ranges of mountains higher and steeper than Monte Scalari rose like a great wall up which the attackers would have to climb; and somewhere among these rugged crags lay the Gothic Line, the first main German defence system since the Adolf Hitler Line.

28th Brigade continued to close in on Incontro Monastery; the Hampshires at Vicchio were already within two miles, to the west, and now the Somersets began to approach from the south. On the night of August the 5th, the Somersets were within striking distance, and mounted an attack through the company positions of the Hampshires, to the south-west of the height. The attack was held off by fierce machine-gun fire.

On the south-eastern spurs of the Incontro range, the Germans were holding fast in spite of pressure by the Reconnaissance Regiment, which at the cost of some losses was drawing up to the right rear of 28th Brigade. The high ground to the right of Incontro was clearly going to be defended, as an eastern bastion to the main position.

Faced by the resolute defence of a naturally strong position, Major-General Ward decided to pass 10th Brigade through 28th Brigade. The Bedfords on the right were to clear the high ground facing the Reconnaissance Regiment; the DCLI on the left were to assault Incontro Monastery, and, having taken it, were to drive on down the hill-side beyond; and the Surreys in the centre were to pass between the two forward battalions, and to clear the last ridge to the north-east of Incontro. The King's and Somersets were to be relieved by 10th Brigade, but the Hampshires were to come under Brigadier Shoosmith's command.

The attack by the Bedfords was eventually cancelled; the battalion came under intense fire while taking up position, and in any case the Germans seemed to have pinned all their hopes on the Incontro Monastery—once that was gone, they would probably withdraw across the Arno.

Lieutenant-Colonel G. R. D. Musson organized the most thorough preparations by the DCLI for their attack on Incontro, which was to begin soon after dawn on August the 8th. During the previous day, company and platoon commanders reconnoitred the approaches to the Monastery. Captain Martyr, the Air Photograph Interpretation Officer, visited Battalion Headquarters and discussed the significant details of German dispositions revealed by camera and stereoscope, and provided air photographs of the Monastery and its grounds.

Information from all sources gave a fairly clear picture of the task which lay before the DCLI. The Monastery could be approached from the south-east, the south or the south-west; German positions on the high ground to right and left prevented approach from any other direction. The south-eastern approach was up an even slope, dominated by the defenders; the southern approach was steep and terraced; the south-western approach was steep, but the convexity of the slope offered the infantry the best chance of forming up within assaulting distance.

The Monastery and its grounds, with a single high tower, were enclosed by a long outer wall. The place was garrisoned by a company of Tank Grenadiers, able and eager troops. Italian civilians had reported a few days earlier that the rest of the battalion was in Villamagna, twelve hundred yards north of Incontro.

Lieutenant-Colonel Musson planned to attack with 'B' and 'C'

Companies, both of which would take the south-western approach. The battalion's pioneers were taking two pole-charges with 'C' Company to breach the Monastery's walls. The artillery programme provided for a long pounding of Incontro and of the flanking hills all through the night of August the 7th, until the moment when the attack went in. Then the fire was to be moved forward in front of the advancing infantry, until only Villamagna and Darwen were under fire. 'B' Squadron of the North Irish Horse, supporting the battalion's attack, would be moving up at dawn to fire-positions hull-down behind a hill-top just over a thousand yards short of the Monastery. An FOO and his party from 22nd Field Regiment, and a representative from the Somerset's mortars, were to be ready with 'A' Company to go up to the Monastery as soon as it was captured.

Early in the morning of August the 8th, 'B' and 'C' Companies of the DCLI, commanded by Major G. Rork and Captain A. T. Tregunno, moved up without trouble, and formed up in good time at the foot of the slope. The attack went in, and a fierce fight began.

'B' Company made the initial attack with 13 Platoon on the right and 14 Platoon on the left, commanded by Sergeant Bray and Lieutenant Whitehorn. The leading sections came under fire a hundred yards beyond the start-line, but the two platoons overran the enemy and reached the west wall by five thirty-five, having taken nine prisoners on the way.

15 Platoon, led by Sergeant Cocks, at once delivered its assault along the south wall, pushed to the south-east corner, turned it and made for the north-east corner. Sergeant Cocks decided to attack the right flank of the Germans on the slope, supported by fire from the left. The only automatic weapon on the left which could reach the German positions was Private Kenneth Carter's Bren gun. As soon as Private Carter opened fire, the German machine-guns replied; he was severely wounded at once—one bullet struck him in the neck and another went through both cheeks, smashing his jaw. In great pain, almost unconscious, he went on firing until his support was no longer needed.

Before the platoon reached the next corner the Germans counter-attacked up the slope on the right, while the Germans behind and on the wall on the left joined in with grenades and small-arms; 15 Platoon was forced back to the south-east corner.

Meanwhile, 17 Platoon of 'C' Company, commanded by Lieutenant Lindsey, had got round behind the Monastery and attacked across the western slope. Under fire from the wall itself, and from a hill-top behind them, seven hundred yards to the west, the attackers reached the north-east corner. There, however, they were stopped; Lieutenant Lindsey was wounded, and a section which tried to push on was destroyed when all its members were either killed or wounded.

At six in the morning, 'C' Company began its second task, the capture of the Monastery itself. 18 Platoon, commanded by Lieutenant Briscoe, prepared the ground for their advance by throwing several Number 77 grenades over the west wall; and then, supported by the fire of 16 Platoon, commanded by Lieutenant P. O. Bodley, forced their way through breaches in the masonry, and advanced through the trees inside to within fifty yards of the main buildings. At this short range, the Germans in the Monastery and the tower opened on them a furious fire, killing Lieutenant Briscoe and inflicting further losses. The survivors went back to the inside of the west wall and dug in there. One section of 16 Platoon was through the wall, and dug in near the north-western corner.

Bombs from the German mortars in the Monastery and outside began to burst among the platoons lining the inside and the outside of the walls. There was obviously no hope of a further advance from the west wall. The British and German troops were in a deadlock; close fighting went on for some time, with a good deal of grenade throwing, but there was no change in the situation.

At a quarter to eight, Lieutenant-Colonel Musson sent 'D' Company, commanded by Major J. T. B. Notley, towards the Monastery, behind a screen of artillery fire. As the company was climbing the steep hill-side towards 'B' Company, the Germans counter-attacked 15 Platoon at the south-east corner. The attackers came storming in from behind the wall and from a position farther down the hill-side. Sergeant Cocks withdrew his men from the corner so that the fire of heavy guns, tanks and machine-guns could be brought down on it.

At ten-twenty, Major Notley reached 'B' Company's headquarters at the south-western corner of the wall. Major Notley and Captain Tregunno arranged that two platoons of 'D' Company, with artillery support, should attack and recapture the south-eastern corner. Two Platoons of 'B' Company would then take over the corner, so that 'D' Company could move along the eastern wall to the main entrance at the north-eastern corner, from which the company could attack the buildings inside.

At eleven in the morning, 7 and 8 Platoons of 'D' Company, commanded by Lieutenants Spurdens and Risdon, attacked along the southern wall. Three-quarters of an hour later, they reached the south-eastern corner. At about ten past twelve the men of 7 Platoon climbed through a gap in the wall at the corner, and moved along the inside of the east wall towards the lodge at the main entrance. The Germans fought back, and the platoon lost men, but reached and surrounded the lodge. By one-fifteen, the lodge's garrison of twenty-five Germans had surrendered.

Meanwhile, 'B' Company had taken over the south-east corner as arranged, and at ten to one 8 Platoon had attacked through the breach towards the Monastery. The platoon reached the buildings, surrounded them, broke in and began to winkle the Germans out of the rooms. There were so many Germans there that 9 Platoon, commanded by Lieutenant Spencer, had to come up and help. By two in the afternoon, there were no armed Germans left in the Monastery.

Tanks came up to the Monastery to strengthen the DCLI's defences there. Patrols went out, and found that no active Germans remained on Incontro hill.

The Germans were beginning to gather themselves together for a counter-attack, and the DCLI warned Sergeant E. Midcalf of the Northumberland Fusiliers. Since the Germans were out of sight of Sergeant Midcalf's platoon of machine-guns, he mounted the platoon in its carriers, and drove up the hill-side through bursting shells, mortar bombs and very fierce small-arms fire, to the Monastery. As the carriers bucketed over the rough ground, the Fusiliers fired their Vickers machine-guns as steadily as possible at the Germans coming into sight. One of the carriers and the machine-gun on it were destroyed by a direct hit, and the whole crew was killed, but the remaining three reached the Monastery and broke up the counter-attack, inflicting heavy losses on the Germans.

The DCLI's action was a model of what a daylight attack by a battalion group on a strong position should be. It was planned in great detail, but the plan was flexible enough to allow of changes to overcome unforeseen obstacles; Lieutenant-Colonel Musson had watched the progress of the battle very closely, but had left to his company commanders those decisions which could best be made on the spot. The men of the assaulting companies had fought hard and well, and had earned their notable success.

The Germans on Incontro had lost ten dead, most of them killed by machine-gun fire in the outer positions. One officer and six others were wounded and captured; two officers and fifty-eight other ranks, unwounded, were taken prisoners. The unwounded prisoners included four sergeant-majors, two staff-sergeants, and representatives from artillery, engineer and signal units.

The DCLI had lost one officer and eighteen other ranks killed, and two officers and seventy-five other ranks wounded.

Some of the German prisoners gave an account of the battle from their point of view. The artillery preparation by 4th Division's guns had done little material damage, since all the German positions were well dug in, but did much to shake the nerve of the defenders. They did not, however, expect an attack until the lifting of the concentrations of gunfire, the significance of which was clear to the artillery FOO, Oberleutnant Fauss.

The garrison commander, Oberleutnant Vittleben, was the only infantry officer present, and he was wounded soon after the attack began. The platoon commanders, who were all sergeant-majors, fought their battle more or less independently.

Oberleutnant Fauss found the line to his battery cut by shell-fire, and at the moment of emergency his wireless set broke down. Since he could not carry out his task of bringing down observed fire, he dismissed his signallers. These signallers may have been the only members of the garrison to escape, though some walking wounded may also have been able to struggle back.

Oberleutnant Fauss had with him an officer new to his battery, an Oberleutnant Schichtel who had been sent to the Monastery to gain experience—which he probably did. Since they were out of touch with their guns, the two officers armed themselves with Schmeisser machine-pistols and grenades, and joined the infantry in the fighting outside the wall.

The fall of Incontro on August the 8th loosened the whole German defence in the bend of the Arno. At dawn on August the 9th, the Surreys advanced past the Monastery to the right and quickly cleared the high ground to the north-east. The DCLI patrolled Darwen and the country beyond and below it; the Hampshires on the left searched the orchards to the north-west of Incontro as far as the Arno. The only Germans about were either dead, asleep or ready to surrender.

On the right of 10th Brigade, the Reconnaissance Regiment found the Germans in front gradually withdrawing. By August the 10th, the regiment had cleared the country between the hills round Incontro and the Arno.

The division had accomplished all its tasks, and was at last due for rest and refitting. 1st Infantry Division had already begun to take over the sector, relieving 12th Brigade during the night of August the 8th. By midnight on August the 10th, the last units of 4th Division had handed over their sectors, and the relief was complete. In pouring rain, the last men out of the line turned their backs on Florence, and began their southward journey of a hundred and eighty miles to the peaceful Vale of Umbria.

21. The Gothic Line

To the civilian, rest may mean a time of relaxation and agreeable idleness. But to a division of the British Army it meant activity of a different kind. There were reinforcements to be absorbed; all weapons and transport and other equipment had to be thoroughly cleaned, overhauled and brought back to first-class condition; and all units had to carry out training indicated by recent experience and by possible experience to come. On the other hand, for the first time for many weeks the whole division was out of range of the enemy—since German aircraft never ventured so far into Allied Italy—and all who had undergone the physical fatigue and mental strain of battle could have the relaxation they needed in long hours of sleep at night, baths, regular and thorough meals, and a general degree of comfort they had almost forgotten. There were also short leave to Naples or Rome, games, stage shows and films, and visits to the famous towns of the valley, Assisi and Perugia.

The division had its own Welfare arrangements to supplement those provided by I District. In Foligno, the largest town in the neighbourhood, the divisional Concert Party appeared at the Imperio Cinema, and the ENSA show 'Eve on Leave' had a popular run of a week. The Black Watch won the divisional football competition in the town stadium, and anyone who wished could use the swimming pool. In Spello, a village north of Foligno, the Concert Party and a small ENSA troupe performed in the tiny theatre, and the Salvation Army provided a canteen. Assisi could offer at first only its own undamaged beauty and quietness, but after a while 10th Brigade opened a canteen and an officers' club there, and one of the cinemas began to work again. To allow as many men as possible to visit Rome, Major-General Ward opened a leave camp under canvas at V Corps Rest Camp at Castel Gandolfo; unit transport which took leave parties to the camp remained to ferry them to and from Rome, and at the camp itself there were films and concerts, and bathing in the nearby lake. Finally, on the shores of Lake Piediluco, the division took over a large empty school, smartened it up with the help of the sappers, and set up a German hut as an annexe. Three hundred men at a time could stay in it for five-day periods; and a staff of local girls was recruited to act as waitresses. The village of Piediluco became the 4th Division's own town; a boat-house and several boats were requisitioned, and various shops were opened, including barber's and photographer's shops, fruit and gift shops and a Post Office. Thirsty soldiers could even conduct a short pub-crawl from the 'Jeep and Trailer' to the 'Peter's Corner', the 'Red Lion' and the canteen run at first by the Church Army and later by the Church of Scotland. Every evening the camp provided a show of some kind, given either by the Concert Party or by a mobile cinema. The Piediluco Rest Camp was entirely successful, and all went well there except for the tragic death of two men of the Hampshires, who were killed when a German booby-trap exploded in the boiler-room just before the Camp was ready for opening.

The advance of the Fifth and Eighth Armies through Italy had all but come to a halt shortly after the 4th Division withdrew from the Florence sector. On the Eighth Army's left, the great mountains behind Florence offered a formidable obstacle to any assault, and, on the right, the Germans had made the difficult country of the foothills near the Adriatic coast even more difficult with emplacements and fortifications. Field-Marshal Alexander decided to hold on the left and to thrust on the right, through the Gothic Line to Rimini and the wide valley of the River Po. The transfer of forces from left to right was carried out with the same speed and secrecy as the division had seen in North Africa and later before Cassino. All divisional signs on clothing and vehicles had been completely erased or cut off before the division left the Florence sector, and some of the advance parties had a bewildering time in the Vale of Umbria, which was already occupied by several equally anonymous formations. While the 4th Division rested, other divisions were already moving across the great mountain-spine of Italy on their way to the Adriatic coast; and, after only a short week's rest, the three field regiments—always the longest in action—followed these divisions on August the 19th to support their assault on the Gothic Line.

The artillery group was made up of Brigadier Kirwan's headquarters, the 22nd, 30th and 77th Field Regiments, provost and postal sections, an RASC transport platoon and REME gun workshops. The group moved fast enough along the main road from Foligno to Fossato di Vico, but, when the narrow country road to Fabriano disappeared into the Apennines, the journey degenerated into a succession of short periods of motion separated by long, silent, unexplained halts. The endless traffic blocks, some of them several miles long, were due to the inadequacy of the road for the weight, width and number of vehicles moving in both directions; worst of all perhaps were the great tank-transporters, two of which were almost as wide as three ordinary vehicles. Some of the field batteries spent sixteen hours on the journey of eighty miles, and several gun-tractors ran out of petrol within a few hundred yards of their concentration area near Jesi.

A few days later, gun-positions were allotted—with some difficulty owing to the number of units crowded together in every fold of the ground—and the guns went into action near Barce. For the first few days they were silent so that the Germans would not know how many guns there were in front of them; and during these hot and dusty days, five hundred rounds per gun were dumped on the positions. During the night of August the 26th, I Canadian Corps began its attack on the Gothic Line by crossing the River Metauro; but the division's guns were ordered to fire less than a hundred of their laboriously unloaded five hundred rounds a gun. During the next five days, the Canadians made good progress through the outposts of the Gothic Line, and on August the 26th the guns moved forward to an area between Urbino and Pesaro. As before, a great weight of ammunition was unloaded on the gun-positions, but the Canadians seemed to have enough guns already, and moved steadily out of range without asking for much of it to be fired off. The guns, kept off the roads by the transport of the attacking divisions, stayed where they were and came out of action.

The rest of the division, meanwhile, between September the 3rd and 6th, had crossed to the Adriatic coast near Senigallia; 10th Brigade, however, did not arrive until four days later. On September the 7th the division came under the command of I Canadian Corps, and began to move towards Tomba di Pesaro. Heavy traffic filled the main coastal road, and the division had to travel by small roads and tracks farther inland; and, while the long columns of vehicles were threading their way over ridges and saddles and round the edges of deep valleys, the weather broke. The clouds thickened around the hill-tops, and burst in torrents of rain; through the haze of mist and water, lightning glimmered like the flashes of distant guns. The sloping roads were filled with foaming yellow streams of water, the surface of every track dissolved under the wheels of lorries, and the River Foglia rose immensely and washed away the Bailey bridges over it. The move took a day longer than had been intended, but by September the 10th was complete.

The divisional sign reappeared, now in the new form designed by Major-General Ward; instead of the red circle with the first quadrant set out from the centre, the sign became a red circle with the fourth quadrant set out, the whole on a square white background.

The force of Eighth Army's attack along the Adriatic coast had taken the Germans completely by surprise; the garrison of the Gothic Line did not even have time to man the fortifications. I Canadian Corps, on the coast, was only ten miles from Rimini—and from the plains of Lombardy, and an end of fighting in mountainous or hilly country. The wide and shallow River Marechia flows down from the Apennines north-easterly to Rimini; and for its last few miles it runs between hills on its south bank and the plain on its north. The task of I Canadian Corps was to cross the river near Rimini and reach the plain beyond.

The corps was to fight towards this objective across the foot-hills of the Apennines, broken by steep slopes and by water-courses running through wide valleys. Farm buildings and occasional small villages clustered on the high ground; and from each ridge the resolute German defenders could see the whole valley and the ridge beyond. The country-side offered little cover; most of the cultivation was plough, vegetable patches, and vineyards planted with low vines set in widely separated rows. The heavy rains had not been enough to fill the water-courses; shallow streams ran through some, and many were dry. Some of these water-courses were formidable obstacles because of their steep banks or deep worn beds, but others were to give the infantry little or no trouble. In general, the bareness of the open fields overlooked by each successive ridge offered considerable advantages to the defenders. They had had a good deal of experience in defensive fighting, and had worked out all the best methods of siting and hiding weapons and positions.

The Germans, although they had by now lost their grip on the Gothic Line, clearly meant to keep the Eighth Army out of the great Lombardy plain for as long as possible, for an armoured thrust from Rimini towards Bologna might outflank their positions in the mountains north of Florence. The 1st Parachute Division, always at the point of most danger, was astride the coastal road at Riccione. On 4th British Division's right flank, the 29th Tank Grenadier Division—which, like several divisions of the Eighth Army, had been brought across from Florence—held a line which included the ridge and the village of Coriano; and south-west of Coriano were the 26th Armoured Division, which still had most of its tanks, and the 98th Infantry Division, which had recently been disgraced by a mass surrender to the Canadians.

The commander of I Canadian Corps planned to break through to the Marecchia by attacking first with one of his three divisions and then with another. As each division attacked, it would have the support of all the guns of the corps which were within range, as well as of medium and heavy bombers directed by Corps Headquarters, and by fighter-bombers which were to be on call for the assaulting battalions. V Corps was to guard the left flank. 4th Division was strengthened for the coming battle by a considerable force of fighting units which were placed under command or in support; these included two regiments of Churchill tanks, five batteries of self-propelled field-guns, five batteries of self-propelled anti-tank guns, a troop of AVREs, three advanced air-support sections, two field regiments, a light anti-aircraft regiment, a medium regiment, two batteries of heavy guns, two batteries of heavy anti-aircraft guns, and a flight and two sections of an air observation-post squadron. Later, a chemical warfare unit was added which specialized in the laying of smoke screens.

The operation was divided into eight phases, of which the first was to be the attack by 5th Canadian Armoured Division on Coriano and the ridge that runs northwards from it, and the last was to be the crossing by 1st Canadian Division and 4th Division of the River Marecchia near Rimini. The first phase began soon after midnight on September the 13th; the division's guns supported an attack by 1st British Armoured Division, which, as part of V Corps, was advancing on the left of I Canadian Corps. After some ferocious fighting, Coriano was cleared by the afternoon, and the first phase was complete.

The division's task in the second phase was to push north-east from the Coriano ridge to the next ridge a mile away; this ridge, running north and south, looks down on the River Marano beyond. Zero hour for 12th Brigade's attack was to be half-past six in the evening, and during the afternoon the Black Watch and the Royal Fusiliers marched to their assembly area behind the Coriano ridge. They were delayed by heavy fire on the roads from German guns and mortars, and on arrival found the assembly area itself under shell-fire. Meanwhile, the tanks supporting the brigade had been prevented by enemy fire from reconnoitring a crossing of the Fornaci ravine which runs between the Coriano ridge and the ridge beyond; and, since the infantry would have had to attack with the evening sunlight dazzling them, the attack was postponed until early next morning.

During the night, patrols from both battalions met Germans on the lower slopes of the Coriano ridge and in the Fornaci ravine itself. A party of sappers, however, working in front of the Fusiliers, found a crossing-place for tanks near a destroyed bridge north-west of Coriano, and an Ark was brought up and placed in position.

Soon after dawn on September the 14th, each supported by a squadron of Churchill tanks, the Black Watch on the right and the Fusiliers on the left began their attack. In less than an hour, all the tanks had crossed the ravine, and shortly afterwards the Fusiliers were consolidating on the centre of the farther ridge. The Germans on the left-hand end of the ridge resisted more vigorously, but by noon the Fusiliers were firm on all their objectives. The enemy on the right-hand end were the most determined of all, and shot up four of the Churchills on the ridge near the Casa Fabbri; the Black Watch destroyed a German tank behind the house with a Piat, but a Tiger lurking behind the Casa Savini got away. By two in the afternoon, the Black Watch had taken most of their part of the ridge, but there were Germans still clinging to the lower slopes to the west. During the afternoon the Germans brought up tanks and attacked the positions on the crest; and, when they failed to shake the Black Watch by assault, they tried to infiltrate into their positions; but their efforts failed and eventually ceased. The Black Watch took sixty-two prisoners during the day, and the Fusiliers sixteen.

Now that 12th Brigade was fairly in position on the ridge looking down on the River Marano, the division could begin its next task; in the third phase of the battle, the division was to cross the Marano beyond the Casa Fabbri ridge and take the three-hundred-foot hill beyond.

Shortly before midnight, the West Kents crossed the ridge on their way to Ospedaletto; they met no Germans east of the river. The bridge across the Marano was blown up as they approached it in the darkness; but, by four in the morning, the West Kents had taken their bridge-head as well as twenty-one prisoners. 'A' Company on the right was three hundred yards north of Ospedaletto; 'B' Company in the centre was astride the two roads leading up the hill to Il Fienile and San Patrignano; and 'C' Company on the left was five hundred yards south of Ospedaletto.

Early the next morning, September the 15th, the two forward battalions of 28th Brigade, each with a squadron of Churchill tanks of the North Irish Horse, passed through the bridge-head to attack the hill. The King's on the right crossed the river near Ospedaletto, and made for the Casa Arlotti and the cross-roads three hundred yards to the left of it. There was little cover between the bridgehead and the objective, and enemy infantry and armour on the hill resisted strongly. Three hours after the attack began, however, the King's had a company on each of their objectives; the two other companies, east of Arlotti, guarded both the battalion's right flank and the bridge-head.

The Hampshires on the left crossed the river south of Ospedaletto, and took San Patrignano and the cemetery two hundred yards farther on. Platoons moving north towards the cross-roads five hundred yards away were pinned down by fire, and had to beat off a counter-attack. Soon after nine o'clock in the morning, the Hampshires finished their task by taking Casa Bagli, three hundred yards beyond the cemetery. During the fighting, 28th Brigade took sixty prisoners. During the rest of the day the brigade's positions were heavily shelled from time to time, since although it was out of the battle for a while it was not out of range.

During the afternoon, patrols of 'B' Reconnaissance Squadron made sure there were no Germans in La Colombarina, four hundred yards down the hill to the north-west of Casa Arlotti, and made contact with 1st Canadian Division on the right flank. When 4th Division completed the third phase of the battle by taking the high ground west of Ospedaletto, 1st Canadian Division on the right began the fourth phase by crossing the Marano to attack San Lorenzo in Corregiano.

The division now held the north-eastern end of the foot-hills which rise between the River Marano and the River Ausa, two miles farther north-west. Its task in the fifth phase was to cross the River Ausa and to link up with 1st Canadian Division on the right. From the cross-roads held by the King's, the ridge runs first north-west, then south-west; and on each side it is divided by deep, wide valleys running north and south. From Arlotti, therefore, the King's looked westwards across an open valley two hundred and fifty feet deep and more than half a mile across, to the Frisoni ridge which hid the River Ausa. As soon as the King's and the Hampshires were on the Arlotti ridge, the Somersets were to have passed through them and taken this further ridge. Heavy shelling by the Germans, however, delayed the preparations for this attack—the Somersets lost forty-five men in the assembly area—and the attack had to be postponed until the night.

By three in the morning of September the 16th, the Somersets had passed through the King's at the cross-roads south of Il Fienile, and, advancing half a mile along the road which runs along the spine of the watershed, had reached a point on it a thousand yards south of Frisoni. Further advances were delayed by fires on other parts of the ridge; haystacks and vehicles were burning furiously and lighting up the whole neighbourhood. Soon after dawn, 'D' Company reached the next height, which from a thousand yards farther south-west overlooks the whole Frisoni ridge. The rest of the ridge remained in the hands of the Germans; a patrol from 'B' Reconnaissance Squadron went on foot towards Frisoni, but was pinned down by mortar-fire six hundred yards from the group of houses.

Shortly afterwards, the Germans brought up infantry in armoured lorries, and, in spite of the defensive fire brought down by 30th Field Regiment, put in a violent counter-attack, with the support of at least one tank, on 'D' Company of the Somersets. The fighting was confused, but at length 'D' Company had to withdraw, and the Somersets had to leave the earlier objective as well, since they were now overlooked from within rifle-range. For the rest of the day, 28th Brigade's positions were heavily shelled and mortared; no movement forward by day over the open ground was possible.

During the afternoon, Major-General Ward decided that he

could not take the bleak and exposed Frisoni ridge or cross the Ausa until he had cleared that part of the watershed farther south-west which looks down on both. After putting out the Frisoni ridge to the north like an arm, the main body of the watershed curves south-west to Cerasolo; this village looks across a valley twelve hundred yards wide and three hundred and fifty feet deep at Casa Bagli, which was then held by the Hampshires. The village and the high ground north-east of it, although outside the divisional boundary, would have to be taken before the division could reach or cross the River Ausa.

The King's on the Arlotti ridge relieved two companies of the Hampshires at Casa Bagli, to release them for the attack on Cerasolo. The attack by the Hampshires was completely successful; soon after dawn on September the 17th the village was taken, and with it about fifty prisoners. Half an hour later, Churchill tanks of the North Irish Horse joined the Hampshires. At the same time the King's, with the help of tanks, attacked and recaptured the high points on the road to Cerasolo which had been lost the day before, and took eighteen prisoners. The King's beat off a counter-attack at seven in the morning, and destroyed a tank. 28th Brigade, however, was still unable to take the Frisoni ridge.

Major-General Ward therefore decided that the Black Watch, temporarily under the command of Brigadier Preston, should put in a night attack. The battalion was heavily shelled on its start-line but pressed doggedly forward; by midnight, after a ferocious struggle, it had captured the ridge.

28th Brigade had now completed its task, after fighting for two and a half days; the four battalions had taken more than a hundred and thirty-five prisoners and destroyed at least eight German tanks, including two Tigers and three Panthers. The relief by 1st British Armoured Division's 18th Infantry Brigade began with the Hampshires while the Black Watch were still fighting for Frisoni ridge, and was completed during the following night. On September the 19th, the brigade moved back to rest near Misano. The Black Watch, still on Frisoni ridge, came under command of Brigadier Heber-Percy again early on September the 18th, but the Germans fired so many guns at any movement that Lieutenant-Colonel G. McP. Smith decided to keep the battalion in position until nightfall.

The divisions on each flank of the 4th Division had also been advancing steadily. On the right, 1st Canadian Division was locked in a fierce struggle with 1st Parachute Division for the village of San Martino, four thousand yards north-east of Frisoni. Farther to the south-east, however, one of its battalions had found the going easier, and had reached the Ausa on the morning of September the 18th. On the left, the 1st London Scottish of 56th Division had pushed across the spur a mile west of Cerasolo; the Germans counter-attacked them repeatedly during the night, but next day the London Scottish were still there and fit to advance again.

The fifth phase of the battle was now beginning; the division was to cross the Ausa and take the high ground beyond. During September the 17th the West Kents on the left moved up from their bridgehead at Ospedaletto to the ridge between Cerasolo and Casa Monte Pirolo. At midnight they started moving down the hill-side towards the Ausa. 'A' Company, on the left, almost immediately came up against a strong force of Germans at the road junction five hundred yards north of Cerasolo; three and a half hours later, when the rest of the battalion was well on the way to the objectives, the company was still pinned down. Since the centre of resistance had by then been by-passed, Lieutenant-Colonel H. P. Braithwaite DSO ordered Major H. N. Raisin to hold his positions and make no further attempt to advance. The other three companies pushed on to the river and crossed it near La Ventura; the tanks had some difficulty in finding a place to cross, but by dawn two troops of the North Irish Horse were on the other side. 'B' Company then attacked and captured the road junction three hundred yards beyond La Ventura, and 'D' Company cleared the houses at La Zingarina, a quarter of a mile farther north. 'C' Company took over the road junction, and 'B', with the help of tanks, pushed on five hundred yards more to the final objective, a group of houses known as Sant' Antima, clustered on a hill-top. This attack on the division's left was finished quickly and neatly; the West Kents took forty-nine prisoners including two officers, and lost twenty-six men wounded.

On the right, the Bedfords assembled north-east of Arlotti, a mile and a half from the Ausa. At eleven o'clock that night, Brigadier Shoosmith ordered them to move off. Searchlights, in position on the Coriano ridge behind, threw their beams over the battle-field, providing a light almost as bright as a full moon; this method of lighting up a battle had not been used by the division before. 'D' Company was to cross the river at the point where the Fossa Budriolo, one of its tributaries, joined it and both were crossed by bridges. Half a mile short of these bridges, the leading platoon—under Lieutenant Gurney—reached the railway line at the same moment as two platoons of German infantry closed in on each side, and a confused fire fight followed. Lieutenant Wells's platoon worked round to the left, and the company went on towards the river. In this scuffle Private Scully was overpowered and carried off by the Germans; two days later he turned up again, leading in twenty-six Germans whom he had persuaded to surrender. By half-past two in the morning of September the 18th, the leading section had reached the river, but was prevented from crossing by heavy fire; the next section made every effort to follow up but was driven back. As there was heavy fire coming from the front and both flanks, Major A. R. A. Wilson MC ordered 'D' Company to dig in about fifty yards from the river to the south of the bridges.

Early next morning a troop of Churchill tanks approached to support the company, which was lying low as any movement drew instant machine-gun fire. When Major Wilson found that he could not catch the attention of the tank commanders, he took a small patrol up to them, but was severely wounded himself. The tanks dominated the German machine-guns, but the company was kept down by heavy shell-fire. Although the company had failed to cross the two rivers, it prevented the Germans from blowing up the bridges, which were later found to be intact with demolition charges laid under them.

'A' and 'B' Company of the Bedfords, meanwhile, passed through the Black Watch, and crossed the Frisoni ridge; by one in the morning of September the 18th they had reached the Ausa half a mile to the north-west. They crossed the river without difficulty, and made for Casa Fagnani, five hundred yards farther on. Lieutenant Quelch's platoon found the house occupied by a detachment of Germans, took them by surprise and after a short fight cleared the place and took twenty-three prisoners. Other Germans nearby were roused by the noise, and opened fire with machine-guns from both flanks. Both 'A' and 'B' Companies were busy with local opposition until just before day-break, when the battalion commander told them to hold until tank support could be provided. An Ark was laid in the Ausa, and at six-thirty in the morning a troop of 51st Royal Tanks joined the two companies and helped them to go on clearing the Germans out of the neighbourhood. Both companies had suffered heavy losses during the night, and had to reorganize as two platoons each. Just before nine o'clock, Major W. Rickman MBE, who was co-ordinating the action of the two companies, decided that they could move on again. The guns of 22nd Field Regiment fired concentrations at the ridge looking down on the Casa Fagnani from beyond the Fossa Budriolo, and the tanks moved forward with the infantry.

The bridge which crosses the Budriolo two hundred yards beyond the Casa Fagnani was intact, and infantry and tanks were soon across the stream. As they came up to the ridge, however, the guns which had been keeping German troops on it quiet had to stop firing for fear of hitting the Bedfords; the Germans at once emerged from their slit-trenches and opened fire with machine-guns, some of them within two hundred yards of the Bedfords. 'B' Company, caught in the open, was halted, and as soon as the German guns and mortars found the range the company began to lose men; both Major Rickman and his Sergeant-Major were wounded, and the company was forced to get back across the Budriolo. 'A' Company on the left was moving across more favourable ground, and made an effort to get on; Lieutenant Trevett's platoon was stopped only fifty yards from the road running along the crest of the ridge. The position was too exposed, however, and the company—whose commander, Captain Francis, had been hit—was placed by Lieutenant Robson in a defensive position round a house near the foot of the ridge. Here the company stayed, shelled from time to time, supported and supplied with ammunition by four tanks.

'B' Company re-formed round the Casa Fagnani, and during the afternoon was joined by 'C' Company, which had been brought up under cover of a smoke screen.

By noon on September the 18th, the Bedfords were clearly unable to move forward; 'D' Company on the right was pinned down east of the Ausa; 'A' Company was across the Ausa and the Budriolo, but could not advance from the foot of the ridge; while 'B' and 'C' Companies were between the Ausa and the Budriolo. Major-General Ward discussed the situation with Brigadier S. N. Shoosmith, and decided that there would be no further advance in daylight, but that 10th Brigade would attack that night to take the Sant' Aquilina ridge, and next morning would take the higher ridge which runs a thousand yards farther north-west, between the Casi Bianchi and Biondi. These two ridges were the southernmost part of the San Fortunato foot-hills, which command the valley of the

Ausa, from the Frisoni ridge to the suburbs of Rimini, four miles away.

That night, searchlights again provided artificial moonlight. Just before midnight, the DCLI crossed the Budriolo in the area held by the Bedfords, and advanced slowly through heavy fire from small-arms, mortars and artillery. By dawn of September the 19th, 'D' Company was half-way up the ridge to Sant' Aquilina, and 'A' Company on the left had joined 'A' Company of the Bedfords near the foot of the slope. Tanks went up to join both companies, followed shortly afterwards by a troop of M.10s, and with their support and the fire of artillery on the ridge, the DCLI made a new effort to gain the crest. 'D' Company took the Casa Brioli at nine in the morning, and consolidated. An hour and a half later, 'A' Company moved on towards Sant' Aquilina, and 'B' Company in the centre moved up the spur that springs from the middle of the ridge; each company was supported by a troop of tanks. Forty minutes later both infantry and tanks reached the crest of the ridge, and began clearing away the remaining resistance; snipers were still firing during the afternoon. 10th Brigade took eighty-five prisoners during the day, including the company commander and two platoon commanders of a Luftwaffe Jaeger Company which was surrounded in Sant' Aquilina.

On the right, meanwhile, the Canadians were fighting hard for San Fortunato; on the left, 1st Armoured Division had taken Monte dell' Arboreta, and its leading troops were behind Sant' Aquilina. The Germans organized a stiff defence, however, and recaptured Monte dell' Arboreta.

10th Brigade's next task was to advance northwards along the high ground until it rose to San Fortunato, where the brigade was to meet the Canadians. Two hills commanding the crest had to be taken first; on one was the Casa Biondi, a thousand yards to the north-west of Sant' Aquilina across a broad open valley; and on the other was the Casa Bianchi, in the middle of the high ground between Sant' Aquilina and San Fortunato.

Later that night 'A' and 'C' Companies of the Surreys took the Casa Biondi, and with it a German 75-mm gun, without meeting any Germans, and consolidated around the house. At dawn two troops of tanks joined the infantry, and helped them to clear the hill of the remaining Germans, a number of whom they captured.

Early in the morning of the 20th, 'D' Company of the DCLI and a troop of tanks attacked the Casa Bianchi. Germans only a thousand yards away on the western slopes of San Fortunato supported the detachment on the hill with small-arms fire and with a gun which inflicted casualties and held up the advance. Major Brown MC eventually found he was the only officer left in his company. He began with determination to reduce the buildings on the hill one by one; as the morning went on, the advancing Canadians silenced more and more of the Germans on the San Fortunato hill; and at eleven in the morning, with the support of the tanks, he led his company to assault the last defended house on the hill. The company took a number of prisoners in this action, and the battalion's total for the day was ninety-one. Since the Canadians had taken San Fortunato itself, the hill and all its ridges were by this time held by I Canadian Corps. The Germans brought down heavy shell-fire on all the forward positions for the rest of the day; one salvo killed every man in a group of eighteen prisoners of war and their escort.

On the left, the advance of 1st Armoured Division was held up by strong opposition from tanks and self-propelled guns on the high spur a mile and a quarter west of the Casa Bianchi ridge. Since the spur was within 1st Division's boundaries, 4th Division's guns had not been allowed to engage it. In the afternoon, however, 1st Division asked for fire on the spur, and the divisional artillery, after harassing it for a while, brought down a final hurricane concentration on it—within one minute, the twenty-five pounder guns fired about thirteen hundred rounds, the 5·5-inch medium guns fired two hundred and fifty rounds and the 7·2-inch heavy howitzers fired twenty rounds; the concentration killed a considerable number of Germans, and must have wounded many more.

In the eighth and last phase of the battle, 1st Canadian and 4th British Divisions were to advance from the San Fortunato hills, first to the Vergiano ridge, three thousand yards farther north-west, which looks down on the many streams of the River Marecchia; and were then to cross the Marecchia itself, and take a bridge-head on the other side.

10th Brigade was to have continued the advance during the night, but the weather broke that evening, and heavy rain fell all night. The ground softened and became slippery and treacherous, and many vehicles were ditched in the darkness. 28th Brigade had great difficulty in coming forward, and the Somersets and Hampshires did not cross the Ausa until the morning of September the 21st. The

King's were unable to move at all, and had to be left at Misano. Major-General Ward had to cancel the night operations.

During the morning of the 21st, the Surreys sent a patrol of platoon strength to Point 112, a hill which stands two thousand yards north-west of Sant' Aquilina, between the San Fortunato hills and the main range of foot-hills farther south-west. Within three hours the patrol had reached and cleared the hill, taking seventeen prisoners of a Luftwaffe Jaeger Battalion and a 75-mm anti-tank gun. 'B' and 'D' Companies moved up to occupy the hill, and during the afternoon the Surrey's battle-patrol reached Monte Fagiolo, which is part of the Vergiano ridge, fifteen hundred yards farther to the north-west, without meeting any Germans.

The battalions of 28th Brigade now began to pass through 10th Brigade on their way to the Vergiano ridge. Only infantry could move across the sodden ground, and the tanks of the North Irish Horse had to wait for the time being at Sant' Aquilina. During the evening, the Somersets reached Vergiano itself and Spadarolo, a thousand yards farther north-east, which stands on the right-hand end of the ridge. The Hampshires reached the ridge a thousand yards south-west of Vergiano, went on down the other side, crossed the river Mavone at the foot of the ridge and took a thousand-yard stretch of the main road beyond. Both the battalions could look across the last obstacle of the operation—the Marecchia.

1st Canadian Division had already crossed the River Marecchia and secured a bridge-head on the other side; and, farther to the right, the Greek Mountain Brigade had taken Rimini, the key to the Lombardy plain.

The crossing of the Marecchia, which might have been the climax of the division's operations, was a comparatively tame affair. During the night of September the 21st, fighting patrols of the Hampshires went down to the river, and found that there was little water in the channels; Germans fired at them from houses beyond the river, and brought down defensive artillery fire. Patrols which went out at dawn found that there were no Germans left south of the river; and, later in the morning, patrols of the Somersets crossed the river and met no resistance in Santa Giustina, a village on the main road more than a mile beyond the Marecchia. This main road is the great Via Emilia, built in the days of the Roman Empire, and still one of the most important roads in Italy; it is known to-day as Route Nine, and runs almost in a straight line from Rimini to

Milan, more than a hundred and sixty miles away. During the afternoon, 'C' Company of the Somersets, with two troops of tanks of the North Irish Horse, crossed the river and reached Santa Giustina without meeting any opposition. On September the 22nd, 'A' Company also crossed the river and took up positions around a cross-roads five hundred yards west of the village. During the night, platoons of the Hampshires crossed the river, and, after some skirmishing, reached Route Nine in the morning a mile to the left of the Somersets. On the right, meanwhile, 2nd New Zealand Division had relieved 1st Canadian Division; and, on the left, 1st British Armoured Division had crossed the Marecchia and was moving towards Sant' Arcangelo, a town on Route Nine a thousand yards to the left of the Hampshires' positions.

5th Canadian Armoured Division was now to pass through the bridge-head taken by 4th Division and push into the plain beyond. During the evening of September the 22nd, all 4th Division's traffic south of the Ausa was ordered to keep clear of the roads to let the Canadians through, and next morning the rest of the division's vehicles, except those needed for essential maintenance, were kept off the roads.

On September the 23rd, the German artillery in front of 28th Brigade was furiously active, and the shelling was so heavy that the Hampshires had to leave the cross-roads west of Santa Giustina. 'B' Reconnaissance Squadron met strong opposition north of Variano —a village six hundred yards north of Santa Giustina—and south of Casale, half a mile farther west, and lost a number of men. That morning 5th Canadian Armoured Division took command of 4th Division's sector.

After stiff fighting, 12th Canadian Brigade took Casale on September the 24th, and that evening the Hampshires were placed under the command of this brigade to guard its left flank from any Germans in Sant' Arcangelo until the town was cleared. Two days later, the Hampshires returned to the command of 28th Brigade, and withdrew to join the rest of the division in I Canadian Corps reserve.

In ten days of stern fighting against a still resolute enemy, the division had advanced rather more than eight miles across the difficult country between the Coriano ridge and Route Nine. The troops had in fact covered a great deal more than that distance while in contact with the Germans; companies had thrust in all directions, from south-west through 120 degrees to north. The division had captured five hundred and eighty prisoners from the German divisions opposing it, and had destroyed or captured a vast number of German weapons and vehicles. The Germans had often resisted fiercely and had continually shelled the division's infantry, guns and communications; but they had been terribly mauled as they withdrew. Most of the German battalions had consisted of only two hundred men when they first faced the division; and ten days later they were disastrously weakened in numbers, quality, morale and equipment.

Every effort the German commanders made to stiffen their line had left them worse placed than before. But they had gained valuable time, and held the Eighth Army back from the plain until the weather broke. The rain-storms increased in frequency, length and force, and the ground ceased to dry within twenty-four hours, as it had after the summer storms, but softened into a slippery morass which could hardly be crossed by men on foot and could not be crossed at all by tracked or wheeled vehicles. The infantry waiting for the next task could see the dry ravines and shallow streams they had walked across being flooded by deep and foaming yellow torrents; and the troops who were under canvas lived on tented islands in seas of slush and lagoons of muddy water. The storm-clouds driving all day across the Italian sky shut out all hopes of a quick advance to the River Po; the rain had not reprieved the Germans, but it had given them a stay of execution.

22. Cesena and the River Savio

Three weeks passed before the whole division went into action again. These weeks, however, were not a time of rest, for the division was often at short notice to move up to the line, and many of the divisional troops were helping other divisions which were fighting.

On October the 1st, the division came under the command of V Corps, and various units were at once allotted tasks in support of other formations in the corps. The three regiments of field-guns went into action behind Sant' Arcangelo, in support of 56th Division; later they supported 46th Division and 10th Indian Division, and were still in action when 4th Division eventually came forward. The change of country-side from the sparsely populated hills to the more civilized plain, and the break in the weather, simplified the choice of gun positions; the advance-parties chose a house each, and fitted the guns round it. The gunners had to give up digging gun-pits, for after an hour or two of rain the gunners in the pit would be ankle-deep in water; instead, each gun stood on a rubble platform in a sangar of earth and timber.

Two days later, the mortars of 'D' Company of the Northumberland Fusiliers went into action in support of 46th Division. On the night of October the 7th, the company supported a brigade attack; heavy rain so softened the ground that base-plates would not hold, and the mortar positions had to be continually changed. The company fired more than two thousand four hundred bombs in two hours; when it returned to the command of 4th Division, it had fired nearly four thousand bombs.

7th and 225th Field Companies were working in the hilly country south of Route Nine, where bad weather was making the maintenance of roads in proper condition an exhausting and important task. 59th Field Company worked on the crossings over the Marecchia. The sappers were helped in their work—and in all the rest of their work during the war—by the Sapper Battery of 14th Anti-tank Regiment. Early in October, 91st Light Anti-aircraft Regiment also sent a Sapper Platoon to be affiliated to each Field Company. The almost complete disappearance of German tanks and aircraft had released the gunners of these two regiments for constructional work which was less exciting than their own role but no less important. 4th Reconnaissance Regiment sent detachments to help the V Corps signallers in line construction; and sections of the Provost Company helped the Corps Military Police with traffic control.

The rest of the division was hard at work training. Town clearing was one of the chief subjects of discussions and sand-model study, for there was a string of towns of various sizes along Route Nine as far as Bologna.

The heavy losses suffered by British formations in the Gothic Line fighting, and the fact that no reinforcements had reached Italy for six months, necessitated a change of war establishment. From this time on, infantry battalions were to consist of thirty officers and seven hundred other ranks. The division's battalions were therefore reorganized as three rifle companies and a carrier platoon at full strength, and a reinforcement platoon or company. In order to provide men for the reinforcement sub-unit, anti-tank guns were taken away from each battalion, and the anti-tank platoon was disbanded. The detachments who had manned the medium machine-guns returned to their original role in the carrier platoon, and their machine-guns were held in reserve by the battalion. To replace the battalion's machine-gunners, the nine machine-gun platoons of the Northumberland Fusiliers were affiliated to battalions. The normal allotment of anti-tank weapons to each infantry brigade was now to be one anti-tank battery, consisting of a troop of M.10 self-propelled guns, a troop of 17-pounder guns and two troops of 6-pounders. Anti-tank batteries had long been affiliated to infantry brigades, but the new organization of the infantry battalion necessitated a more permanent allotment of anti-tank guns.

Having broken into the plains of Lombardy, the Eighth Army set about pushing farther into them, in spite of slippery ground and firm resistance. The Canadian Corps moved into the plain between the coast and Route Nine; V Corps took the foot-hills south of Route

Nine. From these hills, spurs extend north-eastwards towards the main road; and, from between the spurs, streams and rivers run down to pass under the road on their way to the coast. From almost every spur, the Germans could see the attackers as they approached, and could watch Route Nine far behind them. Every canal, dyke, ditch, stream and river was roaring with flood water, and the Germans never failed to blow up a bridge or culvert if they had time. Worst of all, perhaps, all the roads south of Route Nine run down to it, and no roads run parallel with it and across the spurs.

By October the 17th, I Canadian Corps was approaching the River Pisciatello, eight miles north-west of Sant' Arcangelo; and V Corps on the left was fighting hard to clear the Germans from the ridges which look down on the town of Cesena, twelve miles along Route Nine from Sant' Arcangelo. 4th Division was to pass through 46th Division and continue the thrust on the right flank of V Corps.

Before the division as a whole went into action, 12th Brigade was to come under the command of 46th Division to relieve 138th Brigade on that division's right. 12th Brigade carried out its relief on the night of October the 17th; the Royal Fusiliers were on the spur running north-east from Monte Burattini, the Black Watch were round the Casa Baroni, a mile farther south, and the West Kents, farther back, were between Calisese and Montiano. The rest of 46th Division pushed on, clearing the spurs north-west of 12th Brigade, and on October the 19th entered Cesena. 'C' Reconnaissance Squadron took over from 2nd/5th Leicesters the nunnery of Madonna del Monte, which from a three-hundred-foot height looks down on the town three hundred yards away. During the afternoon, the Royal Fusiliers moved up a mile and a half to concentrate just north of Monte Romano, followed in the evening by the Black Watch; the Germans shelled both battalions as they marched up the winding mountain roads, and killed a number of men, among whom was Major W. A. B. Callander, who had been with the Black Watch since the outbreak of war. That afternoon, 12th Brigade came once more under Major-General Ward's command, and a number of other units came under Brigadier Heber-Percy's command, and made 12th Brigade a formidable striking force. These included the 16th Durham Light Infantry and a company of the 2nd/5th Leicesters; 142nd Regiment RAC, and the 10th Hussars; 324th and 150th Anti-tank Batteries (M.10 self-propelled 3-inch guns); and 'C' Company of the Northumberland Fusiliers

(Vickers machine-guns), and part of 'D' Company (4·2-inch mortars, under Captain Kershaw). The brigade was supported by the field-guns of three regiments—77th (Highland) Field Regiment, 5th Medium Regiment and two batteries of 142nd Field Regiment.

The first tasks of this brigade group were to relieve the other two companies of the Leicesters, which were holding the spurs which extended almost into the town; to patrol the River Savio west of the town, from the southernmost of the town's two bridges to the village of Il Trebbo, in the river's valley where it runs through the mountains three miles farther south; to push across the river near the town, if there were a good opportunity; and to clear the town as far as Route Nine, or, if this were impossible, to send out patrols to find out how this might best be done.

The ridge looking down on the Savio and on Cesena was still held by scattered Germans, most of them from the 114th Light Infantry Division; the Leicesters, however, had taken the Capuchin Monastery at its northern end. Before the brigade could begin patrolling, this ridge had to be cleared. 'X' and 'Z' Companies of the Royal Fusiliers drove the Germans off the ridge by midnight on October the 19th, while 'W' Company took over the Monastery from the Leicesters. Patrols that went down to the river reported that it was going to be difficult to cross; the banks were either steep—and in places wooded—or muddy and soft; the bottom was mud and shingle; the width varied between eighty and a hundred and fifty feet; the depth of water varied between four and ten feet; and the current ran at about five knots. The best place to cross was the southern bridge in Cesena; but this had already been knocked about by harassing fire from 77th Field Regiment, and, as a patrol of Fusiliers under Lance-Sergeant Mappley set foot on it, the Germans blew up its central span.

At length Lieutenant A. E. P. Townsend reported that he had forded the river five hundred yards south of the bridge, and Lieutenant-Colonel C. A. L. Shipley decided that the battalion would wade across at the same point. At five in the morning of October the 20th, 'W' Company scrambled down the steep banks into the water, which was chest-deep; the men were laden with weapons, ammunition and equipment, the crossing was difficult and a man was swept away and drowned. The company, wet through, turned northwards along the river bank, and just before dawn reached the village which clusters round the western end of the bridge. The Germans were taken by surprise, and some, sleeping in their billets, were summoned to surrender with shouts of 'Wakey wakey!' One of the Fusiliers captured a horse harnessed to a trailer containing the Germans' breakfast rations; the rations were put to good use, and the horse was afterwards sold to an Italian farmer, to the benefit of company funds. Other Germans, however, resisted, and a sharp street fight began; 'X' and 'Z' Companies, which were following up, joined in. By seven in the morning, the Royal Fusiliers held a bridge-head seven hundred yards wide and five hundred yards deep.

The Germans made every effort to push the Royal Fusiliers back into the river, and German infantry and tanks attacked the battalion throughout the morning. The enemy infantry were quickly scattered and beaten off, but the tanks were particularly dangerous because no anti-tank weapons heavier than a Piat could be carried across the river. During the afternoon, German guns brought down fire on the battalion's positions; this fire was so heavy that one company commander could not visit his three platoons in less than five hours. A counter-attack began to develop during the evening, but was broken up by the fire of 25-pounders and mortars. By eight in the evening all was quiet, except for occasional shells bursting in or near the river; one of these killed Major Galsworthy, who was leading a small party of men carrying sandwiches and tea across the river. This shelling of the river prevented the evacuation of wounded men; they had to stay in the bridge-head for twenty-four hours, but showed great courage and patience. Captain W. F. Caldwell, the medical officer, went about his work as calmly as if he had been in a base hospital, and perhaps more cheerfully.

In order to enlarge the bridge-head, Brigadier Heber-Percy decided to attack across the river that night with both the Black Watch and the West Kents. Soon after nightfall, sappers of 59th Field Company began to clear the eastern approaches to the bridge preparatory to getting a Bailey span across the gap which breached it. Machine-guns of the Northumberland Fusiliers began a programme of harassing fire which lasted for thirty-six hours, but the Germans continued to bring down heavy fire from mortars and guns in the neighbourhood of the bridge.

At midnight 'B' and 'C' Companies of the Black Watch began to cross the river between the two bridges. 'B' Company on the right had to clear the houses one by one; Major Hutchinson broke his ankle, and Lieutenant Steele took command. 'C' Company on the left met little opposition, and pushed forward half a mile in the darkness before halting because of the danger of being outflanked on the left. By dawn of October the 21st, the Black Watch held a narrow bridge-head about four hundred yards deep among streets of small houses; the bridge-head was extended by further street fighting during the morning.

The attack by the West Kents started an hour and a half later than that of the Black Watch. 'B' and 'D' Companies crossed the river near the point where the Fusiliers had crossed; although the assembly area and the river banks were under fire, no men were lost during the crossing. To help the men in wading across, the Pioneer Officer, Lieutenant L. S. Dunmall, stretched a rope from bank to bank; the rope was fixed on the town side to a tree, and held on the far side by Lieutenant Dunmall himself, since there was nothing to which he could tie it. The platoons of 'D' Company had varying success; 17 Platoon penetrated as far as a house half a mile beyond the river, in front of the Royal Fusiliers. 'C' Company took up a position in front of the centre company of the Royal Fusiliers, after having been driven back by a tank from a house four hundred yards farther on. Several hours after the rest of the battalion began its attack, 'B' Company crossed the river and took up a position behind the left flank of the Royal Fusiliers.

The defensive fire brought down by the Germans had prevented the sappers from getting their Bailey span across the breach in the bridge. Three hundred yards farther north, however, the Germans had prepared a ford for tanks, and four Arks were run into the river, connected to each other by their ramps. At dawn of October the 21st, tanks of 142nd RAC had begun to cross into the bridge-head; in spite of damage inflicted by enemy shelling, and various accidents, the crossing remained fit for tanks all day, but could not be made suitable for wheeled vehicles.

By midday, seven tanks had reached the Black Watch, and with their help the battalion began to enlarge its bridge-head. 'C' Company occupied a large block of flats south of Route Nine, and 'B' Company advanced five hundred yards to the north-west. During the afternoon 'A' Company crossed the Ark causeway and cleared the Germans out of the suburb between 'C' Company and the stadium seven hundred yards farther north. After dark, the German ration party, including two cooks, turned up to feed these Germans and were welcomed instead by the Black Watch.

The tanks which joined 'C' Company of the West Kents at noon helped them to reach one of their first objectives, a road junction two thousand yards beyond the bridge. 'B' Company on the left reached houses three hundred yards to the left of the road junction before being halted by machine-guns and an 88-mm gun, but the two companies were not able to link up. 'D' Company reached a house three hundred yards to the right of 'C' Company, from which they had been beaten off earlier in the day.

By night-fall, the bridge-head was considerably deeper than it had been at first, but the men who held it were not having an easy time. The steady shelling and nebelwerfering by the Germans, and the closeness of the country, made communication between platoons and companies difficult, and runners had a bad time dodging back and forth between explosions. The great number of houses in the bridge-head also complicated matters, for in the Royal Fusiliers' sector there were German Jaeger troops in a house next door to one occupied by a Fusilier platoon; and a German machine-gun between 'C' and 'D' Companies caused a great deal of trouble until Lieutenant R. Ternouth silenced it by capturing the detachment of five. There were also some German tanks in the bridge-head, and the arrival of the Shermans of 145th RAC was particularly welcome as no anti-tank guns had yet been able to cross the river. Major E. D. Rae, commanding 324th Anti-tank Battery, and Lieutenant T. G. Vesey, one of his troop commanders, were killed by a shell while trying to find out whether their guns could cross the Ark causeway into the bridge-head.

Five miles south-west of the 4th Division's bridge-head, troops of 10th Indian Division had crossed the river and were approaching a commanding height three thousand yards beyond it; on the right, the whole of I Canadian Corps had not yet reached the river, but two battalions were across in a bridge-head under constant counter-attack by the Germans. The right flank of 12th Brigade's bridge-head, however, was exposed, and could only be protected by harassing fire from artillery and heavy mortars.

Heavy rain fell that night, and the river rose four feet and ran faster; the Ark causeway was awash in turbulent yellow water. Getting supplies across the flooded river into the bridge-head became extremely difficult, for almost everything—food, ammunition, wireless batteries—had to be carried across the river by porters. To supply the Black Watch alone, on their first night west of the river, seventy-nine men were needed. During the night of October the 21st, since the German shelling still prevented the sappers from getting their Bailey bridge across, 7th Field Company began to build a folding-boat bridge just above the Ark crossing. The flood water, however, swept away the bridge and piled it against the Arks, which were already two feet under water; there was also a wide gap between the first Ark and the east bank. Unable to bring forward heavy supplies across the river, 12th Brigade was in no position to mount an attack from the bridge-head. The battalions spent their time patrolling, stalking an occasional German tank and mopping up tenacious parties of the enemy. On October the 22nd, the West Kents sent a standing patrol to keep touch with the Black Watch two hundred and fifty yards to their right; and the Fusiliers extended their front a little to include a big house on the left flank. The accuracy of the enemy's shooting at the river and crossing-places suggested that there might be German observers hidden in the houses of Cesena overlooking the river. 'B' Reconnaissance Squadron, with the help of men of the Field Security Section, searched all the houses overlooking the crossings there, but found nothing suspicious.

The flood had gone down a little by the afternoon of October the 22nd, but the gap in the Ark causeway still rendered it useless. Some amphibious vehicles were brought up, but they were unsuitable for such work and sank. During the night, 59th Field Company built two rafts at the southern crossing; but almost as soon as they were ready, the enemy shelling began with renewed fury and one of them was hit. It was repaired, and hit again, and again repaired; but by dawn of October the 23rd both rafts were riddled and useless. Many of the sappers and porters working at the crossing were lost; two were killed and fifteen wounded within a quarter of an hour. The gap in the Ark causeway, however, had been filled with another Ark, and three troops of Sherman tanks of 142nd RAC crossed to relieve the squadron supporting the West Kents, which by now had only four tanks running. During the night, the sappers built two bigger rafts at the southern crossing, and began to ferry jeeps and carriers across the river. 7th Field Company meanwhile was building up the causeway with rubble-filled sandbags, and by dawn of October the 24th it was fit for jeeps and carriers. By ten that morning the sappers of 225th Field Company, who had at last got the Bailey span across, had it ready for light vehicles, and, before they would guarantee that it could stand anything heavier, several tanks were already crossing.

This solved at last the urgent problem of the evacuation of wounded. Until then, all the wounded had to be carried back from the regimental aid posts across the river by returning porter-parties and German prisoners. These stretcher-bearers had had to wade the river until the assault boats arrived; both banks of the river were still under fire from guns and mortars, and the approaches were soft and muddy. Once across the river, the stretchers were put into ambulances of the Medical Corps or the American Field Service, and driven off to the advanced dressing station of 12th Field Ambulance set up in the town by Major P. K. Walker. The dressing station was within range of the nebelwerfers, but most of the German weapons were firing at the river, and the car posts, at which the ambulances collected the stretchers, were the point of danger. The shelling at one time was so fierce that the ambulances had to keep away from the river for most of the day.

During the morning of October the 23rd, Brigadier Heber-Percy crossed the river in a tank to hold an 'O' Group conference in the house used as a joint Battalion Headquarters by the Royal Fusiliers and the West Kents; as well as the Brigadier, both the commanding officers and a number of other officers were there. There were ten people in the room when a German shell smashed into the wall, and all was dust, rubble and confusion. Lieutenant-Colonels Shipley and Braithwaite, and Major W. I. Thomas—commanding 'W' Company of the Royal Fusiliers—were wounded but able to stay in the bridge-head; Major J. C. D. Jarrod and Captain E. J. Bennett, 'X' Company commander and Intelligence Officer of the Royal Fusiliers, were more seriously hurt and had to be evacuated; Major M. F. W. Tyndall, Captain Caldwell and the two signallers were unhurt, and the Brigadier, as a Fusilier said, 'only needed dusting'.

That evening the Field Company built a folding-boat bridge upstream of the Ark crossing. The Germans seemed unlikely to be able to hold on much longer to the line of the Savio. The German strategy was based on a system of defence lines, each of which ran along one of the many rivers or streams which come down from the hills and cross the plain to the coast. The Savio marked the Erika Line; the Franzeska Line followed the Torrente Bevano, which passes under Route Nine two miles still farther along Route Nine, beyond the village of Forlimpopoli. The Erika Line had now been breached by the Indians on its right, was threatened by the Canadians on its left, and its centre opposite 4th Division was beginning to crumble.

On October the 23rd, Major-General Ward decided to speed up this process with a good hard push by 12th Brigade, now that the Savio was adequately bridged. The brigade was first to deepen the bridge-head to about two thousand yards, and then, if the Germans weakened, to break out of the bridge-head and spread out. Major-General Ward placed the Surreys and 'B' Squadron of the 51st Royal Tanks under Brigadier Heber-Percy's command for this attack, and arranged the support of a great weight of artillery, which included two Canadian and three New Zealand field regiments. German positions at Bertinoro and on Monte Maggio, the two thousand-foot heights which from seven thousand yards to the west looked down on the bridge-head, were to be blinded by repeated air attacks.

The tanks began to cross the river that afternoon, loaded with petrol and with reserve ammunition of all types. The Surreys crossed the Ark causeway during the night, and reached their concentration area by three in the morning.

At the same time, however, the Germans were withdrawing from the Erika Line. 12th Brigade's attack found only a weak rear-guard of Germans, too dazed by the barrage which had preceded the attack to put up much of a fight. The roads, however, were sown with mines, and deeply cratered at awkward points; and the German artillery shelled the advancing troops with accuracy and persistence.

By the end of October the 25th, the Black Watch were nearly two miles along Route Nine from the river; the West Kents were little more than a mile from Bertinoro, from which the Franzeska Line might be overlooked and out-flanked; and the Royal Fusiliers had cleared the ground enclosed by the loop in the Savio on the left of the bridge-head. The Surreys had reached the hills two and a half miles beyond the river, and 'A' Reconnaissance Squadron on the left was in touch with troops of 10th Indian Division.

12th Brigade had reached and passed all its objectives, and had completed its task. 10th Brigade meanwhile had been following up, and during the night of October the 25th began to pass through. By one in the morning, the last weary infantrymen of 12th Brigade had reached the billets prepared for them in Cesena.

The brigade's withdrawal after six days of really hard fighting was marked by the prompt arrival from the rear of a 'Tough Tactics Training Team'; but the hard-earned rest was not to be so strenuous as some past rests had been. The town of Cesena had not been so battered in the fighting along the river that the troops could not be comfortably billeted; and occupation of the town gave the division its first chance of deploying its Welfare services in operational conditions—Welfare work began while the town was still being shelled.

A big hotel was taken over and transformed into a club for 'other ranks', and was called the 'Dutch Cheese'; the facilities of the club included reading and writing rooms, an information room, post office, barber's shop, photographer's studio and restaurant. The restaurant was staffed by Italian waitresses, and an Italian orchestra played there during meals. About fifteen hundred meals were served there every day. A bar was also opened at first, but the customers were so many and so thirsty, and the *vino* was so limited, that it had to close down; the two divisional pubs, the 'Jeep and Trailer' and the 'Red Lion', had to close down for the same reason.

Two mobile film units were installed in local cinemas taken over by the division, and each gave three shows every day. The films were third-rate, but the shortage of film-shows of any kind made these immensely popular. The Opera House had been slightly damaged by shell-fire, but was repaired and taken over; and twice a day the divisional Concert Party put on its show there before a crowded house. For one week, Gabrielle Brune appeared as guest-artiste.

All units of 12th Brigade, and the Royal Fusiliers in particular, were congratulated on their efforts in the battle by Major-General Ward, by V Corps Commander, Lieutenant-General Sir Charles Keightley, and by the Eighth Army Commander, Lieutenant-General Sir Richard McCreery.

23. The River Ronco and Forli

Having relieved 12th Brigade, 10th Brigade continued the advance. From the farthest point reached by the Surreys on October the 24th, the Bedfords pushed on during the 25th, first to the crest of Monte Maggio, and then to the mountain village of Bertinoro, half a mile farther on. From a great height above the plain, Bertinoro dominates Route Nine and the plain for many miles. If the Germans had been less disorganized, they might have made the village the keystone of a defensive position like that of Cassino. The DCLI passed through the Bedfords in Bertinoro; 'D' and 'A' Companies on the left took up positions on a ridge a mile short of the River Ronco, while 'B' Company went on down to the village of Selbagnone in the plain. 10th Brigade's advance so far had been hindered only by mines and demolitions, but 'B' Company had to fight before they could occupy Selbagnone. Later that afternoon, a patrol went out from Selbagnone towards the river, and had a sharp skirmish with some Germans; the enemy retreated across the river by a footbridge west of the village, and the patrol found that this bridge, although partly wrecked, could still be crossed by infantry.

The advance up Route Nine was being continued by three units temporarily under Major-General Ward's command; these were the 60th Rifles, 4th Hussars and 1st Field Squadron RE. The going at first was extremely difficult because of the mines and demolitions left by the Germans. The large crater at Torre del Moro, crossed by the Black Watch the day before, could not be crossed by vehicles until the sappers had put in a great deal of work on it. Once on the move, however, the group advanced rapidly, and by the end of the day a motor platoon had reached the Ronco bridge, more than seven miles farther along Route Nine. The infantry had occupied the small town of Forlimpopoli, on Route Nine, and a company had a firm base only a thousand yards short of the river.

The division had now reached the Ronco and the Gudrun Line on a front of two and a half miles; there had been no resistance on the Franzeska Line. Major-General Ward decided to cross the river and continue the advance that night. Brigadier Shoosmith therefore ordered the DCLI to cross the river with tanks and take a bridgehead extending as far as the road which runs from Route Nine to Meldola, about a thousand yards beyond the river and parallel with it. The Bedfords came up behind the DCLI, ready to pass through the bridge-head.

Lieutenant-Colonel Harding decided to use the foot-bridge west of Selbagnone for the infantry, and patrols found for the tanks a ford which had been used by German tanks a few hundred yards farther upstream.

The evening was gloomy with heavy clouds, and rain fell more and more heavily as time went on; the night was extremely dark, and the low clouds prevented the searchlights from lighting up the scene. From nine in the evening, German guns heavily but intermittently shelled Selbagnone and the foot-bridge which the troops were to cross; the fire was so heavy just before zero hour that the attack had to be postponed half an hour.

Half an hour before midnight, 'A' Company moved off and crossed the river. As the leading platoon reached the far bank, Germans on both flanks opened fire; those on the right had to be ignored, as they were too far away, but those on the left were silenced. In the face of machine-gun and artillery fire, the company went on towards the first objective, a group of houses called Il Capanno, seven hundred yards beyond the bridge; as they moved forward in the darkness, company headquarters and one of the platoons lost touch with the other two platoons. Soon after midnight, the company headquarters group reached the Casa Foschi, two hundred yards south of Il Capanno, and forced the Germans out of the nearby houses; the other two platoons reached and took the objective. Major Ruttledge asked for more light, as fighting was difficult in the pitch darkness, but the searchlights were already doing their best against the heavy clouds. At one in the morning, Major Ruttledge suspected that the Germans were about to put in a counter-attack, and called for defensive fire; within twenty minutes the Germans attacked violently from houses near Il Capanno, and from the track south-west of the Casa Foschi. The two parts of the company, which were not in touch with each other, fought separate battles, and there was close fighting in the darkness and rain as the Germans tried repeatedly to rush and enter the houses. After an hour of this the Germans withdrew, leaving twelve prisoners behind, and their guns began to shell the company area.

'D' Company of the DCLI, meanwhile, crossed the river and lay up on the west bank. When the counter-attack on 'A' Company had been beaten off, 'D' Company moved up to occupy a defensive position on the right of 'A'. By dawn of October the 26th, the two companies were reorganized on the captured positions, with 'D' Company on the right and 'A' on the left, and Major Ruttledge sharing a headquarters with Major J. T. B. Notley DSO.

At dawn of October the 26th, the tanks began to move towards their ford, and after two hours reached the river. With tanks, the DCLI would probably have been able to extend their bridge-head, as planned, to the main road running across the front of their position. But as the leading tank entered the river, it was knocked out by an anti-tank gun, and lay blocking the only crossing by which armour could reach the infantry.

An hour and a quarter later, the Germans opened a fifteen-minute artillery concentration on the bridge-head positions, and, after ten minutes of shelling, launched a strong counter-attack. After an hour's fighting, 'A' and 'D' Companies were both holding firm; Major Notley was wounded but remained in action. German tanks closed on the positions from three sides, and got in among the houses; they fired their guns first at the corners of the top floor and then at the remains of the walls, until nothing was left; and then they started again on the next floor until the whole house came down. There was no basement or cellar, in which the men inside could shelter; as they ran out of the house, they were shot by German infantry waiting outside. Some of the German prisoners tried to escape in the confusion, but were killed either by the DCLI or by the fire of the enemy. The gunner officer's Number 22 wireless set was crushed by falling masonry, and the last Number 18 set was smashed soon after nine o'clock, while Major Notley was using it to describe the situation to Lieutenant-Colonel Harding. The battle broke up into a number of isolated struggles, in which small parties held their ground because they had no orders to withdraw. At half-past nine, however, survivors began to swim back across the river, while the 22nd Field Regiment fired a smoke screen to hide them.

An officer and two other ranks had been killed while patrolling before the counter-attack; another officer and thirteen other ranks, wounded during the battle, had been evacuated across the river; the two company commanders, two other officers and a hundred and twenty-four other ranks were missing. The DCLI were at once relieved by the Bedfords, and withdrew from the forward area.

Months later, the DCLI heard news of one of the missing officers. Five days after being captured, Lieutenant A. J. Spencer MC jumped from a train bound for Germany, and began a long journey towards freedom on foot and by bicycle. After travelling three hundred miles he was recaptured. A fortnight later he escaped again. After a second journey of three hundred miles he reached Yugoslavia, where he was made welcome by partisans. Eventually the partisans helped him to get back to southern Italy.

The 60th Rifles Group on Route Nine, meanwhile, had found on October the 25th that two of the six spans of the bridge crossing the Ronco had been destroyed; but the enemy fire from across the river was comparatively light, as though there were no great strength on the far bank, and the ford fourteen hundred yards upstream of the bridge seemed to be suitable for tanks. The commanding officer of the Rifles therefore decided to cross the river south of the bridge, and to attack the village of Ronco just beyond the far bank. As darkness fell, the German mortars increased their fire, but they were harassing Route Nine rather than engaging a defensive fire-plan. The rain and darkness were more serious, and held up the crossing of the river, which did not begin until after midnight.

The disaster which followed was very similar to that which had overtaken the DCLI. Most of the battalion crossed the river and began to clear Ronco village. The Germans came back with a powerful counter-attack; the Rifles found that the river had flooded while they were fighting, and that they could neither withdraw across it nor be reinforced. Nearly all the men who had crossed the river were lost.

The break in the weather just as the troops of the division were crossing a particularly difficult river, combined with the force and vigour of the Germans on the spot, had inflicted a sharp reverse on the division. The DCLI had been badly mauled, and had suffered heavy losses. The 60th Rifles had been crippled by casualties; it was particularly unfortunate that this battalion should have been so knocked about when serving with a division other than its own. The men of both battalions had shown the greatest gallantry on that unpleasant night.

The torrential rain not only prevented the crossing of the Ronco; it interrupted the communications forward of Cesena. By ten in the morning of October the 26th, the approaches to the folding-boat bridge across the Savio were under water, and before eleven the bridge itself was swept away. Half an hour later, only jeeps could get past the junction of six roads at Sette Crociari, and by midday the road at San Mauro in Valle was flooded. During the afternoon, the bridge across the crater at Torre del Moro sank down into the crater, and all the repaired demolitions on Route Nine were flooded out. The sappers, who less than twenty-four hours earlier had been preparing to bridge the Ronco, were now fully occupied with road repairs; fortunately the 220th and 221st Field Companies of 56th Division were under Lieutenant-Colonel Nelson's command at the time. Early in the evening, the roads were so bad that Major-General Ward had to forbid the movement of all vehicles not needed for road repairs or for taking essential supplies to units; 28th Brigade, which had been about to concentrate west of the Savio, had to stay where it was. The bridge at Torre del Moro was reopened early next day, though it continued to give trouble, and Route Nine between Cesena and the Ronco was not fit for normal traffic for another four days.

4th Division's ban on inessential traffic eased but did not remove the strain on roads and bridges. Route Nine was being used by 1st Canadian Division as well as by 4th Division, and the move forward of guns and of relieving troops weighed heavily on the southern bridge at Cesena; the damaged masonry piers, on which the Bailey bridge rested, began to crumble. On October the 28th the bridge was no longer fit for Churchill tanks, but that afternoon the northern bridge was opened, and both bridges were classified as fit to carry one slow-moving Sherman tank at a time. When the northern bridge was finished on October the 30th, and declared fit for all traffic, the southern bridge was used for light vehicles only.

On the right of 4th Division, 1st Canadian Division had reached the Ronco north of the railway bridge, but had made no crossing. On the left, 10th Indian Division had also reached the river, and some of its troops had crossed into a small bridge-head two miles south-west of Selbagnone.

Lieutenant-General Sir Charles Keightley now planned to relieve 1st Canadian Division on the right with 12th Lancers, who would guard the right flank of 4th Division as the advance went on. The division's boundary was extended a mile and a half to the north of Route Nine so as to include the town of Forli and its suburbs. On the left of 4th Division, 10th Indian Division was to be relieved by 46th Division.

The group of units which, under Major-General Ward's command, had been pushing up Route Nine was relieved by 'C' Reconnaissance Squadron, and left 4th Division. 'A' Reconnaissance Squadron filled the gap between Route Nine and 10th Brigade. There were no other major changes in the division's dispositions. The floods which had covered the fields alongside the river went down slowly, for occasional rain-storms swelled them again; for four nights after its sudden spate the Ronco could not be crossed. The men of patrols who had tried to cross in the darkness were swept off their feet by the swift current, or had to be rescued with ropes from deep and treacherous mud.

For the time being there was stalemate. The Germans on one side of the river and the British on the other harassed each other with fire; 4th Division made feint attacks from time to time, and the Germans maintained a massive defence.

During the night of October the 30th, patrols from the division tried to cross the river; they were prevented, at some points by enemy fire and at others by the depth and swiftness of the water, but patrols of the Surreys found a possible crossing-place a thousand yards north of the foot-bridge used by the DCLI.

Next day, October the 31st, the enemy on the near flank of 10th Indian Division were found to have withdrawn, and the Reconnaissance Regiment and 10th Brigade once more probed the river-line. Reconnaissance patrols tried to cross between Route Nine and the railway, and were held up by chest-deep mud and by fire from Ronco village; but farther south a patrol from 'B' Squadron succeeded in crossing at the ford which had been used by the 60th Rifles five days before. The patrol reached the Meldola road near the north-east corner of Forli air-field, taking five prisoners on the way; two hundred yards farther on towards Ronco village, the patrol met stiff resistance and came to a halt.

Soon after midday, patrols of the Surreys, later followed by the three rifle companies, forded the river at the newly-found crossing-places north of the foot-bridge. In spite of some enemy resistance, the companies reached the Meldola road, and there joined the patrol from 'B' Squadron.

As the Surreys pushed northwards between the air-field and the river, the enemy's resistance grew in strength, and the Scolo Re dei Fossi was found to be too deep and too well defended to be crossed. By nightfall, 'D' Company was in position between the dyke and the river, another company was a thousand yards farther south, and the third was in the loop of the river a thousand yards still farther south-west. The Germans clearly meant to fight for Route Nine; they had withdrawn troops from the flanks of 10th Indian Division's bridge-head only in case they should be cut off by a crossing by 4th Division.

The sappers began to bridge the river that night. They were to have put the main bridge across on Route Nine, but as the Germans were still in the houses only a hundred yards away bridging was impossible. The sappers were able, however, to note the damage to the spans and estimate that an assault bridge would not be enough to make it good. At the Surrey's crossing-place, 225th Field Company began to build a folding-boat bridge two hundred feet long, to carry vehicles weighing up to nine tons. At the same time, the tank ford north of the foot-bridge was prepared for use.

By dawn of November the 1st, the bridge was across and the approaches were fit for traffic. Three-quarters of an hour later, the Bedfords crossed it, and tanks of 51st Royal Tanks were moving towards the tank ford to support the Bedfords and Surreys.

Across the path of the Bedfords lay the Scolo Re dei Fossi, the dyke which had already held up the Surreys farther north. Tanks would hardly be able to cross the dyke itself, but there was a bridge six hundred and fifty yards south of the air-field. If this bridge were to be destroyed, the Bedfords might have to attack without tanks. Major A. E. Richards, commanding 'A' Company of the Northumberland Fusiliers, was therefore given the task of keeping the Germans away from the bridge. He detailed two platoons for this work, and the eight Vickers machine-guns fired in turn for more than twelve hours. One of their bullets exploded a mine, which damaged the bridge slightly, but otherwise the shoot was completely successful, and the Bedfords crossed the bridge with their tanks next morning. They found signs of a hurried withdrawal by the Germans; guns covering the bridge had been abandoned in their positions, and demolition equipment was lying about near the bridge. For some time afterwards Major Richards was known as 'Horatius'.

The tank ford across the Ronco was open by this time, and twenty-five tanks made the crossing, together with Arks, AVREs, anti-tank guns and transport carrying two days' reserve rations and a day's battle expenditure of ammunition and petrol. Between the foot-bridge and the old tank ford, which was still blocked by the derelict tank, 7th Field Company began to build a low-level Bailey bridge, and erected a steel crib pier at the water's edge.

The leading company of the Bedfords pushed forward as far as and beyond Carpena, and was five hundred yards short of the south-west corner of the air-field when German infantry supported by a Tiger tank opened a fierce fire from the corner. The force of the opposition showed that the Bedfords had reached a point on the next German defence line, which ran through Ronco and crossed the air-field to the village of San Martino in Strada, on the Rabbi river south of Forli. The German defence was supported by a number of guns and nebelwerfers as well as by tanks.

Since there was clearly going to be no rapid advance along the north side of the air-field, the Assault Squadron of the Reconnaissance Regiment, commanded by Captain K. C. P. Ive, relieved 'D' Company of the Surreys at the north-east corner, and the infantry company withdrew to the area south-west of the tank crossing; three Churchill tanks, one tapered 2-pounder and one 6-pounder anti-tank gun stayed with the Assault Squadron.

That evening the rain began to fall again, and fell all night. The sappers watched the folding-boat bridge closely, ready to break it the moment the water rose seriously. At eleven o'clock they expected it to last at least an hour longer, but shortly afterwards the full force of the spate arrived without warning. The steel crib pier was bowled over and rolled away downstream; the folding-boat bridge was snatched from its moorings and disappeared in the darkness. Much of it was found later, piled up on a shoal in a confusion of ropes and wreckage.

Once again, the weather had cut off one of the division's bridgeheads, and the division's most urgent task was to get in touch across the river again. The first essential was to get steel wire cables across the river, in order to start a ferry. Men tried to row across in assault boats with one end of the cable, but the boats could not float in the swift and seething flood waters. 7th Field Company, however, tied a length of signal cable to a disarmed Piat bomb, and fired it across the river to men of the Sapper Battery of 14th Antitank Regiment, who had been cut off on the other side. The party across the river reeled in the signal cable, to the end of which the wire rope was fixed. The sappers fired more lines across, and by the next evening, November the 2nd, they had a folding-boat ferry working. At the northern crossing-place, 225th Field Company later used the same method, and opened their ferry on November the 3rd. Farther south, 59th Field Company rigged up an aerial ropeway; its great span and consequent sag, however, made it unable to carry considerable weights. Several amphibious vehicles attempted the crossing; they appeared to be more efficient than those tried out on the Savio, and one of them, with a great deal of manœuvring, crossed the river and emerged with difficulty on the far bank. This trial showed, however, that a regular service with loaded vehicles would not work. In order to supplement the ferries and the ropeways, the division's essential transport was allowed to use two crossings in 10th Indian Division's area—at first an aqueduct, and later a Bailey bridge where the road from Selbagnone to Meldola crosses the river. These crossings, and the supplies which had been brought forward across the river as soon as 10th Brigade's attack began, kept the troops in the bridge-head from running short.

By dawn on November the 4th, the level of the river had fallen low enough to allow tanks to cross at the Surreys' ford. 225th Field Company began work shortly afterwards, and built a new bridge with folding-boat equipment, much of which had been rescued by 59th Field Company from the wrecks of the previous bridges in the Ronco and the Savio. The bridge was ready by midnight, but could not be used until a Bailey span had been set across the crater where the approach road crossed the Scolo Ausa Nuova. The level of the river sank lower still, and on November the 7th some of the folding-boats touched bottom. This made the bridge incapable of carrying its proper load, and trestles had to be wedged under the boats. This bridge was generally known as 'Lords'.

On November the 4th, 7th Field Company began to build a remarkable double-truss, triple-storey Bailey bridge, a hundred and ninety feet long, a little below their previous site. This bridge, known as 'Commons', was finished four days later by 59th Field Company, and the bridge was opened to vehicles weighing up to thirty tons, and less than twelve feet two inches high. A great deal of work had to be done on the approaches to this bridge; with the help of large working parties from the reserve brigades, the sappers had to build a road seven hundred yards long, running beside the river, between the east bank and the flood-bank. The sappers were working hard on the roads in the bridge-head as well as on the river, in order to improve communications and to open up new concentration areas. All this bridging and maintenance work was carried out under fire from enemy guns, which were engaged in harassing or defensive shooting.

The evacuation of wounded men across the Ronco was no less difficult than it had been from the Savio bridge-head. The first stretcher cases had to be brought across the river by boat, before the wire ropes had been fixed up, with men wading and pushing the boat. Although the river had fallen since the spate on October the 26th, the current was still swift enough to carry the men out of their depth and sweep them with the boat nearly a quarter of a mile downstream before they could reach the east bank. No reception centre could be set up on the west bank before the second spate of the river, and wounded men had to be treated as far as possible by the battalion medical officers in the regimental aid posts.

On November the 3rd, 4th Division opened a Bailey bridge on the road from Selbagnone to Meldola, and some of the wounded could then be taken straight to Forlimpopoli. Two days later, when 46th Division's bridge had been enlarged to take two-way traffic, the advanced dressing station moved across the Ronco to the Villa Valeri. At this time, 10th Brigade was being more heavily shelled and mortared than ever before in Italy, and men in the advanced dressing station could see the flash of the nebelwerfers round Forli and hear the whine of the approaching bombs. The main road two hundred yards away was often whipped by machine-gun fire, and the sign at the gate outside the Villa was often punctured by bullets.

The division had been brought to a halt on November the 1st partly by German resistance but mainly by the weather. While restoring its communications, the division was also preparing a fresh attack. On November the 3rd, a day of heavy rain, 'B' Company of the Bedfords put in a local attack, supported by tanks and an artillery programme which included the laying of a smoke screen, partly to cover the actual attack and partly to suggest to the Germans that 10th Brigade was about to push towards Route Nine from the north-east corner of the air-field. The Germans fought back strongly, and brought down heavy defensive fire from nebelwerfers along the whole front of the division; but they did not counter-attack.

'B' Reconnaissance Squadron, commanded by Major J. D. Wigham, relieved 'C' Squadron in the holding positions between the railway and Route Nine. On November the 5th, 'A' Squadron concentrated in Forlimpopoli, where Regimental Headquarters had been working since the end of October. That day some German shells burst outside the orderly room, and the regiment learned with interest that the Orderly Room Corporal had received his baptism of fire and would not be able for some time to resume his seat with comfort.

At this time the 91st Light Anti-aircraft Regiment left the division. The German Air Force, out-numbered and out-fought by British and American aircraft, had long since disappeared from the sky over their Bofors guns; but all ranks of the regiment, under the command of Lieutenant-Colonel Middleton, had worked with enthusiasm at the alternative tasks assigned to them, whether they were firing their guns at ground targets, controlling traffic or helping the sappers.

The Scolo Re dei Fossi, which runs along the eastern edge of Forli air-field, is more than thirteen feet deep, with sloping sides far enough apart and steep enough to be impassable by infantry in wet weather, and impassable by tanks in any weather. 10th Brigade's shortest approach to the air-field buildings, however, was from this eastern side and across the dyke. The Germans realized this, and whenever they felt nervous or suspicious the defensive fire of their guns and nebelwerfers came down heavily on the dyke, on the main road a few hundred yards behind, and in the area between the road and the river. The whole surface of the air-field was covered by German machine-guns and anti-tank guns. The southern edge of the air-field was more vulnerable; good tracks, free from mines, approached it from Carpena, and the ditch along the boundary was not deep enough to keep tanks away from the air-field. Mine-clearing patrols of the DCLI, with representatives from the tank battalion, checked the tracks during the night of November the 6th, crossed the air-field boundary and went forty yards into the air-field itself without finding any mines or anti-tank obstacles.

South-west of the air-field, the German defence was firm and vigilant between the western corner of the air-field and San Martino in Strada; parts of this defence were reinforced by the Scolo Cerchia, which lay across the path of any advance to Forli round the southern side of the air-field. Where the road from Carpena to San Martino crosses the dyke, a patrol of Bedfords found a crater thirty feet across and fifteen feet deep. The German positions were strongly held, and supported by Tiger tanks.

The enemy's resistance in front of the air-field and Forli itself, and farther south along the river Rabbi, was so firm and so advantageously placed that Lieutenant-General Keightley arranged a corps attack, to begin on the night of November the 7th. 4th Division's part was to cross the air-field and capture Forli.

The division at once began a fire programme intended to soften the enemy's resistance and to suggest that an attack was being prepared near the railway bridge or farther north. The harassing fire covered a large area which extended from Ronco to the air-field buildings and to Forli, and the targets included roads, gun and nebelwerfer positions, dumps and suspected headquarters. As the night of the attack approached, the softening programme merged into the fire-plan for the attack.

The divisional and supporting artillery naturally played the largest part in this fire programme. In addition, the Reconnaissance Regiment's battery of self-propelled guns fired fast and often at targets in Ronco village, on Route Nine and north-east of Forli, drawing on itself some German counter-battery fire. 38th (New Zealand) Anti-tank Battery successfully shot up the control tower of Forli air-field, and from the battery's observation post directed the fire of the self-propelled 3-inch guns of 93rd Anti-tank Regiment. Two platoons of 'D' Company of the Northumberland Fusiliers were deployed by Captain P. B. Gorst on each side of the Ronco, where they were firing continually in support of 10th Brigade; the rest of the company, under Captain R. M. Kershaw, was deployed west of the river on November the 7th. The harassing programme gave the battalion a chance to make impressive use of its medium machine-guns. Lieutenant-Colonel F. H. Butterfield, acting as the divisional machine-gun commander, ordered and co-ordinated all the division's machine-gun fire. On November the 7th, Lieutenant-Colonel Butterfield brought a platoon of 'C' Company forward from Cesena to join 'A' Company, which had been harassing the enemy from its positions with 10th Brigade, and which now returned to Lieutenant-Colonel Butterfield's command. Twenty-eight of the battalion's medium machine-guns were now deployed to support the attack. Firing began during the afternoon of November the 7th, and the machine-guns engaged roads up which supplies and reinforcements might move, or down which the Germans might withdraw from the air-field towards Forlì; they also fired at targets north of Route Nine, as part of the deception scheme. The record of ammunition expenditure showed that 'A' Company had fired almost twenty thousand rounds per gun since October the 29th, and that 'B' Company had fired more than twenty-four thousand rounds per gun in three days.

The process of softening 278th Division's resistance was helped by close-support aircraft, which included Kittybombers and rocket-firing Typhoons; on November the 5th and 6th, aircraft on call for 10th Brigade attacked fourteen targets. The large and successful air programme for November the 7th included attacks by light and medium bombers on enemy reserves, headquarters and dumps, by fighter-bombers on twelve targets near Route Nine and between the railway bridge and Ospedaletto, and by 10th Brigade's 'Cab-rank' of aircraft on the northern and south-western sides of the air-field.

Major-General Ward planned to clear the northern edge of the air-field with 10th Brigade, which would patrol towards Ronco and clear the village when he gave the word. 28th Brigade was to be in reserve until called on to carry out one of several possible tasks. The sappers were to build tank crossings over the Scolo Re dei Fossi and the Scolo Cerchia, and to develop forward routes for the advance. The gunners exchanged FOO parties with 46th Division, so that a 4th Division gunner officer and his party moved with the right forward battalion of 46th Division, which would be attacking on the left, and a 46th Division gunner party moved with the left forward battalion of 4th Division. The fire of the 4·2-inch mortars of 'D' Company, the Northumberland Fusiliers, was co-ordinated with that of the divisional artillery.

On the afternoon of November the 7th, the King's and the Somersets crossed the river to their concentration areas near Il Capanno. Two squadrons of tanks of 142nd RAC had preceded them, and a bridge had been built for them to cross the Scolo Re dei Fossi. The Black Watch concentrated around Forlimpopoli, found comfortable billets ready for them, and prepared for the hard work to come by settling down to a full night's sleep. The Hampshires were not due to reach their forward concentration area until November the 8th, but they had already suffered a disaster. On November the 6th, Lieutenant-Colonel F. Mitchell DSO MC, with his second-in-command and company commanders, was looking over the battle-field from the spur east of the river, when one of the party stepped on an 'S' mine. Major G. E. Morgan was killed, and Major Bichard MC was mortally wounded; Major Wakeford VC was wounded for the third time in less than two years; and the second-in-command was severely wounded. Lieutenant-Colonel Mitchell and Major Knight MC were unhurt.

Brigadier Shoosmith decided to clear the northern edge of the air-field with the Surreys, commanded by Lieutenant-Colonel C. G. S. McAlester MC; the battalion was to attack across the Scolo Re dei Fossi. The attack presented the problem of how to get the infantry across the air-field without loss. Brigadier Shoosmith decided to effect this by surprise; the fire-plan was to be so arranged that the Germans would not be warned by it that the attack was about to begin, and the infantry would deliver their assault in the darkness which preceded moonrise. The tanks would have to cross the air-field from the southern edge to meet the infantry at the buildings; because of the Scolo, they could not move with the infantry.

The Surreys started their attack just before eleven on the night of November the 7th; the high wind deadened any sound they made. They were wearing leather jerkins instead of great-coats, in order to travel as light as possible, and they were bitterly cold, particularly as they crossed the dyke. The platoons scrambled across in single file, and the leading man of each stood on the far bank and helped the others up. On the other side, they quickly formed up, with 'C' Company, commanded by Major G. Spencer, on the right and 'B' Company, commanded by Major A. Paskins MC, on the left.

From the ditch across the open air-field to the buildings is about seven hundred yards; the men were too heavily laden with weapons and ammunition to run, but they kept up a steady jog-trot. They were within fifty yards of the first German positions before a single enemy weapon opened fire. Both companies charged at once. Some platoons were beaten off with grenades and machine-carbines, and had to build hurried breast-works of rubble, short of the buildings; but most of the platoons broke into the buildings, threw out the

Germans and consolidated. Before long, the Surreys held Buildings 1, 2, 4 and 5 (*see air-field map on page xxix*).

The uproar of this fighting had, of course, roused all the Germans on the air-field and nearby, and they opened a heavy cross-fire from the north and north-east. By midnight, confused fire seemed to be going off in all directions. The headquarters of both companies were set up near the smashed tower between Buildings 1 and 2, and the company commanders knew that their companies held these two buildings; but they could not find out what had happened anywhere else, because movement in the open was prevented by fire from the north and from Building 3. Visibility was restricted by clouds of dust whipped up by the wind from the heaps of rubble around the bomb-damaged buildings. All three Number 18 wireless sets refused to work, and the only communication across the air-field was by the Number 22 set brought up by Captain K. Peter, of 33rd Field Battery, who with his party had walked unescorted across the air-field. For several hours the platoons in Buildings 4 and 5 were out of touch with company headquarters, and the two companies could get no farther on.

At dawn, however, six tanks of 51st Royal Tanks came charging across the air-field, each towing a tapered 2-pounder anti-tank gun; the infantry fired recognition signals, and joined up with the armour. The platoons which had been repulsed managed to get in touch with headquarters. Majors Paskins and Spencer now had tank support, knew the whole situation, and could make their plans accordingly.

With the help of the tanks, which fired shells through the walls, the Surreys went on to take Buildings 3, 6, 7 and 8 before dawn, and with them a number of prisoners and weapons.

By the time the sun was up, both companies were firmly consolidated, 'C' Company in Buildings 1, 2 and 3, 'B' Company in Buildings 5 and 6. Buildings 7 and 8 were too exposed to be occupied at first. The ambulance carrier was taking the wounded away. The whole operation had run almost to programme.

At eight o'clock, the Carrier Platoon (dismounted) set off to join 'C' Company. The platoon crossed the Scolo at the north-eastern corner of the air-field, farther north than had the two companies, and advanced along the deep subsidiary dyke along the northern boundary. Suddenly a machine-gun opened fire upon them from a well dug-in position only twenty yards away above them and to the right. This post must have been occupied throughout the night—three more were afterwards found farther on alongside the ditch—and might have caught the advancing companies in fire from the flank and ruined the whole operation. Captain Hatt Cook blinded the machine-gun detachment of three Germans with smoke from his 2-inch mortars, got his sections out of the dyke, and leap-frogged them round dispersal-pits on the air-field until one of them was only a hundred yards away from the machine-gun. From this nearest position—he had competed at Bisley before the war—he shot with a rifle one of the Grenadiers manning the gun, mortally wounded the second and after several shots claimed the third, who ran for his life, as a 'probable' at six hundred yards range. Having completed a model platoon action, the Carrier Platoon then got back into the dyke and went on to the buildings.

At about the same time, the Germans, who until this time had brought down less than twenty rounds of defensive fire, began to shell and mortar heavily, and the slightest move by the Surreys for the rest of the day caused the enemy to react with explosive force; two of the anti-tank guns were knocked out by this fire. But the expected counter-attack never developed, and the situation for the Germans in the sector became more and more unpleasant. The positions on the northern side of the air-field were strongly held by infantry and tanks of 10th Brigade; the Germans in the Officina dell' Acquedotto were being harassed by a troop of tanks and M.10s on the southern edge; to the south-west, 28th Brigade and 46th Division were still advancing; and overhead roared the aircraft of the Desert Air Force, bombing and machine-gunning the enemy in depth, giving the infantry the closest possible support and hunting ceaselessly for German tanks.

The 28th Brigade attack had begun at four in the morning, five hours after that of 10th Brigade; as the King's on the right and the Somersets on the left moved forward, the Hampshires in reserve were on their way up to 'Lords' bridge. Each of the forward battalions was supported by three tanks of 142nd RAC; before the rest of the tanks could join the infantry, the southern of the two bridges across the Scolo Re dei Fossi collapsed, and they had to find another way across.

For the first half-hour, the two battalions advanced without meeting any Germans. When the King's reached the south-western corner of the air-field, however, they had to fight hard between the air-field and the road junction a hundred yards farther south-west, the code name of which was 'Cutler'. The Germans in this area resisted fiercely, and the King's could advance little farther for the time being. By the afternoon, after heavy fighting, the King's had taken 'Cutler', and 'A' Company had reached a house two hundred yards to the north-west. 'B' Company consolidated around 'Cutler', and 'C' Company stayed two hundred yards down the road to the south-west.

During the morning's fighting, the Germans had brought down heavy defensive fire, and a shell fired at one of their long-range defensive-fire targets inflicted another disaster on the Hampshires. The shell burst on an ammunition lorry parked outside Battalion Headquarters. The ammunition exploded with terrific force, fires spread and ammunition and petrol exploded all round; the flames and flying splinters of metal for a while prevented the survivors from getting the injured men away. The adjutant, the Headquarters Company commander, the troop commander from 61st Anti-tank Battery, two signallers from 30th Field Regiment and three other men were killed outright; the signals officer and one man were mortally wounded. Nearly thirty other officers and men were also wounded, including the Reverend R. Edwards DSO, Captain R. J. Painter, who was acting commander of 111th Field Battery, the mortar, pioneer and medical officers, the liaison officer from the 4·2-inch mortars, and the signal, cook and intelligence sergeants. Major Knight had another astonishing escape.

On the left of 28th Brigade, the Somersets began their advance with 'A' Company on the right and 'B' Company on the left. The company commanders, Majors A. E. Sutton-Pryce and A. R. Ellis, had some difficulty in keeping touch with all parts of their companies in the advance across flat close country, but both companies moved steadily forward. Before long the advance developed into a fight on the Scolo Cerchia, along which the Germans put up a stout resistance. At seven-fifteen in the morning, both companies were still trying to force their way across the Scolo. 'B' Company was on the road, a thousand yards south-west of 'Cutler', and 'A' Company was six hundred yards farther to the right—there seemed to be strong German positions near the dyke between the two companies. By ten in the morning, however, some platoons had got across the Scolo, and Major Ellis was able to send back forty-four Germans to Battalion Headquarters. Half an hour later, he reported that he had reached his objective, a road-junction seven hundred yards to the right of the point on the dyke where the company had been held up for a while, but that he had no news of 'A' Company.

'A' Company's advance had been complicated by a break-down of communications. Major Sutton-Pryce, with his headquarters and part of one platoon, crossed the dyke and found himself very near 'B' Company's objective. During the fighting on the dyke, the rest of the company had moved north-east along it as far as Busecchio cemetery, and there had come up against the Germans guarding the road-crossing two hundred yards farther on.

At eleven in the morning, 'B' Company was digging in round its objective, and Major Sutton-Pryce was making every effort to gather 'A' Company together. On the right, the King's were fighting hard for 'Cutler'. On the left, 46th Division had captured San Martino in Strada, a thousand yards to the left of 'B' Company.

Wherever the Germans could hope to delay the advance, they had blown up culverts and bridges over rivers, streams and dykes. The division's sappers tried to estimate in advance the nature of these demolitions and to have ready the means of dealing with them. They took their information from the reports of infantry patrols and from air photographs as translated by Captain Martyr and his section of the Military Air Interpretation Unit (West)—generally known as 'Mae West'. For the crossing of the Scolo Cerchia at the point where 'B' Company of the Somersets had crossed it, Lieutenant-Colonel Nelson had brought up an assault group from 1st Assault Regiment RAC/RE, consisting of two AVREs, two Arks and two Shermandozers, protected by one Sherman and three Churchill tanks, and helped by men of 7th Field Company. As the group approached the Scolo Cerchia, early in the morning of November the 8th, the three tanks went forward, leaving the rest of the group a mile behind. The Churchills took cover among some trees on the left of the road near the dyke, while the Sherman laid a smoke screen to cover the advance of the first AVRE, which drew up behind some houses near the Churchills. As soon as the smoke screen had cleared, a Tiger tank half a mile away began firing its 88-mm gun at the houses and at the AVRE, which had left its tail showing. For the next three hours, while the Somersets were fighting for the bridge-head across the dyke, the assault group dodged round the houses to keep out of sight of the Tiger. As soon as 'B' Company of the Somersets crossed the dyke and pushed on, and the Tiger moved away, the sappers began work under intermittent shell-fire, sweeping for mines up to the crater and breaking down its edges into ramps with Wade charges. As soon as the approaches were ready, the first AVRE, covered by the Sherman, rolled forward to lay a fascine, but blew up on a mine twenty yards short of the crater. Nothing else could be done until the sappers had cleared the mines away from a diversion round the disabled AVRE. At length the second AVRE drove round the first and laid its fascine, a Shermandozer followed to improve the approach, and the first Ark was called up to lie on top of the fascine and complete the crossing; but as the Ark was edging past the disabled AVRE it struck a mine which blew off four of its bogies. The sappers made every effort to get it moving again, but after two hours the second Ark had to be called up. This was driven firmly into position, and before dusk the crossing was ready for tanks, though more work had to be done before wheeled vehicles could cross.

Until late in the evening of November the 8th, therefore, tanks could not cross the dyke to support the Somersets; and 'C' Company's attack had to be postponed until the tanks of 'A' Squadron, 142nd RAC, could join the battalion after making a long detour through the 46th Division's area. At three in the afternoon tanks and infantry met, and the attack went in under heavy shell-fire. After an hour and a half, as the evening drew in, 'C' Company took its objective. By nightfall, 'B' and 'C' Companies were firmly in position on their objectives, and most of 'A' Company was accounted for. During the day's fighting, the Somersets had taken more than seventy prisoners from the 278th and 356th Divisions.

The Hampshires meanwhile had reorganized after the grave losses they had suffered before going into action, and were ready to pass through the Somersets and thrust north-eastwards to cut the road between Carpena and Forli. The rapid recovery of the Hampshires from these two severe blows is an indication of the fine spirit of the battalion and of the leadership of its commander. 'A' and 'B' Companies of the Hampshires moved off to the road beyond the crossing over the dyke into the Somersets' area, and formed up for the attack. The Somersets' night patrols, however, had found nobody in front of the battalion, apart from patrols from the King's on the right and from 46th Division on the left; the Germans were obviously withdrawing. Before the Hampshires began their attack, therefore, Brigadier Preston changed his plan; the Hampshires were to make for Forli itself, while the Somersets advanced towards the river south-west of the town, where they were to look for a crossing-place for infantry and tanks. Both battalions began to advance at four in the morning of November the 9th, moving through a thick early morning mist. The Hampshires on the right found that the road from Carpena to Forli was heavily mined, and that a crater had been blown in every cross-roads along it. They captured a few German stragglers and were lightly shelled, but there was no resistance. By six-thirty in the morning 'C' Company, in the lead, had reached the cross-roads half a mile south of the town, and 'A' and 'B' Companies passed through. The Pioneer Platoon was hard at work lifting mines along the road, and reached the town a little ahead of 'A' Company, which had been moving across country. Twenty minutes later, Brigadier Preston and Lieutenant-Colonel Mitchell entered the town, while 'A' and 'B' Companies were still rounding up a few scattered Germans. There was no serious fighting, and patrols reached the western exit from the town across the Montone, where the bridge had been destroyed.

As Major-General Ward had warned Brigadier Preston not to send infantry across the river without tanks and anti-tank guns as well, the Hampshires consolidated where they were. The Carrier Platoon arrived next day to take up positions on the north-western outskirts of the town, with an observation post overlooking the river.

'B' and 'C' Companies of the Somersets had reached the road south of Forli and opposite the junction of the Rivers Rabbi and Montone, and sent standing patrols to points between the road and the river. During the afternoon a patrol reconnoitred the river itself; it found no ford for tanks, and estimated that infantry might get across, but only with difficulty because of the mud, which was up to five feet deep.

Early in the morning of November the 9th, before 28th Brigade began the advance which was to end at the River Montone, 12th Brigade had begun its task of clearing the area between the air-field and Route Nine; when this was done, the brigade was to advance on Forli beside 28th Brigade.

The Black Watch moved off soon after three in the morning of November the 9th. In due course 'B' and 'C' Companies, which were leading, entered Forli without opposition, and reached the great red-brick church which stands in the square in the heart of the town. A patrol from 'C' Company went on through the town to the Montone bridge, and met the Hampshires there. A concentration of nebelwerfer bombs on the western outskirts, and a single machine-gun firing from the far side of the river, were the only signs that there were any Germans within miles. 'A' Company worked northwards through the streets to a row of houses just short of the railway line. Finally, 'B' Company made for the level-crossing north-west of the town; but, as the leading platoons approached it, they were brought to a halt by heavy machine-gun fire.

The West Kents, temporarily commanded by Major D. H. Gwilliam, had moved off soon after dawn, and had cleared first the barracks and then the north-eastern industrial part of the town. They collected some German stragglers on the way, but the only other sign of the enemy was the great number of hastily-laid mines along the roads.

46th Division had crossed the Rabbi the night before, but had not been able to take San Varano, which lies beyond the Montone. Once more the rain-clouds burst and filled the rivers, and by November the 10th the Montone was impassable; troops of the 46th Division, who had been fighting for San Varano, were cut off, like the DCLI and the Rifles at the Ronco, and were overrun by the Germans.

24. North of Forli

Although they had withdrawn from Forli to positions behind the river, the Germans were still in strength on the near side of the river to the north of the town. Until they were pressed back from its outskirts, Forli would be little use as a base or as a centre of communications.

The task of forcing the Germans north-westwards away from the town was given to 12th Brigade. The West Kents cleared the north-eastern part of the town, and came out into the flat, close country beyond. After advancing a mile and a half to the north-west, they reached the Canale di Rivaldino, which flows north from Forli, at the Villa Bondi. At this point, where the road crosses the canal, a deep crater, covered by fire from the front and left, prevented further progress by the main body. 'B' Company, commanded by Major H. B. H. Waring, entered the Villa Bondi itself, and the two leading platoons crossed the canal; but light was failing, and no further advance could be made.

To guard the exposed right flank of his brigade, Brigadier Heber-Percy brought up the Royal Fusiliers to the neighbourhood between Ospedaletto and Forli, some two miles to the right rear of the West Kents.

On the left, meanwhile, the Black Watch had reached the railway-line at the level-crossing a mile to the south-west of the Villa Bondi, but were halted there by a storm of machine-gun fire. Lieutenant-Colonel Smith called off the attack until the following day, and on the right of the brigade the Royal Fusiliers also remained in their positions for the night.

In the centre, however, the West Kents made every effort to push the Germans away from the crater, so that bridging could begin.

During the darkness and rain of the night, 'D' Company attacked along the near bank of the canal beyond the Villa Bondi. Two sections of 16 Platoon, led by Sergeant Lord, reached a factory half a mile farther on. The factory was surrounded by a ten-foot wall, covered by machine-guns on each flank and defended from inside by Germans who lobbed grenades over it; Sergeant Lord's men could not break in, and had to withdraw to the nearest houses. Ammunition was running low, and dawn had come.

During the night, the crater was reconnoitred for an Ark crossing; but the Shermandozers could not work in such darkness, the crater was still under fire from the left flank, and the depth and position of the crater proved singularly difficult. The tanks of the North Irish Horse—six of which were working with the West Kents—were therefore unable to reach the forward platoons until early in the afternoon of November the 10th, and for the time being both sides stayed watching each other.

At noon of November the 10th, the Black Watch opened a battalion attack on the neighbourhood of the level-crossing. The tanks of 'A' Squadron, the North Irish Horse, took on the houses south of the level-crossing one by one, firing shell after shell into them; then the infantry moved in to ferret out the Germans. The enemy put up a fierce defence of every house; this street-fighting was a dangerous business, and losses were heavy—Major A. D. Steel MC was among the killed—but the Black Watch worked steadily up the street. After five hours of their fiercest fighting since the Gustav Line, the Black Watch reached the level-crossing.

Brigadier Heber-Percy now brought the Royal Fusiliers forward to pass through the West Kents. Lieutenant-Colonel Shipley was still convalescent after being wounded in the Savio bridge-head, and the battalion was commanded by Major W. I. Thomas. At half-past three in the afternoon the battalion began its approach march, and before long 'Z' Company, commanded by Major T. C. Howes MC, was passing through the West Kents and through the heavy defensive fire of German guns.

The main body of the company was halted as soon as it came within range of the German garrison in the factory. Major Howes put in an attack with two platoons; the platoon on the right was pinned down by intense small-arms fire at short range, but that on the left, led by Sergeant Carpenter DCM, crossed the canal, worked through the closer country on the other side in a skilful flanking movement, and after a sharp fight captured the first of a group of houses two hundred yards beyond the factory—and with it five Germans. The rest of 'Z' Company fought all night round the factory; the wall was breached, and Corporal E. Eastham's section broke in, but the Germans drove them out again with grenades and machine-guns.

The success on the left was more promising, and Major Thomas sent 'X' Company, commanded by Major P. C. Watling, across the canal to exploit it. The company met stiff resistance, but by dawn of November the 11th had cleared the rest of the group of houses in front of Sergeant Carpenter's section. The German garrison of the factory, outflanked, began to withdraw; 'Z' Company moved in, handed over to 'W' Company and moved on across the canal to relieve 'X' Company of its houses.

During the rest of the day, and during the early part of the night, the Royal Fusiliers, now once more under the command of Lieutenant-Colonel Shipley, maintained their advance in some stiff house-to-house fighting, reached the road junction known as Cathedral, a quarter of a mile farther on, and pressed on up the road to the left for a further quarter of a mile.

Meanwhile, the Ark crossing at the crater was still not working properly, and the roads leading up to the West Kents and the Royal Fusiliers were too narrow for the traffic needed to supply two battalions. Brigadier Heber-Percy therefore decided to open the road leading up towards the factory from the south. This was to be done by a pincer movement; on the right, the West Kents were to send a company from the Villa Bondi to a point on the road near the Casa Fortis, and from there the company was to strike south-westwards towards Forli; on the left, the Black Watch were to advance beyond their level-crossing in Forli towards the Casa Fortis.

'C' Company of the West Kents, commanded by Major Venn Dunn, crossed the fields between the Villa Bondi and the Casa Fortis with some difficulty, owing to failing light and faulty wireless communications. By dawn of November the 11th, however, the company had a firm hold on the road north of the Casa Fortis. During the morning, the company was joined by the Carrier Platoon, commanded by Captain W. Tennant. 13 Platoon attacked and captured the Casa Fortis buildings, driving out the Germans and taking half-a-dozen prisoners without losing any men. 15 Platoon took the houses on the other side of the road; and during the afternoon the company, further reinforced by three tanks, worked its way from house to house down the road towards the Black Watch.

The Black Watch meanwhile had moved forward from the level-crossing to the southern end of the Casa Fortis road, and the Carrier Platoon and a rifle platoon were in action there when the West Kents came down the road from the north and linked up.

Now that the main, northern thrust was equipped with adequate communications, Brigadier Heber-Percy decided to extend the brigade's front by a secondary thrust on the left. He brought up 'C' Reconnaissance Squadron, commanded by Major J. P. Ryan, and sent it along the road which runs at right-angles across the foot of the Casa Fortis road, north-westwards from the positions held by the Black Watch. In spite of tough local resistance and heavy defensive fire, the squadron after an hour's fighting reached a road junction five hundred yards along the road.

In order to keep 12th Brigade's advance going, Major-General Ward now placed the King's under Brigadier Heber-Percy's command, and early in the morning of November the 12th the King's on the right, the Black Watch in the centre and 'C' Reconnaissance Squadron on the left renewed the brigade's attack.

The King's, with tanks of 142nd RAC, passed through the Royal Fusiliers at Cathedral, broke into the enemy positions to the north-west, and in a succession of fights collected prisoners from all companies of the German battalion holding the road. 'A' Company, commanded by Major H. V. Richards MC, reached the road junction (Chancel) twelve hundred yards beyond Cathedral; and 'C' Company, commanded by Major J. H. Tuohy DSO, passed through, turned right, and, after more than four hours of hard fighting, reached the next road junction (Offertory) half a mile farther on.

The Black Watch attack was led by 'A' Company, commanded by Major J. Macdonald MC. The company went quickly forward from the foot of the Casa Fortis road, leaving the road on the right; three tanks of the North Irish Horse could hardly move across the rain-sodden fields, and had to keep to the road. When the Black Watch reached the Casa Pettini, they found that the heavy fire of 77th Field Regiment had apparently driven the Germans out of the house; signs of a hurried departure included an abandoned motor-cycle and a wagon-load of kit.

'B' Company, commanded by Captain P. N. L. Glass, also with

a troop of the North Irish Horse, moved up the road on the right and after a short fight took the Casa Manuzzi, three-quarters of a mile to the north of Pettini.

'A' Company now moved on again, and before long encountered two powerful German tanks. The Air OP drove these off with artillery fire, the Churchills moved forward, laying a smoke screen as they came, and the infantry advanced to within five hundred yards of the road junction known as Aisle. There the company was halted in the gathering dusk by fire from houses overlooking the last few hundred yards of the road leading to Aisle.

On the left of 12th Brigade, 'C' Reconnaissance Squadron had been advancing up the road along the east bank of the Montone, until it was pinned down by fire seven hundred yards short of the Choir road junction. Having heard nothing from his leading troops, Major Ryan drove forward in his jeep with Lieutenant Howe MC. The firing had died down, the troops were hidden in the houses beside the road, and the tank which had been accompanying them was off the road to the left; Major Ryan drove clean through the position without seeing it, and reached Choir without finding his own men or being shot at by the enemy's. A little puzzled, he followed the tracks of a tank into a farm-yard, expecting to find there the Sherman which had been with his squadron; but the place was empty. After a second look at the tracks, he recognized them as German and briskly withdrew. Soon afterwards, German machineguns opened fire from the same neighbourhood, and 'C' Squadron could get no farther forward during the hours of daylight.

By the end of November the 12th, the division's front, from the King's on the right to the Reconnaissance Squadron on the left, lay parallel with, and about a quarter of a mile short of, the long straight road which runs north-east and south-west of the village of San Tome. The German 278th Division, which had been unable to hold against 4th Division the line of the Canale di Rivaldino, seemed likely to attempt a stand along this road.

Brigadier Heber-Percy planned to keep up the pressure on the weakened battalions of the enemy, and shortly before midnight 'C' Company of the Black Watch, commanded by Captain P. Visser, attacked towards Aisle, on the main road a thousand yards to the right of Choir. The Germans met the company's advance with violent bursts of fire, and forced it back to its start-line. Two hours later, however, the company went in again, this time reinforced by a platoon from 'A' Company. For several hours, no report of progress came back to the battalion; but at dawn Captain Visser reported that he had seized a group of houses near Aisle, and had a firm hold on them although the Germans were still in strength in the neighbourhood. The men were tired after fighting all night, but losses had been slight—very much lighter than those of the enemy. With the help of the Carrier Platoon, the rest of the road junction was cleared after several hours of fierce fighting, and its defences were consolidated by tanks of the North Irish Horse and by anti-tank guns.

Now that the Black Watch had reached the main road to the left of San Tome, the King's were to make for the road to the right of the village. 'B' Company, commanded by Major E. Cabrera, began to attack early in the afternoon of November the 13th towards Steeple, a road junction five hundred yards to the right of San Tome.

11 Platoon, led by Sergeant Williams, began to clear the houses on the left of the road leading up to Steeple, but before long was halted. As 10 Platoon followed up, the platoon commander, Lieutenant R. W. Moore, was astonished to see Germans creeping out of the houses on the right of the road to stalk 11 Platoon from the rear. The Germans were equally astonished at the sight of Lieutenant Moore's men—they had mistaken the leading platoon for an unwary patrol. The King's drove the Germans back to shelter behind a haystack, and pinned them down with fire; but the Germans, though trapped and losing men, refused to give in until the haystack was set on fire by a tank brought up by the platoon sergeant.

10 Platoon and the tank moved on towards Steeple, reached it, and cleared the neighbourhood in spite of the fire of a 75-mm gun only four hundred yards away. 'A' Company, commanded by Major Richards, came up to pass through and beyond Steeple, but was held up at first by the gun. The gun was, however, silenced when all the gunners round it were killed by the guns of 30th Field Regiment, in a fire-plan arranged with Major Richards by Captain R. D. Tyler, his FOO. The company reached its first objective, a house half a mile up the road; and, while the infantry were consolidating, Sergeant Cooper carried out a successful though devious artillery shoot on a troublesome mortar position—he sent his directions by his Number 38 set to Major Richards, who passed them on over his 18 set to Captain Tyler.

The right flank of the King's was becoming rather exposed as they advanced, and Brigadier Heber-Percy sent an armoured car patrol from 'C' Reconnaissance Squadron to the main road at the Sedilia road-junction, half a mile to the right of Steeple. The Somersets were also brought in on this flank, and moved up to guard the right rear by occupying the village of Roncadello, a mile to the east of the King's at Steeple.

On the left of the King's, the West Kents had begun their attack early in the morning. 'C' Company, commanded by Major Venn Dunn, started from the Chancel road junction and advanced across country towards San Tome, accompanied by a single tank of the North Irish Horse. Sergeant Gibson led 14 Platoon through some defensive fire towards the first house on the right of the road in San Tome. As it approached the houses it was to assault, the platoon was halted by a machine-gun emplaced in the doorway of one of the houses. This machine-gun, manned by four men, was firing across the line of the company's advance, and might well have inflicted grave losses. But Corporal Whittick, in an act of well-applied courage, charged straight at and into the doorway, blazing away with his sub-machine-gun, and the Germans round the Spandau lost their nerve and threw up their hands.

By ten in the morning, 'C' Company was firmly in position in San Tome, and 'B' Company moved up to the road on the left, between San Tome and the Black Watch at Aisle.

'D' Company of the West Kents, commanded by Major Brock, went on from San Tome along the track that leads towards the next lateral road. A thousand yards farther on, the company reached a house held by about thirty Germans, who were in a state very near panic; the officer in command, with a good deal of bellowing, got them to make a show of resistance, firing wildly in all directions, before the majority broke and ran, leaving five prisoners in the hands of the West Kents. The enemy by this time was probably in no state to counter-attack, but a few determined Germans were still roaming round the house and sniping at the West Kents as they consolidated.

From the northern outskirts of Forli to the line of the road held by 12th Brigade, the battlefield was a dreary waste, with the bodies of British and German soldiers and of many Italian civilians lying in ditches and in the wreckage of smashed houses and ruined farms. Burnt-out tanks and vehicles and spiked guns lay silent in the fields and beside the country roads, among the gathering shadows of the winter night. As darkness fell on this unhappy country-side, a crowd of Italian civilians reached the positions held by 'D' Company of the West Kents; their homes and all they had owned had been utterly destroyed—they had no food or shelter, and little hope or courage left. More than thirty men, women and children were near Major Brock's headquarters when a heavy concentration of German mortar-bombs came rushing down and burst all round. Two men and three women were seriously wounded; the rest gave themselves up to an agony of cries and weeping which went on all night. When first an old man and then a girl died, in spite of all the efforts of the company's stretcher-bearers, the Italians' frenzy of grief drove the nearby British soldiers almost to distraction. Not until morning was it possible to evacuate the survivors.

On the left of the Black Watch, the Germans at Choir had put up a fierce resistance to 'C' Reconnaissance Squadron, although the German defences on their left and even behind them were crumbling under the pressure of the Black Watch, the West Kents and the King's. During the afternoon, however, Troopers on foot worked their way up to the road-junction and consolidated there, though there appeared to be a continuing danger of counter-attack; this, however, was dispelled by the regiment's mortars, which fired four hundred bombs into the area where the Germans seemed to be forming up.

As darkness began to fall, the line of the lateral road which runs through San Martino was marked by the light of countless fires, where the retreating enemy or the 4th Division's guns had set houses, stores and vehicles on fire. 'B' Company of the West Kents, commanded by Major Waring, moved up to within a thousand yards of the road, and sent forward a fighting patrol, which advanced behind the fire of the brigade's mortars and of 77th Field Regiment until it reached the road. A few hours later, 15 Platoon of 'C' Company moved up from San Tome to a house among the fires on the main road, to the left of the fighting patrol, and before long the West Kents held San Martino.

By daylight of November the 14th, 'C' Squadron was able to make a general advance beyond Choir, captured a German 75-mm gun intact, and joined up with the West Kents at San Martino on the right.

The battle of the Montone was entering its last phase. As the already broken battalions of the German 278th Division struggled to get back across the river, the guns of 4th Division shelled the approaches to what reconnaissance aircraft reported to be likely crossing-places. More and more mortars and machine-guns joined in, until, an hour before dawn on November the 14th, heavy anti-aircraft guns fired a finale of air-bursts. To the left of 12th Brigade, 56th Division was already across the river, and held a small bridgehead astride Route Nine. The river line could not be defended much longer. To the right of 12th Brigade, the front of 4th Division's advance to the Montone was beginning to widen. The Somersets moved up to the San Martino road on the right of the West Kents, and farther to the right still the Hampshires came up to the road and occupied the village of Villafranca; both battalions had to deal with sporadic resistance only, and collected a number of prisoners on the way. Farther to the right still, however, the 12th Lancers and the King's Dragoon Guards were still skirmishing with enemy troops who were resisting some distance short of the Montone.

During the afternoon, the Reconnaissance Regiment, commanded by Lieutenant-Colonel A. C. S. Delmege MC, took over from 12th Brigade. 'A' and 'B' Squadrons between them took over the entire brigade front, while 'C' Squadron and 12th Brigade withdrew for a well-earned rest in Forli. Although 10th Brigade had just reached the town that day from Cesena, there were billets for all.

During its six days in the line, the brigade and the battalions under command had captured a hundred and fifty-four Germans from units already very gravely short of men. All the German prisoners had tales to tell of the heavy losses among their comrades as the 278th Division was forced back to the river. One of the German battalions was reduced to forty-two men; in another, one company consisted of forty-three men of all ranks, a second had fifteen men, a third had five and a fourth company had no men at all.

12th Brigade's losses were very much lighter than might have been expected after such fierce fighting; but the Black Watch had suffered comparatively heavily, losing two officers and nineteen other ranks killed, and one officer and forty-six other ranks wounded.

25. Between Forlì and Faenza

Wide and fast-flowing between high flood-banks, and defended by German mine-fields, wire, machine-guns and standing patrols, the Montone now presented a very formidable obstacle to any further advance to the north-west of Forlì. Lieutenant-General Keightley, commanding V Corps, therefore decided to launch his next prepared assault from 56th Division's bridge-head across the Montone astride Route Nine. Eight miles along Route Nine beyond Forlì lies the town of Faenza, the next great objective on the long road from Rimini to Bologna. The town lies immediately behind the River Lamone, which seemed likely to prove an obstacle no less serious than the Montone; and before V Corps could begin to advance towards the Lamone, the River Cosina would have to be crossed—a narrow stream, but capable of being defended by determined troops.

The Eighth Army's drive on the Lamone and Faenza was to start on November the 21st. In the mountains to the south, II Polish Corps was to attack at the same time as V Corps. Between the Poles and the bend in the Montone north of Route Nine, 46th Division on the left and 4th Division on the right were to attack across the Cosina; to the right of the sector just vacated by 4th Division, 10th Indian Division was to cross the Montone by a bridge which had been captured intact.

While the attack was being prepared, 4th Division's front was held by 4th Reconnaissance Regiment on the right, from Villafranca to the bend in the Montone north-west of Forlì; and on the left, between the Montone and Route Nine, by 44th Reconnaissance Regiment, which, under Major-General Ward's command, had relieved 56th Division. Both these regiments were in position by dusk on November the 18th, and behind them the brigades of 4th Division were beginning to move up.

The division became active in its new sector, softening the German defences for the attack that was shortly to be made. Aircraft of the Cab-rank attacked many targets by request, and the divisional artillery was constantly pounding away at suspected enemy guns and mortars. The infantry began to drive in the enemy's outposts on the near side of the Cosina.

The main attack went in during the darkness of two in the morning of November the 21st. On the right of 4th Division, 4th Reconnaissance Regiment put in a feint attack, and drew a furious reply from the Germans; defensive fire came down, the German posts in front of the Montone fought off the approaching Troopers, and machine-guns fired continuously from the far bank of the river.

At the same time, 10th Brigade attacked towards the Cosina between the Montone and the railway-line. The Surreys on the right of the brigade ran into trouble at once. 'B' and 'C' Companies, commanded by Captain Ward and Major Spencer, led the assault, each with two platoons forward. A hundred yards short of the Cosina, the leading platoons of 'B' Company found themselves in a mine-field; enough men were lost to disorganize the advance, and Captain Ward sent forward his reserve platoon. More and more men were injured and killed, and the enemy opened an intense fire on the mine-field from small-arms, and brought down defensive fire from his heavier weapons. Captain Ward brought his men back a hundred and fifty yards, and set them to digging in; even as they withdrew, still more were lost.

'C' Company came to grief even more disastrously. The company seemed to be overrunning the barrage, and Major Spencer brought it to a halt. With his headquarters party, he took cover in a ditch; and within a few moments a chain of explosions—either mines or enemy mortar-bombs—burst all along the ditch. Major Spencer, his batman, a runner and two signallers were killed; Lieutenant Stephenson, commanding the reserve platoon, the company sergeant-major, a second runner and a sniper were wounded. The Number 18 wireless set was wrecked, so that Battalion Headquarters had no report of the situation until Lieutenant Stephenson was carried in.

Of the two leading platoons of 'C' Company, 14 Platoon also ran into the mine-field and came to a halt; the platoon commander, Lieutenant Corcoran, was among the wounded, and died of his injuries before he could be carried back. Lieutenant Street, commanding 13 Platoon, went back to company headquarters for orders, found that he was in sole charge, gathered up the survivors of the company and consolidated round a house two hundred yards short of the Cosina and a few yards from the flood-bank of the Montone.

On the left of the Surreys, the DCLI, commanded by Lieutenant-Colonel A. E. Harding MC, were about to go forward when news came of a German spoiling attack which had crossed the river and reached the battalion's route to the start-line. The Germans soon withdrew, but the whole attack had to be postponed until this was known for certain.

'A' and 'D' Companies, commanded by Majors G. Rork and M. W. R. O'C. Phillips, eventually moved off to the start-line at one-thirty in the morning, taking a short cut across marshy ground where the mud was often three feet deep. 'A' Company reached the start-line on time, and made for the river. Hayricks were blazing round a house on the way, and as the platoons approached the house a German machine-gun opened fire for a few minutes before being silenced. The country-side was dotted with fires, the light of which helped the infantry's advance; the men could even see that trees on the left had wires hanging from them as though they had been booby-trapped.

After the company deployed, about fifteen men were injured by shoe-mines; but the mines seemed to have deteriorated after lying for days in the wet ground, and the explosions did not have their usual shattering effect—the wounded men had legs and ankles broken, but few had to undergo the amputation usually necessary. 11 Platoon lost its commander, Lieutenant Seddon, and its platoon sergeant; the senior section commander, Lance-Sergeant W. Bray MM, took command of the platoon and led it extremely well.

The company advanced quickly, close behind the barrage; five minutes after the reserve platoon had crossed the start-line, down came the enemy's defensive fire behind. Lance-Sergeant Bray's platoon reached the Cosina at two in the morning, and found that although the Germans were not defending the farther bank, a machine-gun firing from the right on fixed lines was whipping the water with bullets. The pauses between bursts of fire, while the German detachment checked the sights of the gun or changed belts, came at regular intervals, and groups of the DCLI began to scramble across the stream between bursts of fire; some of the men only just dodged the first bullets of the next burst as they flung themselves on the farther bank. This machine-gun fire and a single shell which burst nearby were the only opposition to the company's crossing of the stream.

As soon as the whole company was across the river, the two forward platoons went for the company's first objective, a small group of buildings a hundred yards beyond the stream. Against slight opposition, the platoons took the buildings—and with them a couple of prisoners—and the company consolidated there. Nobody else seemed to be across the river, and Lieutenant-Colonel Harding could only tell Major Rork to stand fast for the time being. The situation was quite lively enough; while the uproar of the barrage was still rolling away in the middle distance, the company scattered a small German counter-attack; Lance-Sergeant Bray scored a direct hit with a Piat on a Tiger tank, and frightened it away; a second, larger counter-attack was broken up, and the company took eight more prisoners.

There followed an uncomfortable pause. The enemy's defensive fire was still bursting along the line of the river, there was no news of friendly troops on either flank, and the barrage was moving out of reach. The German prisoners were growing restless; a deputation pointed out to Lieutenant Fowles that under the terms of the Geneva Convention they ought to be evacuated at once from the front line, as a counter-attack was about to be made, and if it failed there would be a more powerful counter-attack at dawn.

By this time, Major Rork knew that his was the only company of the Cosina assault which had managed to cross the stream. 'D' Company of the DCLI had advanced in its turn through the mud, and had been caught on the start-line by the enemy's defensive fire; Major Phillips had eventually been compelled to withdraw his company to re-form. At four-fifteen in the morning, Lieutenant-Colonel Harding sent forward 'B' Company, commanded by Major J. M. Knight MC, to join 'A' Company beyond the river. But 'B' Company too was halted by heavy fire soon after leaving the forming-up place; the fire barred the way, and prevented any advance, except at the cost of severe losses.

Major Rork realized that his company was cut off, and that what the prisoners said about counter-attacks was likely to be true. He therefore called for defensive fire, and 22nd Field Regiment laid a most effective screen of high explosive in front of the position;

medium guns joined in, and one of the heavier shells destroyed a lurking German tank. Major Rork then called for counter-preparation fire on a succession of points where a counter-attack might be forming up, including the track in front, and houses five hundred yards to the south-west and two hundred yards to the north-east, switching the fire from target to target. At Battalion Headquarters, Major G. Goode, commanding 36th/55th Field Battery, translated Major Rork's orders into artillery language and controlled the fire of the guns. Protected in this manner by artillery, 'A' Company held its position, isolated but formidable.

The situation of 10th Brigade at dawn of November the 21st was not very promising. The attack of the Surreys had been wrecked on the mine-field. 'A' Company of the DCLI was holding on to its first objective, but could neither advance nor be reinforced. The only other success had been that of 'D' Company of the Bedfords. 16 Platoon and the Carrier Platoon, under Lieutenants Gurney and Quelch, had crossed the Cosina by the railway bridge. The light of haystacks blazing to the south had revealed the advancing troops to the enemy; they were halted by heavy mortar fire, and at dawn the two platoons were holding on under small-arms fire from three sides. Only a dozen men of 16 Platoon were left; Lieutenant Gurney had been killed, and some of the wounded were too gravely injured to be carried back.

Major-General Ward considered the possibilities of a general advance, and decided that the division's attack would have to be postponed; orders went out for the withdrawal of the foremost infantry.

'B' and 'C' Companies of the Surreys made an orderly withdrawal from the line, and went back to Forli. 'D' Company, which had been in reserve, remained in the forward area under the command of 44th Reconnaissance Regiment, until on the night of November the 22nd 'B' Squadron of that regiment relieved the company. A number of wounded men still lay in the mine-field, and stretcher-bearers could not bring in the last survivor until late in the morning. The German guns were still harassing 10th Brigade's positions, but there was no deliberate shooting at Red Cross parties in the mine-field.

The withdrawal of 'A' Company of the DCLI was as successful as its advance and attack. Soon after six in the morning, the first sections moved back towards the stream, taking the wounded; the movement was most successfully screened by the fire of 22nd Field

Regiment. Five minutes later, the main body followed, escorting ten prisoners. Ten minutes later the rear-guard began to thin out, and made briskly for the Cosina. Two Germans who were too badly wounded to be taken back—one of them was dying—were made as comfortable as possible by the DCLI and left behind. The whole company crossed the stream and concentrated near Battalion Headquarters; Major Rork's batman was wounded on the way back, and was not seen again, and one of the Germans was injured as the party passed through the German defensive fire.

'D' Company of the Bedfords withdrew into reserve, and the battalion eventually relieved 'B' Squadron of the 44th Reconnaissance Regiment.

During the morning of November the 21st, the Army and Corps Commanders, General Sir Richard McCreery and Lieutenant-General Sir Charles Keightley, visited Major-General Ward, and plans were laid for a new assault south of Route Nine. The first preparation for this new attack was that 4th Division was to move farther still to the left, and take over part of 46th Division's sector. 28th Brigade accordingly came forward to take over a sector extending a mile and a quarter from Route Nine to the south. Brigadier Preston ordered the King's—commanded in the absence of Lieutenant-Colonel Robins by Major R. E. Cottingham MC—to take over the whole sector and clear the east bank of the stream. Soon after dark the battalion was in position.

All three battalions of 28th Brigade sent out patrols that night, searching the near bank of the Cosina for German posts and crossing-places.

The attack on the Cosina was to be renewed during the night of November the 22nd; 4th Division was to strike across the stream a mile to the left of Route Nine, and then wheel to the right towards Route Nine and the village of Corleto a mile beyond it. 28th Brigade was to make the crossing this time, and 10th Brigade was to take advantage of the fighting on the left to cross the river in its own sector. 10th Indian Division on the right and 46th Division on the left would be attacking at the same time.

In the vague twilight of searchlights in 46th Division's sector, 28th Brigade's attack went in soon after eight o'clock on the night of November the 22nd, and at once met fierce resistance from Germans all along the Cosina. The Hampshires on the right suffered losses in heavy shelling on the start-line, but advanced steadily across the muddy ground with 'A' and 'C' Companies in the lead. Half an hour later, 'A' Company, commanded by Major R. H. Stevens, had taken a house on the far bank of the river. The full strength of the two companies was unable to cross the stream during the night; until dawn, about one platoon of each stayed on the east bank, working as stretcher-bearers and ammunition porters. At dawn, however, both companies were firmly in position round houses a quarter of a mile apart, on the farther bank, and had taken between them twenty prisoners, including a company commander. From dawn onwards, the forward companies, and Battalion Headquarters half a mile behind the river, were heavily shelled; but the Hampshires were all dug in and lost no more men. All through the fighting the battalion's stretcher-bearers, and the orderlies at the regimental aid post, worked with devotion in darkness, mud and shell-fire, bringing in, tending and carrying farther back wounded men of both the British and German armies.

The Somersets on the left, meanwhile, were having a hard fight. As their attack began, the enemy brought down a curtain of defensive fire, through which the assaulting companies had to advance. 'A' Company on the right, commanded by Major Sutton-Pryce, had nearly reached the Cosina when the left-hand platoon was halted by a storm of machine-gun fire at point-blank range. The company's attack was wrecked; Major Sutton-Pryce was severely wounded and temporarily paralysed, and the reserve platoon, caught in the same fire, lost its commander, became disorganized and could not be found by anyone for a time. 7 Platoon on the right, however, commanded by Lieutenant R. D. W. Strickland, made a detour to avoid the German machine-guns, crossed the Cosina and reached the left-hand of the two houses which had just been taken by the Hampshires. 'B' Company of the Somersets, commanded by Major A. R. Ellis, led by 10 and 12 Platoons, commanded by Lieutenants E. H. Lane and H. Toms, crossed the river before midnight and reached a house about a thousand yards to the left of the Hampshires. An hour and a quarter later, the Germans began to gather for a counter-attack; Major Ellis had defensive fire brought down by 30th Field Regiment, and had it continued at a slow rate of firing. By this means the two platoons across the river were protected while they consolidated round the company's objective.

On the left of 4th Division, 46th Division was also fighting hard, and had forced crossings of the Cosina where the stream curls round to the north-west for a little way. The right forward troops of 46th Division, 139th Brigade, were actually west of the Somersets.

Lieutenant-Colonel Chetwynd-Stapleton decided to send forward 'C' Company of the Somersets across the river to join 'B' Company, and at the same time he had reserve searchlights switched on, to shine up Route Nine. At four-thirty in the morning, Captain J. E. C. Clarke, commanding 'C' Company, sent forward 13 and 14 Platoons, under Lieutenants A. H. G. Morley and E. Middleton, across the river half-way between 'A' Company on the right and 'B' Company on the left. Both platoons met strong opposition, but by eight in the morning were across and firmly in position.

A detachment of 1st Assault Regiment RAC/RE, with tanks of 142nd RAC and sappers of 7th Field Company, had been making strenuous efforts meanwhile to place its Arks at crossing-places behind 28th Brigade's bridge-heads. The way forward from the infantry's start-line lay across country, and the ground was so soft that no tank was to follow in the tracks of another unless the route was proved to be firm. None the less, Arks and tanks became stuck or bogged as they approached the stream; and no crossing-place was ready when daylight came. Soon after seven-thirty in the morning, however, the assault parties managed to open a crossing, and the tanks of 'A' Squadron, 142nd RAC, watched by Major-General Ward, began to cross into the bridge-head held by the Somersets. By eleven in the morning there was a second crossing, and anti-tank guns had crossed into the bridge-head. A third crossing was eventually established.

The second phase of 28th Brigade's attack was to begin at three-thirty in the afternoon of November the 23rd. The enemy's stubborn resistance on the division's left flank, however, had prevented 46th Division from advancing far enough to secure 28th Brigade's left flank. Brigadier Preston therefore proposed to send in 'B' Squadron, 142nd RAC, on the left, to take a house half a mile beyond the river and in 46th Division's sector. The army commander, who was visiting Brigadier Preston's headquarters at the time, approved the plan, and the tanks moved off. They were soon in difficulties in the soft ground, but their appearance was enough for the German garrison, which surrendered shortly afterwards to the Somersets.

Brigadier Preston sent his two battalions forward one after the other. The Somersets opened their attack at half-past three; 'C' Company on the right made for the cross-roads where the Corleto road meets Route Nine, and 'B' Company on the left was to take Cosina, a village on Route Nine, three hundred yards to the left of the same cross-roads. 'C' Company made good progress until halted near the cross-roads by tanks. 80th Medium Regiment at once began shooting at the tanks, but had to stop soon afterwards as 'C' Company was advancing into the target area. By then, however, the O P parties of 30th Field Regiment advancing with the Hampshires on the right had seen a direct hit destroy one of the German tanks. At the same time, the Air OP ranged two M.10 guns of 93rd Antitank Regiment on to a German Mark IV (Special) tank which was coming down Route Nine towards the cross-roads, and was out of sight of the guns themselves. Still without seeing the tank, the guns hit it and set it on fire—an example of the effectiveness of a new tank-hunting drill. Three more German tanks, already withdrawing, were hastened by the shells of 80th Medium Regiment. 'C' Company could see nothing of this shooting, but finding that the opposition from enemy armour had melted away, the company moved on and reached the cross-roads; Captain Clarke, the company commander, was wounded as they advanced.

'B' Company on the left met stronger resistance near Cosina village, where German mortars and tanks opened fire and forced it back. Major Ellis took his company round to the right to make a fresh attack from 'C' Company's area. At the second attempt, 'B' Company took the village after a sharp fight. Lieutenant Toms was twice wounded in the shoulders, and Major Ellis, the third of the battalion's company commanders to be hit in the battle of the Cosina stream, was shot in one shoulder. Both these officers, however, stayed with the company until morning. 'C' Company also reached Route Nine, but could get no farther, and both companies consolidated astride of the main road.

On the right of the Somersets, the Hampshires advanced with 'C' Company on the right, making for the Route Nine bridge over the Cosina, and 'B' Company on the left directed on Piazzetta, a hamlet on Route Nine five hundred yards to the left of the bridge. 'C' Company commander, Major Stevens, had been wounded while conferring with his 'O' Group before the attack, and Lieutenant Pennington was in command of the company; 'B' Company was commanded by Captain Bowers DSO. As soon as the attack began, heavy defensive fire came down on the advancing infantry, and men were killed and wounded as they crossed the start-line. But the battalion pushed steadily forward, and as they approached Route Nine the defensive fire slackened. Lieutenant E. Evans took 10 Platoon through the barrage, penetrated the German positions and overran a German command post and observation post. The platoon captured six Germans in the observation post, including a corporal who was speaking over the wireless when the Hampshires burst in and smashed the set with tommy-gun fire. The supporting fire of 30th Field Regiment had obviously been successful; a direct hit on the command post had killed an officer and several other ranks in the post, and other shells had killed a number of Germans nearby. Soon after four in the afternoon, 'B' Company reached Piazzetta, and began mopping up.

'C' Company, weakened by casualties, reached the Cosina bridge shortly afterwards, and began to clear the neighbourhood. For several hours after dark, prisoners on foot and on stretchers were arriving at Battalion Headquarters. By the time the fighting ended, 'B' and 'C' Companies of the Hampshires had taken thirty-nine prisoners.

By nightfall on November the 23rd, therefore, 28th Brigade had completed the second phase of its attack, and held more than a thousand yards of Route Nine beyond the Cosina. Soon after dark, a great flash of light leaped into the sky to the north-west, followed by the reverberation of a heavy explosion. The flash-spotters reported that all their bearings converged on the bridge by which Route Nine crosses the River Lamone in the eastern suburbs of Faenza. This suggested that the Germans had withdrawn their heavy equipment behind yet another obstacle, and that 4th Division's advance to the river was likely to be obstructed only by rear-guards, mines and demolitions.

The division was active all through the night of November the 23rd. Two troops of 44th Reconnaissance Regiment and the Carrier Platoon of the Surreys crossed the Cosina in the area of 10th Brigade's earlier, unsuccessful attempt at a crossing, and the platoon of Surreys moved on a further fifteen hundred yards, without meeting any Germans, to the road south-west of Corleto. On Route Nine, the sappers were using bulldozers to build a crossing near the smashed Cosina bridge. 51st Royal Tanks, without waiting for the main road to be opened, had already sent two squadrons over this crossing.

Major-General Ward's plan for November the 24th was that 28th

Brigade should continue its north-easterly advance across Route Nine, through Corleto and the hamlet of La Palazzina, a mile and a half beyond Route Nine.

Nearly all the Germans had already withdrawn, leaving the roads strewn with obstructions and debris, and sown with mines. North of Basiago, the Surreys and the Reconnaissance Regiment caught up the German rear-guard and hastened its withdrawal. The Germans, however, did not withdraw far, and during the afternoon halted 'B' Company of the DCLI, commanded by Major J. M. Knight MC, a little farther on. 'D' Company, commanded by Major Phillips, turned left after Basiago and made for the Lamone to the north-west of the village. Both 'D' Company and 'B' Company, on the right, were halted short of the river by machine-gun fire. During the night, however, the Germans pulled back across the river, and 10th Brigade moved up to the near bank, hindered only by heavy shell-fire.

To complete the clearing of the divisional sector right up to the Lamone, the Reconnaissance Regiment came up on the right of 10th Brigade, and swung left to the river between the DCLI and the village of Scaldino. 10th Indian Division, meanwhile, was moving up on the right, and on the left 46th Division had reached the river south of Route Nine.

For some time there had been rumours—probably originating from, and communicated through, the channels usual for army rumours—that 4th Division was to leave Italy altogether. Advance parties were detailed, and rumour began to harden into evidence that as soon as the division was relieved it would go to Palestine for rest and refitting. The betting enthusiasts who had laid long odds on various destinations from every port at which the division had embarked ('Left-hand-down out of Algiers!') now calculated that the division would see no more fighting. The division would hardly go as far as Palestine for a rest of less than six months; and by May next year the war with the Germans was sure to be over; and then the Japanese would hardly be likely to last much longer; and so on. The result of these calculations was a sudden access of caution among even the most foolhardy; and hardened warriors, reckoning to reach home in one piece if they could only survive the next few days, walked a little closer beside the ditch than usual. Caution was not, however, allowed to interfere with the duties to which the men of 4th Division had grown accustomed.

The advance party, commanded by Lieutenant-Colonel W. V. H. Robins DSO, was in fact already on its way to Palestine, and 12th Brigade had left Forli on the first stage of the long journey down the length of Italy to Taranto, where the division was to embark. 28th Brigade was to follow on November the 26th, and the rest of the division, except for the Reconnaissance Regiment, as soon as the sector had been handed over to 2nd New Zealand Division. The Reconnaissance Regiment was to have a short rest before returning to the line under the command of V Corps. When the relief was complete, the Corps and Army troops which had been under Major-General Ward's command were to pass under the command either of V Corps or of 2nd New Zealand Division, which was to relieve 4th Division. These troops included 25th Tank Brigade (the North Irish Horse, 51st Royal Tanks and 142nd RAC), 142nd (Self-propelled) Field Regiment, 150th (Self-propelled) Anti-tank Battery, 80th Medium Regiment, 'A' Flight of 651st Air OP Squadron, 'A' Squadron of 1st Assault Regiment RAC/RE, a platoon of Italian Pioneers and a good deal of supplementary engineer equipment.

At seven in the morning, behind a screen of 'A' and 'C' Reconnaissance Squadrons, 'B' and 'D' Companies of the Surreys moved back to Forli, and shortly afterwards the New Zealand advance parties came forward. Towards the end of the morning, a small German patrol crossed the river opposite 'C' Squadron and occupied positions on the near side of the river; and there, for all that 10th Brigade's guns and mortars could do, the Germans stayed, to the mortification of 'C' Squadron.

During the afternoon, in pouring rain, 5th New Zealand Brigade relieved the two Reconnaissance Squadrons and the DCLI, while a battalion of 6th New Zealand Brigade relieved the Bedfords. In the right sector, some of the roads and tracks were broken and slippery with rain, and the fire of German mortars and machine-guns made movement difficult. By six-thirty in the evening, however, 10th Brigade had handed over its sector to the New Zealanders, and the division had finished with the Germans for the last time.

This relief brought to an end the division's long advance across some of the most difficult country in Europe for fighting, against a most skilful and stubborn defence. There had been many kinds of fighting on the way from the Garigliano in March to the Lamone in November; static warfare in the mountains, a great pitched battle in the valley of the Liri, a long approach march in support, a series of pre-arranged assaults on prepared positions and a pursuit across hilly country; in the hot Italian midsummer, a long advance among the mountains and villages and vine-yards of the Chianti country; hard fighting in rain and mud across the feet of the Apennines near the Adriatic coast; and harder fighting still in the utterly flat plain— muddy, close and divided by many rivers—along the road from Rimini to Faenza. After being conditioned to battle in Tunisia, the division had begun its work in Italy well enough, but with little idea of how much there was to learn; and it emerged from the campaign an immensely efficient fighting machine, built up of men who had been gathering experience all the way.

In its last five weeks of fighting against the Germans, the division had taken six hundred and five prisoners, completed the wreck of the German 114th Light Infantry Division, helped to damage the 256th Infantry and the 26th Armoured Divisions, and destroyed the greater part of 278th Division. The force of 4th Division's attacks during this period drained the Germans of man-power at a time when they greatly needed every man, and when under the repeated blows of the Allied offensive the German brigades were smashed and rebuilt with almost monotonous frequency. But for the Italian winter, the wastage of German troops would probably have outrun the supply of reinforcements, and the final disaster to the enemy in Italy could not have been postponed much longer.

Perhaps at this time the deepest sigh of relief went up from 22nd, 30th and 77th Field Regiments. Most of the division had from time to time withdrawn from the battle for a while, but the gunners had been there all the time. They had enjoyed no rest of any length from the first assault on the Trasimene positions until Faenza, a period of more than five months. In that time, the batteries had fired (and dumped) an enormous weight of ammunition, and had worn out a number of guns. One of the most remarkable differences between the German and British forces engaged in Italy was in artillery. The German guns were often very powerful, usually very accurate indeed, sometimes very wild; but they were always comparatively few. A British company or battalion never had to face the fire of a hundred or more assorted guns, brought down within two or three minutes of the enemy's first sight of the infantry. But the field batteries of 25-pounder gun-howitzers, linked by a complex system of telephone-lines and wireless frequencies, and working in unison through the rapid, elaborate drills for the bringing down of many different kinds of fire—these batteries could all turn their guns on any one target within range, and fire within three or four minutes of the target's having been seen. The Germans, as a result, had very little freedom of movement; and their infantry, mortar and gun positions, supply units, headquarters and reserve battalions could never be sure that a storm of shells would not burst upon them and all round them without more warning than the rush of their approach. The German infantry, forming up for a counter-attack, knew that the curtain of defensive fire would almost certainly shut down in front of their advance, that the shells would search them out as long as their positions were known to the defenders, and that the fire of many guns would pursue them in withdrawal.

The power and flexibility of the division's field artillery was due only in part to the quality of the 25-pounder and the system of observation posts and communications by which the guns were directed. The chief source of the artillery's high quality was the technical knowledge of all ranks, in gun-pits, command-posts and OPs, their constant endeavour for the perfect combination of accuracy with speed, and their sense of duty to the infantry.

The importance of the Italian campaign, and the degree to which it was successful, is clearly described in Field-Marshal Alexander's dispatch. The objects of the campaign were first to knock Italy out of the war, and then to divert as much German strength as possible to a theatre as distant as possible from the vital battle-field—the Channel coast of France. The first of these objects was achieved on September the 3rd 1943, when the Italian army, comprising fifty-nine divisions and amounting to some two million men, surrendered to the Allies. The quality of Italian troops was not usually regarded very highly, but they were quite adequate garrison troops, and at the time of the surrender seven Italian divisions were holding southern France, and thirty-two were doing their best to keep the turbulent Balkans quiet. When they surrendered, these divisions and others had to be replaced by German formations.

The second of the two objects began to be achieved a week later, when the Allies invaded the Italian mainland, and German divisions began to move southwards to join battle.

In Field-Marshal Alexander's words, 'The campaign in Italy was a great holding attack . . . It is the nature and function of a holding force to attack secondary objectives while the main force is preparing to attack the main objective . . . our forces in Italy never at any time enjoyed any but the slenderest margin of superiority over the Germans, and usually not even that.'

At the time of the assault on the Gustav Line, the Allied Armies in Italy consisted of twenty-eight divisions, and the German armies of twenty-three. Soon after the Allies began their advance to Rome and beyond, the invasion of France began, and the Russians came within reach of East Prussia. In spite of the threat to Germany from east and west, the Germans regarded Italy as so important that they strengthened their reeling armies there with a division each from Denmark, Holland and Russia and two from the Balkans. Three other divisions which were being prepared in Germany for the Russian campaign were diverted to Italy, where they took over the title and the survivors of divisions destroyed in the battle for Rome.

4th Division was approaching Palombara when on June the 7th Field-Marshal Alexander wrote 'I have now two highly organized and skilful Armies, capable of carrying out large-scale attacks in the closest co-operation. Morale is irresistably high as a result of recent successes, and the whole forms one closely articulated machine, capable of carrying out assaults and rapid exploitation in the most difficult terrain. Neither the Apennines nor even the Alps should prove a serious obstacle to their enthusiasm and skill.'

A month later, the picture changed; Southern France was to be invaded, and the invasion force of more than seven divisions was to be provided by the Allied armies in Italy. The withdrawal from Italy of more than a quarter of the Allied strength left Field-Marshal Alexander with no appreciable superiority in numbers. 'The Allied Armies in full pursuit of a beaten enemy were called off from the chase, Kesselring was given a breathing-space to reorganize his scattered forces, and I was left with insufficient strength to break through the barrier of the Apennines. My Armies, which had just been built up into a strong, flexible and co-ordinated instrument, inspired by victory and conscious of their own superiority, were reduced once more to the shifts and improvisations which had marked the previous winter, and faced again the problems of overcoming not only the difficulties of the Italian terrain and the stubbornness of the enemy's resistance, but also the lack of manpower on their own side.'

When 4th Division was approaching the Arezzo Line, therefore, the enemy's strength was reckoned as the equivalent of fourteen full-strength divisions, an average strength of 11,500 men; reinforcements from elsewhere were likely before long to bring the figure up to between eighteen and twenty-one divisions. The Allied forces amounted to just over fourteen infantry and four armoured divisions, with seven independent armoured brigades.

The pursuit was, however, maintained until XIII Corps reached the Arno at Florence during the first week of August. Field-Marshal Alexander wrote, 'From the Garigliano to the Arno is two hundred and forty miles as the crow flies; by the shortest road it is two hundred and seventy miles. We had covered this distance in sixty-four days, breaking through three lines of prepared defences south of Rome and fighting two major battles, the Trasimene Line and Arezzo, between Rome and Florence. I consider this a very satisfactory speed in Italian terrain, and the more so when it is remembered that, after the fall of Rome, I was being forced to make detachments to other fronts while Kesselring was being strenuously reinforced.'

When the attack on the Gothic Line began, three weeks later, the enemy had twenty-six German and two Italian divisions, all fairly well up to strength, since the Germans had been reinforced by some sixty thousand men since early June. The Allies had twenty divisions and eight brigades—they had received thirteen thousand infantry replacements in April, and since then no more had come or were to come. This great disparity in the rate of reinforcement between the opposing forces, considered in the light of the steady advance by the Allies in Italy and of the enemy's desperate need of men for the fighting in France, does something to show the success of Allied arms in Italy.

Weakened by losses in the Gothic Line and by the lack of reinforcements, gravely short of ammunition, opposed by a powerful and resolute enemy and hampered by difficult country and appalling weather, the Allies in Italy came to a halt soon after the 4th Division left the fighting. The rest of the story leads on to a fitting conclusion. Allied aircraft smashed the Po bridges behind the enemy, and early in April 1945, the Allied armies drove the Germans back against the river and destroyed them. On May the 2nd, the Germans south of the Po—half a million men—gave up the hopeless struggle, and all the enemy forces remaining in Italy and Austria laid down their arms in unconditional surrender. Six days later, all the remaining German Armies followed suit.

The campaign in which 4th Division had taken a leading part was therefore one of the most difficult and successful of the war. Without the considerable superiority in numbers usually accounted necessary to force an enemy out of strong positions, the Fifth and Eighth Armies had driven back through all the mountains of southern Italy a well-organized force of more or less equal strength, and in the northern plains were to annihilate the enemy and so break open the southern defences of Germany itself. This the Allies were enabled to do by generalship of a very high order—at every major battle, the German commanders, in spite of the high reputation of the German General Staff, had been completely deceived and out-manœuvred —by air power, by mobility and by artillery. But the proudest share in the victory is due to all those men from Great Britain and from twenty-five other countries, who shared the hardships, toil and honour of the great campaign.

26. Between campaigns: Taranto

The withdrawal from the Lamone brought to an end the division's second scheme of well-organized Welfare in the forward area. By the middle of November, the canteens and cinemas of Cesena were out of reach of the men most in need of them. The Welfare services were therefore transferred to Forli; the town was still shelled from time to time by the Germans, but this disadvantage was outweighed by the need for a Welfare organization in just such a place. The 'Dutch Cheese' was shut in Cesena on November the 15th, and reopened at tea-time next day in the Albergo Corso in Forli. As before, it provided reading and rest rooms, an information room, a Post Office, barber's saloon and a restaurant complete with orchestra; as before, tea was served in the morning and afternoon, and there were hot meals at night. The restaurant was bigger than at Cesena, and served many more meals; but there were still more customers than places, and there were long queues at the doors. The civilian staff included the three prettiest and most efficient of the Italian girls who had joined the Piediluco camp as waitresses and who had served there from mid-August until early October; their offer to help again, in winter, within range of German guns, was a credit to their courage and a compliment to the men they served. When the division left Forli, the girls offered to serve in the 'Viking Arms', which had been opened by V Corps in the place left empty in Cesena by the 'Dutch Cheese'.

Two other canteens preceded the 'Dutch Cheese' into Forli. The first, run by Captain and Mrs Roberts of the Salvation Army, who had kept pace with the division's advance for many months, was opened soon after the leading troops reached the town, and while the Germans were still within rifle-shot. The second, run by the

Church of Scotland, arrived shortly afterwards. The Forli Opera House, unlike that of Cesena, had been severely damaged, and the Divisional Concert Party was less comfortably housed. The party had to share a theatre with a mobile cinema, but managed to rehearse and stage one show.

A new venture that began in Forli was the production of a divisional newspaper, the *Quadrant*, under the editorship of Captain P. A. Goodall. A printing press had been requisitioned in Marciano, and a complete set of new type was bought for it in Rome. The first copy was composed and ready for printing when orders for Palestine came through; as the press had to be sent to Rome for storage, only fifty specimen copies could be run off the machine, and publication of the first edition had to be postponed.

Another new Welfare service prepared at this time was a mobile library of two thousand books; as it could not be taken to Palestine, it was lent to V Corps, together with the division's five mobile canteens, against the day when the division would return to Italy.

On November the 15th, the scheme for home leave from the Mediterranean, known as LIAP—Leave in Addition to Python— began for all ranks of the division. A large proportion of the vacancies was allotted to the infantry, so that many of the leave party who cheerfully left the square at Forlimpopoli early in the morning had been fighting in the Montone battle thirty-six hours before.

The Welfare arrangements could not have been more timely than during the fighting of this winter. Living on the battle-field was a nerve-racking, exhausting and dirty business, but the soldier on coming out of the line found there was somewhere pleasant to go while he was off duty—something to give him a change of atmosphere.

Except for the Concert Party, which was first formed in North Africa, and had been performing on many stages ever since, the Welfare services were the idea of the AA&QMG, Lieutenant-Colonel R. D. Judd DSO MC, and were organized by the DAAG, Major R. G. Collet. The success of the 'Dutch Cheese'—and as the people who ran it gained experience it became remarkably successful—was due at first to the hard work of Captain H. Bourgein and later to that of Captain R. E. Fox, and to the able, imaginative and resourceful management of Staff-Sergeant A. E. Harding.

In torrents of rain the troops of the division left their last positions in Italy. One by one the columns headed southwards, at the high speed usual with mechanized troops leaving a battle-field behind. By November the 28th, the last lorries of 10th Brigade had left Forli, and only the Reconnaissance Regiment remained, to make the most of a much-needed rest before returning for a short period to the fighting on the Lamone. By November the 29th, the division had gathered round Pescara, and began to prepare to hand over all but a minimum of its heavy equipment to 5th Division, the advance parties of which were already on the way from Palestine. 12th Brigade had wedged itself into barracks at Chieti, where Captain M. Honey of the Black Watch found himself in familiar surroundings, for the Italians had imprisoned him there after capturing him in 1942.

Leaving its guns and lorries and other equipment (highly polished and in as good order as possible) in the charge of rear parties near Pescara, the division moved southward again by rail and road to Taranto. The rail transport was of the '40 hommes 8 chevaux' type; more than thirty men were crowded into each of the big vans, where they sprawled on top of the baggage and made the best of an uncomfortable journey. By December the 5th the division had gathered again near Taranto, and the troops made themselves as comfortable as possible under rather inadequate canvas. The climate was milder, and there was a long rest ahead; everyone relaxed.

Major-General Ward, meanwhile, had flown from Bari to the Middle East, and in Palestine the division's advance party was making the necessary arrangements with the representatives of the 5th Division. Brigadiers Shoosmith, Heber-Percy and Kirwan were on leave in England, and Brigadier Preston was in command at Taranto.

While the division waited for the ships that were to take it to Palestine, trouble was growing to explosive force in Athens.

While German forces occupied Greece, the nation had been more thoroughly divided by politics than had the people of most occupied countries. As in the days of Saint Paul, the Greeks still 'spent their time in nothing else, but either to tell or to hear some new thing', and to a man were still fiercely and restlessly political. Political differences had enfeebled the nation's resistance to the Germans, for bands of guerillas of several parties had wasted their strength in fighting each other, or had reserved their weapons and their powers for civil war. There had already been serious trouble in Egypt, when left-wing elements of the free Greek forces had mutinied against officers who they said had persecuted them for political reasons. These elements had been weeded out of the Greek Mountain Brigade and the Sacred Battalion, which had returned to Greece with the British forces. The guerillas of all parties had then been required to surrender arms, and the left-wing bands had protested that they would be defenceless against their reactionary compatriots of the regular forces. As in all Greek political affairs, the situation was extremely complicated and difficult, and there was something to be said for both sides—and a great deal to be said against them.

The collective title of the left-wing parties was *Ethnikon Apelefterotikon Metopon* (EAM), the 'National Liberation Front', a resistance movement formed during the occupation and to some extent controlled by the Communist Party. The EAM army was called *Hellenikos' Laikos Apelefterotikos Stratos* (ELAS), the 'Greek People's Liberation Army'; it was a force of some thirty-five thousand men, organized as nine divisions and several brigades. The Communist Party of Greece—*Kommunistikon Komma Hellados* (KKE)—was the disciplined core of the left-wing movement, strengthened with both purpose and ability.

The Athenian Army Corps of ELAS was the main left-wing force in Athens. It was originally organized as a reserve formation composed of civilian members of left-wing movements, and was recruited by districts on a Communist cell basis. It had never been in action against the Germans, and consisted of some eleven thousand men, in addition to artillery and administrative troops. Service in it was unpopular, desertions were frequent and only the press-gang could keep its brigades up to two thousand men—and some women —each. The commanders were apparently powerless to enforce discipline on their men, or to exact obedience from their officers. The complete absence of liaison between fighting units and headquarters prevented the corps from organizing any large-scale action.

Mingled with the militant Communists and the reluctant citizens who made up most of the corps was a nasty element, a riff-raff of hooligans, robbers and murderers, who presumably were responsible for the many disgusting atrocities of which the division was to see evidence. Other improper actions, such as firing on the Red Cross— even when it guarded stretcher-parties carrying women civilians— and using ambulances to carry ammunition, were to be so common

---

[1] The letter H at the beginning of a Greek word is indicated not by a letter but by an apostrophe, which does not appear in initials.

as to suggest that the Athenian Corps recognized no code other than the dictates of impulse.

Neither force nor diplomacy was enough to keep the peace in Athens. During a stormy demonstration in Constitution Square on December the 3rd, a free fight began; shots were fired, and men fell dead. ELAS at once acted on a pre-arranged plan, attacked police stations and other vital points, and made every effort to push the light forces of III British Corps into the sea.

Constitution Square is in effect the centre of Athens. The city is largely modern and European; the relics of the ancient Athenian civilization, of the Roman Empire and of the long Turkish occupation are all but swamped in the crowd of comparatively modern buildings, which range from the up-to-date through the dingy to the downright ramshackle. From among the clustering roofs of the city, each within a mile of Constitution Square, rise two commanding heights—the Acropolis, raising its marvellous ruins two hundred feet higher than the Square; and the towering, pointed Mount Lykavittos, nearly four hundred feet higher still. Through the warren of narrow streets that surround these heights, and along the wide modern boulevards, the fighting spread with the speed and violence of a riot.

But there was nothing riotous about the methodical ELAS assault. Within a week, more than five hundred men of the civil police and gendarmerie had been killed or were missing, and by steady infiltration the guerillas had pressed in close to the heart of the city.

ELAS was apparently trying to fight according to a plan originally framed for use against the Germans. The intention of the plan was to surround the regular troops and force them to fight at a disadvantage by cutting their communications and hemming them in with road-blocks. In this manner, the more powerful weapons of the regulars would be useless, while among the narrow streets and in suburban houses the battle was fought out with small-arms and grenades.

III Corps Headquarters, however, was still protected, and Lykavittos, the Acropolis and Goudi Barracks—in the open country on the lower slopes of Hymettus—still held by Arkforce, which consisted of 23rd Armoured Brigade and 3rd Greek Mountain Brigade (known as the Rimini Brigade, since its capture of that town).

The central position of III Corps was round its headquarters in University Street, which runs from Constitution Square north-west to Omoina Square. ELAS had attacked this position from Omonia, in the poorer quarter of the town, and from Kolonaki, the fashionable suburb at the other end of University Street. Arkforce held off these attacks, but remained closely besieged. Many British detachments such as hospitals, workshops and dumps were cut off, and RAF Headquarters at Kifissia, a wealthy suburb a little way out of the city, was captured. Singros Avenue, the broad highway that leads from Athens down to the coast, was dominated by ELAS but had not been cut. Armoured vehicles could force a passage by day, and convoys from the coast, strongly escorted and travelling fast, could run the gauntlet to reach Arkforce by night.

ELAS held the city waterworks, the electric light plant, the telephone exchange and the greater part of the Piræus. On the northern side of the harbour, however, was a company of Sappers and Miners, and later on a detachment of 57th Light Anti-aircraft Regiment managed to cross the harbour to them and to form a base on the far side. 139th Brigade of 46th Division was holding Kallipolis along the southern shore of the harbour's southern arm. New Faliron, on the shore of the bay east of the base of the southern arm, was held by 5th Indian Brigade of 4th Indian Division. Between this brigade and Hasani air-field, the road along the coast was kept open only by a few British troops, in positions up to a hundred yards in front of it. The air-field itself was adequately guarded, and aircraft of the RAF were based there.

The landing of food, clothing, medical stores and other relief supplies, so greatly needed by the Greek people, had come to a stop. The merchant ships lay idly at anchor in Salamis Bay, among the dull grey ships of the Royal Navy. Small-arms fire rattled among the streets of Athens and the Piræus; sometimes the air shook to the thump of a gun; aircraft swooped over the city, hammering away with their machine-guns, or firing rockets in streaks of smoke. Cowed by the snipers who infested the roof tops, and by rumours of cruelty and murder, the peaceful citizens of Athens hid in their closely shuttered houses, or scuttled across the dangerous streets in search of food. Patrols crept from doorway to doorway, covered by machine-guns on verandas and at bedroom windows. III Corps held grimly and precariously on; ELAS attacked sometimes wildly and sometimes with cunning, but never with entire success.

27. Civil War in Athens

On December the 9th 1944, six days after the fighting in Greece began, Major-General Ward in Cairo was given new orders. The move to Palestine was cancelled; the division was to reinforce the out-numbered Greek and British troops in Athens, and was to join them in subduing ELAS. In Taranto, a hurried conference was called at the large gaunt building on the water-front, where Divisional Headquarters was temporarily installed, and orders were given for the re-equipment of the division. All units were to send parties back to Pescara to collect the guns and vehicles and other equipment which had been left there in so high a state of polish. The advance parties in Palestine were to report for orders at Middle East Headquarters in Cairo.

On December the 11th, the divisional commander and his party flew to Athens, and, after weighing up the situation there, Major-General Ward sent his AA & QMG, Lieutenant-Colonel Judd, back to the division at Taranto with orders for the move to Greece.

By December the 12th, a Tactical Divisional Headquarters had been set up at Old Faliron, near the shore south-west of Athens. The headquarters was absurdly short of all the prosaic stores—such as paper and talc—without which it could hardly work. All communications had to be sent through 139th Brigade, some four miles away by road. Lieutenant-Colonel P. A. Duke, commanding 4th Divisional Signals, took on a variety of jobs which included those of signalmaster, line-maintenance man and exchange operator.

Also on December the 12th, 28th Brigade, less the Somersets, under Brigadier Preston's command, began to arrive by air from Italy, and landed under small-arms fire on Hasani air-field. The troops of the brigade had travelled in the bomb-bays of seventy

Liberator bombers of the Balkan Air Force, and the brigade's essential baggage was carried by nine Dakotas. The King's were at once placed under the command of Arkforce, and moved into Athens after dark. The Hampshires took over the defence of the air-field.

Compared with the campaigns against the Axis, the fighting in Athens was an untidy and confusing affair. The division went into action incomplete and inadequately equipped, but with two brigades —5th Indian and 139th Brigades—and an interesting variety of troops—which included RAF parachutists, a detachment of the Long-Range Desert Group, a squadron of the RAF Regiment and a battalion of the Greek National Guard—under command. The troops under command changed from time to time during the battle, but normally included forces of armour and artillery considerably slighter than those usual in more orderly campaigns. The enemy troops were very slippery customers indeed; they wore no uniform—unless it were British battle-dress or the blue-and-white brassard of the Greek National Guard—and could always slip through the lines as civilians. The battle-ground was naturally full of Greek civilians, who were allowed out of their houses only for two hours in the day, and who were always liable to be stopped and searched. ELAS used children to smuggle messages and ammunition; an old woman was always likely to have a couple of Bren-gun magazines in her shopping-basket, or a girl to have a grenade or two in her handbag—there might even be a bomb sharing a pram with a baby. Ambulances carried reinforcements and ammunition; and a sniper might fire from behind the long, full skirts of a woman standing in a doorway.

Nor was it possible to draw a line to divide friendly country from that held by the enemy. The British headquarters area was surrounded, and the depots of several services cut off; all lines of communication were constantly threatened. The ELAS guerillas —known as Andartes—were always able to filter back into any area that had been cleared by British troops, and every house and street had to be cleared a second time by detachments of the Greek National Guard. The National Guard was a hastily enlisted force, untrained, undisciplined and short of proper weapons, but full of enthusiasm. These Greek troops were much more efficient than the British at extracting information about hidden arms or ELAS soldiers; their methods, however, were better not investigated, and as allies they were useful rather than desirable.

The ability of the Andartes to slip through the cordons of regular troops led to an uncomfortable situation during the night of December the 12th, when a strong force attacked and blew up part of a battalion headquarters of 139th Brigade. On the 14th, resolute attacks threatened the headquarters of both 4th Division and 28th Brigade; Major-General Ward was among those who went out with fighting patrols, and the clerks stationed at the upper windows of Divisional Headquarters, waiting for the order to fire, could see the ELAS riflemen dodging from cover to cover towards the house. Grenades were primed in both headquarters, but were not used, as the attackers were scattered by the machine-guns of low-flying Spitfires.

The division's first tasks were to take the form of consolidation; they were to defend the air-field, secure a beach-head at the foot of Singros Avenue, where all the division's supplies and reinforcements would have to be landed, and keep open the coast road between the air-field and the Piræus. The division was to take the offensive only on the extreme left, where 139th Brigade and 5th Indian Brigade were fighting their way towards each other through the southern arm of the main harbour of the Piræus, clearing snipers and road-blocks as they advanced.

On December the 13th the DCLI arrived, and took over the beach-head. Two days later, two large ships steamed into the bay, and anchored at a discreet distance from the shore; on board were 12th Brigade, commanded by Lieutenant-Colonel Shipley DSO, the rest of 10th Brigade, commanded by Lieutenant-Colonel B. A. Burke, the Somersets and part of the divisional RASC. Assault boats were soon ferrying the newcomers ashore, and by nightfall the line was less thinly held.

On December the 16th, a transport arrived with the Northumberland Fusiliers and four auxiliary companies of infantry raised from the divisional artillery. One of these companies, from 14th Anti-tank Regiment, went off at once to escort two thousand ELAS prisoners to the Middle East, and did not rejoin the division until the New Year. The remaining companies were organized into the RA Battalion, under the command of Major R. A. Hemsworth of the Anti-tank Regiment.

Now that the main body had arrived, and apart from the guns the division's fighting troops were all present, the division began work on its primary task. 10th Brigade on the right at first took over the air-field, 12th Brigade in the centre covered the coastal road between the air-field and the beach-head, and 28th Brigade on the left held the beach-head itself. The DCLI meanwhile had been clearing the comparatively open stretches of ground on each side of the coastal end of Singros Avenue, deepening the bridge-head and providing a firm base for an attack towards Athens.

Farther to the left still, 139th Brigade had done well during the days when 4th Division was gathering its strength. The brigade had cleared the peninsula as far as the Metropolitan Railway, which crosses its base, and patrols had moved down the coast road and reached the DCLI. Now that a large part of the Piræus was clear, the beach-head firmly held, and the road to the air-field and the air-field itself strongly guarded, the British forces in Athens could prepare to expel the Andartes from the city.

Lieutenant-General J. L. I. Hawkesworth CB CBE, lately commander of 4th Division, who had been promoted from the command of 46th Division to that of X Corps, now took charge of operations in Greece, while Lieutenant-General Scobie concentrated on political affairs. The Piræus ceased to be part of Major-General Ward's responsibilities and became that of Blockforce—139th Brigade Group, under the brigade commander, Brigadier Block. 4th Division's next task was to attack from the bridge-head along Singros Avenue, and to open the road between the coast and Athens itself.

Since the divisional artillery had not yet arrived, the attack was to be supported, while within sight of the bay, by the guns of destroyers in the bay; and 25-pounders of 4th Indian Division, which were in action on an island in the bay, were also to fire if called on. A few tanks from 40th Royal Tanks were to accompany the attacking battalions.

Buttersforce, consisting of the Northumberland Fusiliers and the RA Battalion, under Lieutenant-Colonel Butterfield, took over the air-field from 10th Brigade, and 10th Brigade spread along the coast road to release 12th Brigade, which with 28th Brigade was to open the attack.

The Somersets led the way up Singros Avenue in darkness during the night of December the 17th. By dawn of the 18th, they had reached the first crest to which the road rises from the coast, and were two miles inland. At dawn, the Hampshires passed through, creeping up the road in rubber-soled shoes towards the Brewery, half a mile farther on. The Brewery was strongly held, but if ELAS had posted any sentries they must have been fast asleep; not even the three tanks which clattered after the infantry roused any fire. The garrison paid heavily for its slackness; the Hampshires' pioneers blew in the main doors with pole-charges, shells from the tanks knocked holes in the walls, and the infantry burst in through the breaches. The defenders, trying to escape in the open, were cut down by machine-gun fire, and twenty of them were killed. By ten in the morning, the Hampshires not only had a firm hold on the Brewery, but had cleared the houses on each side of the Avenue as far as a point two hundred yards beyond.

The King's, who had joined 2nd Parachute Brigade for the attack, had been working their way, meanwhile, towards the Brewery from the hills round the Acropolis, half a mile to the north, and before long joined up with the Hampshires.

As 28th Brigade advanced up the Avenue, 12th Brigade followed up behind, clearing the suburbs to left and right of the Avenue. In this fighting from house to house and from street to street, against an enemy in civilian clothes, the battalions were compelled to clear the same neighbourhood over and over again, and to secure their rear as well as their flanks against counter-attack. 12th Brigade—followed by a detachment of the Greek National Guard, which cleared all the houses a second time—met little organized opposition, but every house had to be searched from attic to basement, and a single sniper could hold up a section or even a platoon for a while. With the Royal Fusiliers on the right, the Black Watch in the centre and the West Kents on the left, 12th Brigade worked its way slowly towards Athens, astride the Avenue.

On December the 20th, having handed over to a composite force of British static units and to the National Guard, 10th Brigade came up to New Smyrna, behind the Royal Fusiliers on the right of the Avenue. The Royal Fusiliers crossed the Avenue, joined the other two battalions of 12th Brigade on the left, and came in on the left between the West Kents and the River Ilissos, a mile to the left of the Avenue. 10th and 12th Brigades were now one on each side of the Avenue.

On December the 22nd, 12th Brigade completed the clearing of the streets between the Avenue and the Ilissos, as far as the point where the river passes under the road, just short of the Brewery. 10th Brigade finished clearing the suburbs between the coast and the rear of 28th Brigade. 28th Brigade extended its front half a mile to the left, as far as the hill to the south-west of the Acropolis. In all these successful operations, the division suffered few losses. Among the casualties, however, was Brigadier Shoosmith, who had hurried back from leave at home to take charge of 10th Brigade; on December the 21st, while on reconnaissance in an Air O P, he was wounded by small-arms fire from below.

The rest of III Corps was also on the offensive. Arkforce, besieged in the heart of Athens, had attacked and forced its way down the main road towards the Piræus. Blockforce fought hard to debouch from the peninsula it had cleared, and to advance up the road towards Athens. Between Arkforce and Blockforce, troops of 2nd Parachute Brigade, who had been surrounded in buildings on the main Athens-Piræus road, were joined by tanks of 40th Royal Tanks which had crossed the River Ilissos from 12th Brigade's area. ELAS, however, fought back, and on Christmas Day there was a fierce battle in Omonia Square only a few hundred yards from Corps Headquarters. Andartes, loaded with dynamite, crept through the sewers to blow up the hotel in which the temporary civil government was housed; they were caught in time, but others tried again later.

On December the 23rd, the division extended its front to the left across the Ilissos, and relieved the 2nd Parachute Brigade on the Athens-Piræus road. The Somersets occupied Rouf Barracks, and the Royal Fusiliers took over positions a mile farther down the road.

During the night of Christmas Eve, ELAS put in a sudden and violent attack on one of the factories held by the Royal Fusiliers. Small-arms fire tore through the windows on three sides; dynamiters blew a wide breach in the surrounding wall, and later blew in four smaller holes. The few Andartes who scrambled through the breaches were soon driven out again by the steady defence of 'X' Company, commanded by Major P. C. Watling. The battalion's 3-inch mortars inflicted losses on the enemy, but the fierce attacks went on all through the night.

The Carrier Platoon of the Royal Fusiliers, half a mile up the road towards Athens, also had a noisy night. Anyone who showed his head outside was shot at with small-arms from short range, and mortars and guns scored direct hits on several flimsy buildings.

Sergeant McKie's section of 12 Platoon, holding an isolated cottage, had the most exciting time of all. About thirty Andartes attacked the cottage; Sergeant McKie and his six men, crouching behind the front garden wall, used small-arms and grenades to beat off repeated attacks. ELAS placed a pole-charge against the side of a house, and smashed up a room, killing two Greek civilians, but the section's defence held firm. After an hour and a half, ammunition began to run low, and Sergeant McKie ordered a sortie. The seven men sallied out, blazing away at anything that moved, broke through the ELAS cordon and rejoined the main body—Fusilier Light was captured on the way, but the section had suffered no other loss.

The garrison of the besieged factory was reinforced on Christmas Eve by 'Z' Company, commanded by Major M. F. W. Tyndall. The battalion began to prepare to make a sweep to the south-west, to meet Blockforce which was advancing from the Piræus.

During the afternoon of the same day, 104th Field Battery, commanded by Major A. R. Babington, deployed four guns in a small open space among the modern suburban houses of New Smyrna. The technical problems facing the gunners were acutely difficult; there were roofs in the line of fire all round, the electricity cables high up in front of the guns were not to be pulled down, and, somewhere out of sight between the guns and their targets, the Parthenon rose to its great height near the trajectory of the shells—a small arithmetical error might cause a shell to burst on the famous temple. The occupants of the houses round the gun-position welcomed the gunners, and put up with hob-nailed boots on polished floors, sentries clattering in and out all night, and the general discomfort of housing half-a-dozen foreign soldiers in a small and already crowded house; but their smiles faded a little when the first salvo cracked the glass in half their windows.

Christmas Day was no festival for the division. The weather was bitterly cold, and small luxuries such as cigarettes were in short supply. Rations were limited for some time to bully beef, M & V and biscuits. Later on, however, the divisional RASC, commanded by Lieutenant-Colonel A. P. Campbell, supplemented this dry fare with bread of its own baking. Christmas celebrations were officially postponed, in an order by Lieutenant-General Scobie; they eventually took place on February the 3rd, which not unnaturally became known as Scobiemas.

One happy diversion, however, was the party given by 28th Brigade for some hundred and fifty children of New Faliron. The Brigade RASC Officer, Captain Pelling, requisitioned a large café, and enlisted some of the troops as waiters. While parents, noses flattened against the café windows, stared hungrily in, the children sat down to a Christmas feast of M & V, followed by tinned peaches and biscuits. The menu was enormously popular; indeed, it would have been difficult to find a menu which was not, for few of the children had enjoyed a square meal for many months. One little boy of six put away four full plates of M & V before leaning back with a gorged sigh, and other prodigies of digestion were going on all round. When all was done, the children moved drowsily off to their homes to sleep it off and to tell the tale.

The party was a happy one not only for the children and their parents but for the troops, most of whom were spending their second Christmas abroad, and some of whom had not spent Christmas in their own homes for several years. Even in Greece, where the language is difficult to learn, and where Easter is a greater festival than Christmas, and even on M & V, a children's party is still a children's party.

The infantry spent Christmas Day searching the streets, silencing snipers, clearing road-blocks and confiscating dumps of arms and explosives. On the whole, the day was a quiet one—for the ELAS commanders had reckoned on most of the British soldiers being drunk on Christmas night, and were preparing their forces for an attack.

At midnight, ELAS troops came charging in at all 12th Brigade's northern positions, blew a hole in a wall of Rouf Barracks, and engaged 4 Platoon of the Black Watch in a sharp fight. The Andartes were set back on finding the defenders sober and alert, and were further dismayed when the divisional artillery—represented by 104th and 455th Field Batteries—opened fire for the first time; the attacks were driven off after more than an hour's fighting.

Blockforce and Arkforce, meanwhile, had been steadily closing in from each side of 12th Brigade's positions, and had succeeded in joining up so that a strip of safe ground joined Athens and the Piræus.

Now that the siege of central Athens was raised, the next task of the British troops was to clear the southern part of the city. On Boxing Day, while at Corps Headquarters Mr Winston Churchill, Mr Anthony Eden and Field-Marshal Alexander were trying to bring about some agreement between the warring factions, the division regrouped for this task. Blockforce came up from the Piræus and relieved 12th Brigade, and 12th Brigade—once more commanded by Brigadier Heber-Percy—moved up to part of 28th Brigade's sector. The Royal Artillery Battalion came up from the air-field to release 10th Brigade for the new attack.

Before dawn on December the 28th, the Surreys made a silent attack eastwards from New Smyrna, on the right of the Avenue and behind the Brewery. The Bedfords on the right and the DCLI on the left followed up, and by evening the brigade had cleared most of the Drougouti and Katsipodi districts, and held the two low hills that rise among the houses there. ELAS did their best to break into these new positions, and one party, dressed in National Guard uniform, managed to rush two sections of the Bedfords. The positions were held, however, through a night of heavy and intermittent shooting, and on December the 29th, 10th Brigade resumed its advance. The brigade finished clearing the Drougouti and Katsipodi districts, and joined up with the King's, who had attacked from the left across the front of the brigade. Farther to the left front, Arkforce and the Rimini Brigade were attacking at the same time, penetrating deeply into the suburbs east of the Zappion Gardens. ELAS resistance in southern Athens was beginning to collapse.

There was little activity on the left of the division, but ELAS troops were still there in force. Late in the afternoon of December the 29th, Captain R. D. Tyler of 104th Field Battery, in his observation post in the Observatory on Nymph Hill, a little way to the west of the Acropolis, saw the flashes of six enemy guns, and heard the crash of their shells bursting in the lines of the Somersets at Rouf Barracks. The British forces in Athens were restrained by strict orders from any action that could possibly damage the historic parts of the city, and these orders had a particularly restrictive effect on the use of artillery. Wide safety circles, in which no shell was to fall, were drawn on the gunners' maps round every building of importance; and the guns were not allowed to open fire at all until the location of the target and the reason for its engagement had been reported to and approved by Corps Headquarters. On this occasion, Captain Tyler had to wait in the Observatory while afternoon drew into evening, watching the guns firing away at the Somersets, and hoping for permission to silence them. By the time permission was granted, dusk had fallen, and Captain Tyler could no longer see enough to bring down observed fire; he had to content himself with bringing down on the map-reference of the enemy battery the fire of 30th Field Regiment, the rest of which had since been deployed, under the command of Lieutenant-Colonel A. E. Brocklehurst.

On the last day of 1944—the division's most eventful year—28th Brigade went into action on the left of 10th Brigade, and struck eastwards from the neighbourhood of the Brewery into Gouva and Pankrati. The Rimini Brigade advanced across the front of the division from the left as far as Byron; and 10th Brigade, advancing in its turn, penetrated first through Imittos and then through Kopanas to reach Byron and to join the Greek brigade. By dusk on New Year's Eve, the whole of southern Athens was clear.

The role of the British troops in Greece was not only to clear ELAS from the city but to feed the inhabitants. As each district was cleared, the units which occupied it set up distribution centres, and issued soup powder and dried beans to the people, who took them away and cooked them. Far too many meals were needed for the units to do the cooking.

The distribution centres were opened as soon as all violence in the district had come to an end, and they shut down for twenty-four hours the moment trouble boiled up again. Athens at this time was as lively as a shooting-gallery, and local commanders often had difficulty in finding out whether casual fusillades were a resurgence of ELAS defiance or a *feu de joie* by Government supporters.

The Greeks' idea of lining up for rations was to gather in a clamouring mob and fight their way in. The British troops needed all the good humour and tolerance they could muster to induce them to form an orderly queue. The Greek aversion to the mingling in public of men and women—inherited from long years of Turkish rule—made things even more difficult, since two queues always had to be formed, one for men and another for women. After a few days, the Greeks got the idea and formed queues of their own accord, but they tried endless ruses in order to get two rations or to be served first. Expectant mothers were allowed to the front of the queue, and after the first day ladies with cushions under their dresses were being sent to the back.

The northern part of the city remained to be cleared. Lieutenant-General Hawkesworth planned a converging attack, in which 28th Brigade would advance westwards from Goudi Barracks, on the extreme right flank, into the Averof district; Arkforce was to strike northwards from Omonia Square through Vathi and Attiki, across the front of 28th Brigade; and 12th Brigade was to come up on the left of Arkforce, attacking northwards and north-eastwards from Rouf Barracks into Vouthoulas and Plato Academy. Crackforce, commanded by the CRA, Brigadier R. C. H. Kirwan OBE, took over the coastal area from the air-field to New Smyrna, and 28th Brigade moved out to Goudi Barracks.

On the night of January the 2nd, the Hampshires opened the attack from Goudi Barracks. ELAS fought back with fury, but the Hampshires broke through the crust of the defence, the King's and the Somersets went forward in turn, and by dusk the Somersets had reached the farther end of the Averof district, a mile and a half from Goudi Barracks.

A mile farther to the right still, 'A' and 'C' Squadrons of the Reconnaissance Regiment had reached Psychiko Garden Suburb, and had broken the ELAS cordon round 97th General Hospital and Lieutenant-General Scobie's house.

Next morning, on January the 4th, ELAS troops put in a sharp counter-attack, and tried to filter into the regiment's positions. Most of them were driven off, but a few held out in houses at the north-west corner of Psychiko, until fire at point-blank range from the guns and machine-guns of the armoured cars forced them to surrender. The RA Battalion companies of 30th Field and 14th Anti-tank Regiments, together with a battalion of the Greek National Guard, arrived to reinforce the position. The appearance of the National Guard provoked another outbreak of fighting, which was quickly suppressed.

On January the 5th, the Hampshires and the Somersets completed the clearing of the Averof district, while on their right the King's deployed into Kipseli, beyond the gardens round the Military Academy, to the north-west. ELAS resistance in Psychiko had come to an end, and the armoured cars of the Reconnaissance Regiment had passed through and reached Akarnai, five miles to the north-west, and Kalandri, a mile and a half to the north-east.

On the other side of Athens, 12th Brigade had been equally successful. On January the 3rd, the Black Watch advanced a quarter of a mile northwards from Rouf Barracks. At dawn next day, the West Kents on the right began to clear the streets and houses of Plato Academy, while the Black Watch crossed the more open ground on the left towards a crag at Vouthoulous, which rises among the buildings of a brick-works.

Later in the morning, the Black Watch reached and cleared Vouthoulous, handed it over to the Royal Fusiliers, and moved north-eastwards to the outskirts of Kolonos in order to prevent

ELAS from escaping from the city. While 'C' Company was on the move, Captain P. N. Visser was shot dead by a sniper.

On January the 6th, the Royal Fusiliers advanced on the left of the West Kents, and finished clearing Plato Academy. The Black Watch moved a quarter of a mile to the north-west, into the big textile mill at Kolokinthos. A company of 11th Rifles, under Brigadier Heber-Percy's command, moved north-eastwards along the River Kifissos and took the bridge at Three Hills, a mile and a quarter to the north-east of the textile mill.

The whole of the Piræus and of central and southern Athens was now occupied by British forces and the Greek National Guard; the ELAS forces which had survived the battle were streaming out of the northern part of the city, closely followed by mobile columns of British troops. 12th and 28th Brigades spread out into the surrounding districts, rounding up ELAS stragglers and impounding tons of warlike stores.

Once more the division regrouped, as 10th and 12th Brigades prepared to leave the city in pursuit of the retreating enemy. Crackforce merged with Buttersforce, which grew to a strength of some three thousand men, with the Northumberland Fusiliers as the core. The RA Battalion gathered in Psychiko, temporarily under the command of 10th Brigade. Lieutenant-Colonel E. F. H. Key, of 14th Antitank Regiment, took command of the battalion on January the 5th. 22nd and 77th Field Regiments had by this time each supplied an extra company. The whole of 30th Field Regiment's company, on the other hand, had rejoined its regiment to man guns.

As the Rimini Brigade was also to leave the city, its area was taken over by a brigade of the Greek National Guard, which came under Major-General Ward's command. The National Guard had been growing rapidly during the last three weeks of 1944, and Major-General Ward now had under his command three brigade headquarters and eleven battalions; 4th Division had helped to equip many of these battalions, and had provided them with a number of British liaison officers. The National Guard had its shortcomings, but the constant clearing, searching and re-searching of different parts of the city, made necessary by the turbulent remnants of ELAS and the stores of weapons and explosives hidden in the crowded buildings, would have been impossible without the Guard. The National Guard was now to take over more and more responsibilities until it was in complete control of all the cleared districts.

28. The rest of Greece

The forces of ELAS, driven out of Athens and scattered, seemed likely to try to rally in the hills north of Athens and to hold a line across the base of the Lavrion peninsula, from Elefsis on the west coast to the Bay of Marathon on the east.

If this was the intention of ELAS, the British columns were among them before they could carry it out. The Reconnaissance Regiment advanced south-eastwards from the city into the Lavrion peninsula; the King's Dragoon Guards, with the Bedfords—riding in an assortment of half-tracks, White scout-cars and 15-cwt trucks —moved north-westwards from the city into the mountains of Attica.

On January the 6th, the KDG and the Bedfords reached Elefsis, on the shore twelve miles north-west of Athens. The Rimini Brigade followed up to consolidate in the town, and the column pushed inland next day to the mountain hamlet of Oino, twelve miles farther north-east, and to the Kani Kaza Pass, two and a half miles beyond, where there was some sharp skirmishing with ELAS.

The column, now under Major-General Ward's command, entered Thebes, ten miles farther north, on January the 8th, and was welcomed with an ovation. Cheering townsfolk surged round the vehicles; an officer of the KDG, who fell into the hands of the crowd, was swept away and chaired. Major-General Ward arrived shortly afterwards, and nearly suffered the same fate.

The DCLI and the Surreys, meanwhile, had concentrated at Kalandri, one of the north-eastern suburbs of Athens, and 12th Brigade had handed over its sector in the western part of the city to Arkforce. 10th Brigade took over Thebes on January the 9th, and the KDG and the Reconnaissance Regiment went on searching along the mountain roads.

The KDG reached Levadia, at the foot of Mount Parnassus, and the heights above Kalkis, twenty-five miles north-west and fourteen miles north-east respectively of Thebes. Then the battalion returned to Thebes, and cleared the devious eastern road past the Marathon Dam and through Kifissia to Athens, where it ceased to be under Major-General Ward's command.

The Reconnaissance Regiment, having cleared up the peninsula south-east of Athens, began to search the rest of Attica, and had soon reached the borders of the province. On January the 10th, 'A' Squadron, followed up by the 2nd Battalion of the Rimini Brigade, went along the coast road west of Athens, to Megara, twenty-two miles from the city, and to the Corinth Canal, twenty miles farther on. ELAS resistance halted the squadron at the canal, and fighting went on for the next forty-eight hours.

'C' Squadron went towards Kalkis, where there had been some resistance on the previous day, in the hope of arranging a peaceful surrender of the town. The ELAS commander, however, declared that his orders were to defend the place and that he intended to carry them out. However, he told his garrison not to fire unless provoked, and merely opened the swing-bridge between the island of Evvea, on which the town of Kalkis stands, and the mainland. In the interval before negotiations began again, 'C' Squadron cleared the mainland side of the channel.

'B' Squadron meanwhile went out to open the road to Lamia, forty miles north-west of Levadia, and set up its forward base at Amphiklia, halfway between the two towns.

12th Brigade was to have gone to Kalkis, but since the town was still the subject of negotiation the brigade was sent by Major-General Ward to Levadia instead. Leaving the Black Watch to follow next day, Brigade Headquarters and the West Kents entered the town. They found it as silently dangerous as a powder magazine. The few citizens who were not active supporters of EAM were afraid to make the British troops welcome. A few days later, the arrival of a battalion of the Greek National Guard caused a furious riot; the violence was cleverly staged, since all the most offensive demonstrators were children. *Eniaea Panhellinios Organosis Neon* (EPON), the United Panhellenic Youth League, or junior branch of EAM, was lively and well organized. In the hospital lay nearly a hundred ELAS wounded, the care of whom was taken over by 12th Field Ambulance. Large numbers of hostages taken by ELAS, non-combatant refugees from the fighting in Athens, and ex-combatants left stranded by the receding tide of the civil war, had to be sent back to Athens for interrogation and disposal. By firm, just and tactful handling of fiery and belligerent citizens, the British troops eased a very tense situation.

The Royal Fusiliers, meanwhile, had passed through Levadia on their way to the village of Petromagoula, seven miles to the northeast. The advance party was led by two armoured cars, and, to encourage the inhabitants, the Archbishop of Levadia rode in Lieutenant-Colonel Shipley's jeep. Petromagoula's welcome was very different from that of Levadia. The people came tumbling out of their houses, wild with excitement; the Archbishop, without abating the dignity of his bearing, climbed on to the bonnet of the jeep, and in a long and ardent speech introduced 'our gallant British liberators'; and Lieutenant-Colonel Shipley, having made through his interpreter a slightly briefer and less impassioned speech, was presented with a white hen attractively decorated with pale blue ribbon.

At Thebes there was no open activity by ELAS, but the problem of disposing of displaced persons and suspects was serious enough. To deal with these people, 10th Brigade set up a local Hostage Centre and Prisoners of War Cage, both of which eventually became the responsibility of Divisional Headquarters.

As in Athens, the division went on vigorously searching and re-searching the places it had occupied and the country-side all round. Every sweep produced more and more weapons, explosives and prisoners, particularly when Greek troops did the searching while British troops surrounded the neighbourhood.

'B' Reconnaissance Squadron found the road north of Amphiklia cratered in a number of places; many of the demolitions were guarded by ELAS mountain troops in well-chosen positions. On January the 12th, however, the squadron was able to begin to reconnoitre the coast road which leads from Molos, twelve miles north of Amphiklia, towards Kalkis. A large demolition halted the advance, and the squadron leaguered for the night near Atlandi, twenty-two miles south-east of Molos.

On the same day, 'C' Squadron and Regimental Headquarters moved into Amphiklia. 'A' Squadron came back from the Corinth Canal to lend troops to 10th and 12th Brigades.

The civil war had reached its last stage. In Athens, 28th Brigade had become Prestonforce, and had taken over the division's remaining commitments; Divisional Headquarters had moved out to Elefsis on January the 11th. Blockforce had handed over to Jakeforce; 139th Brigade had embarked from the Piræus to take over the garrison of Patras, a hundred and ten miles west of Athens, on the coast of the Peloponnese, where 11th Indian Brigade had spent weeks of uneasy isolation. 4th Indian and 46th Divisions were preparing to move to the Peloponnese and Salonika respectively. In face of these preparations for the occupation of the strategically important towns of Greece, which could not be prevented, and with the ELAS forces scattered and disorganized, retreating as best they could through the mountains, EAM could only begin negotiations for a truce.

The division's rapid advance from Athens had broken so deeply through the ELAS forces that considerable bodies of enemy troops, some of them still disciplined and organized, had been out-distanced, and were still slowly making their way north through the mountains. In these last days of the fighting, troops of 4th Division had some skirmishing with these forces.

The most serious fighting was on January the 13th. A Staghound troop of 'B' Reconnaissance Squadron was ambushed near the village of St Constantine, on the coast road. 'A' Company of the Black Watch was ambushed in the hills south of Aliartos; Lieutenant Sturgey and thirty other ranks were captured, and a number of men were killed and wounded.

A column commanded by Major M. F. W. Tyndall, and consisting of 'Z' Company of the Royal Fusiliers, two troops of the Reconnaissance Regiment, three tanks, two medium machine-guns, two sections of sappers and an assault section of the Fusiliers' Pioneer Platoon, went out along the road to Delphi—twenty-one miles west of Levadia—to intercept an ELAS force said to be moving northwards with a large number of prisoners and hostages. In a narrow pass among the mountains, the advance-guard came under the fire of artillery and machine-guns, and two of the armoured cars were damaged. There was no hope of deploying tanks or armoured cars off the road in such precipitous country, or of catching out the ELAS mountain troops on their own ground, and the column had to withdraw.

That night, 'B' Squadron was unsuccessfully attacked in its

leaguer at Atlandi. Next morning, a column consisting of 'C' Reconnaissance Squadron, 'C' Company of the West Kents and a detachment of 225th Field Company, after opening the Lamia road as far as the summit of the Brallos pass, twelve miles north-west of Amphiklia and above Thermopylæ, was attacked when halted at a demolition on the road down. Low clouds gathering on the mountain-side made the action awkward enough, and the ELAS mountaineers scrambling round the flanks made it worse. The column turned back to Amphiklia that afternoon, and 'B' Squadron also returned from Atlandi. The weather was so bad that 'B' Squadron's last vehicle did not reach the concentration area until morning of the following day.

In Athens, meanwhile, Lieutenant-General Scobie had been working out, with the representatives of the ELAS Central Committee, the terms of a truce to bring the fighting in Greece to an end. Late in the evening of January the 11th, the truce was signed at last.

Its terms provided that fighting was to stop at midnight three nights later. All ELAS troops were to withdraw during the next twelve days from the parts of Greece nearest to Athens—from the northern provinces of the Peloponnese, from Attica, Boeotia, Fokis, and south-eastern Thessaly—and from the islands of the Ionian and the Aegean seas, including the great island of Evvea, which meets Boeotia at the bridge at Kalkis. ELAS were to release all the British and Greek combatants and all the British civilians they had captured, and an equal number of ELAS prisoners would be released in exchange.

From the time the truce came into effect, during the night of January the 14th, parties of ELAS troops began to march through the division's lines on their way over the Brallos pass towards their own zone. Many of these troops were well-armed and adequately dressed—a large proportion in British battledress—and whole battalions marched in a disciplined and soldierly manner. Before withdrawing the ELAS troops who had turned back the British columns on the Brallos pass were good enough to warn the Reconnaissance Regiment that ELAS would not be able to lift the mines from the debris of the demolition on the pass. The troops of the division stood fast to allow the ELAS forces to get clear.

Attempts were being made meanwhile to get ELAS to exchange the men of the Black Watch they had taken prisoner on January the

13th. An hour after nightfall on that day, Lieutenant Sturgey had reached the battalion. He had been wounded, stripped of his battledress—as were all the prisoners—and left behind, in rags and without boots. He found the strength to make his way down the mountain-side; on his way down he borrowed boots from one of three other wounded men still lying at the scene of the ambush; and a little later he met a charitable shepherd, who helped him to the main road near Aliartos and the Black Watch headquarters.

Next day, Lieutenant-Colonel W. H. Valentine, the commander of 12th Field Ambulance, took out a party of stretcher-bearers and a Greek nurse, and sent back the wounded. Lieutenant-Colonel Valentine himself went on, found the regular company of ELAS troops who had carried out the ambush, and saw the Black Watch captives. They were well enough, though already lousy from the ragged clothes they had been given in exchange for their battledress. The ELAS company commander said they had been stripped by irregulars, but he may have been more tactful than truthful. He agreed to set free three men who were wounded but could walk, and said he would make sure that clean clothes and supplies for the rest, sent up from the battalion, would reach them. A quick exchange of prisoners could not be arranged, however, and the ELAS company withdrew beyond the truce boundary with twenty-four men of the Black Watch.

On January the 18th, Lieutenant-Colonel Delmege sent a Reconnaissance squadron over the Brallos pass to occupy Lamia down in the plain beyond. From this base, patrols moved along the truce boundary to Farsala, twenty-seven miles to the north, and others went to meet patrols of 5th Indian Brigade, which had landed at Volos, forty-two miles north-east of Lamia. Volos and Farsala were both near the northerly limit of the zone to be occupied by British troops.

ELAS troops meanwhile were sailing away from Kalkis in caïques, and on January the 20th the Surreys moved into the town; 10th Brigade Headquarters and the DCLI followed next day.

On January the 23rd, Divisional Headquarters moved to Thebes.

At the end of the month, 28th Brigade relieved 12th Brigade round the rich plain which had once been Lake Kopais. The RA Battalion, leaving one company in Psychiko, moved into the village of Vayia, between Thebes and Levadia, and stayed there until it was disbanded in March.

The division had fought its last battle; no violence broke the truce. Large-scale patrolling, house searching and the seizure of arms went on, and a number of suspects and a few armed bands had still to be rounded up.

The division had carried out an unpleasant and thankless task with admirable forbearance. The causes of the civil war were not easy to explain to men who had no time to follow the complexities of Greek war-time politics; and people at home in England were demonstrating against the part played in Greece by British troops. The division lost comparatively few men; but there were times when some of its members sighed for the days of straightforward fighting with the Germans, when a cleared area stayed clear, and enemy troops could be shaken up at sight with a few rounds of gun-fire from the divisional artillery.

The pacification of the country, however, was only the first part of the task, and there was a great deal still to do. Civil government had completely broken down. All over Greece, outside Athens, nobody knew which officials should be in charge of affairs. Prefects and mayors had to be appointed or confirmed in office. Industries and public services had to be started up again, prices had to be fixed and controlled, and food had to be fairly distributed.

The truce had brought the fighting to an end, but had not reconciled the members of EAM with the right-wing statesmen and politicians ranged with the British forces; bitter political feuds were carried on in every town and district. ELAS was disarmed but impenitent; and its wilder men had committed crimes enough during the conflict to leave a legacy of hatred and fear. On all sides and at all times, Greeks of each persuasion clamoured with stories of violence and of reprisal, treachery and espionage. Freedom of speech was vehemently and indignantly claimed by those whose intemperate language provoked some of the very abuses they denounced; and factions loudly demanded protection from opponents whose tempers they had deliberately inflamed.

At this difficult time, the Greek National Guard was harassed ceaselessly with criticism and abuse that would have strained the discipline of far steadier troops. Impartiality could hardly be expected of such a body, for when the civil war began every member of or sympathizer with the left-wing parties had left it. Other recruits had been frightened into deserting; and as a result the battalions raised to replace these losses were drawn from men whose right-wing feelings were firm. The passions of Greek politics burn so hotly that some members of such a force could hardly fail to commit crimes against their opponents, and British formation commanders had to intervene firmly in affairs which the Greeks should have been able to run by themselves.

While the division was restarting the machinery of civil government, public services and industry, it began to work also on the relief of some of the small mountain villages, which were in a desperate state. The Germans had apparently done their best to exterminate many of these villages; they had sent columns of troops on foot miles up the mountain-side to burn and destroy, and to take away the cattle without which the villagers could produce no food. The villagers lacked not only food and shelter but clothes and medicine; malaria and other illnesses of the country had spread rapidly, and struck hardest of all at the children.

The Red Cross civil relief organization had already begun work, and before long representatives of the Scouts and Guides International Relief Services and of the United Nations Relief and Rehabilitation Association arrived.

The divisional RASC, commanded by Lieutenant-Colonel A. P. Campbell, and later by Lieutenant-Colonel K. W. McQueen, helped to transport great numbers of hostages, refugees and ex-combatants back to their homes, and to carry the necessities of life from one community to the next. The RASC had without fail kept the division supplied throughout a most difficult period, and now played a vital part in civil relief. A check had to be kept on the movement of all produce, to make sure that the district from which it came did not go short, and so to prevent artificial shortages, to restrict black market activities and to check rising prices.

In time, this operation of peace, in which all arms and services of the division showed the same team-work that had distinguished them in war, began to show results. Public confidence began to revive, and life became more normal. The country's need, however, was for a strong and energetic government, and this it could not find. No government could be formed which was so firmly and widely supported as to be able to take the drastic action that was essential to put the country on its feet. The left-wing politicians were a disruptive element enough, but the parties of the centre and the right wing could achieve no lasting cohesion of their own.

On February the 12th, the final agreement between the government and EAM was signed. As a result, troops of the division began to move, at the end of the month, northwards into Thessaly and westwards into the Pindus mountains, to take over the dumps of ELAS weapons surrendered according to the agreement. Civil relief was still an important part of the work. The divisional Royal Engineers, commanded by Lieutenant-Colonel J. R. G. Finch MBE, reopened the roads; and 10th and 12th Brigades began a systematic survey of the villages in their districts.

This survey revealed a fearful state of hardship and want in the villages, particularly those to the west of Lamia. 'X' Company of the Royal Fusiliers toiled through the snow to the village of Karpenision, high in the Pindus mountains, thirty-five miles west of Lamia, and found there a desolation like that of Cassino. The Germans, carrying out their unpleasant policy of reprisals, had wrecked all but six of eight hundred homes. The Greek highlanders have always been hardy, but the two thousand villagers had needed more than hardihood during the bitter winter months. The mountain villages everywhere had suffered the same kind of vengeance; village after village had been smashed or burnt, the crops had been destroyed and the livestock driven off. Food, clothing and medical supplies were all scarce. 12th Brigade deployed all its resources in the fight against dirt and disease, and 12th Field Ambulance led the way.

The Greeks themselves laid on the British commanders and their units a heavy burden of responsibility. The Greeks seemed to know nothing of impartiality, and could not understand its practice by the British. Members of the right wing came eventually to think of all the British as rabid Communists, while those of the left wing were convinced they were ardent Royalists. The Greeks of both sides, however, were always friendly to the British, and extremely hospitable. They realized that the British aim was to help in restoring a measure of order and prosperity to the ruined countryside; and to a man, from the Prefects, Presidents, Mayors and military commanders to the humblest peasants, they came to expect as a matter of course that British company commanders would settle their squabbles, organize and supervise the distribution of food, control the prices, inspect the prisons and hospitals, and attend to the cleanliness and sanitation of the towns. To agree among themselves was so far from possible to the Greeks that they were glad to offer to the foreign soldiers the undisputed authority they withheld from the governments they elected.

The tragic civil war that had come to an end with the unwilling surrender of heaps of rusty weapons, had achieved nothing except the increase of hatred between the countrymen of a proud nation, and the delay of help to those who had suffered worst from the common enemy.

Epilogue

The 4th Division's history after the surrender of Germany is for the most part one of routine duties. There was, however, one last contact with the most formidable enemy British soldiers had faced since Napoleon. The German garrison in Crete had surrendered, and the last of an honourable line of Prestonforces—this time consisting of 28th Brigade Headquarters, the 2nd/4th Hampshires and various detachments—went to Crete to protect the Germans and the Cretans from each other and to evacuate the enemy to prison camps in Egypt. Since both the Germans and the Cretans outnumbered Prestonforce by more than twenty to one, as well as being armed to the teeth, this was a particularly delicate mission. It was carried out with admirable tact and firmness, and Prestonforce returned to Greece early in August.

Major-General A. D. Ward CB CBE DSO, who had joined the division just before its greatest battle, and had commanded it throughout its severest campaign, left the division early in May, and Major-General C. B. Callander CB MC took over command. The strength of the division began to drain away; over a thousand of the younger troops were drafted to the Far East, to join in the struggle against Japan, and the older men were being steadily demobilized or sent home on leave.

Japan surrendered on August the 15th 1945, and the war was over at last.

Towards the end of October, 4th Reconnaissance Regiment, which was to be disbanded, left the division, and was replaced by the 17th/21st Lancers.

Early in 1946, the division left the south of Greece for the north, travelling for the most part by sea, to the Salonika area to relieve

4th Indian Division. The released Indian units sailed for India; the British units went to southern Greece, where, with units from 4th Division and others from Italy, they made up 13th Division, which held the region vacated by 4th Division.

The units left behind by 4th Division included the 1st/6th East Surreys, the 2nd/4th Hampshires and the 6th Black Watch. These battalions were replaced by the 1st East Surreys (who thus returned to the division after an absence of nearly four years), the 1st Durham Light Infantry and the 2nd Buffs. 10th Brigade was now reorganized to consist of three battalions of light infantry—the 2nd Duke of Cornwall's, 2nd Somerset and 1st Durham. The 2nd Buffs replaced the Black Watch in 12th Brigade. The Bedfords and the 1st Surreys joined the King's in 28th Brigade. The infantry battalions of the division were now all regular units once more—apparently a sign that the division would continue to exist in peace-time.

The Greek elections, which passed off quietly enough in March 1946, placed in power a government which had—for the time being—a reasonable measure of popular support. The task of British troops in Greece was therefore drawing to a close, and in August the 4th Division began to break up as units sailed from Salonika for the Middle East. At the same time, Major-General Callander was posted to the War Office, and Major-General E. E. Down CBE took over.

The West Kents were the first to leave, and in October the Royal Fusiliers and the King's departed. As units of 13th Division were also leaving, 12th Brigade returned to southern Greece to take their place. Two days before Christmas, the Northumberland Fusiliers left the division; the Lancers, the Somersets and the Bedfords sailed in February.

During March the rest of the division left for the Middle East; and the disbandment of Divisional Headquarters on March the 31st 1947 brought the history of the 4th Division to a close. The division exists no longer as a fighting force; but it lives on—in the memories of all who survived their service in its ranks, and who, together with their comrades who have not survived, enacted the history that has been recorded in these pages.

Appendix A

Order of battle of 4th Division at the outbreak of war in 1939. Certain units left the division before the advance into Belgium; the name of each of these units is followed in parentheses by the name of the unit which replaced it.

DIVISIONAL HEADQUARTERS

10TH INFANTRY BRIGADE
    1st Royal West Kents (1st/6th East Surreys)
    2nd Duke of Cornwall's Light Infantry
    2nd Bedfordshire and Hertfordshire Regiment
    10th Brigade Anti-tank Company

11TH INFANTRY BRIGADE
    2nd Lancashire Fusiliers
    1st East Surreys
    1st Oxfordshire and Buckinghamshire Light Infantry (5th Northamptons)
    11th Brigade Anti-tank Company

12TH INFANTRY BRIGADE
    2nd Royal Fusiliers
    1st South Lancashires
    1st Black Watch (6th Black Watch)
    12th Brigade Anti-tank Company

ROYAL ARTILLERY
    14th Anti-tank Regiment
    17th Field Regiment (77th Field Regiment)
    22nd Field Regiment
    30th Field Regiment

ROYAL ENGINEERS
    7th Field Company
    9th Field Company (225th Field Company)
    59th Field Company
    18th Field Park Company
    4th Postal Unit

ROYAL CORPS OF SIGNALS

ROYAL ARMY SERVICE CORPS
    Divisional Ammunition Company (The divisional RASC was reorganized, before the advance into Belgium, as 21st, 44th and 509th Infantry Brigade Companies and 473rd Divisional Troops Company.)
    Divisional Petrol Company
    Divisional Supply Company

ROYAL ARMY MEDICAL CORPS
    10th Field Ambulance
    11th Field Ambulance
    12th Field Ambulance
    4th Field Hygiene Section

4TH DIVISIONAL SECTION, INTELLIGENCE CORPS

DIVISIONAL PROVOST COMPANY

Appendix B

Order of battle of the division on embarking for North Africa, with the names of some commanders and staff officers.

DIVISIONAL HEADQUARTERS (Divisional commander, *Major-Gen J. L. I. Hawkesworth* CBE; GSO 1, *Lt-Col S. N. Shoosmith*; AA & QMG, *Lt-Col C. J. Kinna*)

10TH INFANTRY BRIGADE (*Brig J. H. Hogshaw* MC)
2nd Bedfords (*Lt-Col D. S. W. Johnson*)
2nd DCLI (*Lt-Col R. B. F. K. Goldsmith*)
1st/6th East Surreys (*Lt-Col H. A. B. Bruno* MBE)

12TH INFANTRY BRIGADE (*Brig R. G. W. Callaghan*)
6th Black Watch (*Lt-Col W. P. Barclay*)
2nd Royal Fusiliers (*Lt-Col M. L. Brandon*)
1st Royal West Kents (*Lt-Col J. M. Haycraft*)

21ST TANK BRIGADE (*Brig T. Ivor-Moore* MC)
12th Royal Tanks (*Lt-Col J. C. Harding* MC)
48th Royal Tanks (*Lt-Col G. H. Brooks*)
145th RAC (*Lt-Col A. C. Jackson*)

ROYAL ARTILLERY (*Brig M. A. B. Johnston* DSO MC)
14th Anti-tank Regiment (*Lt-Col I. V. R. Smith*)
22nd Field Regiment (*Lt-Col G. H. MacCarthy*)
30th Field Regiment (*Lt-Col R. B. Rice*)
77th (Highland) Field Regiment (*Lt-Col W. G. H. Pike*)
91st Light Anti-aircraft Regiment (*Lt-Col B. Middleton*)

ROYAL ENGINEERS (*Lt-Col P. F. Foley*)
7th, 59th and 225th Field Companies and 18th Field Park Company and Divisional Postal Section

4TH RECONNAISSANCE REGIMENT (*Lt-Col P. G. C. Preston*)

ROYAL CORPS OF SIGNALS (*Lt-Col F. W. P. Bradford* MBE)

ROYAL ARMY MEDICAL CORPS (*Col C. H. K. Smith* MC)
10th and 12th Field Ambulances, 6th Light Field Ambulance and 4th Field Hygiene Section

ROYAL ARMY SERVICE CORPS (*Lt-Col W. O. Phillips*)
21st and 44th Infantry Brigade Companies, 107th Tank Brigade Company and 473rd Divisional Troops Company

ROYAL ELECTRICAL AND MECHANICAL ENGINEERS (*Lt-Col N. C. Godfrey*)
10th and 12th Infantry Brigade Workshop Companies and 21st Tank Brigade Workshop Company

DIVISIONAL PROVOST COMPANY

6TH FIELD SECURITY SECTION

Appendix C

Order of battle of the division at the opening of the fighting in Italy.

DIVISIONAL HEADQUARTERS

10TH INFANTRY BRIGADE
  2nd Bedfords
  1st/6th East Surreys
  2nd DCLI

12TH INFANTRY BRIGADE
  2nd Royal Fusiliers
  6th Black Watch
  1st Royal West Kents

28TH INFANTRY BRIGADE
  2nd King's (Liverpool) Regiment
  2nd Somerset Light Infantry
  2nd/4th Hampshires

ROYAL ARTILLERY
  14th Anti-tank Regiment
  22nd Field Regiment
  30th Field Regiment
  77th (Highland) Field Regiment
  91st Light Anti-aircraft Regiment

ROYAL ENGINEERS
  7th, 59th and 225th Field Companies and 18th Field Park Company

4TH RECONNAISSANCE REGIMENT

2ND ROYAL NORTHUMBERLAND FUSILIERS

ROYAL CORPS OF SIGNALS

ROYAL ARMY MEDICAL CORPS
  10th, 12th and 185th Field Ambulances, 4th Field Hygiene Section and 43rd Anti-malaria Control Unit

ROYAL ARMY SERVICE CORPS
  21st, 44th and 509th Infantry Brigade Companies and 473rd Divisional Troops Company

ROYAL ELECTRICAL AND MECHANICAL ENGINEERS
  10th, 12th and 28th Infantry Brigade Companies

DIVISIONAL PROVOST COMPANY

6TH FIELD SECURITY SECTION

Glossary

AA&QMG, (referred to in conversation as AQ) Assistant Adjutant and Quartermaster-General; the divisional commander's chief administrative staff officer, with the rank of Lieutenant-Colonel.

Argoub, (Arabic) ridge.

ADMS, Assistant Director of Medical Services; the divisional commander's adviser on medical services, responsible for all the division's medical units, with the rank of Colonel.

AVRE, Armoured Vehicle RE; an armoured vehicle used by the sappers.

Ark, a Churchill tank, less its turret, equipped with ramps; it can be driven into a crater, and by means of the ramps other vehicles can then be driven over it (picture on page 344).

BGS, Brigadier General Staff; the chief general staff officer of a corps; also a brigadier in the general staff of a higher formation.

Beehive, an explosive implement which can bore a hole several feet deep into hard earth; an explosive charge can then be dropped into the hole, and this breaks up the surrounding earth and makes it easy to dig out.

bazooka, an anti-tank rocket projector.

Colle, (Italian) spur, hill-feature.

Casa, (Italian) house.

Canale, (Italian) canal. *Canale Maestro*, main canal.

Cab-rank, a method of air co-operation in which army formations can call on aircraft already in the air not far away.

DADME, Deputy Assistant Director of Mechanical Engineers; the divisional commander's adviser on mechanical engineering, with the rank of Lieutenant-Colonel.

CRA, Commander Royal Artillery; the divisional commander's artillery adviser, and commander of all artillery units in the division, with the rank of Brigadier.

CRE, Commander Royal Engineers; the divisional commander's RE adviser, and commander of the division's sapper units, with the rank of Lieutenant-Colonel.

CREME, Commander Royal Electrical and Mechanical Engineers; the divisional commander's adviser on electrical and mechanical engineering, and commander of the division's REME units, with the rank of Lieutenant-Colonel.

Djebel, (Arabic) hill or mountain.

DDMS, Deputy Director of Medical Services; adviser on medical services to the commander of certain formations higher than a division, with the rank of Brigadier.

DAAG, Deputy Assistant Adjutant-General; the administration staff officer who deals with personnel matters under the AA&QMG.

double-truss, triple-storey Bailey bridge, a form of Bailey bridge built to take very heavy loads indeed.

ENSA, Entertainments National Service Association.

FOO, forward observation officer; a gunner officer, usually with an infantry company.

Fattoria, (Italian) factory.

Fossa, (Italian) dyke.

fascine, a great bundle of branches tied together, used for filling craters, etc.

GLOSSARY

GSO 1, (referred to in conversation as G1) General Staff Officer Grade 1; the chief of the divisional commander's operational staff, with the rank of Lieutenant-Colonel.

GSO 2, (referred to in conversation as G2) General Staff Officer Grade 2; the operational staff officer next in seniority to the GSO 1, with the rank of Major.

Jaeger, German light infantry.

leaguer, a unit area guarded all round against attack.

LCV, lorry command vehicle; a command-post on wheels.

Mark Four, a German medium tank, armed with a 75-mm gun.

Mark Four (Special), a German medium tank armed with a long-barrelled 75-mm gun.

Monte, (Italian) mountain or hill. Plural, *Monti*.

Mosaic, a series of air photographs, pasted together to form a single large picture.

Massa, abbreviation of *Masseria* (Italian), farm.

M.10, a 3-inch high-velocity anti-tank gun, mounted on a tank chassis (picture on page 344).

nebelwerfer, the German six-barrelled rocket projector.

Number 18 set and *Number 38 set*, two kinds of light portable radio sets for sending and receiving.

Number 22 set, a radio set of medium size, which can be carried by hand but which is usually carried in a vehicle.

Number 77 grenade, a small smoke grenade.

Oued, see *Wadi*.

portee, a lorry equipped for carrying a light anti-tank gun.

Phantom section, an intelligence and signals unit which passes up-to-date information direct from fighting units to the army commander.

PU, personal utility (truck); a light truck.

Ponte, (Italian) bridge.

Piat, projector infantry anti-tank; a light short-range mortar which fires an armour-piercing bomb more or less horizontally.

Panther, a German 88-mm gun mounted on a Mark Four tank chassis.

Python, the scheme for posting home soldiers who had served abroad for a given number of years.

'S' mine, a German anti-personnel mine.

Staff Captain 'Q', a staff officer in charge of supply, quartering, etc.

sangar, a shelter, built up of rocks and earth, etc., when digging is impossible.

scissors bridge, a tank with a folding bridge fixed to its upper works.

San, Santa, (Italian) saint.

Scolo, (Italian) dyke.

steel crib pier, a built-up steel pier.

Shermandozer, a Sherman tank fitted with bulldozer blades, for clearing obstacles under fire.

Spandau, German medium machine-gun.

Tiger, the heaviest German tank, weighing just under sixty tons (against the Churchill's thirty-eight) and armed with an 88-mm gun.

Tedeschi, (Italian) the Germans.

tapered 2-pounder, a light anti-tank gun, the barrel of which narrows towards the muzzle, in order to increase the velocity of the shot.

Val, Valle, (Italian) valley.

Wadi, (Arabic) ravine.

Wade charge, a special made-up explosive charge for placing on a bridge to demolish it.

Index

This index contains only the names of individuals and units.

Adam, Lt-Gen Sir Ronald, 19
Adams, Capt, RA, 49
Air OP Squadron, 651st, 54, 288
Alanbrooke, Field-Marshal Viscount, 6, 17, 18, 28
Alexander, Field-Marshal Viscount, 52, 80, 94, 122-3, 125, 128, 161, 220, 290-2, 307
Alexander, Lt W. G., 189
Allen, Lt-Col, RF, 27-8
Allfrey, Lt-Gen Sir Charles, 43
Amos, Tpr, RTR, 62
Anderson, Lt-Gen Sir K. A. N., 1, 6, 28, 33, 41-2, 79-81, 93
Anti-tank Bty, 38th, 49, 82, 258
— 61st, 263
— 81st, 68
— 150th, 238, 288
— 324th, 238, 242
— 329th, 144
Anti-malaria Control Unit, 43rd, 326
Anti-tank Company, 10th Bde, 324
— 11th Bde, 324
— 12th Bde, 324
Anti-tank Regt, 14th, 18, 96, 109, 133, 164, 237, 255, 302, 310, 311, 324-6
— 20th, 24
— 93rd, 54, 258, 285
Arbuthnott, Lt-Col R. K., 33
Argyll and Sutherland Highlanders, 1st, 97-8
Arkforce, 298-9, 301, 305, 307-9, 312
Armoured Brigade, 1st Canadian, 112, 124, 162, 190
— 23rd, 298
Armoured Division, 1st, 78, 86, 96, 223, 227, 231, 232, 234
— 5th Canadian, 223, 234
— 6th, 42, 66, 78, 80, 84-6, 88, 123-4, 159, 182-4, 194, 196, 208, 212
— 6th South African, 161-2, 165, 174, 177, 183, 187, 200
— 7th, 80-1, 85-6
— 26th German, 223, 289
Armoured Reconnaissance Brigade, 2nd, 17-18
Armoured Brigade Group, 26th, 124
Armoured Regt, 11th Canadian, 177, 188
— 12th Canadian, 109, 165-6, 168-9, 172-3, 186
— 14th, 176, 179

Armoured Regt, 19th New Zealand, 150-1, 154
Army, First, 37-8, 40, 42-4, 64, 79-81, 86, 94
— Fifth, 98-9, 107, 115-16, 123, 158, 159, 220, 293
— Eighth, 80-1, 86, 93, 98-9, 107, 113, 115, 123, 129, 158-9, 162, 190, 220, 222-3, 235, 237, 246, 277, 293
— Salvation, 219, 294
Ashley, Fus, RF, 140
Assault Regt, 1st, RAC/RE, 264-5, 284, 288

Babington, Major A. R., 135, 306
Banfield, Major E. P., 141
Barclay, Lt-Col W. P., 50-1, 325
Barker, Brig, 1, 6
Baxter, Pte J. C., 149
Barden, Fus, RF, 155-6
Beak, Lt-Col D. M. W., 8, 27, 33
Bedfordshire and Hertfordshire Regt, 2nd, *in France and Belgium*, 10, 19, 21, 26, 28; *in North Africa*, 43-9 55-8, 60-1, 63, 66, 82-5, 87; *in Italy*, 108, 112, 125-6, 131-3, 139, 152-3, 155, 159-61, 169-71, 173, 181, 184, 186-8, 192, 194-5, 213, 228-31, 247-8, 250, 253-4, 256, 258, 281-2, 288; *in Greece*, 308, 312, 323-6
Bennett, Capt E. J., 244
Bichard, Major, Hampshires, 167, 260
Black, Major Gordon, 198
Black Watch, 1st, 10, 324
— 6th, *in France and Holland*, 10, 20-2, 24-8; *Home Forces*, 33; *in North Africa*, 50-1, 63, 69-73, 79, 83-5, 89, 338; *in Italy*, 105-7, 117-18, 139-41, 145-8, 150, 152, 154, 160-1, 176-8, 180-1, 183, 197-8, 200-6, 208-9, 219, 224, 227, 229, 238, 240-3, 245, 247, 259, 266-76, 296; *in Greece*, 304, 307, 310-11, 313, 315-17, 323-6
Blackler, Major G. G., 178
Blair, Major C. N. M., 51, 84
Blaker, Major, Hampshires, 167
Block, Brig, 303
Blockforce, 303, 305-7, 315
Bodley, Lt P. O., 215
Bonella, Sgt, Black Watch, 203
Bourgein, Capt H., 295
Bowers, Capt, Hampshires, 285

Bradford, Lt-Col F. W. P., 52, 96, 325
Braithwaite, Lt-Col H. P., 150, 175-6, 198, 228, 244
Brandon, Lt-Col, RF, 68, 325
Bray, Sgt, DCLI, 214
Bray, L-Sgt W., 279-80
Brett, Capt A. R. B., 51
Briscoe, Lt, DCLI, 215
Bristier, Sgt, RE, 71
Brock, Major, RWK, 274-5
Brocklehurst, Lt-Col A. E., 186, 308
Brooke, Lt-Gen Sir Alan, see Alanbrooke
Brooking, Lt J. F., 94
Brooks, Lt-Col G. H., 56, 93, 325
Brown, Capt, East Surreys, 44
Brown, Major, DCLI, 232
Bruno, Lt-Col H. A. B., 43, 49, 61, 63-4, 325
Brunt, L-Sgt, RA, 185-6
Buffs, 2nd, 323
Burke, Lt-Col B. A., 302
Butterfield, Lt-Col F. H., 258-9, 303
Buttersforce, 303, 311
Byrne, Major C. E., 130

Cabrera, Major E., 273
Caesar, Pte, Hampshires, 340
Caldwell, Capt W. F., 240, 244
Callaghan, Brig R. G. W., 50-2, 325
Callander, Major-Gen C. B., 322-3
Callander, Major W. A. B., 202, 238
Calvert, Lt, RE, 26
Calvert, Lt D. G., Bedfords, 155
Campbell, Lt-Col A. P., 306, 319
Carpenter, Sgt, RF, 269-70
Carter, Pte Kenneth, 214
Carthew Yorstoun, Lt-Col, 33
Charkham, Major E., 132
Chemical Warfare Mortar Coy, 68th, 45, 53, 81
Cherry, Fus, RNF, 339
Chetwynd-Stapleton, Lt-Col, SLI, 284
Chinery, Capt John, 199
Churchill, Pte Alan, 192-3
Churchill, The Rt Hon Winston, 94-5, 307
Clark, General Mark, 99
Clarke, Capt J. E. C., 284-5
Clarke, Brig J. G. W., 1
Coates, Major D. E. F., 147
Cobb, Lt S. J., 61
Cocks, Sgt, DCLI, 214-15
Coldstream Guards, 26
Collett, Major R. G., 113, 295
Concert Party, 4th Div, 94-5, 219-20, 246, 295
Cooper, Sgt, RF, 76
Cooper, Sgt, King's, 273

Corcoran, Lt, East Surreys, 278-9
Corke, L-Cpl D., 140
Corps, I Canadian, 123, 152, 221-32, 234, 237-8, 242
— I British, 6, 17
— II British, 6, 7, 15, 18, 22, 24, 26, 28
— II American, 123
— II Polish, 120, 123, 125, 144, 151, 154-7, 277
— III British, 19, 97, 298-9, 305
— V British, 33-5, 42, 44-53, 65-6, 73, 78, 80, 82, 107, 123, 220, 223, 236-8, 246, 277, 288, 294-5
— IX British, 67, 74, 79, 81, 89
— X British, 100, 123, 303
— XIII British, 107, 123, 125, 139, 150-1, 153-6, 158-9, 161-2, 165, 175, 182-4, 188, 191, 212, 292
Cottingham, Major R. E., 282
Cox, Lt, Bedfords, 155, 169
Coxwell-Rogers, Lt-Col, RE, 17, 25
Crackforce, 309-11
Crighton-Pascoe, Lt, 342
Cunningham, Lt T. D., 51

Daniels, Major, RE, 45
Dann, Major E., 72
Darling, Major Lord, 178
Davenport, Lt-Col J. S., 10
Davis, Lt, East Surreys, 130-1
DCLI, 2nd, in France and Belgium, 10, 19, 21, 28; in North Africa, 43, 45, 48-9, 55-7, 61, 63, 65-6, 70, 73, 78-9, 82-4, 87, 89-90, 92; in Italy, 101, 105, 108, 125-6, 133, 140-1, 152, 156, 159-60, 168, 170-3, 181, 188, 213-17, 231-2, 247-9, 250, 252, 257, 267, 279-82, 287-8, 343, 347; in Greece, 302-3, 308, 312, 317, 323-6
Delmege, Lt-Col A. C. S., 190, 276, 317
Dening, Col, 11-12, 31
Dent, Capt, Hampshires, 149
Derbyshire Yeomanry, 85
Dickson, Sgt, South Africa, 160-1
Down, Major-Gen E. E., 323
Doyle, L-Cpl D. E., 208
Drysdale, Lt, 206
Dudding, Lt B. D., 185
Duke, Lt-Col P. A., 96, 300
Duke of Cornwall's Light Infantry, see DCLI
Duke of Wellington's Regt, 1st, 56
Dunmall, Lt L. S., 241
Durham Light Infantry, 16th, 49, 51, 238
— 1st, 323
Durrant, Pte, DCLI, 10
Dutch Cheese, 294-5

INDEX

East Surrey Regt, 1st, *in France and Belgium*, 12, 21, 24, 28-9; *in North Africa*, 79; *in Greece*, 323-4
— 1st/6th, *in France and Belgium*, 12, 19, 21, 28-9; *in North Africa*, 43-9, 55-7, 59, 61-5, 79, 82-3, 39; *in Italy*, 108, 125-6, 130-2, 156, 159, 161, 170-3, 180-1, 184, 189, 191-2, 195, 213, 217, 231, 233, 245, 247, 252-5, 260-2, 278-9, 281, 286-8, 340, 345; *in Greece*, 308, 312, 317, 323
Eastham, Cpl E., 270
Eastwood, Major-Gen T. R., 33, 35
Eden, The Rt Hon Anthony, 307
Edmundson, 2nd-Lt, 75
Edwards, the Rev R., 138, 263
Efford, Cpl, East Surreys, 159
Eisenhower, Gen, 159
Elliott, Brig F. M., 96, 105, 114
Ellis, Major A. R., 263-4, 283, 285
ENSA, 219
Evans, Lt-Col A. F. P., 87, 140, 157
Evans, Lt E., 286

Field Ambulance, 6th Light, 96
— 10th, 45-6, 57, 324-6
— 12th, 60, 244, 314, 317, 320, 324-6
— 185th, 100, 326
Field Battery, 33rd, 261
— 36th/55th, 281
— 104th, 60, 90, 129, 135, 185, 306-8
— 111th, 206, 263
— 455th, 307
Field Company, 7th, 17, 25-7, 70, 72, 126, 236, 243, 254-5, 264, 284, 324-6, 345
— 9th, 9, 324
— 59th, 17, 25-6, 45, 82, 126, 237, 240, 243, 255-6, 324-6
— 220th, 251
— 221st, 251
— 225th, 10, 17, 26, 67, 71, 126, 139, 236, 243, 255, 316, 324-6
Field Hygiene Section, 4th, 324-6
Field Park Company, 18th, 324-6
Field Regiment, 17th, 10, 82
— 22nd, 76, 180-1, 186, 192, 214, 221, 230, 250, 280-1, 289, 311, 324-6, 341
— 30th, 49, 57, 63, 87-8, 178, 180, 193, 221, 226, 263, 273, 283, 285-6, 289, 308, 310-11, 324-6, 341
— 32nd Army, 17-19
— 60th Army, 17-18
— 77th Highland, 10, 21-2, 51, 88, 91, 179-80, 199, 221, 239, 271, 275, 289, 311, 324-6, 343, 348
— 98th (Self-propelled), 190
— 102nd, 54
— 132nd, 82

Field Regiment, 138th, 82
— 142nd (Self-propelled), 190, 239, 288
— 172nd, 46, 50
Field Security Section, 6th, 325-6
Field Squadron, 1st, 247
Finch, Lt-Col J. R. G., 320
Foley, Lt-Col P. F., 52, 325, 337
Folkard, Lt, R W K, 199
Force 125, 37-8
Fotheringham, Capt, Black Watch, 206
Fowler-Esson, Lt-Col, Hampshires, 142-3, 149
Fowles, Lt, D C L I, 280
Fox, Capt R. E., 136, 295
Francis, Capt, Bedfords, 230
Franklyn, Brig G. E. W., 12
Frost, L-Cpl, R F, 156
Fulton, Major R. W., 51

Galsworthy, Major, R F, 240
Gardner, Lt S. C., 75
Garner Smith, Lt-Col K. J. G., 55, 83, 87
Garnons-Williams, Lt-Col, King's, 137
Gibson, Sgt, R W K, 274
Gibson-Horrocks, Capt J. H., 67, 87
Gill, Major C. S., 133
Gillespie, Major, R E, 25
Gilmour, Capt I. E. W., 57
Glass, Capt P. N. L., 271
Gloucester, Major-Gen H R H the Duke of, 11
Godfrey, Lt-Col N. C., 325
Goldsmith, Lt-Col R. B. F. K., 157, 325
Goodall, Capt P. A., 295
Goode, Major G., 281
Gordon Highlanders, 6th, 55, 58, 60-1
Gordon, Major Lord Douglas, 202-5, 207
Gorst, Capt P. B., 25
Gort, Gen Lord, 6-8, 18
Grainger, L-Cpl H., 136
Grant, Cpl G., 146
Grant, the Rev J., 51
Gray, L-Cpl, Hampshires, 340
Green, Lt-Col, Northamptons, 22
Grenadier Guards, 3rd, 105
Gridgeman, Pte, R W K, 141
Grover, Brig T. M. L., 33
Guards Brigade, 1st, 114, 116, 117, 120, 124, 127-8, 190
— 24th, 197
— 201st, 81
Gudgeon, Lt G. H., 159
Gudgin, Lt, R T R, 62
Gurney, Lt, Bedfords, 229, 281

INDEX

Guy, Major R. C., 63
Gwilliam, Major D. H., 267

Hall, Lt, Black Watch, 84
Hampshires, 2nd, 43, 51, 53-5, 61
— 2nd/4th, *in Italy*, 100-1, 105, 107, 112, 126, 136, 138, 141-5, 148-9, 151, 165-8, 177, 181, 183, 189-94, 206-7, 211-13, 217, 220, 225-7, 232-4, 260, 262-3, 265-7, 276, 282-3, 285-6, 340, 342; *in Greece*, 301, 303-4, 310, 322-3, 326
Hansell, Fus, RF, 209
Harding, Lt-Col A. E., 78, 101, 248-9, 279-80, 325
Harding, S-Sgt A. E., 295
Harding, Lt-Col J. C. E., 56
Hardingforce, 101
Harvey, Lt E. A. A., 62
Hatt Cook, Capt, East Surreys, 262
Hawkesworth, Major-Gen J. L. I., 6, 33, 36, 38-9, 43-5, 49-50, 52-4, 57, 66, 70, 72-3, 79, 82, 90, 92, 94-5, 102, 303, 309, 325, 337
Hawkins, Lt S. T., 156
Haycraft, Lt-Col J. M., 52, 325
Hayman Joyce, Major-Gen H. J., 96, 98, 100, 108, 109, 114
Headquarters, Divisional, 1, 6, 18-19, 22, 32, 56-7, 59, 82, 87, 92, 187-90, 300, 302, 323, 324-7
Heavy Battery, 12th/54th, 53, 81
Heavy Regiment, 54th, 53, 77
Heber-Percy, Brig A. G. W., 114, 139, 144-5, 160, 180, 201-2, 209, 227-8, 238, 240, 244-5, 268-72, 274, 296, 307, 311
Hemsworth, Major R. A., 302
Henderson, Capt R. C., 68, 74
Henley, Major E. C., 138
Hermann Goering Jaeger Regt, 55, 58-60, 65, 67, 69, 73, 78
Hermonforce, 101
Hesketh, Capt P., 175
Hogshaw, Brig J. H., 44-5, 48-9, 57-8, 61, 63, 87, 91, 96, 325
Hollick, Major, Bedfords, 153, 194-5
Honey, Capt M., 296
Honeybun, Cpl L., 339
Hope Johnstone, Major H. I. N., 67
Horrocks, Lt-Col, 28
Horrocks, Lt-Gen B. G., 88
Howe, Lt, RAC, 204
Howe, Lt, Recce, 272
Howes, Major T. C., 76-7, 140, 269
Hudson, Capt J. H., 11
Hull, Brig R. A., 56, 59, 69, 70, 72-3, 337
Hunt, Fus, RF, 140
Hussars, 4th, 247

Hussars, 10th, 238
— 15th/19th, 17-18
Hutchison, Major P., 202, 240

Infantry Brigade, 2nd, 54-5, 57, 59, 63
— 5th Indian, 299, 301-2, 317
— 5th New Zealand, 288
— 6th New Zealand, 288
— 10th, *at home*, 1; *in France and Belgium*, 6, 10, 12, 16-19, 21, 23, 26, 28-9; *Home Forces*, 32; *in North Africa*, 44-6, 48-9, 59, 64, 66, 70, 73, 79, 82, 84-5, 87-90, 96; *in Egypt*, 98; *in Italy*, 99-100, 105, 107-9, 124-6, 130, 133-4, 140, 153-4, 159, 168-70, 172, 180, 183-4, 187, 189, 190, 194, 213, 217, 219, 221, 230-3, 245, 247, 252, 255-9, 262, 276, 278, 281-2, 286-8, 296; *in Greece*, 302-5, 308-9, 311-12, 314, 317, 320, 323-6
— 11th, *at home*, 1; *in France and Belgium*, 6-7, 11-12, 16, 18-19, 21, 23, 26, 28; *Home Forces*, 32-3, 37; *in North Africa*, 42, 79; *in Italy*, 152, 154, 324
— 11th Indian, 315
— 12th, *at home*, 1; *in France and Belgium*, 8-10, 16-19, 22-3, 26-31; *Home Forces*, 32-3, 36; *in North Africa*, 45, 49-52, 54, 56, 68, 73, 78-9, 83-4, 88-91, 96; *in Egypt*, 98; *in Italy*, 100-1, 105-6, 108-9, 114, 117, 121, 125, 127, 139-41, 145, 148, 150-5, 157, 160, 171-2, 177-80, 183-4, 187, 190, 197, 200, 202, 206, 208-9, 211, 218, 224-5, 238, 242-3, 245-7, 266, 268, 271-2, 274-6, 288, 296; *in Greece*, 302-5, 307, 309-14, 317, 320, 323-6
— 12th Canadian, 234
— 17th, 7
— 18th, 227
— 28th, *in Egypt*, 97; *in Italy*, 100, 107, 114, 124-7, 133-4, 139, 141-4, 150, 165, 168, 177-8, 183-4, 187, 190, 194, 196-7, 200-2, 206-7, 209, 211-13, 225-7, 232-4, 251, 259, 262-3, 266, 282, 284, 286-8; *in Greece*, 300, 302-5, 307-9, 311, 315, 317, 322-3, 326
— 38th, 50, 151-2
— 128th (Hampshire), 43, 100, 105
— 138th, 238
— 139th, 284, 299-303, 315
— 143rd, 25
Infantry Division, 1st British, 1, 4, 18, 33, 42, 51, 53, 55-60, 65-6, 69, 73, 78-9, 218, 232
— 1st Canadian, 223, 225-8, 232-4, 251-2

Infantry Division, 2nd New Zealand, 106, 112, 122, 153, 182, 234, 288
— 2nd British, 1, 4
— 3rd British, 4, 15-19, 22, 26, 28, 33
— 4th British, *mobilization*, 1-2; *in France*, 3-12; *in Belgium*, 15-29; *at Dunkirk*, 29-31; *Home Forces*, 32-8; *at sea*, 39-40; *in North Africa*, 41-96; *in Egypt*, 97-8; *in Italy*, 99-299; *in Greece*, 300-23
— 4th Indian, 80-1, 84-5, 94, 299, 303, 315, 323
— 5th British, 25-7, 114, 296
— 8th Indian, 123-4, 127, 143-4, 151-2, 157, 161, 190
— 10th Indian, 236, 242, 245, 251-3, 255, 277, 282, 287
— 13th British, 323
— 44th British, 19-21
— 46th British, 42, 44, 46, 95-6, 99, 100-1, 236, 238, 252, 256, 259, 262, 264-5, 267, 277, 282-4, 287, 299, 303, 315
— 50th British, 33
— 51st Highland, 10
— 56th British, 228, 236, 251, 276-7
— 78th British, 37, 42-5, 49-53, 66, 69, 73, 78-9, 81, 84, 123-4, 151-2, 154, 157, 162, 165, 170-1, 174
— 278th German, 259, 265, 272, 276, 289
— 334th German, 164, 168
— 356th German, 164, 205, 265
— Hermann Goering German, 164, 185, 191
Inniskilling Dragoon Guards, 5th, 17-18
Intelligence Corps, 4th Div Sec, 324
Irons, Lt D. M., 51
Ive, Capt K. C. P., 259
Ivor-Moore, Brig T., 37, 52, 56-8, 325

Jackson, Lt-Col A. C., 56, 325
Jakeforce, 315
Jarrod, Major J. C. D., 67-8, 244
Jenkins, Major A. S., 132, 169
Johns, Lt D. B. R., 75
Johnson, Major-Gen D. G., 1-2, 7, 11, 15, 17-18, 23-5, 30-3, 79
Johnson, Lt-Col D. S. W., 43, 45, 325
Johnston, Brig M. A. B., 52, 77, 325, 337
Judd, Lt-Col R. D., 113, 295, 300

Keightley, Lt-Gen Sir C., 246, 252, 277, 282, 347
Kershaw, Capt R. M., 239, 258
Key, Lt-Col E. F. H., 311
Killick, Cpl, DCLI, 10

King George VI, HM, 38, 94, 191, 342
King's (Liverpool) Regt, 2nd, *in Egypt*, 97-8; *in Italy*, 126, 134-7, 143, 165, 168, 171, 177-8, 180, 183-7, 193-4, 200, 207, 213, 225-7, 233, 259, 262-5, 271-5, 282; *in Greece*, 301, 304, 308, 310, 323, 326
King's Dragoon Guards, 101, 276, 312-13
King's Own Yorkshire Light Infantry, 8th, 24
Kinna, Lt-Col C. J., 39, 52, 96, 325
Kinnard, Pte, East Surreys, 159
Kinnersley, Lt-Col, DCLI, 87, 93
Kirkman, Lt-Gen Sir S. C., 123, 165, 171
Kirwan, Brig R. C. H., 114, 124, 221, 296, 310
Knight, Major, Hampshires, 260, 263
Knight, Major J. M., DCLI, 280, 287

Lamond, Lt, Black Watch, 150
Lancashire Fusiliers, 2nd, 11, 19, 24, 28, 33, 79, 167, 170, 324
Lancers, 12th, 252, 276, 323
— 17th/21st, 124-5, 139, 152, 322
Lane, Lt E. H., 283
Larcombe, Sgt-Major, DCLI, 10
Lawton, Major, East Surreys, 21
Lee, Capt A. A., 76
Leese, Gen Sir Oliver, 99, 107, 128, 152, 154
Leicester Regt, 2nd/5th, 43, 238-9
Leventhorpe, Brig G. S., 19
Light, Fus, RF, 306
Light Anti-aircraft Regt, 91st, 39, 45, 164, 201, 237, 257, 325-6
— 57th, 299
Light Battery, 451st, 45
— 456th, 53
Light Field Ambulance, 6th, 325
Lightfoot, Capt T. V., 68
Liles, Sgt, Hampshires, 340
Lindsey, Lt, DCLI, 214-15
Llewellyn Jones, Major W. T., 69, 76-7
London Scottish, 1st, 228
Long-range Desert Group, 301
Lord, Sgt, RWK, 269
Lothian and Border Horse, 140-1, 145, 148, 150-1
Lotinga, Major J. L., 28
Lott, Capt, RTR, 62
Loveday, Major, BM 21st Tank Bde, 57
Lowy, Lt P., 74-5
Loyals, 1st, 55
Lucock, Major T. P., 137
Lyons, Lt, SLI, 136

McAlester, Lt-Col C. G. S., 159, 260
MacCarthy, Lt-Col G. H., 325
Macdonald, Major, RE, 25
Macdonald, Major J., Black Watch, 204, 271
McKay, Lt J. W., 71
McKechnie, Lt-Col, SLI, 166-7
McKie, Sgt, RF, 305-6
Mackley, Lt-Col J. P., 96, 113
MacQueen, Lt-Col K. W., 319
McQuoid, L-Cpl W., 74
McReery, Lt-Gen Sir Richard, 99, 246, 282
Madden, Lt-Col B. J. G., 51, 84, 146-7, 150, 160, 179, 197
Maggs, Major G. G., 64, 130, 156
Mannington, Lt-Col C. H., 59
Mappley, L-Sgt, RF, 239
Marlow, Lt H. N., 63-4
Martin, Major G. V., 132
Martyr, Capt, 101, 213, 264
Medium Regiment, 4th, 17-19
— 5th, 53, 81, 239
— 78th, 170
— 80th, 285, 288
Mellish, Lt P. M., 69
Memory, Fus T., 201-2
Midcalf, Sgt E., 216
Middlesex Regt, 1st, 24-5
Middleton, Lt E., 284
Middleton, Lt-Col, RA, 257, 325
Military Air Interpretation (West), 101, 264
Mitchell, Lt-Col F. J., RF, 33
Mitchell, Lt-Col, Hampshires, 149, 166-7, 206-7, 260, 266
Moberley, Lt-Col, RE, 96
Montagu Douglas-Scott, Brig C. A., 114, 125-6, 148, 165-6, 177, 190
Montgomery, Field-Marshal Lord, 16, 28
Moore, Lt R. W., 273
Moorley, Gnr W. L., 134
Morgan, Cpl, RF, 209
Morgan, Lt A. G., 137
Morgan, Major, Hampshires, 101, 260
Morganforce, 101
Morley, Lt A. H. G., 284
Motor Brigade, 12th South African, 183
Mountain Brigade, Greek, 233, 297-8, 308-9, 311-13
Monsabert, Gen, 108
Muchmore, Cpl, RTR, 62
Murdoch, L-Bdr, 94
Musson, Lt-Col G. R. D., 133, 141, 213, 215-16

Nation, Major P., 137
Nelson, Lt-Col J. E., 96, 251, 264
Newsome, RSM, 149
Newton, Major A. H., 130
Newton-Thompson, Capt C., 60
North Irish Horse, 190, 192, 214, 225, 227-8, 233-4, 269, 271-4, 288
Northamptonshire Regt, 5th, 9, 18-21, 28, 33, 79, 152
North Staffordshire Regt, 2nd, 59
Northumberland Fusiliers, 1st Royal, *Home Forces*, 38-9; *in North Africa*, 81, 95; *in Italy*, 100, 111, 164, 216, 236-40, 253, 258-9, 339; *in Greece*, 302-3, 311, 323, 326
Norton, Capt, RA, 134
Notley, Major J. T. B., 141, 215, 249

O'Brien, Capt A. C., 67-8
O'Neill, Major P. L., 57
Oxfordshire and Buckinghamshire Light Infantry, 1st, 9, 324

Painter, Capt R. J., 263
Palin, Company Sgt-Major W. H., 135
Palmer, Col P. F., 96
Parachute Brigade, 2nd, 304-5
Parachute Division, 1st German, 119, 121, 141, 144, 153, 155-6, 164, 166, 168, 175, 182, 223, 228
Paskins, Major A., 260-1
Pelling, Capt, RASC, 306
Pennington, Lt, 285
Perrins, Fus, RF, 209
Peter, Capt K., 261
Petley, Sgt, RF, 76
Phillips, Major M. W. R. O'C., 279-80, 287
Phillips, Lt-Col W. O., 325
Pike, Lt-Col W. G. H., 325
Pioneers, 203, 266, 288
Plastow, Major M., 130
Platt, Major H., 136
Platt, Lt-Col J. R. I., 136-7
Port, Lt C. G., 76
Postal Unit, 4th, 324-6
Powell, Sgt, RF, 67
Poynting, Lt, 206
Preston, Brig P. G. C., 101, 108, 172, 190, 193, 202, 206, 227, 265-6, 282, 284, 296, 300, 325
Prestonforce, 101, 108-9, 315, 322
Price, the Rev B. D. M., 113
Provost Coy, 4th Div, 70, 164, 237, 324-6, 342

Quadrant, the, 295
Quelch, Lt, Bedfords, 229, 281
Quinnin, Fus M., 339

INDEX

RA Battalion, 302-3, 308, 310-11, 317
RAC, 142nd, 160-1, 190, 203-5, 208, 238, 241, 243, 259, 262, 265, 271, 284, 288, 325
— 145th, 53, 56-60, 81, 242
Rae, Major E. D., 242
RAF, 24, 29, 34-6, 45, 73, 83-4, 87, 164, 179, 299, 301
RAF Regiment, 109-11, 301
Raisin, Major H. N., 228
Ramsey, Vice-Admiral Sir Bertram, 30
Rankin, Capt I. D., 51
Ransome, Gnr, 185-6
RASC, 56, 110, 127, 221, 302, 306, 319
— Div Ammunition Company, 324
— Div Petrol Company, 324
— Div Supply Company, 324
— 21st Inf Bde Company, 324-6
— 44th Inf Bde Company, 324-6
— 107th Tank Bde Company, 96
— 473rd Div Troops Company, 324-5
— 509th Inf Bde Company, 326
Rayner, Major S. F., 132, 153
Reconnaissance Regt, 4th, *formed*, 35; in *North Africa*, 46, 64, 66, 84, 88-92; in *Italy*, 101, 107-8, 157, 159, 162, 165, 172, 177, 184, 190, 194-6, 200, 207, 210, 212-13, 217-18, 225-6, 234, 237-8, 243, 245, 252, 254, 257-8, 271-2, 274-8, 288, 296; in *Greece*, 310, 312-15, 317, 322, 325-6
— 44th, 101, 277, 281, 282, 286-7
REME, 39, 113, 221
— 10th Inf Bde Workshop Company, 325
— 12th Inf Bde Workshop Company, 325
— 21st Tank Bde Workshop Company, 325
— 28th Inf Bde Workshop Company, 326
Rice, Lt-Col R. B., 49, 87, 325
Richards, Major A. E., 253-4
Richards, Major H. V., 271-3
Richardson, Major, RE, 72
Rickman, Major W., 230
Rifles, 11th, 311
— 60th, 247, 250-2, 267
Rimini Brigade, *see* Mountain Brigade, Greek
Risdon, Lt, DCLI, 216
Robins, Lt-Col W. V. H., 207, 282, 288
Robson, Lt, Bedfords, 195, 230
Rork, Major G., 133, 214, 279-82
Rougier, Lt-Col C. M., 22

Royal Engineers, 320
Royal Fusiliers, 2nd, in *France and Belgium*, 17-18, 27-9; *Home Forces*, 33; in *North Africa*, 50, 67, 69-74, 77, 84-5, 87, 91; in *Italy*, 105-6, 117-18, 139-41, 144-5, 154-7, 161, 172-3, 175-7, 179-80, 184-6, 199-202, 208-9, 211, 244, 238-46, 268-71; in *Greece*, 304-6, 310-11, 314-15, 320, 323-6
Royal Tanks, 12th, 56, 69-72, 74, 79, 83-4, 88, 91, 325, 338
— 40th, 303, 305
— 48th, 56, 60-1, 82, 88, 90, 92, 325
— 51st, 159, 161, 190, 197, 229, 245, 253-4, 261, 286, 288
Ruttledge, Major, DCLI, 248-9
Ryan, Major J. P., 271-2

Savage, Sgt J., 193
Savage, Pte L. R. E., 133
Savill, Capt J. A., 74-5
Scobie, Lt-Gen, 303, 306, 310, 316
Scorpion Regt, 71, 82, 83
Scott, Brig P., 96
Scully, Pte, Bedfords, 229
Seddon, Lt, DCLI, 279
Sexton, Lt B. G., 87
Sharpin, Lt-Col J. S., 10
Sherwood Foresters, 5th, 43
Shipley, Cpl, 113
Shipley, Lt-Col C. A. L., 157, 208, 239, 244, 269-70, 302, 314
Shoosmith, Brig S. N., 39, 52, 77, 96, 124-5, 133, 152, 156, 159, 168, 170, 184, 213, 230, 248, 260, 296, 305, 325, 337
Signals, 4th Div, 1, 300, 324-6
Sloan, Lt G., 156
Smith, Brig C. H. K., 96, 325
Smith, Col Evelyn, 31
Smith, Lt-Col G. McP., 197, 204, 227, 268
Smith, Capt H. E., 57
Smith, Brig I. V. R., 96, 108, 325
Smith, Sgt, RF, 209
Snape, Sgt, 153
Somerset Light Infantry, 2nd, in *Egypt*, 97-8; in *Italy*, 108, 112, 126, 135-8, 143, 165-7, 175, 177-8, 180-1, 183, 186, 188-9, 193, 200, 206-7, 211-13, 226, 232-4, 259, 262-6, 274, 276, 283-5; in *Greece*, 300, 302, 303, 305, 308, 310, 323, 328, 326
South Lancashire Regt, 1st, 8, 20, 27, 29, 33, 324
Spencer, Lt A. J., 216, 250
Spencer, Major G., 260-1, 278
Spencer, Capt W. G., 131
Spooner, Capt J. M., 68, 75

336   INDEX

Spurdens, Lt, DCLI, 216
Spurell, Lt, Black Watch, 206
Steel, Major A. D., 269
Steele, Lt, Black Watch, 240
Stephenson, Lt, East Surreys, 278
Stevens, Major R. H., 283, 285
Street, Lt, East Surreys, 279
Strickland, Lt R. D. W., 283
Sturgey, Lt, Black Watch, 315, 317
Support Group, No 2, 108
— 12th, 144
Survey Regt, 5th, 53
Sutton-Pryce, Major A. E., 136, 263-4, 283
Swayne, Major-Gen J. G. des R., 35-7
Sweat, Col, 108
Sykes, 2nd-Lt A. N. H., 76

Tank Brigade, 21st Army, 37, 52-3, 56, 58, 96, 325
— 25th Army, 44, 53, 159, 162, 190, 288
Tank Grenadier Div, 15th German, 105, 164
— 29th German, 213, 223
Taylor, Cpl, King's, 113
Tennant, Capt W., 270
Ternouth, Lt R., 242
Thomas, Lt-Col G. A., 77, 124, 190
Thomas, Major W. I., 140, 154-6, 244, 169-70
Thompson, Lt-Col R. O. V., 130, 132, 63, 79, 159
Titchmarsh, L-Sgt F. W., 210
Toms, Lt H., 283, 285
Townsend, Lt A. E. P., 239
Tregunno, Capt A. E., 214-15
Trevett, Lt, Bedfords, 230
Tuohy, Major J. H., 271
Tyler, Capt R. D., 273, 308
Tyndall, Major M. F. W., 175, 306, 315

Valentine, Lt-Col W. H., 317
Vallard, L-Cpl, 138
Van Rijn, Lt, 101
Venn Dunn, Major, RWK, 270, 274
Venning, Lt M. J., 77

Vesey, Lt T. G., 242
Visser, Capt P. N., 272-3, 311

Wakeford, Major R., 142-3, 149, 191, 260, 342
Walker, Major P. K., 244
Wansey, the Rev P. R., 179
Ward, Capt, East Surreys, 278
Ward, Major-Gen A. D., 114, 124-5, 132-3, 139, 148, 152, 154, 162, 166, 168, 171-2, 177, 180, 194, 196, 198, 213, 219, 222, 226-7, 230, 233, 238, 245-8, 251-2, 259, 266, 271, 277, 281-2, 284, 286, 288, 296, 302-3, 311-13, 322, 347
Waring, Major H. B. H., 268, 275
Watling, Major P. C., 270, 305
Watts, Tpr N., 62
Way, Major W. C. T. N., 101, 138
Wayforce, 101
Weller, Capt W. J. F., 105
Wells, Lt, Bedfords, 229
Welsby, Sgt C. A., 185
Welsh Guards, 3rd, 117
West, Company Sgt-Major, 76
West Kents, Queen's Own Royal, 1st, in France and Belgium, 10, 12; Home Forces, 33; in North Africa, 50, 52, 72-4, 77, 82, 84-5, 88-9; in Italy, 105, 107, 117-18, 140-1, 148-55, 171-6, 179-80, 197-202, 208, 211, 225, 228, 238, 240-5, 267-71, 274-6; in Greece, 304, 310-11, 313, 316, 323
Whitehorn, Lt, DCLI, 214
Whittaker, Lt-Col W. A., 46-8, 132
Whittick, Cpl, RWK, 274
Wiggins, 2nd-Lt, Bedfords, 153
Wigham, Major J. D., 257
Williams, Sgt, 273
Wilson, Major A. R. A., 229
Windsor, Cpl A., 348
Witheridge, Capt H. J., 91
Wood, the Rev H. C., 57
Worsley, Fus, 11
Wynford, Major Lord, 108, 169

Yate-Lee, Major D. T., 47
Yates, Lt-Col D. Peel, 190, 347
Young, Major L. C., 48

A company headquarters moving forward from Hunt's Gap, April 1943.

Brigadier Johnston (CRA), Brigadier Hull (commanding 12th Brigade), Major-General Hawkesworth, Lieutenant-Colonel Shoosmith (GSO 1) and Lieutenant-Colonel Foley (CRE) at 12th Brigade Headquarters on April the 25th 1943, discussing plans for a fresh assault on Peter's Corner.

SIDI MÉDIENE, APRIL 1943

Tanks of 'C' Squadron, 12th Royal Tanks, advancing on Sidi Médiene, April the 24th 1943.

'B' Company of the Black Watch, with tanks of 'C' Squadron, moving up to make their unsuccessful attack on Sidi Médiene.

May the 13th 1944; signallers of an FOO party in their slit-trenches on the slope leading down to the Gari.

A 4·2-inch mortar of 'A' Company, the Northumberland Fusiliers, in action in support of 10th Brigade, May the 14th; manned by Corporal L. Honeybun, Fusilier M. Quinnin and Fusilier Cherry.

German prisoners, taken in the battle of the Gustav Line, being searched by a Provost corporal, watched by the escort of Hampshires—Private Caesar, Sergeant Liles, Lance-Corporal Gray and others.

A patrol from the Surreys searching Gioiella.

A gun of 22nd Field Regiment moving up through Tegoleto.

An armoured OP of 30th Field Regiment has no time to stop for the food and wine offered by an Italian family.

Lieutenant Crighton-Pascoe, 4th Reconnaissance Regiment, takes out a patrol of Troopers and Partisans in search of Italian collaborators.

At Monte Sansavino, near Arezzo, His Majesty the King congratulates Captain Wakeford of the Hampshires, to whom he has just presented the Victoria Cross.

Before the battle. The crew of a DCLI carrier, thoroughly dug in before moving up to Incontro, August the 9th 1944.

The long wait. Two weary gunners of the 77th Field Regiment, on duty in the gun-pit.

Crossing the Savio by a pontoon ferry, October the 24th 1944.

M.10 tank destroyers crossing the Savio by the Ark crossing, October the 24th.

An ambulance carrier of the Surreys crossing the pontoon bridge over the Ronco.

The critical moment. 7th Field Company's bridge, 180 feet long and weighing nearly 100 tons, is about to touch down after being pushed across the Ronco from the farther bank.

The ferry sets out for the farther bank of the Ronco, November the 2nd.

Vehicles of the DCLI at a flooded diversion, October the 26th.

Major-General Ward (on left) conferring with Lieutenant-General Keightley before the attack on Forli. Lieutenant-Colonel D. P. Yates, the GSO 1, is in the background.

Corporal A. Windsor mans a sniping rifle in an OP looking across the Montone, November the 10th.

A gun of 77th Field Regiment being dragged to its platform.

SECOND WORLD WAR
BRITISH DIVISIONAL HISTORIES

All Written Shortly After The Cessation Of Hostilities

Authoritative and scholarly they are essential to any serious study of the Second World War

THE FOURTH DIVISION 1939 to 1945

The British Fourth Division was engaged in World War Two from beginning to end. It was part of the BEF in 1939, left France from Dunkirk in 1940, moved to Tunisia and fought throughout the campaign in Africa. It then moved to Italy fighting all the way up the Italian mainland to Forli and Faenza before being sent off to Greece to aid the civil power during the Greek Civil War. It was an honourable division which through the fortunes of war did not take part in the great adventure in Normandy, being thereby consigned to the relative background in the military history of the Second World War. Such divisions are unjustly given less attention than those which were chosen for Overlord, but their histories are none the less of great importance. This history is one of those narratives. The book is illustrated with a number of photographs and a good set of maps.

SB   9781474536646

HB   9781474536943

THE FIFTH BRITISH DIVISION 1939-1945

The story of the Fifth British Division 1939-1945 begins with the division in the BEF in France in 1940 which it joined from reserve division status. It returned to the UK and underwent training before taking part in the Madagascar operation. Then it went to India and Persia before moving to the Middle East Theatre in 1943 where it took part in the conquest of Sicily before moving into Italy. It fought through much of the Italian Campaign before finishing the war in Lubeck, having made the final move to France and then Germany shortly before the end of the war.

SB   9781783316083

HB   9781783316649

TAURUS PURSUANT
A HISTORY OF 11TH ARMOURED DIVISION

11th Armoured Division is widely recognised as one of the best British armoured divisions in the Second World War, earning its spurs in all of the most famous actions of the North West European campaign and commanded by the desert legend Pip Roberts. Originally printed in occupied Germany soon after WW2 had finished, this is an excellent Divisional History, with good, clear colour maps and a well written narrative. A Roll of Honour by regiment (Name, Date and Place) completes this fine history.

SB 9781783315611
HB 9781783316663

43RD WESSEX DIVISION AT WAR 1944-1945

This is the story of the 43rd Division from its arrival in France during Operation Overlord in June 1944 through to the end of the war with Germany. It relates how the division fought and where, and is illustrated with 21 maps. The division was engaged on the River Odon, and at Hill 112, then in the Seine crossing, the attempted relief at Arnhem, at Groesbeek, in Operation Blackcock and the advance to Goch and Xanten. It also took part in the Battle of the Rhineland and in Operations Plunder and Varsity and made its final move to capture Bremen in 1945. A very readable and an important Divisional History.

SB 9781783316076
HB 9781783316571

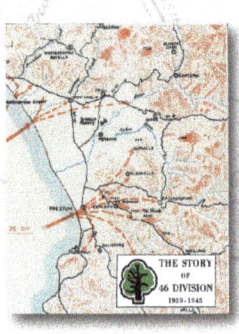

THE STORY OF 46 DIVISION, 1939-1945

Although not one of the D-Day Divisions, like many other formations, it was fundamental to the success of the broad plans for the direction of the war. The fighting in North Africa and Italy is detailed. Good photos, coloured maps, rolls of commands, staff, awards, and an Order of Battle complete this very good contemporary Infantry Divisional that is scarce in its original 1948 printing.

SB 9781783316335
HB 9781783316564

THE PATH OF THE 50TH

THE STORY OF THE 50TH (NORTHUMBERLAND) DIVISION IN THE SECOND WORLD WAR 1939-1945

This is a very valuable history of the 50th (Northumberland) Division in the Second World War. The division fought in France, North Africa, Sicily, and took part in the D-Day landings, finally ending the war in Holland. illustrated with photographs and maps.

SB 9781783316090
HB 9781783316632

THE HISTORY OF THE 51ST HIGHLAND DIVISION 1939-1945

The 51st Highland Division fought and lost in France in 1940, was reborn, and fought and won in the North African desert, Sicily and finally in North Western Europe from D-Day to the end of the war. As a division the men earned the respect of friend and foe alike, and this is their story. Amply illustrated with 36 photographs, 18 maps and battle plans (many coloured) that help the reader to follow the course of the conflict. A good index (persons, units and place names) and a statistical battle casualties list complete this good WW2 Divisional History.

SB 9781474536660
HB 9781474536950

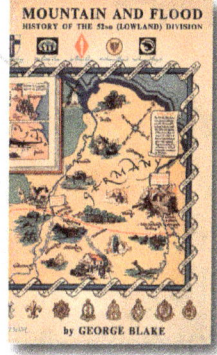

MOUNTAIN AND FLOOD
THE HISTORY OF 52ND (LOWLAND) DIVISION

The 52nd Lowland Division was one of very few "special" divisions of infantry, in that it was trained for mountain warfare, although it spent much time after D-Day locked in battle on the flat lands of the North European coastal plain. This history of the division starts before the war in England, and goes on to describe operations in France in 1940. For four years they then trained and waited, before forming part of 21st Army group, and fighting the Germans in France, Holland and Germany. As with all good divisional histories, it is the story of men in battle that counts, and this volume is no exception.

SB 9781783316069
HB 9781783316588

THE STORY OF THE 79TH ARMOURED DIVISION OCTOBER 1942 - JUNE 1945

A magnificent and fully illustrated official history of Britain's 79th Armoured Division - the specialised unit which developed and operated 'Hobart's Funnies', the adapted tanks which carried out a range of tasks on D-Day and after ranging from mine clearance to bridge laying. Follows the unit from its formation to victory in Europe.

SB 9781783310395
HB 9781783316731

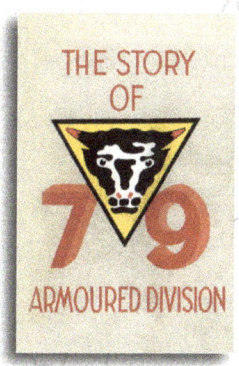

www.naval-military-press.com

The Naval & Military Press offer specialist books and ground breaking CD-ROMs for the serious student of conflict. Our hand picked range of books covers the whole spectrum of military history with titles on uniforms, battles, official and regimental histories, specialist works containing medal rolls and casualties lists as well as titles for genealogists, medal collectors and researchers.

The innovative approach we have to military bookselling and our commitment to publishing have made us Britain's leading independent military bookseller.

www.naval-military-press.com

www.ingramcontent.com/pod-product-compliance
Lightning Source LLC
Chambersburg PA
CBHW041438300426
44114CB00026B/2923